STUDIES OF THE RUSSIAN INSTITUTE
COLUMBIA UNIVERSITY

D0124488

Comintern and World Revolution

1928-1943

Comintern
and World Revolution

1928-1943

THE SHAPING OF DOCTRINE

by KERMIT E. McKENZIE

Columbia University Press

LONDON AND NEW YORK

The transliteration system used in this series is based on
the Library of Congress system with some modifications.

THE RUSSIAN INSTITUTE
OF COLUMBIA UNIVERSITY

The Russian Institute was established by Columbia University in 1946 to serve two major objectives: the training of a limited number of well-qualified Americans for scholarly and professional careers in the field of Russian studies, and the development of research in the social sciences and the humanities as they relate to Russia and the Soviet Union. The research program of the Russian Institute is conducted through the efforts of its faculty members, of scholars invited to participate as Senior Fellows, and of candidates for the Certificate of the Institute and for the degree of Doctor of Philosophy. Some of the results of the research program are presented in the Studies of the Russian Institute of Columbia University. The faculty of the Institute, without necessarily agreeing with the conclusions reached in these works, believe that they merit publication.

The financial assistance given by the Rockefeller Foundation to the research and publication program of the Russian Institute is gratefully acknowledged.

STUDIES OF THE RUSSIAN INSTITUTE

SOVIET NATIONAL INCOME AND PRODUCT IN 1937   *Abram Bergson*

THROUGH THE GLASS OF SOVIET LITERATURE: VIEWS OF RUSSIAN SOCIETY
    Edited by Ernest J. Simmons

THE PROLETARIAN EPISODE IN RUSSIAN LITERATURE, 1928–1932
    Edward J. Brown

MANAGEMENT OF THE INDUSTRIAL FIRM IN THE USSR: A STUDY IN SOVIET
   ECONOMIC PLANNING   *David Granick*

SOVIET POLICIES IN CHINA, 1917–1924   *Allen S. Whiting*

POLISH POSTWAR ECONOMY   *Thad Paul Alton*

LITERARY POLITICS IN THE SOVIET UKRAINE, 1917–1934   *George S. N. Luckyj*

THE EMERGENCE OF RUSSIAN PANSLAVISM, 1856–1870   *Michael Boro Petrovich*

BOLSHEVISM IN TURKESTAN, 1917–1927   *Alexander G. Park*

THE LAST YEARS OF THE GEORGIAN MONARCHY, 1658–1832
    David Marshall Lang

LENIN ON TRADE UNIONS AND REVOLUTION, 1893–1917
    Thomas Taylor Hammond

THE JAPANESE THRUST INTO SIBERIA, 1918   *James William Morley*

SOVIET MARXISM: A CRITICAL ANALYSIS   *Herbert Marcuse*

THE AGRARIAN FOES OF BOLSHEVISM: PROMISE AND DEFAULT OF THE
   RUSSIAN SOCIALIST REVOLUTIONARIES, FEBRUARY TO OCTOBER, 1917
    Oliver H. Radkey

SOVIET POLICY AND THE CHINESE COMMUNISTS, 1931–1946
    Charles B. McLane

PATTERN FOR SOVIET YOUTH: A STUDY OF THE CONGRESSES OF THE KOM-
   SOMOL, 1918–1954   *Ralph Talcott Fisher, Jr.*

THE EMERGENCE OF MODERN LITHUANIA   *Alfred Erich Senn*

THE SOVIET DESIGN FOR A WORLD STATE   *Elliot R. Goodman*

SETTLING DISPUTES IN SOVIET SOCIETY: THE FORMATIVE YEARS OF LEGAL
   INSTITUTIONS   *John N. Hazard*

SOVIET MARXISM AND NATURAL SCIENCE, 1917–1932   *David Joravsky*

RUSSIAN CLASSICS IN SOVIET JACKETS   *Maurice Friedberg*

STALIN AND THE FRENCH COMMUNIST PARTY, 1941–1947   *Alfred J. Rieber*

UKRAINIAN NATIONALISM   *John A. Armstrong*

THE SICKLE UNDER THE HAMMER   *Oliver H. Radkey*

SERGEI WITTE AND THE INDUSTRIALIZATION OF RUSSIA,   *Theodore H. Von Laue*

COMINTERN AND WORLD REVOLUTION, 1928–1943: THE SHAPING OF
   DOCTRINE   *Kermit E. McKenzie*

To Vivian

ACKNOWLEDGMENTS

The interrelationship of ideas and actions poses many a problem for the historian. Whether a knowledge of Communist doctrines is relevant and necessary for the full understanding of Communist activities is a case in point. That such knowledge was of foremost importance, and indeed indispensable to the proper comprehension of the world Communist movement, was always a basic theme of Professor Geroid T. Robinson's seminar at Columbia University on Soviet social thought. This theme is also the fundamental premise underlying this book. Professor Robinson gave the initial impetus to the author's interest in Communist theory. His painstaking and patient guidance accompanied the evolution of research and writing into doctoral dissertation. I am very pleased to acknowledge my great debt to his rigorous tutelage and to the spirit of honest and loyal devotion to truth that permeated it. Whatever usefulness and merit this study may possess are in greatest measure the result of this training.

I wish to acknowledge also the valuable criticisms offered by Professors Alexander Dallin, C. Martin Wilbur, John N. Hazard, René Albrecht-Carrié, and Oliver Lissitzyn, who read the manuscript at the dissertation stage. Informal conversations on many an evening with Professors Allen McConnell and Sidney Heitman provided additional insights and that ingredient of down-to-earth perspective so essential to proper judgment and balance. Mr. Eudocio Ravines and Mr. Douglas Hyde kindly drew upon their own intimate experience with Communist movements to shed light upon obscure aspects of the subject.

My work has been greatly facilitated by the courtesies of many librarians, and especially those at Columbia University and the New York Public Library. Indispensable financial assistance came in the form of generous fellowships from the Social Science Research Council and the Ford Foundation, for which I remain deeply grateful. I wish to thank the staff of the Columbia University Press for very considerable help in the preparation of the manuscript for publication. It is unnecessary to emphasize that none of these persons or institutions are responsible for the views and conclusions expressed herein. Finally, I wish to thank my wife for her many hours of assistance and, most important of all, her constant and refreshing encouragement.

Emory University
April, 1963   K. E. M.

CONTENTS

Contents

PART ONE

Introduction

I. THE PROBLEM

This study is an examination of world revolution as a problem in Communist theory and is based on materials that emanated from the leadership and central institutions of the Communist International between 1928 and 1943. It is not a history of the International but an inquiry into its controlling ideas. The problem of world revolution, or the world-wide Communist struggle for power and use of power to achieve a profound transformation of man and society, is of course the *sine qua non* of all Communist theory. Other elements of the theory are either subordinate to or encompassed within this problem. Yet an examination of the problem of world revolution reveals one special question that must be given proper recognition and emphasis: the relationship that is to exist, according to theory, between the Soviet Union as a Communist-dominated state and the Communist-led world revolutionary movement developing beyond the frontiers of the USSR. Recent events demonstrate that neither the general problem of the Communist struggle for power nor the particular question of the role of the Soviet Union in world revolution has lost any of its earlier vitality and importance. I have undertaken to reexamine these problems in the light of selected but highly significant evidence presented during that crucial period in the history of the international Communist movement when the "Stalinist" type of Communist was forged.

The great historical function of the Communist International, as initially proclaimed at its founding congress in 1919, was the leadership of an anticipated world revolution, the major consequences of which would be the displacement of capitalism and all other existing types of economic systems by a socialist society which Marx had announced as not only inevitable but also necessary for mankind's lasting peace and contentment. This comprehensive, even total, transformation of man and society obviously demanded an equally comprehensive social theory which would answer questions about the principles, aims, and methods of action of the world revolution. Precisely how this great revolutionary effort was to be achieved and precisely what was to be its end result—these are patently indispensable lines of inquiry for the present study. They deal with the means and ends, the methods and goals, of the world revolution.

These lines of inquiry lead to more specific questions. What kind of preparation by Communists and their revolutionary-minded followers was deemed necessary prior to the seizure of power? Under what set of circumstances and at what historical moment might a Communist-led movement seize power? Did the leadership of the Comintern state that Communists could seize power and "build socialism" *only* in societies in which capitalism was highly developed, or that they could seize power, under certain conditions, in underdeveloped societies also? Once having taken power into its hands, how should the revolutionary movement use power to achieve its further aims? What should be the structure and characteristics of the ultimate society for which the revolution had been engineered?

Directly related to these questions is an even more fundamental issue—whether or not world revolution did in fact continue, throughout the period under examination, to be the primary function prescribed for the Communist International and for its member parties, among which was the Communist Party of the Soviet Union?[1] Within the scope of the materials used for the present study, an answer is attempted to this often debated question.

All past and present leaders of the Soviet Union have been willing, on frequent occasions, to voice in public pronouncements their loyalty to and identification with the cause of international revolution. Do the materials produced by the Comintern between

1928 and 1943 help to clarify the true meaning of such generous but often vague endorsements? What contribution should the Soviet Union make to hasten the coming to power of Communists in other countries? Conversely, what should be the obligations of Communists outside the Soviet Union to the "homeland" of the "toilers" of the world? Also, after Communist-led revolutionary movements have successfully wrested power from their opponents, what kind of political, economic, and other assistance should be rendered by the USSR for the protection and development of the new Communist-ruled states? One further and fascinating question: Should the Soviet Union lose its separate identity by merging with other Communist states into a world society of Communism? The compelling nature of these questions requires that special attention be given at each stage in the analysis to the role of the Soviet Union and its Communist Party in the world revolutionary process described in Comintern materials.

All investigations into the realm of theory encounter the thorny and important problem of the meaning of terms, a problem that will receive considerable attention throughout the study; but at this point two such fundamental terms as "world revolution" and "Comintern theory," which recur often, need some initial explanation.

By "world revolution" is meant not a sudden cataclysmic and simultaneous seizure of power by Communist-led revolutionists the world over, but a more or less lengthy process of Communist conquest, encompassing many diverse revolutionary currents. These currents may well vary in degree of force, breadth, and velocity, but they all possess a common denominator in that they are revolutionary movements over which Communists enjoy hegemony or seek to establish hegemony, all to the end of utilizing such movements in the interests of achieving Communist victory on a world scale.

It must be emphasized that the word "revolution" is used by the author to embrace not merely the specific act of *seizing* power but also the prior process of *preparation* for that act, as well as the later process of *utilization* of power to achieve revolutionary goals. Thus two extended periods of political and social activity are hinged to a crucial intermediate axis—the seizure of power—and these three elements taken together constitute the revolution.

The expression "Comintern theory" is employed simply to denote the content of those Communist doctrines and directives that emanated from the *leadership* and through the *central* institutions of the Comintern. Such evidence embraces what is commonly termed theory as well as the practical decisions and directives of everyday policy. The sources of Comintern doctrines and directives include, for example, the utterances and writings of Communists in their capacity as leaders of the Comintern. These sources also include the deliberations of the central governing bodies of the Comintern, as well as the materials to be found in the periodicals published by the headquarters of the Comintern. The focus of this study, then, is on the center of the Communist world-wide organization, and not on the individual Communist parties, which were of course expected to accept faithfully and completely the ideological tutelage of the Comintern leadership. The highly centralized and authoritarian nature of the Comintern justifies the concentration of attention upon the doctrines and directives that flowed from the Comintern center.

It should not at all be inferred that the frequent use of such convenient expressions as "Comintern evidence" or "Comintern theory" denotes or implies a genuine difference in principle between such evidence and other Communist thought. The Comintern's theory is to be distinguished from other Communist theory only in terms of the particular institutional source of the former. Therein lies its special importance as an object of study, since it was largely through the international apparatus of the Comintern that a common stock of Communist ideas became disseminated all over the world and accepted by millions of men and women. It is impossible to investigate the ideological development of any single party during these years without first comprehending the ideological growth of the Comintern.

It is important to realize, then, that in a study of Comintern materials one is examining a set of doctrines and directives intentionally designed for acceptance and application on an international scale. The Communist International was a practical-minded organization, engaged in day-to-day activity while fully conscious of its long-term aims. Created on the insistence of the Russian Bolshevik leader, Lenin, who was above all a political activist, the Communist International lived and worked in full expectancy of ultimate capitalist collapse and revolutionary victory. For almost a quarter of a century—from the spring of 1919 to mid-1943—the leaders of the International exerted guidance and control over the activities of its membership, the Communist parties of the world.

Obviously, the ideological tutelage of the Comintern was the most important factor in the intellectual development of the first generation of Communists to appear on the political scene after World War I. This influence undoubtedly still persists. A considerable proportion of the authoritative leadership in the major Communist parties today is made up of men whose activities for many years were under the direction of the Comintern. Many of these Communists have become rulers of states since the close of World War II.

Comintern ideology thus has a significant place in the genealogy of revolutionary Marxism. Viewed within such a context, the ideology of the Comintern may be regarded, on the one hand, as a spiritual descendant of Lenin's revision of Marxism and, on the other hand, as a forebear of contemporary Communist thought. It may also be helpful to consider Comintern ideology as a revolutionary socialist ideology of the age of Communist rule in one country —the Union of Soviet Socialist Republics. In this sense there is an obvious contrast with both the pre-Comintern and post-Comintern stages in the development of revolutionary socialist theory. During what may be called the classic age of Marxism, prior to World War I and the founding of the Soviet state in 1917, there was as yet no socialist government, anywhere in the world, basing itself upon revolutionary Marxism. After World War II, several Communist-dominated states came into being, and the isolated position of the Soviet Union during the interwar years therefore disappeared.

The impact upon theory caused by this altered situation has become quite apparent in recent years, especially in connection with the anti-Soviet trends of "Titoism" and "national Communism."

The existence, during the life span of the Comintern, of a single[2] Communist-controlled state had a controlling impact upon the nature and development of Comintern doctrines and directives. It is impossible to divorce Comintern ideology from the actuality of the Soviet Union. If today the claims of the Soviet Union and its Communist Party to be the sole model for correct revolutionary theory and action can be effectively challenged and rejected by certain Communists in seats of power, such was not the case during the history of the Comintern. While it is true that the Soviet Union was confronted with opposition within the Comintern, it is also true that this opposition met with uncompromising resistance and defeat. Devastating purges and expulsions rendered such opposition impotent, even in its most developed form of "Trotskyism." On the whole, at any one time during the history of the Comintern, and especially during the period under examination, the great majority of Communists in all countries adhered to the Comintern's presentation of the USSR and its Communist Party as inspiration, guide, and model.

Indeed, Comintern materials frequently and proudly announced that the world revolutionary movement had in the Soviet Union a power base of inestimable value. The unquestionably intimate relationship between the Soviet state and Comintern theory underscores a succinct judgment of Bertrand Russell on the importance of studying Marxist theories. "There is, of course," he writes, "no more sense in Marx's metaphysics than in Hegel's, but one has to treat a metaphysics with respect when it is backed up by the largest standing army in the world."[3] The prestige of the metaphysics contained within Comintern theory was, for many persons living during the interwar years, decisively enhanced, to say the least, by the existence of the enormous "Soviet sixth" of the world.

I have not undertaken to include a detailed treatment of Comintern ideology during its first decade, or, more precisely, before the Sixth Comintern Congress, which met in the summer of 1928.

What is the justification for studying only the final fifteen years of Comintern doctrines and directives? What elements of unity can be found for the period 1928–1943? The decision to restrict detailed analysis to the period after 1928 was determined by several considerations.

First of all, it seems to provide the reader with a description and analysis of Comintern evidence as it developed *during the Stalin era*. It was during 1928 and 1929 that Stalin culminated his struggle for power in the USSR by defeating the so-called Right Opposition in the Politburo. With this victory he emerged as the undisputed leader of the Communist Party of the Soviet Union. The cult of Stalin may be said to have begun with the great celebration of Stalin's fiftieth birthday in December, 1929. For an entire quarter-century, Stalin was to be the dictatorial ruler of the USSR and therefore also the most powerful individual within the ranks of the Communist International. Certainly the ideological guidance of international Communism, from its adoption in 1928 of such a basic document as the Comintern Program, proceeded thereafter under the closest surveillance of the Soviet dictator. Stalin's concept of Marxism-Leninism was the mold within which the Comintern finally hardened after an initial decade of leadership largely by others. Stalin had, of course, participated in Comintern affairs in earlier years, but without enjoying within the USSR the virtually untrammeled personal rule which he clearly wielded from 1928 until his death. If it is permissible to speak of "Stalinist" or Stalin-type Communists today, then one must go to the last fifteen years of Comintern history for the period in which the creation of this type of Communist was completed.

The evidence testifying to the almost unbounded adulation accorded Stalin within the Comintern can only be described as massive and overwhelming. This evidence figures prominently in this study at all points. Even a very cursory examination of Comintern materials for any of the fifteen years from 1928 to 1943 would leave one with the most distinct conviction that Stalin's words constituted the highest possible authority in the Comintern during this time. Thus it would seem entirely proper to characterize the years from 1928 on as the Stalin era in Comintern history. The obvious fact cannot be overemphasized: that it was Stalin—and not Lenin or Trotsky or Zinoviev or Bukharin or anyone else—who ultimately succeeded in shaping the Comintern in his own image.

If Stalin's virtually absolute rule provides an element of unity for the last fifteen years in Comintern history, another element of unity can be perceived in terms of the evolution of capitalism during these years. The period from 1928 to World War II can with good reason be regarded as a time of severe troubles in the capitalist countries, initiated by the Great Depression, which led to novel and often radical experiments in economic, social, and political adjustment. The year 1928 was to be the last year, for some time to come, of more or less widespread confidence and optimism, generated by prosperity, in those countries where capitalism prevailed. Students of twentieth-century history, in their search for definable stages in man's progress, are more than inclined to look upon the period after 1928 as qualitatively different from the earlier postwar years. The development of Comintern doctrines and directives can only be understood against this background of economic and political instability, during which capitalism, as a rival system to Communism, suffered an unprecedented disaster and was in the eyes of many permanently discredited as a viable socio-economic system.

Other points may be mentioned that support the selection of 1928 as a starting point. In the middle of that year the Sixth World Congress of the Comintern met in Moscow. This was the first congress in four years. From the point of view of the development of theory, this Congress took two important steps. First, it adopted the only official Program in the history of the Comintern, and thereby succeeded where earlier congresses had repeatedly failed. The Program was an attempt to achieve authoritative formulations of the fundamental elements of theory. It is the most comprehensive single document in matters of theory that the Comintern ever produced, and it was never formally amended in later years. It gave to all Communists throughout the world a common basic document.

The other important step of the Sixth Congress was the proclamation of the beginning of the so-called third period in the development of world capitalism after World War I. The distinguishing feature of the new third period, according to the Sixth Congress, was to be a profound weakening of the capitalist system, manifested in increasingly severe economic and political crises and culminating in wars and revolutions. Linked with this forecast of a radical change from temporary stability to disintegration in the capitalist countries was the dictating by the Sixth Congress of a new pattern of strategy and tactics, which was to guide international Communist activity for several years thereafter.

One further point may be made to emphasize that the period following 1928 was significantly different from the preceding postwar years. In 1928 the Communist Party of the Soviet Union, dominated by Stalin, terminated the era of the New Economic Policy (1921–1928) and initiated the period of the Five-Year Plans. With the launching of this intensified effort by the Soviet government to obliterate, once and for all, "capitalist elements" in Soviet economy and society, and with the beginning of a full-scale drive for industrialization and collectivization, the Comintern was able with ever-increasing emphasis to expound upon the contrast between "socialist construction" within the USSR and "capitalist disintegration" in the outside world. Comintern literature is replete with effusive statements about the energizing impact of Soviet achievements upon the revolutionary faith of Communists abroad. The "building of socialism" in the Soviet Union was depicted, on an ever grander scale, as verification of the premises of revolutionary Communism.

In order to extract a balanced and accurate picture from the plethora of Comintern resolutions, manifestoes, speeches, articles, theses, and the like, one is inevitably led to construct a hierarchy of values for the source materials. It is, of course, obvious that the remarks of a minor delegate to a congress could never have the weight or importance of a resolution adopted by a congress. The scale of values must take into consideration the origin of a portion of evidence and the importance of that origin, whether it be an individual or a Comintern organ. A hierarchical scale beginning with the most important sources of theory has generally been adhered to and runs somewhat as follows: 1) speeches and writings of Stalin in his specific capacity as a Comintern official, and other speeches and writings of Stalin in so far as these were quoted or reprinted in Comintern materials; 2) works by Lenin, Marx, and Engels, again in so far as these were quoted or reprinted in Comintern materials; 3) the Program of 1928; 4) resolutions, theses, and manifestoes of the Comintern congresses and of meetings of its Executive Committee and Presidium; 5) speeches and writings of certain top-ranking leaders of the Comintern, chiefly Bukharin, Molotov, Manuilsky, and Dimitrov, in their capacity as Comintern spokesmen; 6) editorials in *Kommunisticheskii Internatsional*; 7) other material in the various reports of Comintern gatherings; and 8) other material in the periodicals of the Comintern. In this scale, Stalin's contribution occupies a unique and unchallengeable position above the other sources. The next five categories are all quite important, and are clearly a qualitative notch above the last two.

The plan of the book may now be outlined in brief. The present chapter and the following two constitute an introduction to the detailed analysis of Comintern evidence from 1928 to 1943. In Chapter II the *foundations* of the Comintern are depicted by means of a discussion of its origins, its organizational structure, and the efforts, ultimately successful, to draw up a definitive Program for the International. Chapter III deals, but by no means exhaustively, with certain salient developments in Comintern theory before 1928. These three chapters, constituting Part One of the study, provide the background for an understanding of the pages that follow.

Part Two deals with the problem of *prerequisites* and *preparation* for the Communist seizure of power. For Marxists and for Communists, the problem of prerequisites has its origin in certain restraints imposed upon revolutionaries by Marx himself. Frequently in his writings Marx indicated quite clearly that revolutionary activity would be irrelevant and ineffective if certain preconditions, especially of an economic and social nature, did not exist. Stalin himself, in the Foreword to his *Collected Works*, admitted that as a young socialist at the beginning of the present century he "accepted then the thesis familiar among Marxists, according to which one of the chief conditions for the victory of the socialist revolution was that the proletariat should become the majority of the population."[4] As is well known, Lenin tended strongly to minimize prerequisites and to emphasize, instead, the activity of a revolutionary élite. In Comintern literature, prerequisites were divided into "objective" and "subjective." An "objective" prerequisite, according to the Comintern, developed independently of the will of Communists and as a result of "impersonal laws" of socio-economic evolution, whereas a "subjective" prerequisite emerged as the consequence of the will and activity of Communists. The first big question, then, is: What was the Comintern's concept of the ideal set of "objective" and "subjective" conditions that had to exist before a Communist seizure of power might be attempted?

The problem of preparation for the seizure of power is closely related to the problem of prerequisites and constitutes the second major line of inquiry in Part Two. During the period when the "objective" prerequisites do not yet fully exist—which is the same as saying that conditions are not yet ripe for a Communist seizure of power—the existing situation is to be exploited by Communists with the aim of preparing those prerequisites that are of a "subjective" nature. Time and again, Communists were instructed by the Comintern to make ready for the coming day of struggle for power. In a definite sense, all Communist activity in non-Communist countries may be understood as preparation for the "inevitable" moment when the seizure of power may be justifiably (according to Communist criteria) attempted. Such efforts at preparation are directed: 1) toward the Communist party, which must ready itself ideologically and organizationally and which must seek to gain necessary practical experience in the day-to-day struggle; and 2) toward those segments among the population that are to constitute the mass revolutionary movement. Until, in the "fullness of time," that moment has arrived when the "ob-jective" prerequisites are maturely developed, the Communist parties are to work unceasingly toward the preparation of those prerequisites that lie within the capability of man to control. The choice of a particular pattern of strategy and tactics, to be followed by the Communist parties in the preparation of the "subjective" prerequisites, must always reflect serious consideration of the changing "objective" situation, its trends, and potentialities. Com-intern strategy and tactics between 1928 and 1943 underwent some fairly remarkable shifts. If one examines the period from 1928 to 1943, one perceives four rather distinct phases in Communist activity: 1928 to 1934, 1935 to 1939, late 1939 to mid-1941, and mid-1941 to mid-1943. These phases, exhibiting different patterns of strategy and tactics and therefore different ways of preparing the "subjective" prerequisites for a seizure of power, have been treated in separate chapters in Part Two.

In Part Three, the problem of the actual seizure of power by the Communist-led revolutionary movement is discussed. Despite the crucial character of this phase of Communist activity, or perhaps because of it (i.e., the desire for flexibility and secrecy), only a rather small body of evidence revealing Comintern thought on this subject exists in Comintern literature.

Part Four treats the period of time following the Communist seizure of power. Two component aspects of this period are discussed: 1) the initial phase, during which immediate steps are to be taken to set in motion the transformation of a society away from its non-Communist past and toward its newly imposed Communist goals; and 2) the final phase, i.e., the ultimate world society of Communism.

In Part Five are set forth the conclusions of this study. The results of the present investigations should properly transcend a mere increase in the factual knowledge of the content of Com-munist doctrines and directives. It should be possible to draw conclusions concerning the elements of continuity and the elements of change between 1928 and 1943 in the body of evidence as found in Comintern materials. Some ideas did remain fairly constant

throughout the fifteen years from 1928 to 1943, while others exhibited a high degree of evolution. The constants may, but do not
necessarily, demonstrate a rigidity in thought patterns, a knowledge of which would be helpful in anticipating Communist
response to specific situations. The variables may indicate the
degree of flexibility in Communist thought.

It should also be possible to draw useful conclusions concerning
the overall consistency, completeness, and clarity of Comintern
doctrines. How free of contradictions is the body of evidence? Does
it provide reasonably adequate answers to the important questions
that should be put to it? How clear is the language and meaning?

Given Stalin's position in the Comintern as its supreme living
theoretician, it should be possible to determine with some degree
of accuracy those particulars of Marxism-Leninism that Stalin
singled out as requisites for the individual Communist's understanding and carrying out of his role in world history. It is one
thing to understand *generally* what philosophical orientation is
professed by a group of militant reformers; it is another matter to
know *precisely* in what articles of faith they have been most dili-
gently instructed—in this case, by the educative faculties of the
Comintern.

The Comintern's doctrinal development was the product of a
conscious effort to refashion Marxism in a meaningful and effective
way. As such, it bears similarity to several other attempts undertaken since the original publication of the *Communist Manifesto*
in 1848. The promulgators of Comintern theory claimed an exclusive title to Marxist orthodoxy. They are neither the first nor
the last to do so. But irrespective of the question of orthodoxy, it
seems safe to say that the ideological development of the Comintern from 1928 to 1943—set against the background of world
economic and political turmoil and coinciding with an economic
and social revolution within the USSR—deserves serious consideration by any student of twentieth-century revolution.

II. FOUNDATIONS OF THE COMINTERN

In 1914 there occurred, as one result of the outbreak of World War I, a dramatic exposure of the weakness of the concept of proletarian internationalism. In its most radical definition, this concept meant that the supreme loyalty of the working class in the various countries was to the international proletarian movement, and not to anything else. Proletarian internationalism, based on a highly developed sense of common interests and aims, was in theory a greater force than patriotism. But confronted with the pressure of patriotic sentiment in 1914, the supposed anti-war solidarity of the European proletariat was revealed as a sham. At the same time, powerful impetus was given to schismatic tendencies already existing within the leadership of the international socialist movement. The beginning of war did not in itself destroy the unity and internationalism of the socialist movement; but it did accelerate the process of disintegration that had been developing in preceding years. Ultimately this process was to lead to a division of the socialist movement into hostile camps, adhering to rival international organizations.

THE ORIGINS

The international socialist movement in 1914. Precisely a half-century before 1914, supporters of the ideas of proletarian unity and internationalism had achieved a remarkable success in their efforts to create an organization for the European movement. There then came into being the Workingmen's International Association, which later became known as the First International.[1] Founded on

September 28, 1864, in St. Martin's Hall in London, the Association sought, in the words of Karl Marx, "to afford a central
medium of communication and cooperation" for those organizations aiming at the "protection, advancement and complete
emancipation of the working classes."[2] By no means a thoroughly
Marxist organization, the International, after a tumultuous
existence during which Marxist, Proudhonist, anarchist, and
other radical philosophies vied for control, finally dissolved in
1876. Yet it was not without significance as an effort to implement the idea of proletarian internationalism. It was for the
purpose of celebrating the golden anniversary of the founding of
the Association that the Second International, the successor to the
First, was to have held a congress in Vienna during August of 1914.[3]
The anticipated festivities never took place, and the fiftieth anniversary of the Association witnessed, instead, another baleful
example of the weakness of proletarian internationalism—the collapse of the Second International.

The year 1914 rounded out a full quarter-century in the history
of the Second International, which had been founded on Bastille
Day, 1889.[4] In contrast with the experience of the First International, the Second successfully rejected efforts at infiltration by
the anarchists and became quite closely identified with Marxism
in its outlook. In the Second International were included the
working-class parties of Europe called variously Socialist, Social-
Democratic, or Labor. After 1900 the International had its headquarters in Brussels and gave guidance to the socialist movement
through an International Socialist Bureau. By 1914 there had been
eight congresses, not counting the special anti-war Congress of
Basel, which met in 1912.

The Second International could hardly be described as a monolithic organization. It embraced many diverse strains of Marxist
thought, of which three broad groupings—right, center, and left—
are usually perceived. The right, or reformist, wing of the International was strongly influenced by revisionism, the chief ex-
pounder of which was Eduard Bernstein.[5] Although it is difficult
to describe in brief fashion the characteristics of revisionism, for

purposes of identification it may be said that the revisionists openly
challenged Marx's law of increasing misery and held instead a
belief in the possibility of a progressive improvement of working-
class conditions within the framework of capitalist society; this
peaceful and evolutionary process would, it was believed, ultimately succeed in replacing capitalism with socialism. The revisionists insisted upon the efficacy of the democratic method in the
struggle on behalf of the workers, and looked forward to democracy
—not class or party dictatorship—as the political foundation of the
future socialist society. Furthermore, Marx's assertion that the
working class had no fatherland was rejected; the correctness of
proletarian patriotism, even under capitalism, was recognized.

For these notions, the rightists or revisionists were sharply
criticized by the centrists, who insisted upon the continuing validity of Marx's "laws" and vigorously defended what they considered to be orthodox Marxism. However, the conduct of the
centrists, among whom Karl Kautsky was perhaps the dominant
figure,[6] was in general considerably less revolutionary than their
vocabulary.[7] It has been pointed out that, while the "orthodox"
centrists clung faithfully to the terms used by Marx, they gave
these terms new content. For example, the concept "proletarian
revolution" meant for them not a bloody struggle but a tame and
civilized process.[8] Holding firm to the Marxist idea that socialism
was inevitable and predetermined, the centrists tended to await
passively the coming fulfillment of Marx's prognosis and to find no
contradiction between orthodoxy and inactivity.[9]

To the left of the centrists stood the radicals or extremists, who
insisted upon "revolutionary" Marxism and criticized both the
revisionists and the centrists. Lenin and the Russian Bolsheviks
were an important element here, as were the followers of Rosa
Luxemburg and several other small groups. These radicals by no
means constituted a cohesive group. There was, for instance, the
profound difference in viewpoint between Lenin and Luxemburg
on the relative importance of the revolutionary roles to be played
by the proletarian masses and by their enlightened leaders.[10] Yet
there was agreement among the radicals that both the revisionists

and the centrists had transformed Marxism into a mild type of reform movement, not particularly dangerous for capitalism.

Despite the existence of three opposing currents in the Second International, each with its own understanding of the proper meaning of Marxism, there was not, before 1914, a demand for the displacement of the Second International by a new organization that might provide more correct leadership of the socialist movement. Such a demand, however, was urged after the outbreak of World War I in 1914 and the accompanying collapse of the Second International. The Bolshevik Revolution of 1917 in Russia, bringing to power representatives of the left wing of the old International, further divided the ranks of the socialist movement.

The struggle for a new International, 1914–1918. What E. H. Carr has designated as the "pre-history"[11] of the Communist International began with the impact of World War I upon the Second International.[12] The majority of the socialist leaders in most of the belligerent countries rendered patriotic support to their respective "bourgeois" governments, despite the objections of a strongly anti-war minority. The latter stood faithfully by the famous anti-war resolution adopted by the Stuttgart Congress of 1907, a document originally drawn up by August Bebel and strengthened by the adoption of amendments offered by Luxemburg, Martov, and Lenin.[13] In Russia and in Serbia, but not in Germany, France, England, Belgium, or Austria-Hungary, the small Social-Democratic parliamentary groups unanimously opposed support of the war effort, refusing to yield to prevailing popular emotion.

The commencement of World War I in 1914 thus created an opportunity and, to a minority among European socialists, a justification for extremely bitter criticism of the majority leadership in the Second International. It must not be assumed, however, that those socialists who opposed support of the war were united on the proper solution of the crisis within the International. This point is inescapable when one examines the history of the Zimmerwald movement, as the anti-war socialist movement came to be called.

The Zimmerwaldists constituted a minority among European

socialists. Within this anti-war minority, there existed yet another minority of extremists, whose criticism of the conduct of the "social-patriots" extended to an outright rejection of the Second International and to the demand for a new and purer world organization. This drastic position was not shared by the more moderate majority within the Zimmerwald movement. Some of the extremists also demanded a revolutionary struggle against war, with the aim of abolishing war by means of working-class revolution. The dominant figure in this group was Lenin, who was supported by some—although at that time by no means all—of the Russian Bolsheviks, as well as by a few non-Russian socialist leaders.

On his arrival in Berne early in September, 1914, Lenin had outlined his position on the war in a set of theses which were discussed at a meeting with other Bolsheviks in the city. Lenin's theses unequivocally condemned the war as "bourgeois" and "imperialist."[14] With respect to socialist support for the war effort, the fourth point of Lenin's theses read: "The betrayal of socialism by the majority of leaders of the Second International (1889–1914) means an ideological collapse of that International."[15] During the discussion which immediately followed, Lenin's theses were revised to make reference to a "future International."[16] In this manner Lenin made his first public endorsement of a new, third International. This is not the place to discuss in detail the evolution of Lenin's thought between 1914 and 1917.[17] But, in relation to the question at hand, it may be sufficient to note here that two pertinent demands persist in Lenin's writings during the war years: the transformation of the "imperialist" war into a revolutionary civil war and the outright rejection of the old Second International in favor of a new International. On his return to Russia in April, 1917, Lenin once again reiterated these themes and called for a "new revolutionary proletarian International" to be formed by the Bolsheviks without delay.[18]

Lenin, to be sure, was not alone in voicing an early plea for a new International. Trotsky, perhaps inspired by Lenin, likewise appealed for a third International.[19] Among non-Russians, the well-known Dutch poet and Left Socialist, Hermann Gorter, wrote a brochure within a few weeks after the war began, in which he spoke of the need for a "new International."[20] But no one can question the vital and perhaps indispensable role of Lenin in the movement for a third International.

The Zimmerwald movement drew its strength chiefly from the prewar left wing of the Second International. Communist writers have been eager to emphasize that within this left wing only the Bolsheviks represented unblemished Marxist orthodoxy; other political groupings in the Second International might approach but not equal the Bolsheviks in terms of consistency and correctness in Marxist theory and practice. In the opinion of one Communist historian of the Second International, "the only current that approximated Leninism was the current headed by the 'left radicals' in Germany and the so-called Tribunists in Holland."[21] The German "left radicals" were the followers of Rosa Luxemburg and Karl Liebknecht.[22] The Tribunists, an interesting group associated with the periodical *De Tribune*, had established in 1909 the Dutch Social-Democratic Party, standing to the left of the older Social-Democratic Labor Party.[23]

At the Zimmerwald Conference in September, 1915, thirty-eight delegates from eleven countries attended. Besides Lenin, Zinoviev, and Trotsky, the Russians were also represented by Mensheviks and Socialist-Revolutionaries. Other delegates came from Italy, France, Holland, the Balkans, Scandinavia, and Switzerland. The majority, while condemning support for the war, refused to endorse Lenin's exhortation to turn the war into a revolutionary struggle. Likewise, they rejected the demand for a break with the Second International and the creation of a new one in its place.[24] Lenin's minority, known as the Zimmerwald Left, counted only eight adherents at Zimmerwald.[25] After the meeting, the Zimmerwald Left was strengthened by the adherence of the Dutch Tribunists and others.[26] The Zimmerwald Conference chose an executive committee of four, called the International Socialist Committee, which established its seat at Berne.[27] With these steps the Zimmerwald adherents clearly demonstrated the depth of their reaction against the war and against the right-wing socialists of the Second International. While not severing ties with the Second International, as Lenin demanded, the Zimmerwald movement did make the necessary arrangements to ensure its perpetuation after its first conference.[28]

At the Kienthal assembly, in April, 1916, the Zimmerwald Left was accorded more support, but still failed to command a majority of the gathering. The crucial question at the meeting was that of the attitude to be taken toward the International Socialist Bureau, the governing body of the Second International. The Bureau had not met since the beginning of the war. Here again, Lenin failed to force a rupture with the old International,[29] but did increase his following, especially among the left-wing German socialists.

The third and final meeting of the Zimmerwald movement took place at Stockholm in September, 1917, during the quickening of the revolutionary currents in Russia. The Stockholm Conference counted for little in the struggle for a new International, for precisely those elements in the Zimmerwald movement who were most determined to create such an organization—the Russians—were now concentrating on the problem of seizing power in Russia. None of the leading Bolsheviks attended. With the successful October Revolution the Bolsheviks were well on the way in Russia toward acquiring the requisite basis of power, hitherto lacking, for the creation of a new International.

The founding of the Communist International. Like the outbreak of World War I, the Bolshevik Revolution of November, 1917, provoked among European socialist leaders varying reactions, which again served to illustrate a basic absence of consensus within the international movement. The rightists condemned the Bolshevik seizure of power and Bolshevik political behavior in general; the centrists initially preferred to suspend judgment, claiming inadequate information, but in subsequent months split badly amongst themselves in their reaction to Bolshevik rule in Russia; the radicals greeted the Bolshevik victory as the first example in a series of revolutionary actions which they intended to carry out in other countries.[30]

After their seizure of power from the weakly supported Kerensky regime, Lenin and the other Bolshevik leaders did not immediately seek to construct a new International. Indeed, sixteen months were to elapse before the convening of the founding congress of the Comintern. During this period the Russian leaders did try to "internationalize" their victory in various ways. Propaganda on behalf of world revolution figured heavily in Soviet diplomacy. Contacts were developed with representatives of the Left in other countries. In January, 1918, an international conference in Petrograd was attended by Left socialists from Sweden, Denmark, Britain, the Balkans, Poland, Armenia, and the United States (the American Socialist Labor Party).[31] In May of that same year a Federation of Foreign Groups, attached to the Central Committee of the Russian Communist Party, was created. This organization embraced groups sympathetic to the Bolsheviks among the former prisoners of war in Russia.[32] The chairman of the Federation was Bela Kun,[33] later to become famous as the leader of Communist Hungary in 1919. Its propaganda activity was intense, and many prisoners of war returned to their native countries full of the desire to emulate the Bolshevik seizure of power in their own homelands. It may be noted that during this period Communist parties were created in Germany, Finland, Poland, Austria, Hungary, and elsewhere; and in several countries strong sympathy for the Bolsheviks was expressed by the more left-wing socialists in the various Socialist or Social-Democratic parties.

It was on January 24, 1919, that an invitation in the name of eight parties[34] was issued from Moscow, calling upon revolutionaries in thirty-eight parties and groups to send delegates to Russia to organize a new International. Lenin and Trotsky signed the appeal for the Russian Communist Party. The reasons for making such an appeal at that time seem to have been these: 1) the desire to exploit social unrest in various parts of the world, but chiefly in Europe, by organizing the world revolution which seemed imminent; 2) the need to get support from foreign workers in order to hinder any anti-Soviet actions by the big capitalist countries; and 3) the desire to counter efforts being made by Right socialists to revive the Second International. The most immediate cause was the third, for an international socialist conference at Berne had been scheduled by the Right socialists for January 27, 1919.[35]

The Communist International was actually founded on March 4, 1919, at the third session of the conference which had convened in response to the Moscow invitation of January 24. The Russian delegation dominated the gathering, at which fifty-one representatives in all took part.[36] Thirty-five of these, representing nineteen parties and groups, had full voting rights. Initially, the conference decided to consider itself as only a preliminary assembly, preparing the way for a future, more representative congress at which a third International would be created. This decision was due to the opposition of the German delegate Eberlein, who had been instructed to oppose the immediate founding of a new International.[37] But on March 4 this objection was overridden, and with Eberlein abstaining the other members voted unanimously to transform the conference into the First Congress of the Communist International. An Executive Committee was elected, which in turn chose a bureau of five, including Lenin, Trotsky, and Zinoviev. The Congress issued a Manifesto, which proclaimed the new International to be the true spiritual heir of Marx and Engels. Thus there came into being, in Russia and under the impetus of the Bolshevik Revolution, a new international organization, militantly hostile not only to capitalism but to "reformist" socialism as well.

ORGANIZATIONAL STRUCTURE

Much has been written about the dictatorial methods employed by the leaders of the Communist International against their followers to achieve compliance or to suppress and silence opposition. Without entering upon an examination of this controversial literature, one has only to investigate the formal constitutional structure of the Comintern to understand the opportunities for authoritarian control within it. The importance of the body of doctrine emanating from the central institutions of the Comintern is, of course, directly proportional to the importance of those central

institutions within the Comintern structure and to the ability of
the central institutions to enforce doctrinal uniformity throughout the Comintern. The following paragraphs are designed to
show that, even without any abuse by the Comintern leadership
of the constitutional arrangements of their organization, the
Comintern would inevitably have been a highly centralized and
highly undemocratic institution.

The Statutes. During the brief First Congress no effort was made
to draft a set of governing rules for the new organization. This task
was performed at the next Congress, in 1920, when the first version
of the Statutes *(Ustav)* was adopted.[38] This initial version of the
Statutes comprised seventeen articles, headed by a rather lengthy
preamble devoted to the principles and aims of the Comintern.[39]
Acting upon a decision of the Fourth Congress, the Comintern later
revised the Statutes to take into consideration organizational
changes since the Second Congress.[40] The new Statutes, which
were adopted at the Fifth Congress, retained the original preamble,
but now numbered thirty-six articles.

A third and final version of the Statutes was adopted in 1928 at
the Sixth Congress.[41] There is no evidence that the Statutes were
again revised before the dissolution of the Comintern in 1943.[42]
Thus, as far as available evidence indicates, the formal structure of
the Comintern remained unchanged during the period embraced
in the present study.

The governing bodies of the Comintern. The central organs of the
Third International were the World Congress, the Executive
Committee, the Presidium, the Political Secretariat, the Inter-
national Control Commission, and the offices of Chairman and
General Secretary. These various organs will be discussed in the
order listed.

The World Congress was consistently defined in Comintern
statutes as the supreme organ of the Comintern. Seven World
Congresses were held.[43] According to the Statutes of 1920, a congress was to meet at least once each year,[44] but this rule was
changed in the new Statutes of 1924 to once every two years—a rule
that was repeated in the Statutes of 1928.[45] Provision was made for

extraordinary congresses which might be called by any group of
Communist parties having no less than half of the votes at the
preceding congress. According to the Statutes of 1928 the World
Congress had the following powers: to judge and decide on programmatic, organizational, and tactical questions in the International and in its member parties; to change the Program and
Statutes of the Comintern; to elect the Executive Committee and
the International Control Commission; and to determine the seat
of the Executive Committee.[46]

As noted above, the First Congress was attended by only fifty-one
delegates. At succeeding congresses the number of delegates aver-
aged about 400. Not all of these delegates were empowered to vote
on Comintern decisions; a considerable proportion had only a
consultative voice.[47] The number of votes which each member
party should enjoy at the Congress was to be "determined by a
special decision of the Congress itself, in accordance with the
membership of the given party and the political importance of the
given country."[48]

It is obvious that the World Congress, meeting only twice during
the period under study, could not in this period live up to its
designation of "supreme organ," if, indeed, it could be maintained
that the Congress was the Comintern's leading body before 1928.
No serious effort was ever made to justify the violations of the
Statutes involved in the failure of the Congress to meet more
frequently.

The Executive Committee of the Communist International
(the ECCI) emerged at the First Congress. According to a decision
of that Congress, the first ECCI was to include representatives
from Russia, Germany, Austria, Hungary, the Balkan Social-
Democratic Federation, Switzerland, and Scandinavia. It was also
stipulated that other national Communist parties that joined the
Comintern before the Second Congress would receive a place on
the ECCI.[49] By the Statutes of 1920, the ECCI was to be composed
of five delegates from the country in which the ECCI had its
headquarters (Russia) and one representative each from ten to
twelve of the largest Communist parties.[50] Other parties had the

right to send delegates with a consultative voice only. At the Third
Congress, the membership of the ECCI was increased. While Soviet
Russia continued to have five representatives, other large parties
now received two each, and smaller parties one each.[51] Subsequent
versions of the Statutes did not define the composition of the ECCI
in any manner whatsoever, either as to allocation of representatives
or as to total membership.[52]

An important change in the electoral procedure occurred at the
Fourth Congress in 1922. At that time the Comintern frankly
sought to eliminate certain federalistic aspects in the ECCI in favor
of greater centralization. Previously the congresses had determined
only the number of representatives from each country, and had not
actually, as a body, elected the personnel of the ECCI. Each party
had separately chosen its own representatives. This practice, it was
pointed out in 1922, "did not correspond to the whole spirit of the
Communist International, which was not simply a gathering of
separate national sections but a united world organization."[53]
Henceforth the congress as a whole was to elect the ECCI, and the
individual party lost the right to choose at its own discretion its
representatives in that body.

Throughout the history of the Comintern the powers of the
ECCI were considerable. According to Article 12 of the Statutes
of 1928, "the leading organ of the Communist International in the
period between two congresses is its Executive Committee, which
gives directives *to all sections of the Communist International* and controls their activity."[54] Article 13 pointed out that the decisions of
the ECCI were obligatory for all sections of the Comintern and
were to be promptly executed.[55] The specific powers of the ECCI,
and also of its Presidium, over the Communist parties within the
Comintern are discussed in detail in the next section. Among the
other powers of the ECCI were: the publication in not less than
four languages of a central journal of the Comintern (Article 12),
the election of a Presidium (Article 19), and the acceptance of
applications for admission to the Comintern from organizations
and parties sympathetic to Communism (Article 18). Such "sympathetic" organizations and parties were given only a consultative

vote.[56] The ECCI possessed a large apparatus, which in 1928 included the following specialized departments: organization, agitation and propaganda, information, cooperatives, women, publications, the editorial board of *Kommunisticheskii Internatsional*, and the bureau of the Secretariat.[57]

More important for the purposes of the present study is the function of the ECCI as a molder of policy. In 1928, addressing the Presidium of the ECCI, Stalin made a noteworthy pronouncement on this matter in the course of castigating the Italian Communist Serra, whom he charged with attempting to usurp the rightful role of the ECCI. "The interpreter of the decisions of the VI Congress," Stalin emphasized, "is the Executive Committee of the Comintern and its Presidium."[58] In addition to this role as interpreter, the ECCI was also the forum for the proclamation of important new policies. This was certainly true for the period between the Fifth and Seventh World Congresses, when ten plenums were held.[59] Four of these ten were called enlarged plenums and were in effect small congresses.[60] Enlarged plenums differed from regular plenums; they were attended by a considerable number of delegates who were not members of the ECCI but who were given the privilege of a decisive vote.[61] Apparently a decisive vote was rarely given to nonmembers attending regular plenums. The practice of convening enlarged plenums was discontinued by the Sixth Congress.[62]

Just as the ECCI was to exercise supreme authority between meetings of the World Congress, in like fashion the Presidium, elected by the ECCI, was to be the supreme Comintern organ when the ECCI was not in session. In actual fact, the changes recorded in the Statutes of 1928 enhanced the position of the Presidium in the Comintern hierarchy and weakened that of the ECCI. Henceforth the ECCI was to meet only twice a year (Article 23) instead of monthly. It no longer elected the Secretariat, nor did it elect the editorial board of *Kommunisticheskii Internatsional* and of other publications; these powers now fell to the Presidium (Articles 25 and 26). The Presidium was to meet not less than once a fortnight (Article 24).[63] Originating at the First Congress as a small bureau of five persons, the Presidium grew by 1935 to include nineteen full members with decisive vote and twelve candidate members with consultative vote.[64]

The evolution of the Comintern Secretariat is interesting, for in the beginning the various secretaries had no special importance in the Comintern. Among the early secretaries were Karl Radek, who performed that function at the First Congress, and Angelica Balabanov, a former leader in the Zimmerwald movement.[65] Later, the Secretariat expanded, and by 1926 it comprised fourteen persons.[66] In that same year it became known officially as the Political Secretariat. According to the Statutes of 1928, wherein the Political Secretariat is mentioned only briefly, it was a "deciding organ" *(reshaiushchii organ*[67]*)* which also had the tasks of preparing questions for the meetings of the ECCI and the Presidium and acting as their executive body (Article 25). The Political Secretariat appointed Länder-secretariats, which were permanent commissions organized on a geographical basis and entrusted with the preparation and working out of questions concerning individual Communist parties.[68] The Statutes offer no elucidation of the actual powers of the Länder-secretariats.

The Political Secretariat elected in 1935 was composed of seven full members and three candidates. The seven full members have all become well known even in the non-Communist world: Dimitrov, Ercoli (Togliatti), Manuilsky, Pieck, Kuusinen, Marty, and Gottwald.[69] Dimitrov as General Secretary became the titular head of the Comintern.

These four organs—the World Congress, the ECCI, the Presidium, and the Political Secretariat—constituted the official policymaking bodies of the Comintern. To aid them in the enforcement of Comintern decisions, there was created in 1921 an International Control Commission.[70] Elected by the World Congress, the Control Commission had two major tasks: the enforcement of Communist discipline and the auditing of Comintern accounts.

From 1919 to 1926, Gregory Zinoviev was the Chairman (sometimes translated as President) of the Comintern. He was elected to this position at the founding congress and reelected at each succeeding congress until 1926.[71] The Statutes of 1920 made no

provision for the office of Chairman, although it was included in the
revised Statutes of 1924. As a consequence of his unsuccessful struggle
with Stalin in the Russian Communist Party, Zinoviev was forced in
1926 to resign as Chairman of the Comintern. He did so in a letter,
dated November 21, 1926, to the Seventh Enlarged Plenum of the
ECCI.[72] The Seventh Plenum not only accepted Zinoviev's resig-
nation but also abolished his long-held office.[73] In the final Statutes
of 1928, no provision was made for a chairman of the Comintern.
Accordingly, it seems incorrect to attribute this specific title to any
of Zinoviev's successors as Comintern leaders. There is no available
documentary evidence to indicate that Bukharin, who was clearly
the leading spokesman in 1927 and 1928, was ever the titular head
of the Comintern, as he has been termed in several works.[74] During
the next few years after 1928, no single individual seems to have
acquired the position of prestige once held by Zinoviev and
Bukharin. It appears, however, that Molotov was in 1929 and 1930
at least one of the most powerful men in the Comintern if not the
actual successor to Bukharin.[75] With Molotov's promotion in
December, 1930, to the chairmanship of the Soviet Council of
People's Commissars, the chief remaining figures at that time
included Dmitry Manuilsky, Otto Kuusinen, A. Lozovsky, and
Osip Piatnitsky. Manuilsky, a Ukrainian, and Kuusinen, a Finn,
both were major Comintern spokesmen down to 1943. Lozovsky
was head of the Red International of Trade Unions, an affiliate of
the Comintern, while Piatnitsky occupied himself with organizational and financial matters within the Comintern.

In 1935 George Dimitrov, the veteran Bulgarian Communist
and hero of the famous trial in Germany that followed the burning
of the Reichstag in 1933, received the title of General Secretary[76] of
the Communist International. No great dignity had previously
been attached to membership in the Political Secretariat, and the
singling out of Dimitrov as General Secretary and therefore as the
titular leader of the Comintern was a novel development. Dimitrov
received widespread publicity as the spokesman of the Comintern,
but there is no evidence to suggest that he did not remain firmly
under Stalin's control.

Relationship between the Comintern leadership and the member parties.
What resources, it may be asked, were available to Comintern
headquarters to compel the acceptance and, more important, the
actual implementation of its doctrinal interpretations? The obverse
or negative side in this struggle to produce conformity was the
constant effort by the Comintern to hinder or eliminate divergent
and rival theories. In terms of constitutional provisions, there are
three documents which are basic here: "Conditions of Admission
into the Communist International," adopted in 1920, "Organizational Structure of the Communist Parties, the Methods and
Content of Their Work," adopted in 1921, and the Statutes of 1928.

Upon entry into the Comintern, each member section had to
signify its acceptance of the twenty-one conditions drawn up by
Lenin and Zinoviev in 1920 and adopted by the Second World
Congress.[77] These twenty-one conditions played the historically
important role of splitting the Socialist parties of Europe. While
losing for the Comintern a goodly number of sympathizers, the
conditions did ensure that each member section of the International possessed a certain standard of Leninist orthodoxy in fundamental principles and aims, as well as in matters of organization,
strategy, and tactics.

Those conditions that dealt especially with the relations between
a member section and the central organs of the Comintern may be
noted. The fifteenth condition stipulated that the program of each
party should be drawn up not only in the light of the special
situation existing in the country of that party, but also in accordance with Comintern resolutions. The program was subject to the
approval of a Comintern congress or of the ECCI. The sixteenth
condition declared that all member parties were bound by the
decisions of the International. According to the eighteenth condition, all parties were required to publish all the most important
documents of the ECCI. The twenty-first condition called for the
expulsion by Communist parties of those members who rejected
their obligations and disobeyed the theses issued by the Comintern.

The Third Comintern Congress in 1921 elaborated upon the
theme of a properly constituted and functioning Communist party

in its rather lengthy theses entitled "Organizational Structure of the Communist Parties, the Methods and Content of Their Work."[78] Chapter VII of the theses emphasized that a Communist party "is *under the leadership of the Communist International*," and that the "directives and decisions of the International are binding upon the party, and also, it is evident, upon each member of the party."[79] Furthermore, the central committee of a Communist party is "responsible to the congress of the party *and to the Executive Committee of the Communist International*."[80]

The Statutes of 1928 continued the spirit of the twenty-one conditions. Part V of the Statutes, entitled "The Relationship between the Sections of the Communist International and the ECCI," revealed a heavy concentration of authority in the ECCI and its Presidium. Article 29 required the central committee of each Communist party and of each sympathizing party to submit to the ECCI minutes of its meetings and reports of its work. Article 30 asserted that elected officials in the leading bodies of the Communist parties might resign only with the consent of the ECCI; the consent of the central committee of the party concerned was insufficient. Article 31 indicated the desirability of close organizational and informational contact among the sections, i.e., the member parties, but required the consent of the ECCI for any "exchange of guiding forces."[81] Article 32 stipulated that the formation of federations among parties for the purpose of coordinating activities required the permission of the ECCI, and such federations had to work under its guidance and control. Article 33 required the payment of regular dues to the ECCI. More importantly, Article 34 stated that the ECCI must give its consent before any congress of a party might be held.[82]

In 1935 the Seventh World Congress called upon the ECCI "as a rule to avoid direct intervention in internal organizational matters of the Communist parties," and to revise the Statutes with this point in mind.[83] However, the degree to which the parties were "emancipated" by this directive is not at all clear. The resolution of the Congress did not exclude intervention in *external* organizational matters—the relationship of a party to the ECCI or to another party—nor did it exclude intervention in *doctrinal* matters. At any rate, the decision of the Congress to amend the Statutes apparently was never implemented, and there is no evidence that intervention by the ECCI in the affairs of the Communist parties diminished after 1935.

Such were the statutory provisions. As for the actual cases of interference by the ECCI and its organs in the affairs of the Communist parties, there exists, of course, a considerable body of literature, very little of which is documented and much of which is highly subjective. This is not the place to embark upon a lengthy account of ECCI intervention in national parties, a subject that must bulk large in any future, definitive history of the Comintern.[84] But it is pertinent to the present study to attempt at least a brief examination of the principles and techniques of such intervention, which, it may be added, although not begun during the Stalin era of the Comintern, was certainly continued and developed.

Underlying the relations between the Comintern center (the ECCI, the Presidium, and the Political Secretariat) and the several Communist parties was the oft-cited principle of international proletarian unity and discipline. According to this basic principle, the relationship between the ECCI, on the one hand, and any member party, on the other hand, was not one between equals, but emphatically one between superior and inferior. Consider, as an example, a resolution of the Comintern Presidium on a dispute within the Czechoslovak Communist Party in 1929, wherein the Presidium declared that relations between the Comintern and its sections "are not relations between two partners who are negotiating with each other but are based upon the principle of international proletarian discipline."[85] Here is clearly implied a demand for the subordination of the party to the central Comintern organs.

The Comintern center took frequent advantage of its constitutional right (Article 22) to send emissaries to meetings of the national parties. At the Fifth Congress of the Czechoslovak Party, which met in February, 1929, Ziegler, as Comintern representative, supported the struggle against the right wing of the Party, led by Jilek and Neurath.[86] This is merely one instance of intervention by an emissary at a time when widespread purges were being undertaken against the "rightist" opposition within the International. In like manner, the ECCI in 1929 sent Harry Pollitt of the British Party and Philip Dengel of the German to the convention of the American Communist Party, where they opposed the "right deviationists."[87] Emissaries were delegated from Comintern headquarters to the national parties not only to eliminate opposition to current Comintern interpretations and applications of doctrine, but also to provide guidance for the correct formulation of theory in basic documents of the national parties. If the sending of emissaries did not produce the desired results, the Comintern could refer a case of oppositional recalcitrance to the International Control Commission (the ICC), or to a special commission appointed by the ICC.[88]

According to the Statutes, the ECCI might expel from the Comintern individuals, groups, or even entire parties.[89] The ECCI was sufficiently powerful in some cases to effect the dissolution of a party, although authority to do so was not explicitly given in the Statutes. The Korean Communist Party, which had been admitted into the Comintern at the Sixth World Congress, was dissolved only a few months later, in December, 1928, by a special decision of the Comintern.[90] In 1938 the Polish Communist Party was dissolved.[91]

Other means of achieving and maintaining orthodoxy existed. Training foreign Communists in Soviet schools was one such method. According to Tito, he himself lectured in Moscow at the International Lenin School[92] and at the Communist University for the National Minorities of the West (KUNMZ).[93] The former institution, Tito remarks, was set up expressly for higher party cadres from foreign countries.[94] Tito also testifies to the influx of money from Moscow, which he claimed had only a "harmful effect."[95] Financial dependence of member parties of the Comintern must have exerted its own indirect pressure toward obedience.

In the pursuit of its all-important goal of maintaining, continuously and undeviatingly, a state of orthodoxy throughout the far-flung ranks of Communism, the Communist International was obviously well equipped with a variety of constitutional and extra-constitutional means, ranging from advice to penalties and expulsion. It is, of course, to be expected that the exalted position of certain leaders would permit an exaggerated misuse of the power concentrated at the center.[96] It is also to be expected that such a misuse of power would be even greater in the period under study than during the first decade of Comintern history. The sinister implications of the rapid progress toward authoritarian centralization in the Comintern were made explicit when many Comintern officials, Russian and foreign, disappeared during the great purge trials of the late 1930s in the USSR.[97] The above evidence gives full support to the conclusion that the Comintern, a highly centralized and disciplined institution, could effectively enforce adherence to its doctrines and policies. The only practical alternative for the dissident Communist was withdrawal from the Comintern and the Communist party.[98]

GENESIS OF THE COMINTERN PROGRAM

Like the Comintern Statutes, the Program of 1928 is a basic document for any investigation of the Communist International, and indispensable in a study of Comintern theory. Adopted at the Sixth Congress in 1928, the Program constitutes an outstanding landmark in the history of the Comintern. Authoritative pronouncements are to be found in the Program on the most fundamental problems of Communist theory. In this section the Program will be treated in terms of its antecedents, authorship, and evaluation within the Comintern; the ideas contained within the Program are presented and analyzed in detail in subsequent chapters.

At the First Congress of the Comintern no effort had been exerted to formulate an exhaustive statement of principles. The vital significance of that Congress did not, of course, lie in any contribution it may have made to theory, but in its founding of the Third International. However, a short document of a programmatic nature was drawn up at this Congress, bearing the title "Platform

of the Communist International."[99] By Comintern authors it has
been regarded as a "preliminary draft of the program of the Communist International."[100] The Platform began with a description of
capitalist decay and anarchy, and announced the birth of a new
era of Communist revolution. Only a world-wide victory of the
proletariat, it claimed, could end further capitalist attempts to
exploit mankind. The Platform summarized Leninist attitudes on
such subjects as imperialism, labor aristocracy, the necessity of
violence, the definition of democracy, and other matters. Castigating those socialists who opposed the coming revolutionary actions
of the world proletariat, the Platform unmistakably sounded the
note of imminent world revolution.

Later, in less inflamed times, the question of the preparation and
adoption of a more comprehensive program for the Communist
International was first seriously raised at the Second Enlarged
Plenum of the ECCI in June, 1922. This Plenum decided to create
a program commission of thirty-three members, which was to
report to the next congress.[101] At the Fourth Congress, November
and December, 1922, Bukharin in his official capacity as reporter
submitted a draft of a program, as did also Thalheimer, one of the
leaders of the German Communist Party, and Kabakchiev, a
founder of the Bulgarian Communist Party.[102] Yet no program was
adopted, presumably on the grounds that many Communist parties
had not been able to study the drafts sufficiently.[103]

In June, 1923, the Third Plenum of the ECCI created a second
program commission, which was directed to draw all sections of
the Communist International into the discussion of a suitable
program and to elaborate a draft for the next congress.[104] Shortly
before the Fifth World Congress, Zinoviev, in a circular letter to
the Comintern sections, pleaded earnestly for the adoption of a
program by the coming congress.[105] At the Fifth Congress (June–
July, 1924) a new draft was presented by Bukharin and is generally
considered to have been his work.[106] Bukharin himself suggested
that no decision on the draft should be taken by the Congress, but
that instead yet another new program commission should be created
by the ECCI to guide the discussion of the draft throughout the

International.[107] These proposals were unanimously accepted.

Almost four years later, on May 25, 1928, the program commission of the ECCI adopted the document usually known in Comintern circles as the Draft Program.[108] In July, 1928, it was approved by the Plenum of the Central Committee of the CPSU[104] —apparently the first instance of approval by a section of the Comintern. Both before and during the Sixth Congress the Draft Program became the focus of discussion and criticism by the various sections of the Third International.

The Draft Program varied considerably in length and in content from the old version of 1924, which had been designated the original point of departure for the work of the program commission. Besides being many times longer than the version of 1924, the Draft Program differed from it in these important points: 1) the version of 1924 did not mention, much less analyze, the phenomenon of fascism, which received major attention in 1928; 2) the Draft Program added a new, detailed section, devoted to the USSR and the mutual obligations of the Soviet state and the revolutionary movement beyond its borders—subjects which had received almost no attention in the version of 1924; 3) unlike the version of 1924, the Draft Program presented a detailed classification of the various countries and areas of the world according to their stage of economic development and the type of revolution appropriate for each nation; 4) the Draft Program added several paragraphs on the problem of rival ideologies in the international labor movement; 5) whereas the 1924 version failed to raise the question of the universal applicability to future proletarian dictatorships of the Soviet Russian pattern of economic development, this subject was treated at length in the Draft Program. In general, the Draft Program devoted far greater space to the existence and achievements of the Soviet Union than did the version of 1924, which, in fact, mentioned the USSR only twice. In this respect, the version of 1928 was a good deal more "sovietized" than its counterpart of 1924.

As the Draft Program was first published in the official organs of the Comintern at the beginning of June,[110] the Communist parties

were allotted only eleven weeks for the examination of this fundamental document prior to the opening of the forthcoming Sixth
Congress. During the months of June, July, and August, the journal
Kommunisticheskii Internatsional, in its several editions in various
languages, sought to stimulate interest by running a series of
articles on specific aspects of the Draft Program. Such Comintern
dignitaries as Eugene Varga, Clara Zetkin, and Bukharin contributed material.

The decisive pre-Congress discussion of the Draft Program took
place at the July Plenum of the Central Committee of the CPSU.
Stalin's summary of this discussion touches upon a variety of points
and testifies to a fairly vigorous debate within the Central Committee.[111] The following issues were examined: the length and scope
of the Program, the sequence of the chapters, the nationalization
of land, the "Russian" character of the Draft,[112] the classification of
societies according to socio-economic development, and the applicability to non-Russian societies of "War Communism" and the
"New Economic Policy."

Having received an advance endorsement by the Soviet Party,
the Draft Program was presented to the Sixth Congress by Bukharin, the chairman of the Program Commission. Subsequently it
was debated, on the floor of the Congress, in patently energetic and
belligerent fashion, during the course of five sessions. In this
connection, it is important to appreciate that the Sixth Congress
stood roughly midway between the purge in 1926 and 1927 of the
Soviet "Left Opposition" (headed by Zinoviev, Kamenev, and
Trotsky) and the future purge in 1929 and 1930 of the "Right
Opposition" (led by Bukharin, Tomsky, and Rykov). During the
Sixth Congress it was impossible to use openly a "Trotskyite" argument; at the same time sinister rumors of the imminent ousting of
Bukharin created an atmosphere of tension.[113] One development at
the Congress clearly signified the limitations of the debate. It was
the refusal to permit Trotsky, then in exile at Alma-Ata in Soviet
Central Asia, to submit to the delegates his severe criticism of the
Draft Program. A partial text of Trotsky's criticism was apparently
obtained by some delegates although it was not discussed on the

floor of the Congress.[114] Trotsky followed up his criticism with an open letter entitled "What Now?" but this letter never saw the light of the Congress.[115]

After the discussion on the floor of the Congress and Bukharin's closing words in answer to the debate, the Draft was sent to a new program commission, elected at the fourth session of the Congress on July 19, 1928. Soviet chiefs among the membership were Bukharin, Stalin, Rykov, Molotov, Manuilsky, Skrypnik, and Osinsky.[116] Other delegations were represented on the Commission by such outstanding Communists as Ercoli (Italy), Thorez (France), Cannon (U.S.A.), Katayama (Japan), Koplenig (Austria), Kolarov (Bulgaria). In their personal capacity, Otto Kuusinen, Clara Zetkin, and Eugene Varga also were members of the Commission.[117] The Commission held a total of fifteen sessions, during which more than one hundred speeches were made.[118]

The Program of the Comintern was adopted on September 1, 1928, by the Sixth Congress. It turned out to be quite similar in form and content to the Draft Program. The Program was only slightly longer than the Draft and, like it, contained an Introduction followed by six major chapters bearing the following headings: I. The World System of Capitalism, Its Development and Inevitable Downfall; II. The General Crisis of Capitalism and the First Phase of World Revolution; III. The Ultimate Goal of the Communist International—World Communism; IV. The Transitional Period from Capitalism to Socialism and the Dictatorship of the Proletariat; V. The Dictatorship of the Proletariat in the USSR and the International Socialist Revolution; and VI. The Strategy and Tactics of the Communist International in the Struggle for the Dictatorship of the Proletariat.

The content of the Program is, of course, treated in many places in this study, and no summary will be attempted here. As a part of the work of the Sixth Congress in 1928, the Program properly belongs to the main body of this study and not to the Introduction. But the differences between the Draft and the final version may be noted at this point. According to Bukharin, there was considerable reworking of the Draft in the Program Commission of the Sixth Congress, so that only about 40 percent of the text was carried over unchanged in the final version.[119] Yet, in fact, although there was a good deal of rewriting and shifting of material from place to place, there were few changes in major ideas. In Chapter I, the Program differed from the Draft in adding these points to the discussion of capitalism: 1) capitalism in its most advanced stage causes degeneration of the cultural life of mankind; 2) competition, although more and more restricted by the growth of monopolies, never completely dies out but persists until the downfall of capitalism. Thus antagonisms remain within each capitalist country as well as between capitalist countries.[120] Chapter II of the Program remained essentially the same as in the Draft, but some points were developed more fully. Chapter III reveals no important differences between the two versions. In Chapter IV of the Program there were some significant changes in the treatment of a few subjects: 1) the need for violence in the overthrow of capitalism was more clearly and insistently urged; 2) the specific policies to be implemented following the seizure of power were listed in a more comprehensive fashion; 3) the categorization of types of societies and revolutions, a very fundamental problem, differs somewhat in the two versions. Chapter V, which deals with the interrelation of the USSR and the world revolutionary movement, shows no real change. Finally, in Chapter VI, perhaps the only important difference was the much sharper condemnation accorded social democracy in the final Program. The conclusion would seem to be that the work of the Program Commission of the Sixth Congress was in the direction of refinement and greater precision; no overall recasting of the Draft was involved.

The authorship of the Program cannot be established with absolute certainty. However, much circumstantial evidence exists to support the view that Bukharin, the most outstanding theoretician among the members of the Program Commission elected at the Sixth Congress, was very probably the chief architect of the Program. As indicated above, since the founding of the Third International, Bukharin had been closely associated with the task of defining the fundamental theoretical tenets of the Comintern.

Bukharin himself never seems publicly to have claimed authorship of the Program of 1928. His intimate participation in its drafting is, however, undeniable. Ex-Communists have generally concurred in saying that Bukharin was the major author of the Program.[121] Many non-Communists have also agreed. Bukharin is accepted as the chief author by Alexander Schifrin in his commentary on the Program in the German socialist periodical *Die Gesellschaft*.[122] The Serbian writer, Branko Lazitch, also credits Bukharin with the elaboration of the "definitive" Program of the Comintern.[123]

Difficult to assess accurately are the scope and importance of Stalin's collaboration. Two questions may be asked here. First, to what extent did Stalin contribute to the Program? Second, irrespective of Stalin's contribution or lack of it, to what degree did he accept or reject the completed Program, both in 1928 and in subsequent years after the ousting of Bukharin from his position as chief spokesman of the Comintern?

To the first question no definitive answer can be given, because of the absence of any published records of the Program Commissions appointed by the Fifth and Sixth World Congresses and of memoirs or personal accounts by any of the members of the Program Commission. It may be noted that in 1930 a curious plea was addressed to the Department of Agitation and Propaganda of the ECCI by the mid-European sections of the Comintern, calling for the publication, "as soon as possible," of the minutes of the Program Commission of the Sixth Congress.[124] Apparently, these invaluable minutes were never published. In their absence, it is very difficult to gauge Stalin's role. Some writers have confined themselves to brief references to Stalin and Bukharin as the chief authors, without attempting to evaluate the relative importance of each. Professor Florinsky, for example, simply states that the Program "was largely the work of Stalin and Bukharin."[125] Martin Ebon offers a similar brief judgment.[126] One biographer of Stalin, Boris Souvarine, claims that Stalin sought to assume the role of chief theoretician and hampered Bukharin's work. Souvarine's statement must, of course, be evaluated in the light of his bitter opposition to Stalin. Bukharin is quoted by Souvarine as follows:

"Stalin has messed up the Programme for me in dozens of places....
He is eaten up with the vain desire to become a well-known
theoretician."[127]

We know that Stalin was a member of the Program Commissions
appointed by the Fifth and Sixth Congresses and that he discussed
the Program in his report to the July Plenum of the Central Committee of the CPSU and in a later report before members of the
Leningrad organization of the Soviet Communist Party.[128] In these
reports, Stalin, of course, was dealing with the Draft Program prior
to its scrutiny by the Sixth Congress. None of the positions he took
at the July Plenum were altered by the Sixth Congress. The
question, basically, is whether Stalin, in giving his general endorsement of the Draft Program at the July Plenum, was endorsing his
own or Bukharin's or someone else's views.

Even if Stalin's precise activity in the drafting of the Program
cannot now be determined, on the basis of the available material,
the other important issue—Stalin's attitude toward the completed
Program—can be settled easily. There is no evidence that Stalin
ever repudiated the Program or any part of it, either in 1928 or at
any time thereafter; rather Stalin ordered or permitted Comintern
writers to create the impression of an intimate association between
himself and the Program. In 1934 an editorial in *Kommunisticheskii
Internatsional* asserted that "Comrade Stalin took the leading part
in working out the Program of the Communist International."[129]
Some twenty years after the Program's appearance, the editors of
Stalin's *Collected Works* were impelled to credit him with having
guided the work of the program commission that had produced
the Draft Program of 1928.[130] Yet Stalin himself does not seem ever
to have claimed sole authorship, either of the Draft or of the final
version.

In what light did the Comintern regard its Program? Certainly
no other Comintern document had similar prestige. In 1929 the
Bulgarian historian of the Comintern, Khristo Kabakchiev, ac-
claimed the Program as a "most valuable guide and powerful
weapon in the revolutionary struggle of suppressed classes and
peoples."[131] Molotov, in his report in 1930 to the Sixteenth Congress

of the CPSU on behalf of the Soviet delegation in the ECCI, referred to the Program in these words:

The great perspectives of the Communist International have found their best expression in the Program of the Comintern adopted by the Sixth World Congress. This Program represents the progress of the struggle for the world dictatorship of the proletariat; this is a Program for the overthrow of imperialism and the liberation of the toilers of the whole world from imperialist oppression. This Program already is being made a reality in the victorious contruction of socialism in the USSR.[132]

In 1934, when the strategy and tactics of the "popular front" were being initiated, the Program of the Comintern was given reindorsement by the Comintern. Dimitrov, the leading spokesman of the Comintern in 1935 and thereafter, identified himself closely with the Program. In his speech before the Nazi tribunal during the famous "Reichstag fire" trial in 1934, he declared boldly: "It is true that for me as a Communist the highest law is the Program of the Communist International."[133] Referring to a characterization given him by a German newspaper during the trial—"Dimitrov is the Programme of the Communist International become flesh"— Dimitrov affirmed, "I cannot think of a better description of myself."[134] He was to speak even more dramatically that same year: "When I stood at the bar in Leipzig and Berlin, I kept in one of my hands, the left one, the penal code of the German state, and in my right hand, the Programme of the Comintern."[135] It may again be emphasized that the Program was never at any time criticized or rejected by the leadership of the Comintern. Above all, it should be remembered that the Program of 1928 became a *universal* guide for correct Communist thinking on many problems of the revolutionary movement, for the programs of all the Communist parties were modeled after the Comintern Program.

III. REVOLUTIONARY PROSPECTS
AND STRATEGY, 1919-1928

Although the detailed analysis of Comintern doctrines and directives in this study begins with the work of the Sixth Congress in 1928, a sketch of certain salient features in the ideological development up to 1928 seems appropriate. Such a summary, albeit brief, should provide a helpful overview of the first decade in the evolution of Comintern doctrines.

During the period from 1919 to 1928 undoubtedly the major conditions shaping the doctrinal evolution of the Comintern were the survival and strengthening of Communist rule in the Soviet Union and the failure of Communist efforts to seize power in other countries. Both factors could not but serve to maintain and reinforce the hegemony of the Communist Party of the Soviet Union within the Comintern and therefore within the world Communist movement.

An examination of the history of the Comintern permits the construction of a sequence of phases that has a considerable coincidence with the well-known sequence of phases in Soviet history. To illustrate, the first broad phase of Soviet history was terminated in March, 1921, with the adoption of the New Economic Policy by the Tenth Congress of the All-Russian Communist Party; and in mid-1921 the Third Comintern Congress acknowledged the close of the first "round" of world revolutionary actions that had been initiated by the revolutions of 1917 in Russia. Just as NEP represented a conservative, though temporary, retreat in Soviet Russia, so the new directives of the Comintern in mid-1921 emphasized the need for considerable *preparation* before the Communists could seize power. The earlier expectancy of immediate and easy victories was reluctantly abandoned. To continue the parallel, in 1928 the First Five-Year Plan inaugurated in Soviet Russia a strenuous effort to end the relatively easy going days of NEP and to establish the foundations of a socialist society. In 1928, also, the Comintern announced the advent of the second "round" of postwar revolutions and defined a new and radical pattern of strategy and tactics to meet the changing situation. Thus, in 1928, the "swing to the left" in the USSR was paralleled by a similar "swing to the left" in the Comintern.

Although the Comintern Congress of 1928 considered the terminal point of the first phase of postwar revolutionary development to be the fall of 1923, it seems that a more accurate date, from the point of view of a significant change in Comintern expectations and strategy, is mid-1921. This date is used below to delimit the two broad phases of Comintern history before 1928.

THE FIRST "ROUND" OF REVOLUTIONS

A whole series of political and social disturbances occurred throughout the world in the closing months of World War I and in the immediate postwar years down into the spring of 1921. Civil war in Finland in 1918, the overthrow of monarchy in Germany and Austria-Hungary in late 1918, the "rice riots" in Japan in 1918, the establishment of a Communist regime in Hungary in 1919, the nationalist movement of Mustapha Kemal in Turkey from 1919 on, the seizure of factories by Italian workers in 1920, and the uprising of the German Communists in March, 1921—all these developments evoked an enthusiastic response in the Comintern, which was prone to see in them clear proof of the imminent collapse of world capitalism and imperialism.

The Manifesto and the Platform issued by the First Congress in 1919 presented the essential interpretations of the new International respecting contemporary society and social change.[1] These ideas may be briefly summarized. Broadly speaking, the perspective was Marxist. Existing societies in 1919 stood at different stages of historical development: some were in the capitalist stage, others were still in a pre-capitalist stage, and one society—that of Soviet Russia—was entering upon the post-capitalist stage, socialism. The capitalist system, which controlled the non-Soviet world, was described as decaying and unprogressive, though still powerful. The less advanced societies, i.e., colonies and other dependent countries, were subordinated economically, and therefore politically, to the capitalist system. The two documents sketched a world-wide conflict, in which the bourgeoisie, i.e., the social class dominating in the capitalist world, was confronted by a host of enemies including Soviet Russia, the working class in the capitalist countries, and movements for independence in the colonies. The Manifesto and the Platform claimed that the Russian working class in 1917 had overthrown the exploiting and predatory bourgeois and landlord classes in that country, and stood in 1919 beside the working class of capitalist society and the "exploited" masses in the colonies in a united international movement destined to overthrow decadent capitalism and establish socialism on a world-wide scale. The terms "finance capital" and "imperialism" were used interchangeably at the First Congress to denote this supposedly final phase of capitalism before the advent of the socialist era.[2]

Since the outbreak of World War I, the capitalist system was said to be in an epoch of prolonged crisis, which was at the same time the *"epoch of the Communist revolution of the proletariat."*[3] The establishment in Russia of what the Comintern was satisfied to call "proletarian" rule was pictured as immeasurably significant for the subsequent course of world revolution. The world was henceforth confronted with the inescapable and undeniable fact of the existence of a developing system of economy and government that, according to the Comintern, was intrinsically more progressive than the capitalist system. A threshold had been crossed, an irretraceable step had been taken, by which the formerly unified world economy was now split into two antagonistic systems. Further revolutions that would extend the territory under Communist leadership were confidently expected by the First Congress.

How was the Communist revolution to be accomplished? Both

the Manifesto and the Platform stated the bare essentials: the inevitability of violent struggle, the necessity of the expropriation and eradication of the bourgeoisie, and the socialization of the means of production.

It may be noted that the First Congress followed Marx in rejecting outright the idea of an alternative to the downfall of capitalism through a "reform" of the capitalist system. The capitalist world was inherently unable to resolve its difficulties, or so-called contradictions; it could never realize the level of organization and cooperation necessary for stability. It was inescapably doomed to collapse. The First Congress here accepted one of the basic—and unprovable—assertions of Marx: that capitalists would never be able to cooperate in a sustained and fruitful manner for the purpose of solving the problems of modern industrial society. Like Marx, it asserted that the struggle for profits had shattered and would continue to shatter all efforts at stability of the capitalist system. It is an interesting commentary on the Comintern's system of anthropology—if it can be said to have had one—that, under a system of private property, not only was human nature considered to be vulnerable to the impulses of greed and rapacity, but even the most astute and successful capitalists were regarded as driven blindly by the profit motive into a self-inflicted doom.

What Communists have termed a major contribution to Comintern theory was made at the First Congress with Lenin's theses on "Bourgeois Democracy and the Dictatorship of the Proletariat."[4] Zinoviev, the Comintern President, called this the most important document of the Congress.[5] In his theses Lenin rejected as indisputably fallacious any abstract concept of democracy or of dictatorship, which were never to be treated as absolutes but as variables in relation to the class in power. There could be, for the revolutionary proletariat, no such thing as defense of democracy in general. Democratic liberties existing in capitalist countries were liberties essentially for the bourgeoisie. Therefore, institutions of "bourgeois" democracy were not to be defended, as they were in fact instruments of dictatorship. In all this, there is nothing particularly new; the relativity of political ideals and systems is as old as Marx.

But what is worth noting is the total and absolute repudiation of the value of "bourgeois" democracy. In later years, as we shall see, the Comintern discovered much of value in parliamentary government as distinguished from fascist rule. The uncompromising rebuff of "bourgeois" democracy in 1919 reflected the high hopes then held for world revolution.

Lenin assigned to the Communist movement the task of replacing "bourgeois" democracy with "proletarian" democracy, which would be implemented by a "dictatorship of the proletariat." This term in Communist theory signifies the presence of genuine political rights for the proletariat and other "toilers," who exercise a dictatorship over class enemies (bourgeoisie, great landowners, etc.), who have been overthrown. In actuality, it has always meant a dictatorship of a Communist party over all segments of the population.

The Second Congress, held in July and August of 1920, coincided with the advance of Russian armed forces against Warsaw during the Russo-Polish War. Lenin, believing that the international situation was still ripe for revolution, gave considerable attention to the question of the Communist parties. In the months of April and May before the Second Congress he wrote his well-known brochure, *"Left-wing" Communism, an Infantile Disorder*, which has been compared for its force and realism with *The Prince* of Machiavelli.[6] In this work, Lenin insisted upon Communist participation in and utilization of parliaments and trade unions, and condemned those who shunned such channels of activity. The Second Congress adopted the ideas of Lenin on these matters, in two resolutions,[7] and thereby rejected what would have been an unnecessary and unwise policy of self-isolation from two major arenas of political activity.

In line with Lenin's obvious interest in creating the proper kind of Communist party for the carrying out of imminent revolutions, the Second Congress adopted a resolution entitled "The Role of the Communist Party in the Proletarian Revolution."[8] The Communist party was defined in this resolution as the "most advanced, most conscious, and, therefore, most revolutionary part" of the working class. The resolution pointed out that, before the Communist seizure of power, the party would as a rule have only a minority of the working class in its ranks, but under favorable circumstances it could exercise political influence "over all the proletarian and semiproletarian elements of the population." According to the resolution, the Communist party was an absolutely necessary organ of leadership and control—before, during, and after the seizure of power. The primacy of the party over other "proletarian" organizations after the seizure of power was especially affirmed; the party was to guide the victorious proletariat both in the governing soviets and in the trade unions.

The famous twenty-one conditions of admission into the Third International were also adopted at the Second Congress.[9] Besides treating the relations between member parties of the Third International and the latter's governing bodies—a question which was discussed in Chapter II—the conditions incorporated Lenin's views on the nature of Communist parties, their organizational structure, and the fields of activity in which they should participate. The parties were to adopt the name "Communist," were to disassociate themselves publicly from all "reformist" elements and views, and were to stand openly for a revolutionary overthrow of capitalism and the establishment of the "dictatorship of the proletariat." Thus the Communist party was to be clearly distinguishable from a Social-Democratic party. Organizationally, each Communist party was to exemplify the Leninist principle of "democratic centralism," which in effect meant a highly centralized and disciplined party, governed undemocratically from above. Each party was also to create a parallel illegal apparatus, in recognition of the transitory nature of bourgeois liberties, and was to conduct periodic purges of its membership. In all these respects, the organization pattern followed closely that of the Bolshevik Party in Russia, which had, of course, been the creation of Lenin. The Communist party, while directing its chief effort toward winning the proletariat, was also to work in the armed forces and among the peasantry and colonial "toilers." The important fourteenth condition specified the obligation of the Communist parties to render all possible aid to Soviet republics in their struggle against counter-revolution.

Two other major doctrinal matters were treated at the Second Congress with the direct participation of Lenin. First, Lenin developed his views on the revolutionary potential of the national and colonial question, which had been largely ignored by the Second International.[10] He called for Communist support of the colonial movements for independence, even to the point of temporary agreements with the revolutionary bourgeoisie of the colonies. Yet, he warned, the Communist party in the colonies should never merge into the bourgeois-led movement, but should "unconditionally preserve the independence of the proletarian movement, even in its most embryonic form."[11] The theses adopted by the Second Congress emphasized the impossibility of a complete solution to the nationality problem except through the establishment of Communism.

Second, the agrarian question was treated extensively by Lenin at this Congress, and indeed more thoroughly than it was again to be until the Sixth Congress in 1928. The theses[12] of the Congress on the agrarian question adopted the customary Bolshevik division of peasants into three categories: 1) the rich or big peasants, who were "capitalist entrepreneurs in agriculture" and therefore enemies of the revolutionary proletariat; 2) the middle peasants, who were able at times to realize a small profit and, in good years, to hire labor outside the family; and 3) the "laboring and exploited masses," who constituted a majority of the rural population and who were essential allies of the proletariat in its revolutionary activity. The "laboring and exploited masses" in the village included as subcategories the agricultural proletariat, the semi-proletariat or peasants with "dwarf" holdings who worked part-time as hired labor, and the petty peasantry, whose small holdings barely supplied the needs of their families. The theses insisted that, without the support of the "laboring and exploited masses" in the village, the proletariat could not be a truly revolutionary class. The experience of the Russian Revolution had shown the value and necessity of Communist work among the poorer peasants.

EBB OF THE REVOLUTIONARY TIDE

In mid-1921, when the Third Congress met, the failure of the revolutionary movement up to that time to spread successfully beyond the confines of the old Russian Empire led the Comintern leadership to adopt a more cautious outlook and to insist upon the need for serious preparation before attempting to seize power. In its theses on "The World Situation and Our Tasks," the Third Congress acknowledged that the "first period of the postwar revolutionary movement . . . appeared in significant measure completed,"[13] and offered the explanation that world revolution did not develop "in a straight line."[14] The theses admitted that the greater part of the working class still stood outside Communist influence; they set as the major task of the International the winning of exclusive influence over the majority of the working class and the drawing of its most active part into direct struggle against the bourgeoisie.[15] The slogan of the Third Congress was "To the Masses."

As years passed the Comintern became even less optimistic. Although the Fourth Congress in 1922 insisted on the continuing existence of crisis in the capitalist world, it conceded that the Communist parties were still far from achieving their necessary aim of persuading the majority of the proletariat to follow the Communist path.[16] The Fifth Congress in 1924 granted that since 1921 "the bourgeoisie had succeeded almost everywhere in carrying out successfully its attack upon the proletariat."[17] The Fifth Plenum of the ECCI in March, 1925, went even further and took note of a "certain partial stabilization" of capitalism.[18] The Sixth Plenum, meeting in February and March of 1926, confirmed the view that capitalism had made a kind of limited recovery from the severe crisis of the immediate postwar years. Yet the Sixth Plenum insisted that capitalist stabilization was only temporary and quite precarious.[19] Essentially, such stabilization as had been achieved rested upon three factors: unheard-of pressure on the masses in the capitalist countries, increased exploitation of the colonies, and the American loans to Europe, which in the final analysis meant that

America was enslaving Europe.[20] The Seventh Plenum, meeting in November and December of 1926, and the Eighth, meeting in May, 1927, continued to acknowledge a partial and temporary stabilization in the capitalist world.

In line with the Comintern's recognition of the ebbing of the postwar revolutionary tide and the achievement of temporary stability in the capitalist world, the tactics of the "united front" were developed. An extensive discussion of the new tactics was given in the form of the theses on the "United Labor Front," adopted by the Fourth Congress in 1922.[21] The united front was envisaged as a temporary alliance between Communist and non-Communist workers to achieve short-term, immediate aims that would benefit the proletariat, such as better working conditions. By these tactics, the Comintern hoped to achieve the strategic goal of unity within the working class under Communist leadership. The united front did not mean that Communist parties were to give up their independence, nor did it mean an abandonment of plans for ultimate Communist control over the revolutionary movement. But the uncompromising, "go-it-alone" attitude of earlier days of the Comintern was displaced by a more flexible approach to non-Communist proletarian organizations. It is important to note here that, although the united front tactics were used henceforth until the dissolution of the Comintern in 1943, the precise manner of implementation varied. Broadly speaking, two forms of the united front alternated in Comintern history. One form, called the united front "from below," was an attempt to achieve working class unity by means of separating non-Communist proletarians from their socialist, anarchist, or anarcho-syndicalist leadership and bringing them under Communist control. This variation of the united front was always accompanied by vicious and uncompromising attacks upon rival non-Communist leaders claiming to represent the working class. The alternative form was the united front "from above," which accepted and indeed sought temporary rapprochements with non-Communist leaders in the proletarian movement. That form of the united front to be employed depended upon the prevailing mood and general policy of the Comintern. In the colonial countries the counterpart of the united front was the collaboration between Communist parties and the anti-imperialist native bourgeoisie. The most famous case of such collaboration was that between the Chinese Communist Party and the Kuomintang from 1924 to 1927.[22] The failure of this collaboration, which was terminated forcibly by Chiang Kai-shek in 1927, led, as will be seen, to a radical change in Comintern thinking about the problem of colonial revolt.

It should be noted that, despite these reversals, the Chinese revolutionary movement assumed increasing importance in the eyes of the Comintern. In the absence of any victories in the capitalist world, the persistent unrest and revolt in China took on impressive and, to be sure, not unjustified dimensions of importance. The Eighth Plenum in May, 1927, pictured the world situation in terms that markedly deemphasized the revolutionary movement in the capitalist countries and extolled the importance of the Chinese revolution. The Plenum divided the world into two camps: "in one—the Union of Soviet Socialist Republics and revolutionary China; in the other—the whole capitalist world." The USSR and revolutionary China were the key points of the international situation. "The significance of the Chinese revolution for the world proletariat is enormous." According to the Eighth Plenum, victory for the workers and peasants in China would be " a powerful stimulus in the revolutionizing of the world labor movement. . . . It would create an objectively revolutionary situation for the most profound mass movements throughout the world."[23] If at one time in the past the Bolsheviks in the economically backward Russian Empire had been fond of speculating on the impact of a successful Russian revolution upon the proletariat in the more advanced capitalist countries, then in the late 1920s the Comintern was beginning to consider an even more serious impact, caused by revolution in the colonial areas, upon the Communist movement in the rest of the world.

The Soviet Union and its ruling Communist Party gained increasing status and importance in Comintern theory during this period. Two developments illustrate this point. First, the Soviet

Union came to be regarded, not as a backward country that had
temporarily risen to occupy the leadership in the world revolutionary movement, but as a vital bulwark of revolution to which
the world movement should give all possible support and defense.

This change in attitude toward the USSR, in the opinion of
E. H. Carr, crystallized at the Fourth Congress in 1922. For the
Communists in other countries, support of the USSR became the
"paramount duty of the sincere revolutionary. From the Fourth
Congress onward this could be openly proclaimed."[24] In the relationship between the Soviet Union and the world revolutionary
movement there had developed a "reversal in the balance of
obligation, from which there would henceforth be no turning
back."[25] This vitally interesting assertion will, of course, be examined later in terms of its appropriateness for the period after
1928. It is certainly true that initially the Comintern regarded the
preeminence of Soviet Russia in the world revolutionary movement
as only temporary, and firmly expected that leadership would pass
soon to the more industrialized countries of the West, especially
Germany. Indeed, one Comintern resolution of the Third Congress
referred to the help to be given by the German working class to
Russia after a German Communist victory had brought about the
unification of "agricultural Russia and industrial Germany."[26]
On this theme, the comments of Trotsky at the Third Congress on
the permanence of the Russian hegemony in the world revolutionary movement are extremely interesting:

Yes, Comrades, we have erected in our country the bulwark of the world
revolution. Our country is still very backward, still very barbaric....
But we are defending this bulwark of the world revolution, since at the
given moment there is no other in the world. When another stronghold
is erected in France or in Germany, then the one in Russia will lose
nine-tenths of its significance; and we shall then go to you in Europe to
defend this other and more important stronghold. Finally, Comrades,
it is sheer absurdity to believe that we deem this Russian stronghold of
the Revolution to be the center of the world.[27]

The Fourth Congress in 1922 passed a resolution stating the
obligation of workers in other countries "to fight for the Soviet
Union."[28] Succeeding congresses continued this theme. During the

"war scare" of 1927, the Eighth Plenum in May passed a special resolution calling for the defense of the USSR from the attacks supposedly being planned by the capitalist countries.[29] Believing that capitalism inevitably bred war and convinced that an anti-Soviet war was always threatening, the Comintern regularly instructed its followers to display their revolutionary zeal by fighting for the defense of the USSR.

The second development enhancing the status of the USSR and its Communist Party was the program of "bolshevization" undertaken in the Comintern at its Fifth Congress in mid-1924. A major drive was launched to ensure a greater degree of conformity to the ideas and practices of the Soviet Communist Party. Only briefly described at the Fifth Congress, "bolshevization" was more fully elaborated at the Fifth Plenum in the spring of 1925. Essentially, it had as its aims the consolidation of the Soviet Party's control over the Comintern and, at the same time, the creation outside the USSR of an improved type of Communist party which could more effectively exploit revolutionary situations. Of course, only the latter purpose was publicized in Comintern materials. The name "bolshevization" explicitly gave a Russian label to the prescription cf reform considered necessary for the various Communist parties.

"Bolshevization," according to the Fifth Congress in 1924, did not mean a "mechanical transferring of the entire experience of the Bolshevik Party in Russia to all other parties."[30] Yet "bolshevization" was defined (in terms so obviously vague as to permit misuse) as the incorporation by the other Communist parties of "that which in Russian Bolshevism was and is international and of general significance."[31] Since the term "bolshevization" recurs subsequently in this study, it is advisable at this point to summarize completely the characteristics of a "bolshevized" party, as given in the theses at the Fifth Congress. Such a party, according to the theses, must be closely and constantly linked with the masses; it must be able to maneuver, unhampered by dogmatism or sectarianism; it must be centralized, without factions, monolithic; it must regularly conduct propagandistic and organizational work in the military forces; it must be "essentially revolutionary, Marxist,

unhesitatingly advancing to its goal" of overthrowing the bourgeoisie.[32] In his authoritative history, Kabakchiev stated that
"bolshevization" meant the "utilization of the experience of the
Russian Communist Party, but equally the revolutionary experiences of the world proletarian movement";[33] yet he failed to
discuss any experience worth imitating other than that of the
Russian Bolsheviks. In another definition, Kabakchiev equated
"bolshevization" with the irrevocable acceptance of the principles
and tactics of Leninism.[34]

Leninism as another name for correct Marxism came into usage
at the Fifth Comintern Congress in mid-1924. It will be recalled
that the Bolshevik leader had died in January of that year. At the
Fifth Plenum of the ECCI in the spring of 1925, the now familiar
definition was made for all the Communist parties to accept:
*"Leninism is Marxism of the era of monopolistic capitalism (imperialism),
imperialist wars, and proletarian revolutions."*[35] According to the Fifth
Plenum, Leninism "enriched" the teaching of Marxism by working
out the following questions:

1. the theory of imperialism and proletarian revolution;
2. the conditions and mechanics of realizing the dictatorship of
   the proletariat;
3. the mutual relations of the proletariat and peasantry;
4. the significance of the national question in general;
5. the significance in particular of national movements in the
   colonial and semi-colonial countries for the world proletarian revolution;
6. the role of the party;
7. the tactics of the proletariat in the epoch of imperialist wars;
8. the role of the proletarian state in the transitional period;
9. the Soviet system, as the concrete type of proletarian state
   for this period;
10. the problem of social strata within the proletariat itself as the
    source of the split of the labor movement into opportunistic
    and revolutionary tendencies, etc.;
11. the overcoming of right social-democratic tendencies as well
    as left deviations in the Communist movement.[36]

The above material on Leninism was incorporated in the theses of the Fifth Plenum on "The Bolshevization of the Parties of the Communist International," a lengthy document spelling out in detail the full meaning of "bolshevization" for the Comintern.[37] The ideological conquest of the Comintern by the Communist Party of the Soviet Union was thereby made even more explicit.

Within the Comintern truly "bolshevized" parties were accorded special recognition and prestige. Less fortunate parties were regularly enjoined to "bolshevize" themselves. The preeminence of the Soviet Communist Party and of its ideas and political experience reached an unprecedented level. It should be remembered, of course, that the program of "bolshevization" developed against a background in which the chief political facts were the continued existence and the increasing power of the USSR (in Comintern eyes the only "proletarian" state) and the failure of the Communist-led revolutionary movement to win power in other countries.[38]

In 1928 a new, third period in the postwar development of capitalism was proclaimed at the Sixth Comintern Congress. Thus, at the beginning of the fifteen-year span of time covered in this study, the Comintern made a fresh appraisal of the possibilities of world revolution and defined a fresh pattern of strategy and tactics for Communists everywhere.

PART TWO

Prerequisites and Preparation
for the
Communist Seizure of Power

IV. PREREQUISITES

Under what set of conditions, in the opinion of the Comintern, should the seizure of power be attempted by the Communists? Posed in this form, the question is somewhat simplified, but it is sufficient to suggest that there did exist for the Communists in the Third International, as well as for any follower of Marx in general, a problem of prerequisites with respect to the seizure of power.

NATURE OF THE PROBLEM

The meaning of "prerequisites." The Communist did not believe that he operated in a vacuum, as it were, in which the sole precondition of action was his own will to act. Definite prerequisites were to be fulfilled before the seizure of power might be placed on the agenda. The problem is one of the "legitimacy," in Communist eyes, of an effort to transfer power from the ruling groups in a society to the Communists.

Two points may be made at the outset with respect to the further definition of the phrase, "prerequisites of the attempt to seize power." First, it is obvious that the spokesmen of the Comintern were thinking in terms of the prerequisites of an attempt to seize power that would offer at least reasonable prospects of *success*. While avoiding claims that under certain conditions any given revolutionary attempt would of necessity be victorious, the Comintern clearly sought to identify those conditions or prerequisites *without which* the revolutionary attempt would be doomed to failure. Second, the phrase would seem to apply only to a seizure of power over a significantly large political-territorial unit. In most cases, and this especially is true of the capitalist countries, the unit is the whole sovereign state. Comintern spokesmen do not appear to have entertained seriously the possibility, for example, of a successful seizure of power in only one half of Germany; no prolonged stabilization between revolutionary and counterrevolutionary forces was considered possible in such a situation. In a capitalist state with its excellent communications systems, it would be patently difficult to perceive an alternative to an "all-or-nothing" outcome of an armed uprising. But for backward areas, especially where communications were lacking and terrain was difficult, it was thought that a seizure of power could be successful on a regional basis, as in the case of Soviet China in the 1930s.[1]

An inquiry into the problem of prerequisites must inevitably take into consideration the general view or philosophy of history held by the leaders of the Comintern. This philosophy of history ought to indicate, more or less clearly, the relative importance of the sphere of activity allocated to the free human will, on the one hand, and the sphere of activity allocated to impersonal forces or "laws," on the other. These spheres exist unless the particular philosophy is either wholly deterministic or wholly void of any appreciation of nonpersonal factors in the process of social change. In the writings of Marx, the precise frontiers of these two spheres are not clear, but it is agreed by all that Marx does assert the reality of certain "laws" of socio-economic development. According to some commentators, these "laws" have such an unquestionable primacy for Marx that he appears as a thoroughgoing determinist, completely subordinating human will and activity to the dictates of impersonal forces. On the other hand, Marx showed from time to time an explicit hostility to the reduction of all human activity to mere puppetry, and insisted on more than one occasion that man makes his own history. In this light, Marx may be seen in part as a voluntarist, who reserved some meaningful scope to the sphere of free human will and activity. This is not the place to try to decide whether Marx was primarily a determinist or primarily a voluntarist, but it is important to recognize that this basic problem exists in the broad philosophy claimed by the Comintern as its own.

The problem of prerequisites may be restated in more elaborate fashion to include: 1) the problem of the effect of impersonal "laws" in determining a revolutionary seizure of power; 2) the problem of the degree of free and conscious self-direction on the part of the revolution-promoting individuals and groups in society as well as on the part of their opponents and of neutrals.

An authoritative statement of Marx's position is in the Introduction to his *Critique of Political Economy*, written in 1859. In this Introduction, Marx laid down certain fundamental propositions outlining his theory of history.[2] Especially relevant is the following:

No form of society can perish before all forces of production which it is large enough to contain are developed, and at no time will outworn conditions be replaced by new higher conditions as long as the material necessities for their existence have not been hatched in the womb of the old society itself.[3]

In Marx's famous five-stage outline of human history, capitalist society (the fourth stage) was to be succeeded by socialist society (the fifth stage). The European Marxist in the nineteenth century was thereby confronted with an unavoidable question: Is capitalism in such-and-such a country fully mature and therefore ripe for displacement through a proletarian revolution and the establishment of a socialist system? The Russian Mensheviks, asking this question in 1917, concluded that it was incorrect at that time to work for the immediate overthrow of capitalism in Russia.

The degree of maturity of a particular economic system within a given society is, of course, very difficult to judge. One simple criterion often used by Marxists in judging the maturity of capitalism was the *numerical size*, in relation to the rest of the population, of the proletariat (the wage-earners who own no means of production and who exist by selling their labor power to entrepreneurs). In the *Communist Manifesto*, Marx and Engels had predicted that two complementary social developments would accompany the maturing of capitalism: the disappearance of the middle class and the polarization of the rest of society into two classes, one composed of an ever-diminishing number of capitalists, and the other of a ever-increasing number of proletarians. The proletariat would constitute the large majority of the population in the later phases of the capitalist stage of history, and therefore would be in a large majority on the eve of the socialist revolution.

Marx contributed further to the problem of prerequisites by insisting that with the full development of the productive capacities of capitalism there would be created in the ranks of the proletariat the necessary *will* to seize power. Leaving aside the question of the role of a Communist party in the creation of this revolutionary will, we can yet perceive another extremely important prerequisite to the seizure of power. In thus making pronouncements on a difficult problem, Marx compelled his spiritual heirs, the Comintern leaders, to face the same question.

The Comintern's view on prerequisites. In later sections of this chapter the problem of prerequisites will be discussed in detail in relation to specific types of societies and revolutions. Here it will be useful simply to indicate the broad features of the Comintern's viewpoint between 1928 and 1943 on the prerequisites of a Communist seizure of power.

First of all, it must be said that the Comintern did not accept Marx's proposition, stated roughly, that a given society in a certain stage of development must exhibit full maturity of its productive forces before that stage can be superseded by another. Rather, it adopted the concept of the "weakest link." According to this concept, revolutions establishing Communist power and leading sooner or later to the creation of a socialist economy would break out wherever the capitalist system was weakest. The "weakest link" of capitalism was not necessarily that country in which capitalism was most highly developed; it might be a colonial country with only the rudiments of a capitalist economy. Stalin in 1924 suggested India and Germany as possibly the "weakest links."[4] In 1917 Russia had enjoyed this distinction. In that year, according to the Comintern Program, the "imperialist front was broken at its weakest link—in tsarist Russia."[5] In Stalin's *Foundations of Leninism,* a work vigorously praised in Comintern literature, the author specifically rejected the view that revolution must come first "where capitalism is more developed, where there is such-and-such a percentage of proletarians and such-and-such a percentage of peasants, and so on."[6] Indeed, those who held such an opinion were the object of unconcealed contempt. In 1933, for example, one of the editors of *Kommunisticheskii Internatsional*, A. Martynov, delivered a severe attack upon the "fatalism" and "tailism"[7] exhibited by the leadership of the Second International in the years before World War I. He wrote:

Bowing before the spontaneity of the historical process, they considered that material conditions for socialist revolution mature only at that remote time... when large-scale capitalist production has completely crowded out small-scale, when the majority of the peasants are pro-letarianized, when the proletariat in the capitalist countries comprise the great majority of the population, when Social-Democratic parties have won a majority in parliament, etc.[8]

The authoritative Comintern Program, while recognizing that the "exploited" segments of society comprised a majority of the population, nowhere stated that the proletariat should itself constitute a majority of the population, or even a majority of the "exploited." The rejection of the belief that in an advanced capitalist society the working class would ultimately outnumber all other classes combined was a clear denial of a viewpoint long popular in Marxist circles. Prior to the Bolshevik Revolution of 1917, as Isaac Deutscher has pointed out, it was a "common Marxist notion that the working class could not and ought not to try to seize power before it had become a majority of the nation."[9]

Intimately related to the concept of the "weakest link" was the concept of the "world system of capitalism." This was a basic term in Comintern literature[10] and it helps to explain the idea of the "weakest link." In Comintern theory, the existence of a "world system of capitalism" was a feature of capitalist development in its last stage, i.e., in the so-called era of imperialism. Capitalism is properly to be understood in this final era not as a collection of separate *national* economic systems, but as a *world* economy, increasingly transcending the political frontiers of states and aiming, albeit in vain, at a kind of world trust capable of managing an international economic network. As a "world system," capitalism is decadent and moribund, despite the fact that in specific political-territorial units the development of capitalism might yet be in its infancy, or, if further advanced, still not at full maturity. The *world* decadence of capitalism permits the Communist party to try to seize power, under certain conditions, within the *national* framework, regardless of the maturity or immaturity of the capitalist development of the country in question. Countries penetrated to any degree by the capitalist mode of production comprise so many links in the world chain of capitalism. If capitalism is an integral world system and if that world system is decadent, then any of its links is ripe for revolution. So runs the Comintern argument.

The concept of the "weakest link" is truly remarkable. Its emancipating character is obvious. No longer is there a question, for the Communists in a particular country, of deferring an attempt to seize power until such time as the capitalist system of that country becomes fully, demonstrably mature. Revolution breaks out at the "weakest link," and the "weakest link" at any given moment is simply that country most victimized by the inevitable and inherent difficulties of the capitalist system of production.

Those who might question this interesting concept of the "weakest link," and the related notion of a "world system" of capitalism, were confronted with a dilemma if they accepted the Bolshevik Revolution of 1917 as a genuine proletarian revolution. For it could not be maintained that before 1917 capitalism in Russia had attained an advanced level of development or had reached parity with Western European capitalism. Nor could it be ignored that strong remnants of "feudalism," as this term is understood by Marxists, persisted in the Russian economic order down to 1917. That the concept of the "weakest link" offered a kind of rationalization for the Bolshevik seizure of power in semi-backward Russia is obvious.

In laying down the proposition that the maturity of the productive forces in a society was irrelevant to the question of a seizure of power, the Comintern did not take the position that *no* prerequisites whatever existed. On the contrary, Comintern doctrines and directives during the whole period from 1928 to 1943 insist upon the presence of three prerequisites before an attempt to seize power may be undertaken. These prerequisites are: 1) a situation of severe crisis, seriously jeopardizing the position of the "ruling circles" in the given society; 2) the presence of a Communist party possessing certain specific attributes; and 3) mass support from substantial parts of the discontented classes or groups in the society. As the Comintern usually spoke of the maturing or growth of these prerequisites, there is involved here also the factor of time. These prerequisites had to reach a certain level of development, extremely difficult to define, before the seizure of power could be attempted with prospects of success.

Of the three prerequisites, the first two may be called *constant* prerequisites, as they held true without change or variation for all types of societies; the third may be called the *variable* prerequisite, because the kind of necessary mass support varied from society to society and depended upon the given stage of economic development. These convenient terms—constant and variable prerequisites—will be used subsequently in our detailed examination of the three prerequisites of the seizure of power. But here we may briefly recall the Comintern's terminology, which was somewhat different.

The habit of Comintern ideologists was to divide prerequisites into "objective" and "subjective," the former embracing the situation of extreme crisis and the latter embracing the Communist party and its "organization" of mass support. This terminology could be misleading, for spontaneous feelings of resentment and hatred on the part of the masses against the capitalist system fell into the category of "objective," not "subjective," factors. Only when such feelings became translated into a class-consciousness that accepted Communist leadership did they constitute "subjective" factors. Evidence abounds in Comintern literature that the subjective factor was always associated with the Communist party or, by extension, with a class or classes which accepted its doctrines and its leadership. Through such acceptance, a class became "class-conscious," or subjectively aware of its role and duty. Its resistance to the existing regime was no longer blind and spontaneous, but perceptive and disciplined.

Essentially, then, the subjective factor was the Communist party. "*Objective conditions*," it was stated in an editorial in 1931 in *Kommunisticheskii Internatsional*, "are very favorable for us, but the subjective factor (the readiness of Communist parties for impending great battles, at the head of the working class) strongly lags behind the tempo of unfolding events."[11] Lozovsky, the head of the Red International of Trade Unions and a member of the ECCI, spoke at the Tenth Plenum in 1929 on the British situation in these words: "But the British proletariat cannot get rid of its illusions automatically. The objective situation is, of course, favorable for this, but to accelerate the process, the intervention of a subjective factor is necessary—the Communist party."[12] Another editorial in the Comintern's theoretical journal distinguished between "objectively favorable factors" and the "insufficient maturity of the *subjective factor*—the Communist parties."[13]

The prerequisites briefly outlined here are discussed below at much greater length. But at this point, as a necessary and preliminary part of the detailed study of prerequisites that is to follow, the various types of revolutions and the various types of societies within the Comintern panorama of world revolution must be identified.

REVOLUTIONS AND SOCIETIES

"*Bourgeois-democratic*" *revolution and* "*proletarian-socialist*" *revolution.* A cursory reading of almost any Communist material reveals the frequent usage of the terms "bourgeois-democratic" revolution and "proletarian-socialist" revolution. A frequent substitute for "bourgeois-democratic" revolution in Comintern usage is "bourgeois" revolution; likewise, "proletarian" revolution and "socialist" revolution are often found in place of "proletarian-socialist" revolution. These terms are among the most confusing and misleading of all those used by the Comintern. They require careful definition here, and subsequently throughout the text they will always be found within quotation marks, to indicate that the meaning of these terms as used in Comintern literature differs radically from the meaning usually given to them elsewhere. This difference between Comintern usage and normal usage will now be discussed. But it may be pointed out immediately that, whatever the usage, the two terms reflect the view that at a given time not all societies are alike; rather, they are at different stages of development and require different types of revolutions.

To understand the terms "bourgeois-democratic" revolution and "proletarian-socialist" revolution it is necessary to refer once more to Marx, because the Comintern leaders claimed him as their chief ideological ancestor and because with Marx these terms had a special definition and meaning. Marx used the term "bourgeois" revolution to denote the revolutionary process by which his third (feudal) stage in the development of human society was replaced by his fourth (capitalist) stage. The term "proletarian" revolution signified the revolutionary process by which his fourth (capitalist) stage was replaced by this fifth (socialist) stage. Marx's usage of these terms gave to them a fairly clear meaning, and subsequently they were widely used by his followers in the socialist movement. It is probably safe to state that most non-Marxist scholars are in general agreement about the meanings which Marx meant to convey by these terms.

The broad distinctions between the "proletarian-socialist" and the "bourgeois-democratic" revolution, commonly recognized by Marx and his professed followers—other than Communists—may be summarized at this point.

1. *Politics*. The "bourgeois-democratic" revolution is pictured as terminating royal absolutism or the rule of the nobility. The succeeding rule of the bourgeoisie exhibits the typical devices of a bill of rights, a parliament, and an independent judiciary. The classic case for Marxists is the French Revolution of 1789. The "bourgeois-democratic" revolution is closely associated in time with the development of capitalism in each political-territorial unit. The "proletarian-socialist" revolution overthrows bourgeois rule and establishes the "dictatorship of the proletariat," a temporary form of government intended to be "democratic" toward all "toilers" and "dictatorial" toward the propertied classes. Ultimately the proletarian state "withers away."

2. Economics. The "bourgeois-democratic" revolution is a revolt against feudalism and mercantilism, and a demand for a minimum of interference in the economic sphere by the government and for a strengthening and clarification of the concept of private property. Land reform, in the direction of a division of great estates into small private holdings for distribution to land-hungry peasants, is also a common feature. The "proletarian-socialist" revolution is a revolt against the general "anarchy" of capitalism arising from the private ownership of natural resources, machines, and other means of production. Private property is abolished by the transfer to public ownership of the means of production. The "anarchy" of capitalism is abolished by the inauguration of a planned economy. The goal of production is to be not profit, but the satisfaction of human wants and needs. Ultimately, no coercion is necessary; voluntary associations for production are formed.

3. Society. The "bourgeois-democratic" revolution destroys the privileges existing under the *ancien régime*, in the name of equal rights for all men, but, in the opinion of Marxists, actually only for the benefit of the bourgeoisie. The "proletarian-socialist" revolution ends the supremacy of the bourgeoisie and endows the proletarian class with the greatest social power and prestige. One of the ultimate goals of the "socialist" revolution is the further transformation of all classes into the one all-embracing category of freely cooperating "toilers."

These contrasts between the "bourgeois-democratic" and the "proletarian-socialist" revolution by no means exhaust the differences between them, but they should serve to clarify the content of these terms as non-Communist Marxists have been accustomed to use them. It is indispensable to appreciate that when Marx used the term "bourgeois-democratic" to characterize a society in a given era, he meant that the bourgeois class was the ruling class during that era in that particular society. It may appear that the point is being labored here; however, the reader will realize how markedly Communist usage departs from conventional usage, when he discovers that Communists, in speaking of a coming "bourgeois-democratic" revolution, actually mean a revolution led by

Communists on behalf of the proletariat and other nonbourgeois segments of society.

The general content of these terms—as used in Comintern materials—must now be briefly stated. The "bourgeois-democratic" revolution is one that occurs in societies in which capitalism as a rule has reached only a modest level of development. The leadership of the "bourgeois-democratic" revolution must come into the hands of the Communist party, if such a revolution is to be successful. In the phase of world capitalist development after World War I the bourgeoisie no longer can be counted upon to play a genuinely revolutionary role. The revolution, under Communist leadership, is not made on behalf of the bourgeoisie, but on behalf of the proletariat, the broad masses of the peasantry, and other segments of society that may reasonably fall within the broad category of "toilers." The goals of the "bourgeois-democratic" revolution do not include the establishment of individualistic capitalism, but rather the setting up of a controlled economy that will move toward socialism through a prolonged transitional phase.

The "proletarian-socialist" revolution occurs in societies in which capitalism has reached mature development, in the opinion of the Comintern. The leadership of the "proletarian-socialist" revolution is in the hands of the Communist party. The revolution is made on behalf of the proletariat and the poorer elements among the peasantry. The goals of the revolution include the abolition of private property in the means of production and an immediate effort to reach socialism through a short transitional period.

The above definitions are admittedly oversimplified, but their full content will be set forth as the study unfolds. The Comintern's usage of these terms remained consistent from 1928 to 1943, and the above summary holds true for the entire period under examination.

The advanced capitalist society. The Comintern Program of 1928 outlined four broad types of societies in which the world revolutionary process was to unfold: 1) highly developed or advanced capitalist societies; 2) societies of medium capitalist development;

3) dependent, semi-colonial, or colonial societies; and 4) very backward, primitive societies.[14] In Comintern discussions, the first three types are by far the most important; the fourth type received virtually no attention in Comintern literature. The questions to be asked here about each of the four types of societies are: What were the characteristics of the given type of society according to the Comintern? What was the type of revolution—"bourgeois-democratic" or "proletarian-socialist"—that was appropriate for each type of society?

We may begin with the society of highly developed capitalism. In Comintern literature from 1928 on, including the Program of 1928, one searches in vain for a completely satisfactory definition. In fact, one finds definitions for the second and third types of countries that are more satisfactory. Apparently, the Comintern regarded the term "advanced capitalist country" as so familiar and self-explanatory that it considered an extensive definition unnecessary.

In its most complete attempt at a definition, the Program stated that an advanced capitalist society was one in which there prevailed "powerful productive forces, highly centralized production, with small-scale production having relatively little significance, and with a long established bourgeois-democratic political order."[15] The specific countries mentioned in the Program as examples of this category were the United States, Germany, and Great Britain.

In so far as economic conditions are concerned, the Program does not make explicit anything more than the preponderance of "highly centralized production" over small-scale enterprises. Tendencies toward centralization and concentration are, of course, familiar features of Marx's own picture of capitalism in its mature state. As to other economic criteria of an advanced capitalist society, a number of questions, however, remained unanswered by the Comintern. What percentage of its production should be industrial, as against agricultural? To what degree should heavy industry exist? What level of development should have been attained by the so-called tertiary[16] sector of the economy, i.e., those occupations devoted to distribution, transport, etc.? No attempt was made in Comintern literature to provide even approximate answers to these questions. The impression is that the Comintern spokesmen in general preferred not to make precise commitments on such points.

The type of revolution deemed appropriate for an advanced capitalist society was the "proletarian-socialist" revolution.

The society of medium capitalist development. The Program of 1928 offered only a brief and highly unclear definition of a country with a medium development of capitalism. Such countries were those with "significant remnants of semi-feudal relations in agriculture, with a certain minimum of the material prerequisites necessary for socialist construction, and with a yet uncompleted bourgeois-democratic revolution."[17] By "significant remnants of semi-feudal relations in agriculture" was meant any or all of the following: widespread peasant indebtedness and landlessness; inadequate or "dwarf" holdings by peasants coupled with a predominance of large-scale holdings by nonpeasants; and the absence of legally defined rights of the peasantry to their land. A "certain minimum of the prerequisites necessary for socialist construction" must mean —and here again the Program is quite vague—at least the beginnings of large-scale industry in several fields, including the production not only of consumer goods but also of capital goods. It is difficult to perceive how a country could possess the minimum basis for the development of a socialist economy without having some capital-goods industry. The "uncompleted bourgeois-democratic revolution" may indicate the failure of the bourgeoisie to become the ruling class. It may also indicate the absence or the incomplete emergence of "bourgeois" rights, such as freedom of speech, assembly, and press, and of "bourgeois" institutions, such as a parliament, the secret ballot, an independent judiciary, and the like. Finally, it may indicate the failure to solve national minority problems. As examples of this second type of society, the Program singled out the following: Spain, Portugal, Poland, Hungary, and the Balkans.[18]

The society of medium capitalist development posed many problems for the Comintern theoreticians. From the evidence it is clear that the task of determining the correct type of revolution for this category was for them a difficult one. Originally, in the Draft Program of 1928, the second category of societies was assigned a "bourgeois-democratic" revolution which would "grow over" into a "socialist" revolution.[19] Neither the nature nor the rate of the process of "growing over" was made clear. The solution offered in the Draft provoked a good deal of debate, both on the floor of the Sixth Congress and in the Program Commission. Especially was this true with respect to Poland and Bulgaria. Some delegates argued that a "socialist" revolution was on the agenda for both of these countries. Bukharin replied to the criticism of the Draft Program by acknowledging the objections raised concerning the classification of Poland and Bulgaria. He proposed that a "more elastic formula" be adopted for the type of revolution suitable to countries in the second category.[20]

The "more elastic formula" was given in the final Program. Here the simple alternatives of "bourgeois-democratic" and "proletarian-socialist" revolution were abandoned for the countries of medium capitalist development. Instead, the Program outlined a fairly complex revolutionary process, in which two paths were possible: "In *some* of these countries, there is possible a process of a more or less swift growing over of the bourgeois-democratic revolution into the socialist revolution; in *others*—types of proletarian revolution [are possible], but with a great number of tasks of a bourgeois-democratic character."[21]

Broadly speaking, there were two possibilities in the case of the society with a medium development of capitalism. One was that such a society might not be sufficiently developed, economically and politically, to permit an immediate advance toward socialism after the Communist seizure of power. Here there would have to be, therefore, a distinct period of transition, which was called in Comintern phraseology the "growing over" of the "bourgeois-democratic" revolution into the "socialist" revolution.

The other possibility was that a society of the second category might be sufficiently advanced to permit a revolution that would be "proletarian" from the beginning although it might face a considerable amount of unfinished business of a "bourgeois-democratic" nature. It is obvious that those societies to which the Comintern assigned a "proletarian" revolution ranked higher in terms of Comintern criteria than did those societies to which a "bourgeois-democratic" revolution was assigned.

For which countries lying within the second category of societies was a "proletarian" revolution considered appropriate by the Comintern? And for what reasons? Poland, Hungary, and Bulgaria fall into this category.

The Polish Communists at the Sixth Congress had objected strongly to the passage in the Draft Program that placed Poland in the second category of societies and assigned to her a "bourgeois-democratic" revolution. A favorite argument of the Polish Communists was that Poland had reached (by 1928) a higher stage of development than Russia had attained by 1917. If the Bolshevik Revolution of November, 1917, was "proletarian-socialist" in nature, as the Comintern claimed, then, the Polish Communists argued, Poland was certainly entitled to such a revolution. A reading of the speeches of the Polish delegates leaves one with the impression that they believed Poland's national honor to be at stake in this debate. The Poles argued as follows: 1) in Poland capitalist relations were more strongly developed in the countryside, and differentiation amongst the peasantry had proceeded much further, than in Russia before 1917; and 2) the Polish political system was in harmony with bourgeois interests, whereas in pre-1917 Russia there had been deep hostility between the liberal bourgeoisie and the tsar who, together with the landed gentry, had dominated Russian political life.[22] The German delegate Dengel pointed to other and more specific factors in recent Polish history: the existence of large-scale capitalist farming in the western lands of Poland that had formerly been within the German Empire; the experience of the Polish proletariat in the Russian Revolution of 1905; the development of fascism in Poland and the proletariat's belief that the bourgeoisie rather than feudalism was its chief enemy; and lastly, the existence in Poland of a mass Communist Party having a considerable influence among the proletariat and part of the peasantry.[23] All these factors indicated, Dengel said, the appropriateness of a "socialist" revolution.

An authoritative statement of the nature of the revolution that would be suited to Poland was given in 1932 in the draft of the program of the Communist Party of Poland, drawn up with the help of the central organs of the Comintern. Here a "proletarian" revolution linked with the completion of "bourgeois-democratic" tasks was stated to be necessary for Poland. The explanation for this decision followed:

The confiscation of the land of the landlords and its distribution to the peasantry and the liberation of exploited nationalities are the historic tasks of the bourgeois-democratic revolution. In contemporary Poland in view of the well-developed stratification of the peasantry, in view of the fusion of the landlords with the urban bourgeoisie, in view of the bourgeois order of the Polish state—the bourgeois-democratic revolution is already a bygone stage. However, the fact that a significant, and among the oppressed nationalities an overwhelming, number of tasks are still unfulfilled, creates in Poland a special interlacing of historical conditions, thanks to which the socialist revolution of the proletariat must fully complete and carry to conclusion the tasks of the bourgeois-democratic revolution.[24]

The case of Hungary is especially interesting. The Program of 1928 had classified the Hungarian Communist Revolution of 1919 as "proletarian"[25] and other Comintern materials had defined the short-lived Communist rule in Hungary as a "dictatorship of the proletariat."[26] However, some members of the Hungarian Party, led by a Communist named Blum, expressed in 1929 the view that the appropriate future revolution in Hungary was "bourgeois-democratic" in nature.[27] In an open letter of October 26, 1929, addressed to the Hungarian Communist Party, the ECCI took an authoritative step toward the elimination of this latter view. Blum's position was condemned. The ECCI envisaged for Hungary a "proletarian" revolution that would liquidate in its course "a number of remnants of feudalism."[28] For this "proletarian" revolution, the most significant tasks of a "bourgeois-democratic" nature would lie in the field of the "distribution and structure of landed property and the organization of labor in agriculture." Precisely what is meant here is not clear, but it can be conjectured that this statement referred to the breakup of large landed estates. But the revolution was to go much further, and was to overthrow the capitalist system. The open letter noted that a decisive circumstance in determining the character of the revolution in Hungary was the fact "that the working class has already once won state power and established its dictatorship." The authors of the open letter were apparently impressed chiefly by the actuality of the Hungarian Revolution of 1919, which had been customarily interpreted as a "proletarian" revolution. Not wishing to contradict the traditional view and obviously sensing the awkwardness of proposing a "bourgeois-democratic" revolution where once a "proletarian" revolution had for a time succeeded, the Comintern once more opted for the latter type of revolution.

The Bulgarian Communist Kolarov had objected to the classification of the future Bulgarian revolution as a "bourgeois-democratic" revolution. Kolarov's main argument in favor of a "proletarian" revolution was that Bulgarian agriculture was without any "semi-feudal" elements whatsoever. "In Bulgaria," Kolarov declared, "the agrarian revolution was already completed a half-century ago."[29]

A summary of the Comintern's position might run as follows: a "proletarian" revolution that would perform some "bourgeois-democratic" tasks in addition to its "proletarian-socialist" tasks was appropriate for a society of medium capitalist development if that society had completed *most* of the customary tasks of the "bourgeois-democratic" revolution. The major tasks of the "bourgeois-democratic" revolution were: 1) the attainment of a certain level of industrial development; 2) an agrarian reform, including the eradication of "semi-feudal relations" and the breakup of large estates; 3) the establishment of democratic institutions of government; and 4) the solution of the national minority question, in those countries where it existed.

Turning now to those countries to which was assigned a "bourgeois-democratic" revolution that might fairly rapidly "grow over" into a "proletarian-socialist" revolution, we have Spain and Japan as major examples.

The nature of the contemporary Spanish revolution was indicated by the Spanish Communist Urtada at the Twelfth Plenum of the ECCI in 1932. "The basic characteristic of the Spanish revolution," he declared, "is the incomplete nature of the bourgeois-democratic revolution and above all of the agrarian revolution."[30] In Spain the "bourgeois-democratic" revolution was incomplete in at least three respects: in the system of land tenure, in the question of national minorities, and in the governmental system (the persistence of feudal monarchical government up to the revolt of April, 1931).[31] The "bourgeois-democratic" character of the Spanish revolution was reaffirmed in 1936 by Ercoli (Togliatti), who pointed out that the Spanish people were solving the tasks of the "bourgeois-democratic" revolution under the special conditions of the Spanish Civil War.[32]

The case of Japan was more complicated. Rather surprisingly the considerable industrial progress made by Japan did not put it in the category of countries destined to have a "proletarian" revolution. The chief characteristics of Japan were its "backward, Asiatic, semi-feudal" system of agriculture and its peculiar political regime headed by a monarchy resting upon the support of the landlords and the bourgeoisie.[33] The strong proletarian component of the population—asserted to be about 50 percent of the total[34]— failed to win Comintern recognition of Japan as ready for a "proletarian" revolution.

The Comintern had in 1927, under the direction of Bukharin, drawn up new theses respecting Japan in which the "bourgeois-democratic" revolution was singled out as applicable at that time.[35] Subsequently, the theses underwent revision, and in 1931 a "proletarian" revolution was considered appropriate for Japan in a project issued by the Japanese Central Committee.[36] The project of the Japanese Central Committee was criticized in a document entitled "On the Situation in Japan and the Tasks of the Communist Party of Japan," which emanated from the West European Bureau of the Comintern and was published in *Kommunisticheskii*

Internatsional in March, 1932. The purpose of the document was to correct the designation of the Japanese revolution as a "proletarian" revolution. In raising the question of the nature of the Japanese revolution, the West European Bureau directed its major attention to the "uniqueness of the ruling system in Japan, which represents a linking of extraordinarily strong elements of feudalism with a far-advanced development of monopoly capitalism."[37] The Japanese ruling system was led by the monarchy, which rested not only upon the "feudal, parasitical class of landowners," but also upon a "predatory bourgeoisie" that was fast becoming rich. At the same time, the monarchy preserved "its own independent, relatively large role and its absolute character, concealed only by pseudo-constitutional forms."[38] The mistake of the Japanese Communists had been in underestimating the role of the monarchy, and in looking upon the Japanese parliament and ministries as state institutions independent of the monarchy. The monarchy was a "bourgeois-landlord monarchy," which "rather cleverly" represented the interests of both classes.[39] What the West European Bureau was trying to say appears to be that the monarchy was not a mere tool of the two classes which supported it, but rather a partly independent political force continuing to exercise arbitrary power behind a parliamentary façade.

The nature of the Japanese revolution was also examined in a report by Otto Kuusinen, a top-ranking Comintern figure, at a special session of the Presidium on March 7, 1932.[40] Kuusinen admitted the "extremely difficult task" of formulating the character of the revolution that would be appropriate in Japan. Referring to the now condemned attitude of the Japanese Party, he pinpointed its error as one of seeing only a single aspect of the economy of Japan—that of finance capital.[41] Such an incomplete view of the Japanese economy had led to an underestimation of the Japanese monarchy and of the survivals of feudalism in Japan and to an erroneous conclusion about the suitability of a "proletarian" revolution for Japan.[42]

Having made these points, Kuusinen supported the attitude of the West European Bureau, which had insisted upon a partly

independent role for the Japanese monarchy and the civil and
military apparatus headed by it. What, in Kuusinen's opinion, was
the relation of the monarchy to the classes supporting it? "The
monarchical state apparatus represents the solid skeleton of the
existing dictatorship of the class of exploiters; it rests upon these
classes, it represents their interests, it exists in an intimate bloc with
the upper groups of the bourgeoisie and landlords." But was the
monarchy merely a figurehead whose actions were determined by
the bourgeois and landlord groups? Kuusinen answered in the
negative, saying that the monarchy "develops its own independent
and relatively great role and its own absolute character, hidden
only by external, pseudo-constitutional forms."[43] Kuusinen's argument is not wholly consistent, for he claimed that the Japanese
monarchy represented two sets of interests, its own and the interests
of the bourgeoisie and landlords. The "relative independence" of
the Japanese monarchy was at least as great as that of the Russian
monarchy in the opinion of Kuusinen, who asserted that Lenin
himself had called it a mistake to equate the Russian monarchy
with the rule of the possessing classes.[44]

For Spain and Japan, the major considerations that led the
Comintern to insist upon a "bourgeois-democratic" revolution
appear to be the need for a sweeping agrarian reform and the
weakness of the bourgeoisie vis-à-vis the big landowners and the
monarchy. Yet it must be said that the Comintern never offered a
convincing set of criteria by which to judge the appropriateness of
a "bourgeois-democratic" revolution for this type of society. The
indecision of the Comintern in 1928 in the cases of Poland and
Bulgaria, as well as later in the case of Japan, point clearly to a
serious weakness in Comintern efforts to establish useful criteria.

The colonial, semi-colonial, and dependent societies. Besides those
countries which exhibited either a high level or a moderate level of
capitalist development, the Comintern Program of 1928 also sought
to categorize those areas of the world in which capitalism had
made only a rudimentary appearance. In the Draft Program, this
third category was labeled "colonial and semi-colonial countries,"
and the examples given were China and India.[45] No attempt was

made to distinguish between "colonial" and "semi-colonial." These terms are always found grouped together in Comintern literature. Apparently the use of the term "semi-colonial" was a recognition by the Comintern of the *formal* independence of such countries as China, which was regarded by the Comintern as in fact no more independent of foreign control than, say, India. In the Program as finally adopted, the label is extended to include "dependent countries," of which Argentina and Brazil were cited as typical.[46] The use of the term "dependent countries" was probably adopted because of the suggestion of Ricardo Parades, a delegate representing the Communist and Socialist parties of Ecuador. Pointing to the variation in the degree of dependence of Latin American countries upon imperialist states, he suggested that a new subcategory, to be known as "dependent" countries, should be set up.[47] This term would encompass those areas which had been penetrated economically by imperialism but which still retained a higher degree of political independence than did the colonies and semi-colonies.

According to the Program, the countries in the third category had the following major characteristics: 1) a rudimentary, or in certain instances, a significant development of industry, which was, however, insufficient "in the great majority of cases for independent socialist construction"; 2) the predominance of "feudal-medieval relations or relations of an 'Asiatic mode of production' in the economy of the country as well as in its political superstructure"; and 3) the concentration in the hands of "foreign imperialist groups of the most important industrial, trade, and banking institutions, the basic means of transportation, latifundia and plantations, etc."[48] By "independent socialist construction" was meant the building of socialism in a particular country without outside help from a more advanced country. As is well known, Stalin in his struggle with Trotsky, insisted upon the capacity of Russia to build socialism without outside help. According to the Program only a minority of the colonies, semi-colonies, and dependent countries might expect to build socialism without the help of more advanced societies and then, as indicated

below, only after a long period of "bourgeois-democratic" revolution. The terms "feudal-medieval relations" and "relations of
'an Asiatic mode of production'" refer, respectively, to the third
and first stages in Marx's five-stage periodization of human
history.[49]

In the colonial, semi-colonial, and dependent countries, the
Program stated, the appropriate type of revolution was the
"bourgeois-democratic" revolution.[50] It must be remembered that
this term meant for Communists a revolutionary process under the
leadership of Communists and not under the leadership of the
bourgeois class. Here the term "bourgeois-democratic" referred to
the nature of the tasks of the revolution and not to the leadership of
that revolution.

Two very important forms of revolutionary activity in the colonial, semi-colonial, and dependent countries received a good
deal of attention from the Comintern and were embraced within
the category "bourgeois-democratic." These were the peasant
revolutionary movement, directed against "feudalism and pre-
capitalist forms of exploitation," and the national independence
movement, directed against foreign imperialism.[51] As will be shown
later, both of these movements, popular in the true sense of the
word, were regarded by the Comintern as powerful forces that
were to be harnessed to Communist leadership.

The very complex "bourgeois-democratic" revolution in the
colonies, semi-colonies, and dependent countries was eventually
to "grow over" into a "proletarian-socialist" revolution. The
Program did not state the duration of the "bourgeois-democratic"
phase. It emphasized that entry into the "proletarian-socialist"
phase could, in the majority of cases, come about only with help
from outside, i.e., with help from more advanced countries that
were already socialist.[52]

Finally, it may be noted that the Comintern rejected the idea
that colonial, semi-colonial, and dependent countries were ready
for a "proletarian-socialist" revolution, for such societies, having
not yet undergone a "bourgeois-democratic" revolution, could not
simply skip a necessary stage of historical progress. In 1928, the

Ninth Plenum, in its resolution on the Chinese question, condemned tendencies to "leap over" the phase of the "bourgeois-democratic" revolution in China; the Plenum explained the necessity of this phase on the grounds that several major tasks of the "bourgeois-democratic" era had not been completed—the agrarian revolution and the abolition of feudal relations, the unification of China, and the national independence of China.[53] The impossibility of "skipping" stages in the evolution of society, however, did not mean that such stages might not be shortened by the "growing over" of a lower stage into a higher. But these points must await fuller treatment in Part IV.

The very backward societies. The Comintern Program completed its categorization of societies by distinguishing yet a fourth group of "still more backward countries."[54] Only one paragraph of the Program was devoted to this category, which received almost no attention in other Comintern literature. Evidently this category was to embrace the most primitive parts of the globe—areas in which tribal institutions still prevailed. The Program suggested that some parts of the African continent belonged to this category.[55] It was pointed out that these areas possessed almost no proletarians and almost no "national bourgeoisie."[56] Foreign imperialism played the role of military occupier and governor. In these areas, the struggle for national liberation was regarded by the Comintern as of central significance.

The Program briefly suggested a most interesting future for such backward areas: "A national uprising and its victory can open here a path of development toward socialism without passing through the stage of capitalism in general, if in fact the powerful aid of the countries with proletarian dictatorships is rendered."[57]

THE CONSTANT PREREQUISITES

The constant prerequisites for the Communist seizure of power were the existence of a revolutionary situation and the existence of a Communist party having certain minimum characteristics (as to size, ideological purity, organizational correctness, contact with

the masses, etc.). These prerequisites were considered necessary in
any and all societies.

The revolutionary situation. The definition consistently used by the
Comintern throughout the period from 1928 to 1943 to convey
correctly the nature of a revolutionary situation was taken from
Lenin's pamphlet *"Left-wing" Communism, an Infantile Disorder*,
published in 1920.[58] The following passage, written in 1930 by
A. Martynov, a member of the editorial board of *Kommunisticheskii
Internatsional*, may serve as an example of the frequent endorsement
of Lenin's definition:

> Lenin gave the methodological prerequisites for the solution of the
> problem of political crisis . . . in this fashion:
> "Only when those below do not wish the old way and when those at
> the top cannot go on in the old way, only then can revolution conquer.
> This truth is expressed in another way: revolution is impossible without
> a national crisis (affecting both the exploiters and the exploited)."
> Such a "national crisis" Lenin identified with a revolutionary situa-
> tion. On the characteristics of a national crisis, i.e., a revolutionary
> situation, Lenin wrote in this sense even earlier, in 1915, in his article,
> "The Collapse of the Second International":
> "What, generally speaking, are the signs of a revolutionary situation?
> We surely will not be mistaken if we point to the following three chief
> types: 1) Impossibility for the ruling classes to preserve their rule
> unchanged . . . 2) Unusual intensification of the demands and wants of
> the oppressed classes. 3) A significant increase, in view of the indicated
> reasons, of mass activity . . . ." Such are the objective signs of a revolution-
> ary situation.[59]

Martynov in this quotation presented the essential elements in
one of the two constant prerequisites. Lenin's statements, brief and
undetailed as they were, constitute the classical definition customarily resorted to by the Comintern. These quotations from Lenin
are to be found with great frequency in Comintern materials. In
fact, they always remained the core of the official Comintern viewpoint on this question.[60]

The quotation from Lenin's *"Left-wing" Communism* stresses the
national character of the crisis, which must embrace not only the
"oppressed" classes, but also the "ruling" groups in society. Thus
a revolutionary situation is one reflecting not only severe instability

at the apex of society but also profound discontent, leading to mass activity, among the lower echelons of society. Rudolf Schlesinger points out that the situation of crisis, to be at all meaningful in a revolutionary sense, must involve at least two things: 1) the outlook of the lower classes within the existing society must be so hopeless that they are prepared to make "serious sacrifices for the cause of their emancipation"; and 2) prospects for successful revolution must exist through "the evident inability of the present rulers to handle the situation, due to cleavages within their own ranks and between them and their former supporters."[61]

Is it not safe to assume that Lenin believed the "ruling classes" would be so seriously disunited as to policy and action that they could no longer rely upon the traditional instruments of coercion— the police and the armed forces? The impossibility of effective decision-making and the impossibility of decision-enforcement— these would appear to be reasonable characteristics of the crisis "at the top." The effectiveness of the armed forces at the moment of the Communist attempt to seize power is a factor of obvious importance. While the Comintern materials do not explicitly state that one prerequisite of the attempt to seize power must be a favorable attitude on the part of the armed forces, it seems safe to conclude that the bulk of the armed forces must be in a state of disintegration, and at least indifferently disposed toward the "ruling classes" even if not favorably disposed toward the Communists. Especially in conscripted armies it could be expected that the national crisis among the "exploited" would have grave repercussions in the rank-and-file of the fighting forces. It may be added that the Comintern Program simply states that armed uprisings against ruling groups must have as "an obligatory prerequisite . . . strengthened revolutionary work within the army and navy."[62]

Lenin's phrase, "when those below do not wish the old way," is obviously vague. It must mean, at the minimum, that the resentments and dissatisfactions produced by the national crisis have created a profound resolve throughout the population to alter radically and in wholesale fashion the existing situation. The strength of this desire for a change is expressed in Lenin's words, "significant increase . . . of mass activity."

There was no quarrel within the ranks of the Comintern as to the ultimate origin of a revolutionary crisis, which, as might be expected, was accredited to the malfunctioning of the capitalist system. The accentuation of misery and the inevitability of economic crises under capitalism were basic prophecies of Marxism. That capitalism breeds wars, with accompanying political and social crises, was also an elementary lesson of Leninism.

Comintern materials are quite precise on the point that the revolutionary situation, as described above, would itself be insufficient to cause a victorious Communist seizure of power. The situation of crisis was, of course, a necessary part of the Comintern's picture, but not its whole picture. The revolutionary situation represented that special conjunction of economic, social, and political processes and events which was to be exploited by the Communist party. But no situation, however severe, was thought to be a *cul-de-sac* for the ruling classes. The Communists were not to be installed in power, so to speak, mechanically, whenever a revolutionary situation existed.

The Communist party and its characteristics. In addition to the presence of a revolutionary situation, a second prerequisite of the Communist seizure of power that the Comintern considered necessary in any society was the existence of a Communist party possessing certain minimum attributes.

In the discussion of the structure of the Comintern in Chapter II, it was shown that the Statutes of 1928 created a highly centralized organization, with a maximum of control concentrated at the center and a minimum of autonomy exercised by the individual Communist parties. These Communist parties were in fact regarded merely as "sections" of a *single* world party, the Communist International. The purpose of such a centralization of control was, of course, to make each section of the International the most effective possible instrument of the will of the Comintern.

The character of the Communist party and its all-important place in the revolutionary movement can be summed up briefly by posing and answering a few basic questions. First, what is the Communist party? "The party is the vanguard of the working class, consisting of the best, most class-conscious, active, and courageous members of the class."[63] Such is the definition in the Program of 1928. Next, is the party necessary for the achievement of the aims of Communism? The Program states: "The successful struggle of the Communist International for the dictatorship of the proletariat presupposes the existence...of a Communist party in every country."[64] And finally, why is the party necessary? The answer to this question is based solidly on Lenin's famous pamphlet *What Is To Be Done?* published in 1902, in which Lenin in one of his most consequential writings laid down the proposition that the working class could not "spontaneously" effect its own salvation and could by itself achieve only a "trade-union consciousness"; the proletariat would always stop short of the act of destroying the capitalist system unless it were properly led and directed by an élite vanguard, the Communist party.[65] Lenin's position always received full endorsement by the Comintern.[66]

At the Seventeenth Congress of the CPSU in 1934, Stalin further explained the need for a Communist party in his attack upon mechanistic belief in an automatic downfall of capitalism. At this Congress he made a pertinent statement that was repeatedly quoted at the Seventh Comintern Congress in 1935 and subsequently during the late 1930s in the Comintern press. Since it was so publicized and of such obvious authority, it is well to present Stalin's statement here, as quoted verbatim in Wilhelm Pieck's speech at the Seventh Congress of the Comintern:

Some comrades think that as soon as a revolutionary crisis occurs the bourgeoisie must drop into a hopeless position, that its end is predetermined, that the victory of revolution is assured, and that all they [the Communists] have to do is to wait for the bourgeoisie to fall, and to draw up victorious resolutions. This is a profound mistake. The victory of revolution never comes by itself. It has to be prepared for and won. And only a strong proletarian revolutionary party can prepare for and win victory. Moments occur when the situation is revolutionary, when the rule of the bourgeoisie is shaken to its very foundations, and yet the victory of the revolution does not come because there is no revolutionary party of the proletariat sufficiently strong and authoritative to lead the masses and take power. It would be unwise to believe that such "cases" cannot occur.[67]

The Communist party, then, was indispensable. It was to direct the transition from capitalism to socialism throughout the world. It was to lead even the "bourgeois-democratic" revolutions in the less developed countries. In fact, as will be shown below, the Comintern moved close to the point of claiming that all future social change, to be fully progressive, had to be undertaken under the direction and control of a Communist party.

If the necessity for and the importance of the Communist party were never questioned in Comintern history, what, then, were the attributes of an ideal Communist party, able to lead and control the revolutionary movement? A reading of Comintern literature leaves no doubt that the Communist party was expected to attain certain standards of ideological growth and of organizational strength before it could exploit successfully a revolutionary situation. These standards—ideological and organizational—were universal, irrespective of the types of society and of revolution that might be at hand. A single mold was to fashion the Communist parties of such diverse countries as, for example, the United States, Bulgaria, and the Dutch East Indies.

Taking up first the matter of ideological rectitude, we may present the Comintern's definition of an "ideal" Communist party in terms of: 1) its acceptance of orthodox theory; 2) its rejection of erroneous beliefs; and 3) its attitude toward the Soviet Union.

The Bolshevik version of Marxism was accepted in the early years of the Comintern as one form of orthodox Marxism. The Russian Bolsheviks were regarded as the most successful interpreters and developers of classical Marxism. In later years, in large measure because of the failure of any successful revolution elsewhere and the consequent absence of a rival group of Marxists in a seat of power, orthodox Marxism tended to be equated exclusively with Russian Bolshevism. Twice in its history the Comintern explicitly altered its definition of orthodox Marxism to include, first, the contributions of Lenin, and later, those of Stalin.

As pointed out in Chapter III, Leninism as a term in Comintern usage seems to date from the Fifth Congress, which met in mid-1924, a few months after Lenin's death. To be sure, Lenin's ideas dominated Comintern theory from the beginning. But it was only after his death that the Comintern leadership evidently considered it permissible to enunciate publicly two equations: that of orthodox theory with Marxism-Leninism and that of a genuine Communist party with a "bolshevized" party. Later, in 1928, the Introduction to the Comintern Program expressly welded Marxism to Leninism, stating that the Comintern "in its theoretical and practical work stands wholly and unconditionally upon the point of view of *revolutionary* Marxism, which received its further development in Leninism, which is nothing other than Marxism in the era of imperialism and of proletarian revolution."[68]

Three possible inheritors of Lenin's position as chief propounder of "orthodox" theory for the Comintern—Trotsky, Zinoviev, and Bukharin—all failed to establish themselves for any length of time. Trotsky and, to a lesser extent, Bukharin did contribute major "heresies" that had some support for a time not only inside Russia but outside. Weakened and discredited in turn by Stalin, these three potential successors to Lenin as chief theoretician of the Comintern were forced into helplessness, leaving Stalin free to initiate his era of dominance in the Comintern as well as in the Soviet Union.

The rise of Stalin to the role of chief continuator of Marxism-Leninism was by no means clearly foreseeable, even by the time of the Sixth Congress in 1928. Here he received public praise from only a handful of delegates. But in the immediately succeeding years his ability as a theoretician was accorded greater recognition, a development intimately linked, of course, with the consolidation of his political ascendancy within Soviet Russia. In the early 1930s the Comintern began to single out Stalin as its "leader," but with relative restraint in comparison with subsequent years. Typical of this early acknowledgment was Togliatti's remark at the Thirteenth Plenum in December 1933: "We have a guide, comrade Stalin, who continues in the field of theory and practice the great cause of the revolutionary leadership of Marx and Lenin."[69] The unrestrained and wholly uncritical adulation of Stalin at the Seventh Comintern Congress in 1935 defies both belief and summary, but perhaps Manuilsky's effusion may be selected as reasonably characteristic. He declared that "in short, every pronouncement *Stalin* makes is not only a landmark on the road of socialist construction in the USSR; it is also a landmark in the enrichment and deepening of Marxist-Leninist theory."[70] Stalin's writings, he affirmed, were the material from which the advanced workers of the world were acquiring their knowledge—which was true enough at that time, if "advanced" means Communist.

Thus Communist theory was not looked upon as a completed body of doctrine, fixed for all time by the deaths of Marx and Engels. "Owing to historical conditions," Manuilsky pointed out at the Seventh Congress, "Engels, like Marx, was *unable* [to create], and *did not create*, a complete science of the strategy and tactics of the revolutionary proletariat."[71] But Lenin and Stalin were the only individuals, in the entire quarter-century of Comintern history, to be singled out as having made original and substantial contributions to Communist theory. The theory might well be as yet uncompleted, but those Communists who were able to develop it further turned out to be appallingly few. No other figures were ever dignified in Comintern materials by the title of "theoretician."

Heretical and false doctrines within Communist ranks were attacked by the Comintern as corrosive, if not destructive, influences upon correct Communist strategy and tactics. The link between correct theory and correct revolutionary conduct had been emphasized by Marx and Lenin, and was endorsed repeatedly by the Comintern. Incorrect ideas and resultant incorrect practices were classified by the Comintern as either "right" or "left" tendencies, which, if developed strongly, would become deviations.[72] Although "right" (conservative) and "left" (radical) deviations seem to have existed during most of Comintern history, the relative importance of these two categories varied. For the period 1928–1934 the official view of the Comintern was that the "right" deviation was the more serious. According to the Comintern, the "right" deviation involved an underestimation of the revolutionary potential of these years and an inadequate struggle against social democracy.[73] The "leftist" form of heresy in this period was described as a continuation of Trotskyism, and was regarded as a relatively secondary problem. During the mid-1930s, with the initiation of the period of the popular front, the major deviation was to the "left," and was termed "left sectarianism" or "left doctrinairism." Briefly stated, this term was used against those Communists who, resisting the general ideas and strategy of the popular front, believed that the Comintern, in part by its rapprochement with non-Communist socialists and liberals, was losing its revolutionary character and idealism. After the "left sectarianism" of the mid-1930s, there would seem to have been no further widespread deviations, unless the opposition to the Nazi-Soviet Pact of August, 1939, might be so labeled.[74]

The source of deviationist tendencies, in the Comintern's view, had to lie in capitalism, or within the USSR, in "capitalist survivals." The Comintern insisted that erroneous thought must have an explanation in terms of Communist materialist philosophy. Manuilsky in 1931 cited the following causes of the "right" deviation: the pressure of capitalism on the working class, the existence of reformist social democracy (which, he said, until completely rooted out, would inevitably foster reformist recidivism in Communist ranks), and the intensification of the class struggle, which led unstable elements in the Communist parties to lose faith.[75] This rationalization may be considered typical of the Comintern's explanation of the appearance of heresy within the Communist parties.

Among the ideologies condemned by the Comintern as false and inimical, one may mention the following: social democracy, "petty-bourgeois" radical ideologies, secular ideologies of ruling classes (outside the USSR), and religions. All were considered dangerous to the revolutionary movement in that, first, they competed for and split the allegiance and unity of the working masses and, second, they detoured the masses away from the correct revolutionary path into byways that were at best roads to compromise with the class enemy and at worst blind alleys leading only to political emasculation and defeat. The Communist parties were instructed to combat ruthlessly any appearance of these ideologies within their ranks. The Communist-led movement could never be successful if its own leadership, so vital to the success of world revolution, were penetrated by false doctrine. "It is our duty," said Eugene Varga at the Seventh Comintern Congress, "to defend the revolutionary theory of Marx, Engels, Lenin, and Stalin against every revisionist falsification. This is one of the prerequisites for our victory."[76]

"Social democracy" was a term used to label the non-Communist brands of socialism that were advocated by various Socialist, Social-Democratic, and Labor parties. Most of these parties by 1928 held membership in the Labor and Socialist International, which was created in 1923 as the successor to the Second International. Social democracy, regarded by the Comintern as essentially nonrevolutionary and treacherously reformist, was feared as a dangerous competitor for the loyalty of the working class. Various special tendencies (Fabianism, guild socialism, Austro-Marxism, and others) within what the Comintern loosely termed social democracy were described—and condemned—in the Program of 1928.[77]

"Petty-bourgeois radicalism" was a label used by the Comintern to include anarchism and revolutionary syndicalism,[78] as well as anti-colonial ideologies such as Sun Yat-sen's Three Principles, Gandhi's pacifist nationalism, and Garvey's "Back to Africa" movement in the United States.[79] In the Comintern Program the philosophy of Sun Yat-sen was condemned for, among other things, its un-Marxist conception of socialism and its failure to understand the class struggle. Gandhi's philosophy, the Comintern believed, incorrectly rejected the class struggle, was imbued with pacifism and harmful religious notions, and offered a solution not in terms of an advance to a highly industrialized socialist economy but in terms of a return to backward techniques of production. Garveyism, according to the Comintern Program, was "a unique Negro 'Zionism,'" propagating the "aristocratic attributes of a nonexistent 'Negro kingdom.'"[80]

Besides combating the harmful influence of socialist and radical theories, the Comintern sought to block off any influence of secular ideologies fostered by capitalist ruling groups. These ideologies ranged from the loosely defined, informal cluster of beliefs that might best be summed up by the term "capitalist folklore" to the more explicit, dynamic, and counterrevolutionary doctrine of fascism.[81] The latter was adjudged to be the ideology of "finance capitalism," i.e., of capitalism in its last, decadent phase.[82]

Regarding the Comintern's attitude toward religions, it is perhaps necessary simply to note that the Comintern was rigidly hostile toward all forms of religion and idealistic philosophy.

These, then, were the pernicious influences to be fought within and outside the party, and to be eradicated wherever they appeared in Communist ranks. The continuous campaign to immunize the Communist parties against these false doctrines bore the label, as we have already seen, of "bolshevization." Endlessly repeated in Comintern literature was the claim that only a "bolshevized" party could successfully direct a revolution. A leading editorial in the Comintern theoretical journal in 1934 traced the history of the "bolshevization" of the Communist parties and registered the causes of the successes achieved in advancing toward this goal.[83] The editorial began by reiterating the familiar claim that only the Russian Communist Party had been truly "bolshevized" at the time of the founding of the Comintern.[84] The later victories of "bolshevization" in other Communist parties it attributed to these factors: the revolutionary experience of the Communist parties, the leadership of the Comintern under Lenin and Stalin, and more pointedly, "the direct intervention of Comrade Stalin, who came to the aid of the parties at every difficult moment," and lastly, the "victories" that had been won by the Soviet Communist Party.[85]

The "bolshevization" of a party was considered a prerequisite to its success in the revolution. The appeal issued by the ECCI on the tenth anniversary of the Comintern declared that, without "bolshevization," the parties would be unable to produce real leaders "capable of preparing the masses for the coming revo-

lutionary struggles and leading them in the fight for the establishment of the dictatorship of the proletariat."[86]

If Marxism as developed by Lenin and Stalin constituted orthodox doctrine and if "bolshevization" was the means of attaining
and preserving a state of orthodoxy, there yet remains a third
feature of orthodoxy, which although implicit, needs emphasis. This
feature of orthodoxy was the necessity that a positive and favorable
attitude be held by every Communist party toward the USSR and
the Soviet Communist Party. It is patently impossible, in the light
of the overwhelming evidence the Comintern has to offer, to
conceive that a Communist party could be regarded as an effective
revolutionary force if it were critical of the USSR or in any wise
unfriendly toward it. All congresses and plenums, all May Day
manifestoes, all official proclamations of the Comintern agreed
upon a central formula: a complete harmony of interests existed
between the various Communist parties and Communist-led revolutionary movements, on the one hand, and the USSR and the
CPSU, on the other. The Comintern Program of 1928 enjoined the
proletariat of the world to defend the USSR as the bulwark of the
world revolution.[87] The case was put more explicitly in 1935, in a resolution adopted by the Seventh World Congress of the Comintern:

Both under peace conditions and in the conditions of war directed
against the USSR, the strengthening of the USSR, the increasing of its
power, and the assuring of its victory in all spheres and in every sector
of the struggle coincide fully and inseparably with the interets of the
working people of the whole world . . . ; they are the conditions for, and
they contribute to, the triumph of the world proletarian revolution, the
victory of socialism throughout the world.[88]

Perhaps the most striking statement of the implications of this
doctrine was made at the Seventh Comintern Congress by Togliatti
in a speech in which he, in effect, denied the necessity for similar
tactics on the part of the USSR and on the part of the revolutionary
movement in other countries. Having asserted that there was a
"complete identity of aim" between the "peace policy" of the
USSR and the policy of the Communists and the working class in
the capitalist countries, Togliatti went on to state:

But this identity of aim by no means signified that at every given moment there must be complete coincidence in all acts and in all questions between the tactics of the proletariat and Communist Parties that are still struggling for power and the concrete tactical measures of the Soviet proletariat and the CPSU (B), which already have the power in their hands in the Soviet Union.[89]

Of course, almost any action of the CPSU and the USSR could be explained and defended by the Comintern as an action that was intended to preserve and strengthen the USSR as the bulwark of the world-revolutionary movement. So long as the Comintern proclaimed the Soviet Union to be a part of the world-revolutionary Communist movement—and this was done repeatedly and repetitiously—the preservation and strengthening of the Soviet Union meant also the preservation and strengthening of the Communist world movement. Thus an accommodation between the USSR and Nazi Germany, at a time when Communist parties were fighting against fascism, could be explained as an effort to safeguard the Soviet Union from a dangerous war and therefore to preserve unharmed the bulwark of the world revolution. The problem becomes basically a matter of faith—the faith of the foreign Communist in the USSR and the CPSU as genuine and loyal participants in the world-revolutionary process. If this faith remained unshaken, the Communist would accept any and all actions of the USSR and the CPSU as correct actions. As we have seen, one of the attributes of an ideal Communist party was precisely this kind of unshakable confidence and faith in the Soviet Union and in its Communist Party.

Ideological correctness was not the only prerequisite for party leadership in a seizure of power, however. If doctrinal purity would enable the Communist party to judge accurately the shifting forces of economics and politics, good organization was necessary to translate party strategy and aims into the aims of a mass movement. Otherwise the Communist party would run the risk of failing in its attempt to seize power, despite the presence of favorable circumstances (a revolutionary situation). As the German Communist Wilhelm Pieck put it, organizational weakness might mean that "the Communist parties may not be equal to the tremendous tasks which the political situation imposes on them in the matter of leading the masses."[90]

The organizational principles of the individual parties had become fully fixed in the years before 1928 and the major pertinent documents belong to that earlier period.[91] Those principles were faithfully advocated and followed throughout the period from 1928 to 1943; hence it is necessary only to summarize them here. It is important to bear in mind that the Comintern insisted upon principles of organization that it considered applicable to all Communist parties. The organizational theses of 1921, while briefly acknowledging that national peculiarities would to some extent promote organizational differentiation among the parties, strongly emphasized the need for universal standards binding upon all parties alike.[92] These standards and principles are as follows:

1. Democratic centralism. This term, employed to designate the principles governing internal party relations, was defined ambiguously as "the uniting of centralism and proletarian democracy."[93] It was described as the highly preferable alternative to the evils stemming from an inflexible, bureaucratic party structure on the one hand, and from an anarchistic approach to organization, on the other. Comintern materials as a whole leave no doubt that democratic centralism meant centralized control exercised by a small party leadership over a well-disciplined rank-and-file membership.

2. Labor duty. Each Communist should be a daily worker in the revolutionary process, intimately linking his activity with the life of the "toiling masses." Mere verbal acceptance of the Communist program was seen as "only a declaration of intention to become a Communist," and had to be backed up by deeds.[94] Faith without works was dead.

3. Production cells as the best form of organization. The party was to be built where the proletariat and other "toilers" actually worked. "The center of gravity must lie *in the chief cities and centers of the masses working in heavy industry.*"[95] This demand, applying to all parties, of course, serves to underline the leading role of the proletariat, whether the existing society was predominantly capitalist, semi-capitalist, or even feudal. The factory cells, or factory nuclei, were the preferred units of primary party organization. Comintern insistence on this point has a long history, and the merits of the factory cell as against the demerits of street or residential cells, are extolled time and again.[96] The special difficulties of the task of creating factory cells in colonial and semi-colonial areas are well illustrated by the history of the Chinese Communist Party, which was cut off from urban centers during most of its history before World War II.[97] In very backward countries where a proletariat virtually did not exist, no factory cells of course existed; here the party normally did not take the name "Communist" and was admitted to the Comintern only as a "sympathizing" member.[98]

4. Combining legal with illegal work. The legal Communist parties were not to be limited in their activity by the framework created by "bourgeois" laws; "revolutionary" legality was to override the restraints imposed by "bourgeois" legality. The illegal parties were not to neglect opportunities for any legal activity, however small in scope. In effect, the Comintern sought to create parties able to function on either side of any line drawn by "bourgeois" legality.

The above presentation of the characteristics—ideological and organizational—of an "ideal" Communist party, according to Comintern standards, should not of course convey the impression that such "ideal" parties existed between 1928 and 1943 (with the exception of course of the Soviet Communist Party, itself, however, the object of purges). Comintern materials offer considerable evidence that an unsatisfactory state of affairs prevailed throughout the sections of the Comintern. Yet the characteristics discussed above are useful to have in mind as the desiderata to be realized by each Communist party in its struggle toward the seizure of power.

The examination of those common prerequisites necessary for the Communist seizure of power in *any* society has now been completed. Those prerequisites which *vary* according to the stage of development of the society must now be discussed.

If it acted without nonparty support, a Communist party was adjudged to be incapable of engineering a seizure of power in any society. It had to possess mass support drawn from certain social classes and groups. Consistent in its repudiation of *putschist* adventures, the Comintern repeatedly affirmed the importance of mass activity in any Communist-led attempt to take power. Although not precise in its description of the particular social categories from which the party must draw support, the Comintern always stated very strongly the indispensable nature of such support.

The role of the several supporting groups in the seizure of power may be discussed under three headings: 1) the proletariat, 2) the allies of the proletariat, and 3) the "neutralized" groups.

In the advanced capitalist societies. Here, as we know, a "proletarian" revolution was on the agenda. The Communist party was to possess leadership and control over the proletariat and over all other revolutionary forces as well. The proletariat was described as the main "driving force" of the revolution. It required the leadership of a Communist party, the active support of certain other social groups, and the neutralization (reduction to inactivity) of yet other social groups. Needless to say, the belligerent opposition of certain elements, especially of the bourgeois class, was fully expected and indeed regarded as inevitable, for the Comintern always denied the possibility of a peaceful transition from capitalism to socialism (see Chapter IX).

It is clear from a reading of Comintern materials that the Comintern held faithfully to Marx's general notions of the proletariat. The proletariat was simply that social group which provided the labor force of modern capitalistic enterprises; it did not own any significant means of production and its livelihood was gained exclusively or almost exclusively by receiving wages in return for its labor. The term was always used to designate industrial workers (wage-workers in agriculture were always designated as the *agricultural* proletariat and never simply as the proletariat). The authors of the Program of 1928 apparently considered the term so well under-

stood that they offered no formal definition.[99] The term "workers,"
or "working class," was often used in Comintern materials as an
alternative form. But by "toilers" or "toiling masses," the Comintern signified a broader grouping that included, in addition to the
proletariat, other "exploited" categories of the population.

The Comintern's evaluation of the political function of the
proletariat was, of course, made unequivocally clear time and
again: it was considered to be by far the major revolutionary force
in the advanced capitalist countries. What, then, did the Communist party need from the proletariat at the moment when power
was to be wrested from the bourgeoisie, the ruling class in capitalist
society? The answer, endlessly repeated throughout Comintern
literature, was that the party must have the active support of the
majority of the proletariat. As shall be demonstrated below, the
term "majority" should not be taken literally. The Comintern
Program stated that "in order to fulfill the historic task of winning
the dictatorship of the proletariat" the party as the vanguard of the
proletariat must bring under its influence "*the majority of the members
of its own class*, including the women workers and the working
youth."[100] The Comintern undeviatingly employed this formula.
In doing so, it sought to make absolutely clear one prime prerequisite of the seizure of power. "It is wrong," stated Manuilsky in
1935, "to think that . . . there is no need to rely on the majority of
the working class."[101]

What, then, is meant by winning the support of the majority of
the proletariat? What evidence might convince the Comintern
that a particular Communist party enjoyed such support? (Another
question, by what *means* was the majority to be won, is a matter of
strategy and tactics and is deferred for treatment in Chapters V
through VIII.)

The term "majority" was not explained in the Program. The
impression was very probably created among many rank-and-file
Communists that a simple numerical majority, statistically demonstrable, was meant. However, Comintern writers and speakers
frequently equated the term "majority" with the term "most
decisive strata" of the proletariat. For example, Manuilsky in 1928

wrote of the "task of winning the majority of the working class, that is, its most important sections."[102] A leading editorial in the Comintern journal in 1929 used the term "basic decisive strata" as the equivalent of "majority."[103] A Leninist origin for this kind of interpretation was often claimed. For example, an editorial in *Kommunisticheskii Internatsional* drew upon Lenin's defense of the Bolshevik seizure of power in 1917. "Lenin answered repeatedly both before and after the October Revolution . . . in the decisive struggle for power it was quite sufficient to have secured a majority among the most important sections of the proletariat in the decisive centers of the country."[104] Martynov, a member of the editorial board of the Comintern journal, endorsed this viewpoint in a subsequent article, in which he defined majority in "the Leninist sense of the word, the sense of winning the decisive strata of the proletariat."[105]

At the Tenth Plenum in 1929, Manuilsky delivered an interesting speech wholly devoted to the problem of winning a majority of the proletariat.[106] His remarks clear up a number of points. Raising the question of whether, under capitalism, the Communist party could itself embrace the majority of the working class "organizationally," i.e., as party members, he answered that this would be impossible.[107] The question was one of influence, and the necessary influence over the majority of the proletariat could be established through nonparty organizations under party guidance. Manuilsky also rejected the validity of any statistical measurements of working class support. The Communist party did not need a formal majority support; besides, under capitalism no fully free elections could be expected. Manuilsky's criteria were stated chiefly in terms of results: if the Communist party could lead mass strikes, marches, and other demonstrations in which great numbers of workers participated, on those grounds alone the party might make the claim that it represented the sentiments of the majority among the working class.

Thus the term "majority" was rendered vague and unverifiable. As such, it could be employed carelessly and misleadingly in all kinds of propagandistic and hortatory party literature. According to Knorin, a member of the ECCI, no Communist party had up to 1931 won the support of a majority of the workers; but the German Communist Party, the most successful, had come "to the brink of winning the majority of the working class in its most decisive sections."[108] In 1933, Piatnitsky attempted to explain away the absence of a Communist-led proletarian uprising in Germany on Hitler's accession to power by asserting, among other things, that the German Communist Party did not then enjoy the support of the majority of the proletariat.[109] Having dispensed with verifiable data, the Comintern could ignore any challenge to this claim.

One question remains. Where were the "decisive strata" of the proletariat to be found? In his answer to this question, Manuilsky listed the following as the most decisive strata: workers in the metallurgical, transport, chemical, and electrical industries, as well as miners, and workers in the munitions industries. Geographically, the party should seek strength in the key industrial centers, where proletarian victories would have a tremendous effect on the rest of the country. Manuilsky believed that strong proletarian support in two or three revolutionary centers in a Western capitalist country was not sufficient, as it had been in old Russia, for a successful seizure of power by the Communist party; the revolution now needed such support in dozens of such centers.[110] Workers in communications were also important, e.g., those in postal, telegraph, and telephone services, as well as those working at harbors and railroad junctions. In general, Manuilsky advocated the winning over of those workers who were most essential to the normal functioning of a given enterprise.[111]

The most important economic branches in the United States were listed by one writer as mining, automotive, metallurgical, textile, and sea transport; and the most important centers as New York, Pittsburgh, Cleveland, Chicago, and Detroit. The author warned that without winning over the workers in these industries it would be impossible to speak of winning a "majority" of the proletariat in America.[112]

We may now inquire about those social groups which the Comintern considered necessary as secondary supporting forces in the seizure of power in the "proletarian-socialist" revolution. These allies were to be drawn from nonproletarian but "toiling" and "exploited" categories. To use the expression favored by the Comintern, the Communist party and its proletarian supporters were to exercise "hegemony" over these allies. According to the Comintern Program,

The winning of the dictatorship of the proletariat presupposes also the realization of the hegemony of the proletariat over *wide circles of the toiling masses*. To accomplish this the Communist party must win influence over the masses of urban and village poor, the lower strata of the intelligentsia, and the so-called little man, i.e., the petty-bourgeois strata in general. Especially great significance attaches to the work of securing the influence of the party among the peasantry. The Communist party must obtain the full support of the village strata closest to the proletariat, namely, the agricultural workers and the village poor . . . . The solving of all these tasks by the proletariat . . . is an obligatory prerequisite of the victorious Communist revolution.[113]

The Program, then, laid down as an essential condition of victory substantial support from the lower echelons among the bourgeoisie, the intelligentsia, and the peasantry. Comintern materials never state quite clearly just how broad and inclusive the support among the nonproletarian groups must be in order to make possible a Communist seizure of power. The term "hegemony" of course implied that the Communist party, the "vanguard" of the proletariat, would enjoy leadership and control over social categories regarded as intrinsically incapable of independent political activity. The Program spoke of the realization of such hegemony "*over wide circles of the toiling masses*"; it also spoke of the "full support" of the agricultural workers and village support. It is impossible to state precisely what percentage of each of the nonproletarian toiling groups had to give support to the Communist party and its proletarian followers before it could take power. On one occasion Manuilsky did state explicitly that the proletariat could overthrow the bourgeoisie before winning a majority among the nonproletarian "toilers."[114]

The urban petty bourgeoisie, as a subdivision of the bourgeois class, was commonly understood to include such categories as small

traders and shopkeepers, self-employed artisans and handicrafts-
men, and office workers and "white-collar" workers in general, as
well as part of such professional groups as teachers, lawyers,
doctors, and dentists, and the lower ranks of the intelligentsia in
general.[115]

From a reading of Comintern materials certain supposed characteristics of the urban petty bourgeoisie emerge. This social category,
according to the Comintern, generally had a low, or at best a
modest standard of living, demonstrating that it had not profited
from the capitalist system but rather had been "exploited"; was
for the greater part not in a position to "exploit" in turn the
working class and could be persuaded that it shared certain common interests with the workers; and was not an "independent"
political force, as were the upper bourgeoisie and the proletariat,
but was a vacillating element that might follow either the bourgeoisie or the proletariat in time of crisis.[116]

The peasantry presents a more complicated picture. As pointed
out in Chapter III, the Comintern had drawn up in 1920 an
elaborate statement entitled "The Agrarian Question," in which
the peasantry was separated into three main groups. This system
of classification was used also during the period from 1928 to 1943.
The three categories were the "toiling and exploited" peasants, the
middle peasants, and the big or well-to-do peasants, often called
"kulaks." The economic interests of these groups varied, although
they shared a common peasant culture. It is in the category of
"toiling and exploited" peasants that the Program of 1928 saw the
basic *rural* allies of the proletariat in the Communist seizure of
power in advanced capitalist society. This category included the
landless agricultural proletariat, who, as wage-workers in capitalistic agricultural enterprises, were considered to be the closest in
circumstances and spirit to the industrial proletariat; the semiproletarian or "dwarf" peasants, whose small landholdings compelled them to supplement their income with wage-work; and the
small peasantry, who owned or rented sufficient land to feed their
families but were unable to hire extra, nonfamily wage-labor.[117]

Substantial parts of these three subdivisions of the "toiling and exploited" peasantry were considered to be indispensable allies in the "proletarian" revolution. The importance of the peasantry was asserted time and again. A lengthy analysis of the question of peasant allies was offered at the Eleventh Plenum of the ECCI by Kolarov, who was a major Comintern authority on the whole peasant problem. He emphasized carefully the necessary relationship between the proletariat and its village allies as one of mutual dependency. "For the toiling peasantry," he affirmed, "there can be no salvation from poverty and oppression . . . without the struggle under the leadership of the proletariat." Likewise, "the proletariat cannot secure its victory over the bourgeoisie without the support of the exploited and oppressed part of the village."[118] It is certainly safe to say that the Comintern attributed far more value to the winning of peasant allies than to the winning of nonproletarian urban allies. To Knorin, at the Eleventh Plenum, this was the central question in the whole matter of recruiting support from other classes for the proletariat.[119]

While building support from parts of the urban proletariat and other sectors of the "toiling masses," the Communist party was expected to weaken the opposition forces by "neutralizing" certain sectors of society. Neutralization meant the reduction of these social groups to a passive role, so that when the seizure of power was attempted the neutralized groups would not give aid to the bourgeoisie. The Program of 1928 did not indicate which categories were to be neutralized, other than the middle strata of the peasantry.[120] This category, whose members were able to enjoy an adequate living standard from farming and sometimes even to make a small profit and to hire some wage labor, was not considered a potential ally of the Communist party in the advanced capitalist countries, but, at best, a neutral bystander. The economic interests of the middle peasant made him an undependable force, but with careful work it was thought possible to neutralize the influence which capitalism exercised over him as a property owner.

The Program is silent respecting the neutralization of any urban groups. In fact there is almost nothing on this point in Comintern literature. However, on one occasion an editorial in the Comintern journal called for the neutralization of the "middle section" of the urban petty bourgeoisie.[121] Presumably, the Comintern may have considered that the battle lines between the revolutionary and the nonrevolutionary forces would be much clearer in the cities than in the rural districts, and that a middle ground of neutrality would be less likely to exist. Also, the Comintern undoubtedly considered that the importance of a neutralized sector would be much less in the towns, where the revolutionary forces of the proletariat would be concentrated, than in the countryside.

In summary, it may be said that the Comintern insisted upon the necessity of broad mass support for the Communist seizure of power in an advanced capitalist country. Yet it refused to commit itself to any quantitative criteria respecting the scope of such support, and thereby reserved for itself a maximum of liberty and a minimum of restraint in the matter of judging whether a seizure of power might be attempted. To remain faithful to the Marxist heritage, it was essential not to reduce the seizure of power to a *coup d'état* or *putsch*. At the same time, the existence of mass support was not intended to restrict the leadership and control of the party, which, as the professed vanguard of the proletariat, was to exercise hegemony over the rest of the proletariat and, in addition, was to exercise "proletarian" hegemony over nonproletarian supporters.

In the societies of medium capitalist development. In this second category of societies, the problem of the Communist organization of the revolutionary forces that were required for the Communist seizure of power is considerably more complex than in the case of the advanced capitalist societies. In the first place, the available Comintern materials are imprecise and incomplete in their treatment of all problems pertaining to the middle category of societies. Apparently most Comintern speakers and writers thought in terms of two major divisions—capitalist countries (including all types) and colonial countries—and tended to regard societies with a medium development of capitalism as a special subdivision of the capitalist world, to be discussed only in so far as they showed variations from the characteristics of the advanced capitalist country.

The second complicating factor is, as we have seen, the existence of two possible paths of revolutionary development for the societies of medium capitalist development. One path was that of the "socialist" revolution, in which Communist-led revolutionists were confronted, in the early period following the seizure of power, with the immediate task of completing certain unfinished business of the "bourgeois-democratic" revolution (such as the abolition of feudalism), in addition to the major task of achieving socialism and communism. The other path (appropriate to societies with a more limited development of capitalism) was that of the Communist-led "bourgeois-democratic" revolution, capable of crossing, relatively soon after the Communist seizure of power, the frontier separating "bourgeois-democratic" tasks from "proletarian-socialist" tasks.

In both types of revolutions, the Communist parties were to lead and control the revolutionary movement. The major driving force of both revolutions was to be the proletariat, small as it might be. These features were true not only for the "proletarian-socialist" revolutions which were on the agenda, for example, in Hungary[122] and in Bulgaria,[123] but also for the "bourgeois-democratic" revolutions in, for example, Spain[124] and Yugoslavia.[125] Thus it is clear that the Comintern rejected leadership by the bourgeois class in the "bourgeois-democratic" revolution.[126] The Communist party, and the proletariat, under its control, were to ascend to a position of hegemony not only in the "proletarian-socialist" revolution, but even in the "bourgeois-democratic" revolution that was to grow over into the "proletarian-socialist" revolution. This increased role for the proletariat obviously constituted a radical departure from the so-called bourgeois revolutions of the nineteenth century, such as those of France in 1830 and 1848, in which the proletariat had played only a supporting role under the leadership of the bourgeoisie.

Before seizing power in a country of medium capitalist development, the Communist parties were directed to bring the "majority" of the proletariat under its influence. This "majority," as in the case of the advanced capitalist countries, was usually equated with some such term as the "decisive strata" of the proletariat. The Bulgarian Communist Party had the unique distinction of being the only party which, according to available evidence, was specifically credited with having brought under its influence the majority of the proletariat in its country.[127]

As far as nonproletarian allies were concerned, the peasantry and the national minorities received the major attention in Comintern materials. The Comintern Program emphasized the revolutionary importance of peasant revolts, which were seen as generally playing "a very great—and sometimes decisive—role."[128] This statement is backed up by a wealth of evidence. It is indeed the special importance attributed to the peasantry as an ally in both the "bourgeois-democratic" and the "proletarian-socialist" revolutions that distinguishes the second category of societies. This is to be expected, since this category embraced the countries of eastern and southern Europe (excepting Italy and the USSR) where the proletariat was relatively small and where agriculture was the overwhelmingly dominant form of economic endeavor. In relation to the rest of the population, the peasantry was of course proportionately much larger than in the more advanced capitalist countries.

It is impossible to determine precisely what categories of the peasant population would have to be brought under the hegemony of the proletariat before the Communist seizure of power could be attempted. The Program of 1928 did not so specify. Comintern materials are vague here, and most writers and speakers simply referred to hegemony over the "basic masses" of the peasantry, without further definition. Some light was shed by Martynov in an article in 1932, in which he repeated the class formulation of the problem of peasant allies as given by Lenin and Stalin. In the "bourgeois-democratic" revolution, he asserted, the proletariat is allied with *all* of the peasantry against the monarchy, the landlords, and feudalism. In the "proletarian-socialist" revolution, the peasant allies are restricted to the lowest peasant groups, while the middle peasant is neutralized and a fierce struggle is directed against the big peasant or "kulak."[129] This degree of clarity was rare in Comintern materials. Even in countries said to be destined for a "bourgeois-democratic" revolution, almost never were the peasant allies defined as all the peasantry, but rather as the "toiling" peasants or "broad mass" of the peasants. For example, in Yugoslavia where a "bourgeois-democratic" revolution was on the agenda, the Communists were expected to bring under their influence not only the poorest strata of the peasantry but also the middle peasant. The kulak, or well-to-do peasant, was not included.[130] It is probably safe to conclude that, for the societies of medium capitalist development, those to undergo a "proletarian-socialist" revolution required as a prerequisite of the Communist seizure of power widespread support only from the poorest strata of the peasantry; those to undergo a "bourgeois-democratic" revolution would require the support of both the poorest and the middle strata of the peasantry.

In countries of medium capitalist development, in addition to establishing its hegemony over a broad peasant movement, the Communist party had to establish hegemony over the national minorities. Most of these countries had minority problems—for example, the Ukrainians and Belorussians in Poland, the Croats, Slovenes, and Macedonians in Yugoslavia, and the Catalonians in Spain. "One of the most essential conditions for the victory of the revolution in the Balkans" was seen as "the linking up of the national revolutions with the proletariat and the revolutionary struggle of the toiling peasants."[131] The leadership of the movement of the national minorities, struggling to achieve autonomy or even full independence, was not on any account to be left to the national bourgeoisie. The Communist party and its proletarian supporters, both of the "oppressing" nationality and of the "oppressed" nationality, were to come forward as the only true, consistent, and incorruptible champions of national independence. The nationality question in these countries was, in Kolarov's opinion, "essentially a peasant question."[132] By this he meant that an oppressed national minority usually was overwhelmingly peasant. According to a report of Kuusinen to the Presidium of the ECCI, the Communist parties were to link up the national question with the social questions of the revolution and were to come out unequivocally on the side of full national independence for the minorities.[133]

Allies were also to be found among the lower echelons of the urban petty bourgeoisie. But the paucity of material respecting this social category, contrasted with the heavy emphasis on allies amongst the peasantry and the national minorities, suggests that the Comintern saw the revolutionary movement as a struggle of the Communist-led industrial proletariat, possessing hegemony over a poorly defined mass movement of the peasants and backed up by the support of the national minorities.

From the very scanty material available no worthwhile conclusions can be drawn respecting the neutralization of particular social groups in societies of medium capitalist development.

In the colonial, semi-colonial, and dependent societies. As we have seen, the distinctive features of these societies were, from the Comintern's standpoint, their subjugation to foreign imperialist control and the resultant absence of genuine national sovereignty; a predominantly feudal, pre-capitalist economy, primarily agrarian, within which, however, an elementary development of capitalism had already begun; and a largely peasant population, together with a numerically insignificant bourgeoisie and proletariat. The Comintern held that, for these societies, a "bourgeois-democratic" revolution under Communist control was on the agenda.

The first important question to be answered is that of the leadership in the revolutionary movement in these countries. Historically, the driving force behind such revolutionary movements—involving a struggle for national independence—had been derived largely from the ranks of the educated, urban middle classes, i.e., from the native bourgeoisie. Intellectuals and merchants and, in some cases, military officers had comprised the leadership of such emerging national anti-colonial movements in the late nineteenth and early twentieth centuries. The Wafd Party in Egypt, the Indian National Congress, and the Sarekat Islam in the Dutch East Indies are examples.[134] The Comintern admitted that the post-World War I wave of nationalist disturbances in Egypt, India, Turkey, the Dutch East Indies, and elsewhere had arisen under the leadership of the bourgeoisie, with the proletariat playing as yet only a supporting role.[135] But, by 1928, the Comintern had concluded that the native bourgeoisie must inevitably go over sooner or later to the counterrevolutionary camp without completing the tasks of the "bourgeois-democratic" revolution (including particularly the parceling of large holdings among the peasants), and that the Communist party, supported by the proletariat, must come forth as the leader of the revolution and must exercise hegemony over a group of allies which should include as its most vital component the peasant masses to whom the Communist party would promise a land partition.[136]

These conclusions were in great part the result of the failure of Kuomintang-Communist collaboration in China in 1927. The Chinese revolution had been reexamined at the Ninth Plenum early in 1928, and loomed large in all the deliberations of the speakers at the Sixth Congress of the Comintern. The action of Chiang Kai-shek in terminating the collaboration that began in 1923 cast the most serious doubts upon the whole theory of cooperation between bourgeois nationalists and the Communist-led forces in any of the dependent and colonial areas.

The Sixth Congress suggested that the "bourgeois-democratic" movements in these countries would pass through two stages before the Communist seizure of power, a first stage of bourgeois hegemony with the proletariat playing a subordinate role, and a later, higher stage of Communist and proletarian hegemony, with the bourgeoisie passing over into the camp of counterrevolution.[137] The rapidity of the transition from one stage to the other depended upon the growth of the Communist party and upon the revolutionary experience of the working class and the peasantry and the extent to which they were brought within party-controlled organizations.[138] Kuusinen regarded the Chinese revolution as having reached by 1928 the higher stage—the Canton uprising of December, 1927, being an example of independent proletarian (Communist) leadership—while he considered the Indian revolution to be still in the first stage.[139] The Yenbay uprising in February, 1930, in Indo-China was depicted as the last revolutionary effort in that colony to be led by the bourgeois nationalists, who, having turned to conciliation with French imperialism, had forfeited leadership to the Communists.[140]

The alignment of social forces in the colonial, semi-colonial, and dependent countries may be analyzed in terms of anti-revolutionary, vacillating, and revolutionary elements.[141] The anti-revolutionary forces were in Comintern literature labeled the "feudal-imperialists" and were said to include the foreign imperialist power, the native feudal lords and great landowners, and, in most of these countries, that part of the native middle class known as the *comprador* bourgeoisie. The *compradors*, largely engaged in commerce and trade, were economically dependent upon the imperialists. The vacillating elements included the remainder of the native bourgeoisie, usually called "national-reformist" bourgeoisie, said to be based economically upon industry rather than commerce and characterized as "opportunistic, prone to great waverings, and teetering between imperialism and revolution."[142] This class, the Comintern warned, would inevitably abandon the revolution and capitulate to the imperialists. Their weak-kneed opposition to the imperialists might, however, be utilized for a time by the Communist parties.[143] The petty bourgeoisie and the petty-bourgeois intelligentsia were regarded, especially in so far as their lower strata were concerned, as possible allies of the Communist party and the proletariat in the seizure of power.

The revolutionary forces were to be under the hegemony of a Communist-led proletariat. The terms "majority of the proletariat" or "decisive strata" were used here, with the same vague connotations that were noted above in the discussion of the advanced capitalist countries. In the peasantry the proletariat was to have its most important ally.[144] The colonial theses indicate the possibility "that in the first period of struggle of the peasantry against the landlords, the proletariat can carry with itself all the peasantry. But in the further course of struggle, some upper strata of the peasantry may cross over into the counter-revolutionary camp."[145] It is clear that the Comintern expected the overwhelming mass of the peasantry to support the proletariat and the party in the initial phase of the Communist seizure of power. Among the allies of the proletariat in the support of the Communist party, the greatest importance, by all odds, was attached to the peasantry.

Having discussed the Comintern's theory on the prerequisites of a Communist seizure of power in each type of society, we may turn to an analysis of the Comintern's view as to how these prerequisites might best be achieved or approximated by the Communist parties.

V. PREPARATION: STRATEGY
AND TACTICS, 1928-1934

The day-to-day activity of a Communist party in a non-Communist country has a twofold purpose—the winning of short-term, partial goals and the preparation for the eventual attempt to seize power. Time and again Comintern materials emphasize the interrelationship between current Communist policies and practices and the future paramount effort to wrest power from non-Communist hands. For the winning of partial aims, such as better working conditions, could well mean the winning of influence over important strata of the population. Unlike most political parties which accept the existing arrangements of society and seek to operate within that milieu, the Communist party displays an uncompromising hostility to all non-Communist societies and boldly proclaims its fundamental estrangement from the basic institutions of these societies. The members of the Communist party are ever kept conscious of their major purpose—the overthrow of existing social arrangements and the implementation of a Communist society. The current strategy and tactics of Communist parties, at any given moment, must then be understood in terms not only of immediate issues but also of preparation for the future Communist attempt to seize power.

As evidence of the Communist effort to prepare those prerequisites within the power of human beings, the changing pattern of strategy and tactics of the Communist International will be analyzed. The pattern of Comintern strategy and tactics, of course, reflected the Comintern's interpretation of the evolution of the non-Communist world and the Communist world. The non-Communist world, dominated by the capitalistic economic system, was in Communist theory inherently hostile to the existence, activity, and aims of the Communist-led world revolutionary movement. The Communist world—the USSR—was by definition benevolently disposed to the world revolutionary movement, of which it considered itself an inseparable component. In the ultimate sense, it can be said that the conditions under which the Communist parties developed their strategy and tactics were jointly created by the changing fortunes of these two irreconcilable worlds.

Comintern strategy after 1928 is divided into four distinct periods: 1928 to 1934, 1935 to 1939, late 1939 to mid-1941, and thereafter to May, 1943. This periodization reflects successive major changes in the Comintern's outlook during the fifteen years under consideration. For each of the four periods there will be given: 1) an overview of the period, in which will be briefly noted as background material the main developments in the non-Communist world and in the USSR; 2) the Comintern's evaluation of developments in the non-Communist world and in the USSR, in terms of their impact upon the revolutionary movement; and 3) the Comintern's broad pattern of strategy and tactics for the period. No effort is made to write a detailed history of Communist strategy and tactics; the purpose is only to extract the pattern and to relate it to the larger question of world revolution.

OVERVIEW OF THE PERIOD

The situation in the non-Communist world. Clearly the most important and consequential development in the capitalist economic system during the period 1928 to 1934, and indeed during the whole era since World War I, was the Great Depression that began in the United States in 1929 and subsequently spread to Europe and other parts of the world.[1] There ensued manifold economic, social, political, and intellectual reactions throughout the world. The catastrophic plunge of values on the New York Stock Exchange in October, 1929, acted to detonate the underlying weaknesses of world capitalism, causing explosions that reverberated throughout the world. It was no longer possible, either for Americans or for others, to "regard the present with satisfaction and anticipate the future with optimism," as President Coolidge had suggested to Congress in December, 1928.[2]

America and Western Europe, the strongholds of world capitalism, were badly weakened. Neither the American economy nor that of Europe had been wholly sound in the first decade after World War I, despite the general recovery from the immediate postwar depression. A chronic slump plagued agriculture for the entire two decades between 1920 and 1940. After 1926 unemployment in Europe was on the increase. Long before 1929, the tide of prosperity which followed the depression of 1920–1921 was ebbing away. But the fairly rapid shutoff of the export of American capital, especially to Europe, caused world-wide difficulties of a profoundly serious nature. In particular, the foundations of the postwar economic revival in Germany were largely destroyed, with widespread repercussions in Europe. Another American action, the erection of the highest tariff wall in United States history (the Smoot-Hawley Act of 1930) had untold harmful effects. "It is in no sense an exaggeration of fact," declare two specialists in international relations, "to say that the Smoot-Hawley tariff, more than any other single thing, was responsible for the most devastating depression which the world has yet known."[3] Capitalist Europe became progressively more embroiled in economic disaster. The collapse of the European financial system was dramatized by the failure of the Austrian Kredit-Anstalt Bank early in 1931, followed shortly by that of the great Danatbank in Germany.

The pattern of the depression is well known. The world economy sank to its lowest level in 1932–1933, then pulled upward painfully until 1937, then again slipped back somewhat. In terms of world manufacturing production (excluding the USSR), if 1929 is taken as 100, there was a steady decline to 63 in 1932, followed by a rise to 104 in 1937 and a decline again in the following year to 93.[4] Unemployment during these years reached unprecedented proportions. In the United States, the major capitalist state, the total production of the economy in 1933 was nearly a third less than in 1929 and about thirteen million persons, or almost one in every four in the labor force, were out of work.[5]

In total or partial reaction to the world economic crisis, there appeared a number of important developments. In the realm of economics, countries failed to achieve any worthwhile international cooperation to counter the disaster and, consequently, resorted to severely nationalistic solutions. The increased role of governments in economic and social matters was clearly visible, both in the democratic and in the undemocratic countries. Moreover, countries became intensely competitive and strove for economic self-sufficiency as far as possible. International trade declined drastically.

In the field of politics, a great stimulus was given to the growth of radical and totalitarian movements. The instability and insecurity of the economic world had crossed over into the domain of politics. After 1929 the trend to dictatorship or totalitarianism, already initiated in the 1920s, spread rapidly over the greater part of Europe. The almost bloodless accession of Hitler to power in January, 1933, was only the most direful example among the successes of the rising anti-democratic tide.

In the arena of international politics, the period from 1928 to 1934 witnessed a transition into a more disquieting and inflammatory stage, marked by the failure of the League of Nations either to achieve effective international disarmament or to preserve the peace. The outbreak of open war between Japan and China in 1931, coupled with the appearance of an aggressive and revisionist Nazi Germany, indicated the passing of the era structured upon the Versailles settlement, the Locarno Pacts, and the Nine-Power Treaty.

The situation in the Soviet Union. Turning now to the Soviet Union, we have between 1928 and 1934 a period often designated as "Stalin's revolution." This label is usually meant to apply to the great economic transformations—high-tempo industrialization and rapid collectivization—that Stalin successfully led the Communist Party of the Soviet Union to accept and implement. This program was Stalin's answer to specific economic difficulties that were becoming increasingly acute in the USSR, especially the declining amount of marketed grain, as well as his plan for building a socialist economic system. In many ways the Soviet Union's economic revolution of this period was a more profound social upheaval than the Bolshevik conquest of power between 1917 and 1921. The First Five-Year Plan, from October, 1928, to the end of 1932, largely completed the structural outline of the rapidly growing socialist economy. In 1934 the authority of the Party was placed behind the claim that socialism was "victorious" in the USSR.[6] This proclamation, jubilantly endorsed at the Seventeenth Party Congress in February of that year, resounded abroad in all Comintern and Communist party publications, which contrasted the "building of socialism" in the USSR with the quite negative features of capitalism during the Great Depression.

The beginning of Stalin's revolution, wrought at the cost of uncounted lives and incalculable human suffering, was accompanied by the concluding phase of his political revolution—the concentration of power into his own hands and out of the hands of the major comrades-in-arms of Lenin. With the expulsion of Trotsky from the Party in October, 1927, and his subsequent removal from the ECCI, Stalin eliminated his chief rival. A purge against "Trotskyites" removed the followers of the brilliant revolutionary leader. There followed the destruction of the "left" deviation,[7] in which effort Stalin had the support of the "rights" in the Politburo, led by Bukharin. Subsequently, Bukharin and the "right" deviation, both within the Soviet Party and throughout the Comintern, were purged in 1929-1930.[8] Stalin and his co-thinkers formed a truly Stalinist Politburo by 1930.[9]

In the conduct of its foreign policy during these years the Soviet Union appeared to be strongly motivated by an acute sense of isolation and by a dread of an anti-Soviet war. In reaction, the Soviet Union sought to identify itself firmly with the cause of peace. The outward manifestations of the peace policy included the signing of the Kellogg Peace Pact, the Litvinov Protocol, and the several neutrality treaties of the period. Accommodating itself to the aggressive presence of the Japanese in Manchuria, the Soviet Union negotiated and completed the sale of its interests in the Chinese Eastern Railway during 1933-1935. The USSR likewise sought to maintain normal relations with Nazi Germany in 1933 despite the blatant anti-Bolshevism of Hitler. Finally, it may be mentioned that the Soviet Union had hoped, in the early part of this period, to secure beneficial trade arrangements with other countries in order to facilitate the achievement of the First Five-Year Plan.

It should be noted that during 1933 and 1934 a more active search was made by the Soviet leaders for friends to balance the danger presented by the more aggressive states. Overtly, the Soviet Union expressed a willingness to identify itself responsibly with the *status quo* and to enter into commitments for collective security. In November, 1933, diplomatic relations were established with the United States; during 1934 the Soviet Union sought to create a viable security system in Eastern Europe; and in September of that year it entered the League of Nations. The period of isolation was rapidly fading away by 1934.

VIEWS OF THE COMINTERN

Comintern evaluation of "world capitalism": the third period. According to the Comintern the first period in the postwar development of capitalism had come to an end by the late months of 1923.[10] The failures in Germany and Bulgaria that year terminated the first round of postwar revolutions. The following period, from 1924 to 1928, was characterized as a phase of temporary, partial stabilization in the capitalist world, during which the proletariat stood mainly on the defensive. In 1928 the concept of a new, third period in the postwar development of capitalism was given its official world-wide debut at the Sixth Comintern Congress.

The essential characteristics of the third period were described in the Comintern theses entitled "The International Situation and the Tasks of the Communist International."[11] In terms of the prospects for revolution during the third period, the theses predicted two basic developments: the disintegration of the temporary and partial stabilization achieved by world capitalism during the second period of its postwar history, and the approach and inevitable occurrence of a new round of wars and revolutions. It was predicted that the crumbling of stabilization within the capitalist system would be accompanied by the passing of revolutionary forces from the defensive positions of the second period to a renewed offensive, expected by the Comintern to be more successful than the uprisings of the first period.

The Comintern's view of the development of capitalism during the third period was complex. Capitalism was to exhibit both positive and negative aspects, although the latter were ultimately to triumph. As for the positive side of the picture, capitalist production, having already exceeded prewar levels, was expected to continue for a while to grow, stimulated by rapid developments in technology.[12] But, unlike the situation that prevailed during the second period, the negative tendencies of capitalism were no longer to be held in check, and, once having become severely intensified, were to destroy the temporary, partial stabilization of the earlier period. According to the prediction of the Comintern, the very successes of capitalism were to lead to profound difficulties, for capitalism was to be confronted with an increasingly serious "contradiction" between the growth of productive forces and the failure of markets to expand correspondingly. The so-called reconstruction period in the USSR, initiated in 1928 with the First Five-Year Plan, was to embarrass the capitalist countries further by continuing to deprive the latter of a vast market area.

Structurally, capitalism was expected by the Comintern to manifest two major tendencies during the third period. One tendency was to be the greater development of business combinations, a process labeled in Comintern verbiage as "cartelization" and "trustification." This tendency was to transcend national limits and appear on an international level.[13]

The other expected line of development was described by the Comintern in the phrase "tendencies toward state capitalism." This phrase was loosely employed by Comintern orators to cover a number of institutional arrangements within the capitalist system. Two forms of state capitalism were identified in the theses mentioned above. State capitalism, in the proper sense of the word, entailed state ownership of enterprises, such as electric power stations. This form of state capitalism is readily understood. The other form mentioned in the theses was characterized as the "ever greater growing together[14] of business organizations with the organs of state power."[15] This ambiguous statement raises certain questions. What exactly is the meaning of the "merging" or "growing together" of business and state organs? Is this process of merging visible (i.e., is it the consequence of perceivable organizational changes), or is it merely a more intimate association between business and government personnel? In view of the familiar assertion of Marxists that capitalists dominate the mechanism of government throughout the capitalist era, what new kind of relationship between economics and politics was signified?[16]

To make the term even more confusing, Bukharin at the Ninth Plenum earlier in 1928 had suggested, as a form of "growing together," the increasingly intimate contact between anti-revolutionary labor organizations and the governments of capitalist countries.[17]

It is obvious that state capitalism was used loosely by the Comintern to denote a variety of phenomena. Perhaps the essence of the idea of state capitalism, as understood by the Comintern, was a conscious and coordinated struggle on an unprecedented scale by government, business, and anti-revolutionary labor leaders against economic disorder and revolutionary movements, for the purpose of acquiring greater profits on the basis of a more harmonious and regulated capitalist system. It was, therefore, an effort to control by political decisions the impersonal economic power of "blind" market forces.[18]

That such efforts by capitalism to organize itself during the third period would end in failure was considered inevitable by the Comintern. The contradictions within capitalism, though temporarily controlled and abated during the second period, were to become immeasurably intensified during the third period. Increased production was to lead to an unprecedentedly desperate struggle for markets, during which the capitalist states were to resort to violence against each other, against the "toiling masses," and against the Soviet Union. The predicted results were wars and revolutions.

Two other processes, primarily political, characterize the gigantic struggle that was said to be at work in the third period. They were summed up in Comintern terminology by the terms "fascization" and "radicalization." These words occur frequently in Comintern literature of the period. The former process was operative amongst the "exploiting" capitalists, the second process, amongst the industrial workers, and, more generally, within the "exploited" segments of society. Taken together they may be seen as manifestations of a political polarization within society.

Fascization, as defined in the Program, was the "terroristic dictatorship of big capital."[19] It was the result of an increasing tendency on the part of the ruling groups of a society to depart from parliamentary rule and to employ methods of "direct dictatorship, ideologically masked by an 'all-national idea.'"[20] The fascists employed techniques of social demagogy (e.g., anti-Semitism) and designed their many-sided doctrine for appeal to the middle classes of society, to intellectuals, and even to a certain part of the working class. The function of fascism was counterrevolutionary. "The chief task of fascism is the destruction of the revolutionary proletarian vanguard, i.e., the Communist strata of the proletariat and their cadres."[21] Fascism might, temporarily and before coming to power, utilize anti-capitalist sentiments. In 1928, of course, the model of a fascist state was still Mussolini's Italy. From the viewpoint of the Comintern, the recourse to fascist methods was provoked by the so-called general crisis of capitalism, which was considered to have begun with World War I.

The process of radicalization was pictured as a simultaneous development among the proletariat and the "toilers" in general. Their persecution and exploitation by the "fascists-capitalists" was expected to provoke a resurgence, in progressively greater scope and intensity, of proletarian struggle against capitalism. Signs of radicalization were demonstrations, strikes, riots, and other activities which indicated both a determined resolve on the part of the working class and other "toilers" not to submit to "bourgeois" law and a willingness on their part to break the law in defense of their supposed interests.

The origin of the concept of a third period in the postwar development of capitalism cannot be known with certainty from Comintern materials. The spirit of the third period obviously coincided nicely with the spirit of the First Five-Year Plan. Both represent swings to the "left."[22] The "war scare" in mid-1927 would appear to have set the stage for the great fear expressed within the Comintern of an anti-Soviet war to be waged by capitalists during the third period. The "war scare" also helped set the stage for the mobilization of opinion within the USSR in favor of the Five-Year Plan.

At the Fifteenth Congress of the CPSU in December, 1927, both Stalin and Bukharin delivered speeches in which they described a new period of capitalist development marked by intensified "contradictions," sharpened class struggles, and the outbreak of war.[23] It was Bukharin who presented the major exposition of the concept at the Sixth Comintern Congress, but he was shortly thereafter to be accused of "errors" concerning the third period. There is no evidence that Stalin ever addressed the Sixth Congress, although he was present as a delegate. In 1929, after Stalin had publicly accused Bukharin of being a "right deviationist," a campaign was begun by Comintern spokesmen to establish Stalin as the originator of the basic ideas in the concept of the third period.[24] In any case, there can be no doubt that the idea of a new, third period originated in the Politburo of the CPSU and not elsewhere.

The concept of the third period is, therefore, intimately linked to the broader story of Stalin's struggle for mastery, both within the CPSU and within the Comintern. The attack upon Bukharin's allegedly erroneous position on the nature of the third period was initiated by Stalin's broadside delivered in April, 1929, at a high-level CPSU meeting.[25] Subsequently, the criticism was taken up by several high-ranking Comintern dignitaries at the Tenth Plenum of the ECCI in July, 1929, and also in the pages of the Comintern's theoretical journal.[26] The consequences of this campaign included Bukharin's demotion both from the ECCI and from the Russian Politburo and a purge of his followers throughout the Comintern.[27] The final phase in the "Stalinization" of the Comintern had begun.

The "errors" of Bukharin may be briefly noted, to clarify the Comintern's concept of the third period. Stalin's chief allegation was that Bukharin did not accept the basic idea that there would be during the third period a disintegration of the partial stabilization achieved by capitalism during the second period.[28] The Tenth Plenum of the ECCI added more detailed charges: 1) that Bukharin believed in the capacity of capitalism to organize itself within the confines of each capitalist country, and to eliminate within each such country the "anarchy" of the capitalist system; 2) that Bukharin thus believed in the possible end of "contradictions" *within* a capitalist country and the continuance of "contradictions" only in the sphere of relations among countries; 3) that Bukharin held a pessimistic and distrustful attitude toward the power of the working class.[29] Obviously, if "contradictions" existed only in the sphere of relations among nations, the possibilities for Communist-led revolution were to be created henceforth solely by wars arising from "external contradictions" among capitalist countries, or between one or more capitalist countries and the Soviet Union, and no longer by peacetime economic crises arising from "internal contradictions." To the Comintern such a hypothesis appeared harmful and erroneous. For Bukharin allegedly asserted what Marx had always denied—the capacity of capitalists to cooperate with each other and eliminate, even within the confines of a single country, the supposed anarchy of the capitalist mode of production. Bukharin's alleged views would have seriously restricted the possibilities for revolutions by making them dependent on the prior occurrence of war. The Comintern, in rejecting the "errors" of Bukharin, drew a perspective of increasing instability in the capitalist economic system, which would lead to revolution in time of peace as well as in time of war.[30]

Having enunciated the doctrine of the third period and having condemned the heretical interpretation offered by the "right deviationists," the Comintern subsequently looked for evidence in the capitalist countries that its predictions were correct. Each plenum of the ECCI made appraisals, and the leading Comintern economist, Eugene Varga, offered informative and interesting quarterly economic analyses in the pages of *Inprecor*.

The Tenth Plenum of the ECCI, meeting in July, 1929, simply repeated the general ideas respecting the third period as given by the Sixth Congress. The Plenum, the last before the great American financial crash of the coming October, in no wise forecast this event, and confined itself to an unoriginal discussion of the "sharpening of the basic contradictions of capitalism."[31] In May, 1929, Varga, a good deal more scholarly in his analysis, saw during the first quarter of that year some evidence of economic improvement in several large capitalist countries, but also saw increasing unemployment.[32] Turning his attention to the United States, he noted the wide-scale speculation in the stock market and observed, with accuracy: "Inevitably, sooner or later . . . there is bound to be a great stock exchange crash, which may well become the starting point of a serious crisis."[33] Three months later, Varga returned to the issue of speculation on the stock exchange, which he said, along with a crisis in American agriculture and an overproduction of oil and possibly of automobiles and buildings, marred the current business boom.[34] He felt that the boom in the United States would "probably last till well into the autumn, if not till the end of the year." At the same time, he asserted, indications were already apparent of a coming serious crisis, which would occur "not later than one year's time at the most."[35]

In February, 1930, an Enlarged Presidium of the ECCI met for almost three weeks, evidently to discuss the international economic crisis which was then unfolding. It found in the American crisis important confirmation of the views of the Comintern, and refutation of all alternative views. "The economic crisis which began three months ago . . . in North America," it stated, "while accelerating to an extreme degree the tempo of intensification of the basic contradictions of world capitalism, liquidates the bourgeois legend of the 'permanent prosperity' of the North American United States (Hoover) and deals a crushing blow to the Social-Democratic theories of 'organized capitalism.'"[36] There is no doubt that the Comintern, jubilantly witnessing an early confirmation of its prediction concerning the breakdown of capitalism, became exceedingly confident that its analytical tools were trustworthy. History appeared to verify in generous fashion its concept of the third period. This apparent confirmation and the self-confidence it bred must be kept in mind if one is to understand fully the Comintern's later reluctance to abandon the strategy and tactics of the third period. Varga was gleeful in his report in February, 1930, in which he pointed out that America had been the chief hope of the European bourgeoisie and of those renegade Communists who had believed the United States to be an exception to the coming general decline of capitalism. The reasons for the past successes of American capitalism, he wrote, had been the great natural wealth of the United States and the gigantic consumptive capacity of the home market; now the latter had been shattered, and the "contradiction between the consumptive and productive forces of society has become altogether disastrous."[37]

Later Comintern pronouncements attempted to specify the time when temporary stabilization had ended in the capitalist world. At the Eleventh Plenum, in March–April, 1931, Manuilsky announced that the capitalist world was "approaching the end of capitalist stabilization."[38] It remained for the Twelfth Plenum, meeting in September, 1932, to declare flatly that the end of capitalist stabilization had indeed come.[39] The Thirteenth Plenum, meeting in December, 1933, not to be outdone, announced that the world crisis was leading to a further "shattering of the capitalist system in the whole world."[40] However, it was conceded by Kuusinen that there had been some growth in industrial production in certain countries during 1933.[41] In February, 1934, Manuilsky, reporting to the Seventeenth Congress of the CPSU on behalf of the Russian contingent of the ECCI, admitted that "the lowest point of the economic crisis" had been passed in 1932.[42]

The revolutionary potentialities of the serious predicament of world capitalism seemed immense to the Comintern. The capitalists, confronted by growing social unrest and the impossibility of maintaining their former, relatively easygoing system of social controls, were increasingly compelled, according to the Comintern, to unmask their hitherto veiled dictatorships and to resort to the promotion of fascist movements. In this fluid and unstable social milieu the Comintern perceived serious difficulties for capitalism and remarkable opportunities for itself.

Comintern evaluation of the CPSU and the USSR in the world revolution. Much emphasis has been given elsewhere in this study to the strong ties that existed between the Comintern and the USSR. It has been stressed that the Comintern, aiming to achieve a Communist-led world revolution, accepted and sought to apply the same philosophy—Marxism-Leninism—as that endorsed and interpreted by the Communist Party of the Soviet Union. It has also been stressed that the Comintern looked upon the Soviet Union as the base of the Communist-led world revolution, and that the Comintern upheld the theory of an identity of interests between the USSR and world revolution. The Comintern's insistence upon the reality of an all-important and many-sided interrelationship between world revolution and the Soviet state under Communist rule seems unmistakably clear. How, then, did the Comintern define the revolutionary role of the CPSU and the USSR?

The salient features of this definition are grouped under the following three headings: 1) Stalin's personal role as the leading theoretician of the Comintern; 2) the didactical and inspirational value of the internal Bolshevik-Soviet experience; and 3) the international impact of the USSR—diplomatically, economically, and militarily—upon the surrounding non-Communist states. The obvious justification for the separate section devoted to Stalin lies in his unique status during this, the Stalin era of the Comintern.

It may be noted that, despite the virtual silence of Comintern sources on the question of direct practical aid from the CPSU to other Communist parties, the CPSU did provide important practical aid in the form of much of the personal leadership of the Comintern, financial support to other parties, physical headquarters of the Comintern (including buildings, secretarial staff, equipment, and the like), the training of foreign Communists in Soviet Party schools, and the publication of the Comintern periodicals.[43]

1. Stalin's personal role. It may be noted that after 1929 there was no publication of any speeches made by Stalin in his capacity as a Comintern official. He, however, remained a member of the Presidium of the ECCI and indisputably maintained a supervisory interest in the Comintern.

It was during this period (1928–1934) that the adulation of Stalin by the Comintern began. Certainly this was largely absent at the Sixth Congress, where Bukharin even more than Stalin was the recipient of applause. But after Stalin's victory over the "rights" in the USSR and in the Comintern during 1929, the Comintern initiated on the occasion of Stalin's fiftieth birthday in December, 1929, an era of adoration of the Soviet leader. Within the Soviet Union a similar worship of Stalin developed at the same time. This adoration by the Comintern was terminated only by its demise in 1943.

In December, 1929, a leading editorial in the theoretical journal of the ECCI proclaimed Stalin the "leader" of the Communist International and proceeded to spell out his five major contributions to the international revolutionary movement. These were as follows: his work on the national question, his struggle against Trotsky and the theory of "permanent revolution," his treatment of the question of building socialism in one country, his struggle with the "right" deviation in the Comintern, and, finally, his "leading role and direct participation . . . in the preparation of the Program of the Communist International."[44]

The ascendency of Stalin as supreme ideologist of the world revolution materialized with speed. His major speeches, even those pertaining exclusively to internal Soviet affairs, were reprinted in the Comintern organs. Stalin became "the best interpreter of Lenin," and the sin of ideological deviation was foretold for the Communist who did not "carefully study everything said and written by Comrade Stalin and everything said and written by Comrade Lenin."[45] Stalin was especially credited with having stimulated the study of revolutionary theory in the Comintern by his article in the Soviet journal *Proletarskaia Revoliutsiia* (Proletarian Revolution), in which he defended Leninism against alleged distortion.[46]

Between 1929 and 1934 the assertions of Stalin's merits were legion. Stalin was uniformly worshiped, and had no rival. A summary of this mass of adulatory testimony would reveal that Stalin was praised for these things: his threefold activity as the leader of the USSR, of the Comintern, and of all "toiling" humanity; his original contributions to Marxism-Leninism; his lucid interpretations of Marx and Lenin; and, in general, his role as *defensor fidei*.

2. *The value of the Bolshevik-Soviet experience.* As might be expected, Comintern materials during these years from 1928 to 1934 contain much about the achievements of the first Five-Year Plans. This period of Comintern history coincides roughly with the so-called reconstruction period in the USSR, i.e., from the beginning of the first Plan in October, 1928, to the proclaimed "victory of socialism" at the Seventeenth Congress in January–February, 1934. The transition to a socialist economy was portrayed as a tremendous victory for the proletariat of all countries and as a remarkable effort in the solution of the practical tasks of the transitional period.

According to the Enlarged Presidium[47] of February, 1930, the First Five-Year Plan was "a very great achievement not only of the toiling masses of the Union of Soviet Socialist Republics, but also of the entire international proletariat." Among other aspects of the Soviet experience the Presidium praised the "success of the mass kolkhoz [collective farm] movement," which the Presidium considered could not "fail to become a fighting summons to the proletariat and to the oppressed peasant masses of all countries to struggle for the world dictatorship of the proletariat." All sections of the Comintern were enjoined to master the "irreplaceable experience" of the CPSU in the problem of socialist construction. The stronger the USSR became economically, the stronger would be the attraction of socialism and the revolutionary path for the proletariat and "exploited" of the capitalist countries now entering upon a serious economic crisis.[48]

Evaluations similar to the above are quite numerous in all Comintern materials of the period. The Comintern leadership could hardly be blamed for drawing the maximum profit from the very evident distress in the non-Communist countries by its emphasis and doubtless exaggeration of the economic achievements within the USSR. If the strongholds of capitalism were crumbling, the "base" of the world revolution was being strengthened, for, as the Twelfth Plenum claimed, the "grandiose victories of the workers and kolkhoz farmers of the Soviet Union are the best support for the struggling masses of the capitalist and colonial countries."[49]

3. The impact of the USSR upon the non-Communist states. From 1928 to 1934 the Comintern painted the picture of an increasingly powerful—economically and militarily—USSR that was forcing the capitalist powers to acknowledge its importance in world affairs. Recognition by the capitalist countries in 1932 took the form of nonaggression pacts, which were interpreted as evidence of the consistent peace policy of the USSR and of the temporary postponement of an anti-Soviet war.[50] The postponement of war was considered beneficial for two basic reasons. It enabled the USSR to move further toward socialism, and it permitted the Communist parties abroad to develop. In this sense, the pacts were said to represent gains for the world revolution. The diplomatic recognition of the USSR by the United States in November, 1933, was interpreted as another sign of the growing importance of the USSR in international relations. Moreover, the economic growth of the USSR had, in the judgment of the Comintern, a baleful effect upon the weakened economies of the non-Communist world. By *not* succumbing to imperialist pressure, the USSR deprived the system of world capitalism of an immense market precisely when such a market was desperately needed. This circumstance, significant enough in earlier years, was thought to be especially potent during the Great Depression.[51]

One further question respecting the role of the USSR in the world revolutionary process may be raised. Did the Comintern ever indicate that the USSR should wage an offensive war for the purpose of creating revolutionary situations in other countries and helping Communist parties to seize power? Certainly the Comintern consistently took the position that wartime conditions were much more favorable than peacetime conditions to the development of a revolutionary crisis. "The maturing of an actual revolutionary situation in this or that country," asserted a Comintern writer in 1928, "is possible not only as a result of war *(as a result of war it is inevitable)*."[52] In the Comintern's analyses of the third period, war and revolution were always linked. But on no occasion did the Comintern state or suggest that the USSR should undertake an offensive revolutionary war. Nor was it suggested that Communists should not oppose war among capitalist countries or war between a capitalist coalition and the USSR, on the grounds that such wars would create favorable revolutionary situations.

The theses of 1928 on the war question, entitled "Means of Struggle with the Danger of Imperialist Wars," were the most elaborate treatment of the war question in the years 1928–1934. Despite their affirmation of the belief in the inevitability of war under the capitalist system, the theses rejected as "senseless calumny" the accusation that Communists encouraged war, hoping thereby to accelerate the revolutionary process.[53]

THE PATTERN OF STRATEGY AND TACTICS

In capitalist societies. It will be convenient in the discussions of Communist strategy and tactics to combine the advanced capitalist societies and the societies of medium capitalist development. Much repetition—and little profit—would result if these two categories were treated separately, for the concern here is solely with the broad pattern of Communist strategy and tactics, and this is largely the same for both types of societies.

In each such society, the Communist party had, besides the job of increasing its own strength, the following tasks regarded in Comintern materials as indispensable: 1) to bring under its control a significant part of the proletariat, although not necessarily a majority, as has been shown in Chapter IV; 2) to create a popular base, necessarily including the additional allies required for a future seizure of power; and 3) to defend the USSR.

These tasks were integrated into an overall pattern of strategy and tactics that corresponded to certain fixed notions in respect to the foreseeable future. In 1928, and on down into 1934, the Comintern held rather rigidly to an outlook based on the following beliefs: 1) no intrinsic difference existed between bourgeois democracy (e.g., in England) and fascist dictatorship (e.g., in Italy)—both were genuinely dictatorial systems of bourgeois class rule, one masked, the other open; 2) bourgeois democracy and its system of representative government and civil rights were meaningless to the proletariat and not worth defense by it; 3) no real alternative to fascism existed except the struggle for socialism via a Communist seizure of power. These points should be noted, for they contrast markedly with the assumptions of the following period, 1935–1939. They are embodied explicitly or implicitly in the resolutions of every plenum from the Ninth in February, 1928, through the Thirteenth in December, 1933, as well as in the resolutions of the Sixth Comintern Congress of 1928.

In the light of the Comintern's expectations respecting capitalist crises, wars, and intensified oppression of the proletariat, what did the Comintern insist upon as the "way out"? Essentially the answer is that the Comintern ordered the Communist parties to prepare for armed revolt against the capitalist order, such a revolt being contingent, of course, upon the existence of a "revolutionary situation." The Communist parties were to hasten to make ready those prerequisites that could be created by Communist activity.

Advocating the above "way out," the Comintern rejected the choice of the "lesser evil." That is, the Comintern refused to imitate the Social Democrats who undertook a defense of democratic institutions (parliamentary representative government, civil rights, etc.) lest this milder form of bourgeois class rule succumb to fascist dictatorship. Bourgeois rule in any form, whether democratic or fascist, was rejected by the Comintern. The Thirteenth Plenum, December, 1933, examining the events that had occurred since the Twelfth Plenum of the preceding year, perceived no choice between fascism and bourgeois democracy, despite the success of German fascism in January, 1933, and the resultant ruin of the German Communist Party. In its "Theses on Fascism, the

War Danger, and the Tasks of the Communist Parties," the Plenum summarized its outlook in the slogan "For a revolutionary way out of the crisis—for Soviet power." [54] This was the outlook as the year 1934 opened, during the course of which this view would undergo essential modifications.

How was the problem of winning influence over a significant part of the proletariat to be solved? Two lines were followed. One was negative—the reduction to a minimum of non-Communist influence over the proletariat; non-Communist influence included that exercised by Social-Democratic parties, or by "reformist" trade-union leadership, or by fascism. The other line was positive— the activity of the Communist party on behalf of the proletariat to win its support.

In 1928 the Comintern called for the creation amongst the proletariat of a "united front" from below. By this was meant the uniting of the proletariat under the Communist party alone, as a party acting independently of, and belligerently toward, all other political parties or movements. The Ninth Plenum in February, 1928, had instructed the French and British Communist parties to initiate the united front "from below." [55] The Sixth Comintern Congress had made this form obligatory throughout the Comintern. [56]

The united front "from below" was a radical departure from the strategy of the preceding years when the united front *from above* had been looked upon as a useful arrangement. In effect the united front "from above" had involved short-term agreements between the leaderships of Communist and Social-Democratic parties for joint action in defense of working-class interests. Now the Communist attitude stiffened toward the Social Democrats, who were severely criticized for allegedly defending the capitalist order. The Sixth Congress perceived a developing process of "fascization" among the socialists. The Twelfth Plenum in 1932 accused the Social Democrats of being the "chief social support of the bourgeoisie." [57] At the Thirteenth Plenum in 1933 Kuusinen asserted that the socialists and fascists agreed on the same goals, and differed only in that the socialists preferred "bourgeois-democratic" forms of rule. [58]

The terms "social-fascist" and "Social Democrat" were employed as synonymous. Especially treacherous was the left wing of social democracy, which, according to the Comintern, maliciously deceived the workers with talk, but not deeds, of revolution. On the whole, social democracy and not fascism was regarded as the most serious enemy of the Communist party within the labor movement. The Comintern reasoned as follows: no revolution without support from the proletariat, no support from the proletariat without the eradication of Social-Democratic influence. The "main blow," according to the Twelfth Plenum, was, therefore, to be directed against the Social Democrats.[59]

By its independent leadership of strikes, demonstrations, and other forms of protest, the Communist party was expected to win the confidence of the proletariat and to demonstrate the "treacherous" nature of social democracy, as well as to educate the proletariat in class militancy. In fighting for concise partial demands, i.e., the immediate wants of the proletariat, the party was to draw the proletariat to an ever higher level of class consciousness. The line of independent action was to be followed by the party in the trade unions, the factory councils, and other organizations of the working class.

The Tenth Plenum of July, 1929, further developed the line of independent action in the labor movement. In those countries where the trade-union movement was already split and there existed a well-developed Communist trade-union organization alongside one that was "reformist" (anti-Communist), the weight of Communist activity was to be placed behind the strengthening of the Communist trade-union movement as the sole independent and reliable defender of the working class. All efforts were to be made to draw membership away from the "reformists." Where the trade-union movement was not seriously split but was largely in the hands of "reformists," the Communists were to work inside the "reformist" organization and seek to create a trade-union "opposition" under Communist control. On the eve of strikes, the Communists were to form "committees of struggle" for the purpose of leading the strike. Such committees, created on a temporary *ad hoc* basis, were to deprive the "reformist" leadership of any chances to betray the strike. Where workers were largely unorganized, special efforts were to be made to create new, Communist-controlled unions. Communists were also to attempt to win control over factory councils, which, as permanent organizations of all workers of an enterprise, could most effectively hamper or promote labor opposition to management.[60]

It is worth noting that the Comintern's strategy of directing its "main blow" against social democracy as its most dangerous enemy, and not, for instance, against fascism, aroused some misgivings in the Comintern. For example, at the Thirteenth Plenum in December, 1933, Manuilsky recognized that some had questioned the condemnation of social democracy as the "chief social support of the bourgeoisie" in view of the severe punishment given it in Germany by Hitler. Manuilsky answered that German social democracy remained the chief social support of the German bourgeoisie for, although ousted from the Reichstag, it had not altered its attitude toward the Communist party, the Soviet Union, or proletarian revolution and the class struggle, and therefore continued to split the labor movement and thereby helped the bourgeois class.[61] Manuilsky did not permit social democracy the luxury of opposing *both* fascism and Communism. So long as it did not come over to the side of the Communist party, social democracy remained "objectively" the chief supporter of bourgeois rule over the working class.

The line of independent action, i.e., action apart from and against social democracy as the chief rival of the Communist party for influence over the working class, was carried over to the other major tasks of winning nonproletarian allies and of defending the Soviet Union. Of course, absolutely no relationship with bourgeois parties was maintained. The Communist party was to create organizations under its control among the peasantry and the urban petty bourgeoisie. By working closely with the masses for limited aims desired by them, and by linking the struggle for these limited aims with a campaign for the defense of the USSR, the Communist party expected to achieve two goals at the same time—greater influence for itself and greater sympathy and support for the Soviet Union.

Shifts and waverings in this general line may be detected in statements issued during the years 1928 to 1934. The Tenth Plenum of July, 1929, and the Enlarged Presidium of February, 1930, reflected an extremely leftist and sectarian phase; not only was social democracy, especially its left wing, harshly condemned, but within the Communist parties the main heresy by far was considered to be "right" deviationist tendencies (including manifestations of Social-Democratic influence).[62] In contrast, a somewhat more moderate position was sought by the Eleventh Plenum of March–April, 1931, and the Twelfth Plenum of September, 1932; careful distinction between the Social-Democratic leadership and the rank-and-file was insisted upon, and the Communist parties were enjoined to struggle against symptoms of "left," as well as "right," deviationism.[63] In Germany, the more moderate and less sectarian slogan of a "people's revolution" was employed.[64] In March, 1933, following Hitler's accession to power, the ECCI moved even further right. Its manifesto "For the United Front against Fascism!" instructed the Communist parties to make "yet another attempt" to achieve the united front, through proposals directed to the executive committees of the Social-Democratic parties.[65] Thus the united front "from above" again became permissible, although for only a short time. Several Communist parties did make proposals, but with virtually no success; the much-abused Social Democrats displayed great skepticism of the Communists' good faith.[66] The subsequent May Day Manifesto of the ECCI reflected its keen disappointment at the lack of fruitful response; the most serious charges were again leveled at the socialists, and the united front "from below" was restored.[67] This hostile line was continued by the Thirteenth Plenum at the end of 1933. Blaming social democracy for the fascist victory in Germany, the Plenum labeled "right" opportunism as the main heresy and called for the united front "from below."[68]

In colonial, semi-colonial, and dependent societies. As mentioned in Chapter IV, the disastrous experience of the Kuomintang-Communist collaboration in China, which was forcibly terminated by Chiang Kai-shek in 1927, necessitated a reappraisal of Communist strategy and tactics in the colonial sphere.[69]

In 1928, the Comintern held important discussions on the Chinese question at the Ninth Plenum of the ECCI in February and at the Sixth World Congress in July, at which time a new pattern of strategy and tactics was generalized for all countries in this category.

The prime results of these discussions were: 1) condemnation in the strongest terms of the vacillating and inconsistent nature of the native bourgeoisie, which, it was claimed, would inevitably betray the revolutionary movement by crossing over into the counter-revolutionary, imperialist camp; and 2) insistence upon the necessity of the "hegemony of the proletariat," i.e., the hegemony of the Communist party, in the colonial revolutions.[70]

The new line permitted only temporary and cautious collaboration with "national-reformist" bourgeois and petty-bourgeois parties in the colonial sphere. Such collaboration was not to carry with it any loss of independence by the Communist party. The bourgeois parties were to be viewed with the utmost suspicion, and collaboration with them was to rest upon a genuine struggle on the part of the bourgeoisie against imperialism. The Communist party was to be constantly on guard to expose the first signs of bourgeois wavering. It was emphasized that sooner or later the bourgeois parties would shift support to the counterrevolutionary camp and therefore in no wise could be regarded as consistent and permanent supporters of the aims of the so-called "bourgeois-democratic" revolution.[71]

In China, the Kuomintang had previously been viewed by the Comintern in 1924–1927 as the proper movement within which the Chinese Communist Party should operate. The Kuomintang had been initially defined as a four-class coalition of bourgeoisie, petty bourgeoisie, peasants, and workers.[72] Later, after the anti-Communist actions of Chiang Kai-shek in April, 1927, the Kuomintang was redefined as a three-class coalition of the petty bourgeoisie, peasants, and workers.[73] Already during the period of the three-class coalition, the Communist Party was instructed by the Eighth Plenum of the ECCI in May, 1927, to secure "the hegemony of the working class in the revolutionary struggle," by means of achieving that hegemony *within* the Kuomintang.[74] In 1928, as noted above, the strategy changed. The new pattern of strategy called for the winning of Communist hegemony over the Chinese revolution independently and *outside* the Kuomintang.

The Chinese example is stressed here because the Comintern gave it foremost attention and advised the other Communist parties in the colonial world to study the experience of the Chinese Communist Party.

How were the Communist parties to achieve their basic tasks of winning support among the proletariat, and of extending their influence among nonproletarian classes and groups in society, while conducting simultaneously a struggle for the defense of the USSR? According to the theses on the colonial question adopted by the Sixth Comintern Congress, the Communist parties were instructed to strive for the independent leadership of the proletarian struggle through strikes, demonstrations, and the like, to conduct revolutionary propaganda in the trade unions controlled by the bourgeoisie, and to create new, Communist-controlled unions among the unorganized workers.

Among the peasant masses, as the most important nonproletarian ally of the Communist party, the party was to attempt to work within peasant leagues and committees. However, the party was not to build itself as a two-class (proletarian and peasant) party, but was to strive for a primarily proletarian base. In certain cases, however, revolutionary committees of action, coordinating the activity of workers' and peasants' organizations, were to be created. In the period of an uprising, soviets (councils) of workers' and peasants' deputies could be elected.[75]

The Sixth Congress in its theses also singled out for special party work such categories as youth, women, and children, all quite significant elements in the labor force of the colonial countries.[76]

It is clear that the Comintern came out boldly in 1928 for

Communist party leadership over the revolutionary movement in colonies, semi-colonies, and dependent countries. The term used to designate this hegemony of the Communist party was "hegemony of the proletariat." The highest development in any country of this new pattern of strategy and tactics was certainly that in China, where in 1931 a Soviet Republic, embracing a significant area, was proclaimed on the anniversary of the October Revolution of 1917 in Russia.[77]

Subsequent Comintern directives endorsed these policies. The Tenth Plenum called for independent Communist leadership of colonial labor struggles, and for purging strike organs of any "national-bourgeois and social-reformist elements."[78] The Eleventh Plenum, expressing gratification at the growth of the Chinese soviets, enjoined the Indian Communists to seize control of the "revolutionary-liberation" movement, and claimed that in northern Indo-China, "where the influence of the Chinese revolution is especially strong," soviets were already being formed.[79] The Twelfth Plenum issued similar injunctions to the colonial Communist parties. Emphasizing the recent Japanese aggression in Manchuria, it appealed to the Communists in China, Formosa, and Korea to cooperate with the Japanese Party in achieving Communist control over the anti-imperialist and national-liberation movements in their countries.[80]

There is an obvious parallel between the struggle for independent leadership for the Communist parties in the capitalist countries and the similar struggle in the colonial orbit. The broad pattern of Communist strategy and tactics for the period beginning in 1928 and ending in 1934, faithfully reflected in all the resolutions and theses of the various plenums of the period, indicated a bold (or rash) "go-it-alone" attitude, certainly reinforced after 1929 by the optimism generated in Communist ranks by the Great Depression. No attempt has been made to describe the historical application of this broad pattern of Comintern strategy and tactics in each major country, for such a task lies outside the proper scope of this study. But, as Borkenau states, the "essential features of the new tactics were the same everywhere."[81]

A new pattern of Comintern strategy and tactics began to emerge during 1934. The "go-it-alone" policy was abandoned, and perhaps without too much regret, for the period from 1928 to 1934 failed to record Communist successes other than the establishment of the Chinese Soviet Republic in 1931. The same period witnessed the disastrous failure of Communist strategy in Germany and in other Western countries.[82]

VI. PREPARATION: STRATEGY
AND TACTICS, 1935-1939

The half-decade preceding World War II constituted the baleful terminal years of the interwar armistice. Stability, law, and peace rapidly lost out to violence, aggression, and war. In both the non-Communist and Communist worlds the proposition *homo homini lupus* seemed to be unpleasantly supported. Fascist brutality in Nazi Germany and Communist terror in Soviet Russia were merely the most extreme cases of man's irrationality. One great contrast between the two worlds was clearly evident by 1939: Disunity riddled the capitalist camp, but an ever-higher degree of monolithic totalitarianism was being attained in the USSR.

OVERVIEW OF THE PERIOD

The situation in the non-Communist world. Perhaps the most notable trend of the 1930s was the marked and widespread movement from democracy to dictatorship. By 1935 almost all of central and central-eastern Europe had moved to the right. In Spain, where civil war lasted from 1936 to 1939, there was yet another victory for fascism. In western and northern Europe, in Czechoslovakia, and in the United States and the British dominions, democratic institutions continued to function, though perilously at times in France. Political stability was increasingly difficult to maintain in that key country, where successive governments attempted to cope with financial ills and the threat of an aggressive Germany. Among the chief capitalist countries, the United States and Great Britain most successfully maintained their democratic systems.

The Great Depression, beginning in 1929, created trouble in

every country in the non-Communist world during the entire decade before the outbreak of World War II. Unemployment, financial muddles, agricultural depression—these continued to plague the world. The painfully slow rise in the level of industrial production only in 1937 advanced beyond the 1929 level. Confronted by the persistence of economic ills, states continued to resort to increased governmental controls over their economies.

International politics during this period witnessed the unsuccessful and at times halfhearted efforts of those countries that wished to preserve the status quo against the aspirations of the aggressive countries—Italy, Germany, and Japan. Soviet Russia and the United States, hitherto somewhat isolated, directed increasing attention to the international imbalance. The prevailing mood of isolationism restrained the American nation from playing a large role in the worsening political situation. On the other hand, the Soviet Union moved to identify itself with efforts at collective security and the solution of international problems by peaceful means. Having joined the League of Nations in 1934, it salvaged from its unsuccessful efforts to create a security system in Eastern Europe two pacts of military alliance—those with France and Czechoslovakia, both signed in May, 1935.

For the aggressive states the period was one of success—Italy in Ethiopia, Japan in China, Germany in Austria, in Czechoslovakia, and finally in Poland. Exploiting a frontier incident of 1934, Italy invaded Ethiopia the following year from Italian Somaliland and, despite the approval and application of economic sanctions by the League of Nations, defied world opinion and ruthlessly extinguished the independence of its poorly matched opponent. In July, 1937, a Japanese force attacked Chinese units near the Marco Polo Bridge in Peiping, and thus began the long undeclared war that ended only with the defeat of Japan eight years later at the close of World War II. In Europe, Hitler annexed Austria in March, 1938, bullied France and England into appeasement at the Munich Conference in September, 1938, whereupon he acquired vital border areas of Czechoslovakia, and in March, 1939, completed the destruction of that state. The aggressive powers were only weakly opposed. Memel and Albania were final prewar victims.

The Soviet Union perhaps felt most keenly the failure of its policy of collective security at the time of the Munich Conference, to which it was not invited. Statesmen in the West distrusted the Soviet pledge to aid Czechoslovakia, questioned the effectiveness of the Soviet armed forces in the light of the great military purge trial of 1937, and in general doubted whether a Communist-ruled country could be a reliable partner against Hitler. There were some, also, in the West who viewed with satisfaction the prospect of a German expansion at the expense of the Soviet Union. During 1939 the Soviet leaders worked for a rapprochement with Nazi Germany as an alternative to collective security. The resulting Nazi-Soviet Pact of August, 1939, was the most cynical indicator of the perilous state of world peace and world democracy.

The situation in the Soviet Union. Two broad developments stand out in the history of the Soviet state during this period. One was the continued and impressive growth of the economy, and especially of its industrial base. The First Five-Year Plan was succeeded by the Second and, in 1938, by the Third. Emphasis continued to be placed by the Soviet leaders upon the production of capital goods at the expense of consumer commodities. Having claimed in 1934 at the Seventeenth Congress of the CPSU that socialism had been attained in the USSR, the Soviet leadership in 1939 regarded the country as on the path toward communism.

The other major development was the further consolidation of the personal rule of Stalin. With the assassination of Kirov, a member of the Politburo, in December, 1934, a period of ruthless and undiscriminating investigation, arrest, and purge began. The most extreme manifestations of this blood bath were the Great Purges of 1936, 1937, and 1938. Most of the notable "Old Bolshe-viks" of the October Revolution of 1917 and the Civil War of 1918–1921 became its victims. Zinoviev and Bukharin, former leaders of the Comintern, were perhaps the best known. Trotsky, in exile, was condemned to death *in absentia.* Well over 50 percent of the senior officers of the Red Army were removed by the purge.[1]

The absolute dictatorial rule of Stalin was more complete, more terroristic than ever. The Stalin Constitution of 1936, announced as the most democratic in the world, proved to offer in practice no limitation to the despotism of Stalin. But quite aside from the matter of Stalin's personal rule, the power and functions of the Soviet state greatly increased during these years, with a correspondingly greater impact—both positive and negative—upon the life of every Soviet citizen.

VIEWS OF THE COMINTERN

Comintern evaluation of world capitalism: the threat of fascism. In its analyses between 1928 and 1934 of the situation in the "capitalist world" during those years, the Comintern had emphasized economic rather than political factors. In the following period, from 1935 to 1939, a major switch in emphasis is very sharply revealed. Political factors become primary and remain so throughout these years. The reason for a preoccupation with politics, rather than economics, may in great part be explained by the fact that a most serious threat to the security of the USSR was then becoming increasingly manifest. The threat was Nazi Germany, whose leaders made no effort to conceal their desire to conquer and exploit the "socialist fatherland."

However, the Comintern did continue to comment upon the economic ills of world capitalism, and repeated some familiar ideas. These may be mentioned briefly. The Comintern regularly maintained that capitalism could not recover that degree of temporary stabilization which it had attained in the later 1920s. In 1935 it was claimed that the cyclical recovery normal in past capitalist depressions had not been repeated, even though six years had passed.[2] Varga predicted in March, 1937, that a new crisis would occur either during that year or certainly in 1938.[3] Reviving an old theme, he rejected the notion that a capitalist economy could be planned in such a way as to avert crises.[4] Capitalism under the rule of the bourgeoisie was incapable, he said, of organizing itself to the point of becoming a viable system.

A much more extensive discussion was devoted to fascism, which in Comintern theory was always viewed as proof of capitalist instability. Fascism, it was stated, pointed to the existence of weakness and panic within the ruling circles, who could no longer control matters by "normal" means. Fascism had been defined at the Thirteenth Plenum of the ECCI in 1933 as "*the open terrorist dictatorship of the most chauvinistic and most imperialist elements of finance capital.*"[5] Dimitrov endorsed this interpretation at the Seventh Congress of the Comintern in 1935. But whereas at the Thirteenth Plenum and during the whole preceding period the Comintern saw the solution to fascism in the immediate struggle for "proletarian revolution" and the destruction of the capitalist system, Dimitrov was to outline a fresh approach, providing for a victory over fascism within the context of the capitalist system. Dimitrov's program, which gave the basic character to the strategic pattern for 1935–1939, will be discussed below. But it is important to note here that the Comintern made in this period a careful distinction between bourgeois parliamentary democracy and bourgeois rule through a fascist dictatorship. This distinction, as we know, had not been made in the preceding period.

If the Comintern began to perceive a qualitative difference between the traditional form of bourgeois rule and the fascist dictatorships, it also began to discriminate in international politics between the role of the aggressive fascist states (Germany, Italy, and Japan) and the nonaggressive capitalist states (Britain, France, the United States, and others). No longer were all international groupings amongst the imperialist states viewed as equally bad. The distinction began to appear early in 1934, when *Inprecor* reprinted a speech of Litvinov before the Soviet Central Executive Committee, in which he pointed out that "not every capitalist state has equal desire for war at all times."[6] States, however imperialistic, might become for a time deeply pacifist, in one period or another. Soon Germany and Japan were singled out as the chief instigators of war.[7]

By 1935 there had unfolded in Comintern statements the drama of a great struggle between the "war-mongering" forces of world fascism (the fascist dictatorships and movements) and the anti-fascist forces. The category of the anti-fascist forces included the Communist parties, the USSR, the international proletariat and other elements of the "exploited masses," and under certain conditions the nonaggressive states, the Social-Democratic parties, and even various strata of the bourgeois class.[8]

As part of its conception of a gigantic world-wide struggle between the forces of peace and the forces of war, the Comintern abandoned its hitherto wholly negative view of the institutions of the bourgeois world. We have noted its new-found, but limited, appreciation of traditional bourgeois democracy. The Comintern also conceded some modest value to the League of Nations, taking its cue from Stalin's qualified support for the League as expressed in his interview with the correspondent Walter Duranty.[9]

The Comintern moved to the position that neutrality was impossible. The neutrality of small states, such as the Scandinavian countries was attacked as, in effect, a sign of hostility to the cause of democracy and peace.[10] Such neutrality was senseless, for the aggressive states aspired not only to colonial conquests but also to parts of Europe itself. Just as a colony's anti-imperialist war was considered a just war, Dimitrov declared that for a capitalist state a national, anti-fascist war would also be just.[11]

Against this background of political instability in the capitalist world, the Comintern continued to speak between 1934 and 1939 of the "maturing" new "upsurges" in the revolutionary movement.[12] The important thing to note, however, is that the Comintern did not demand the exploitation of the instability in world capitalism for the immediate purposes of a Communist seizure of power but for more moderate, albeit temporary, aims. These points, as elements in the new pattern of Comintern strategy, are discussed below.

Comintern evaluation of the CPSU and the USSR in the world revolution. Having described the Comintern's views on the chief trends in the "capitalist world," we may now turn our attention to the Comintern's evaluation of the role of the CPSU and the USSR during this period.

1. Stalin's personal role. At the Seventh Comintern Congress in
1935 the adulation of Stalin was unrestrained. His preeminence
within the Comintern was accorded even greater recognition than
ever before by the speakers. Practically every speech expressed
deference to Stalin. He himself, although a Soviet delegate to the
Congress and reelected by it to the ECCI, did not address the
gathering.[13]

Stalin was later to be given credit for the basic features of the
new general line enunciated by the Seventh Congress and followed
for the next four years.[14] However, it may be noted that there was
no campaign to publicize Stalin's role. No explicit personal
identification of Stalin with the new line—that of the "anti-fascist
people's front," to be discussed below—was made at the Seventh
Congress. Rather, such identification was made with Dimitrov, the
General Secretary of the Comintern.

Of the publications of Stalin during this period, that which
almost certainly received the greatest circulation among the Communist parties of the world was the *History of the Communist Party
of the Soviet Union (Bolsheviks): Short Course.*[15] This work, attributed
to Stalin until his death, was actually written by a commission of
the Party Central Committee, according to Khrushchev in his
"secret" speech at the Twentieth Congress of the CPSU.[16]

Another writing singled out as of especial importance for the
guidance of Communists was Stalin's *Foundations of Leninism,* which
Bela Kun termed the "handbook for the Bolshevization of the
Communist International and its sections."[17] Manuilsky at the
Seventh Comintern Congress similarly identified it as the "handbook of proletarian revolutionaries all over the world."[18] This basic
work by Stalin first appeared in 1924. Stalin's speeches before the
CPSU were repeatedly designated as required reading throughout
the Communist parties in the Comintern.[19]

In an important address before the Seventh Congress, com-
memorating the fortieth anniversary of the death of Friedrich
Engels, Manuilsky portrayed Stalin as especially the theoretician
of the phase of socialist development following the "proletarian"
revolution. His contribution to the theory of this transitional phase

to Communism was judged superior to that of Marx, Engels, and Lenin. "Neither in the *Critique of the Gotha Program* [by Marx], nor in the works of Engels, nor in Lenin's *The State and Revolution* were the concrete problems of the first phase of communism raised which Stalin raised and solved with the greatest boldness and profundity."[20]

In his role as a Soviet statesman Stalin was praised in Comintern publications for the so-called Stalin Constitution of 1936. Certain democratic articles in this Constitution, such as those providing for universal suffrage and the secret ballot, fitted in nicely with the anti-fascist struggle then being waged by the Comintern, avowedly on behalf of democratic institutions. A new role emerged for Stalin as not simply the leader of the "toiling masses" but more broadly as "the leader of progressive, anti-fascist humanity." The shift in terminology here is just one example of the terminological innovations of this period, to be discussed more fully below.

The great purge trials in the Soviet Union of 1936, 1937, and 1938 received extensive coverage in *Inprecor*. The full endorsement by this Comintern periodical of the official Soviet explanation of the purges shows the Comintern's willingness to accept Stalin's methods of eliminating his opposition. It is perhaps unnecessary to add that a clear picture is thereby drawn of the Comintern's understanding of Stalinist democracy.

2. *The value of the Bolshevik-Soviet experience.* Traditional appreciations were readily reaffirmed in this period respecting the universal applicability of the Bolshevik-Soviet experience, the superiority of the CPSU over other Communist parties, and the didactical and inspirational contributions of pioneering Soviet socialism. "The doctrine of Marx and Engels," declared Manuilsky at the Seventh Congress, "rules unchallenged over one-sixth of the globe, backed by a powerful state, by a socialist economy with wealth amounting to billions."[21] And elsewhere the same doctrine was at work. "In all countries this doctrine is breaking the chains of the slaves, in order that it may embrace the whole world."[22] Yet the growing experience of other Communist parties did not eliminate the need for a careful study of Russian Bolshevism. As an

editorial in the theoretical journal of the Comintern declared,

It is natural that every congress, every plenum of the Central Committee
of the CPSU is for all sections of the Communist International an event
which compels them to ponder again and again their own problems and
endeavor to draw from the experiences of their great brother party
practical lessons for themselves also.[23]

Besides reaffirming in familiar fashion the continuing universal
value of Bolshevik-Soviet experience, the Comintern concentrated
upon Soviet economic achievements and the Soviet Constitution of
1936 as the most important contribution of the period. The further
construction of socialism in the USSR demonstrated, according to
the Comintern, how practical problems could be solved. The
USSR, paving the way for other Communist parties, was in effect
facilitating the future work of these parties after their own conquests of power. Soviet socialism also had the more immediate
effect of aiding the world revolution through its inspirational impact upon workers and "toilers" the world over. For these people,
"socialism is not merely some magically invented doctrine, a
doctrine that has still to be tested by experience; it already exists
on an extensive territory stretching from the Berezina to Vladi-
vostok."[24] A Comintern Manifesto on the twentieth anniversary of
the Bolshevik Revolution declared that the "victory of socialism"
in the USSR "imbues the masses of the capitalist countries with
the flame of ardent enthusiasm." Proletarians, peasants, and
"toiling intellectuals" alike were becoming confident that their
salvation lay only along the path already paved by Bolshevik
experience.[25] Such confidence, the Manifesto claimed, would
continue to grow with the growth of the material might of the
USSR.

The impact of the adoption of a new Soviet Constitution in 1936
was viewed similarly. The decision to extend "proletarian democracy by the introduction of equal and direct suffrage and the
secret ballot" was a "powerful weapon that the Communist parties
in the capitalist countries may wield in their struggle against
fascism."[26] Stalin's own emphasis upon the international revo-

lutionary significance of the new Soviet Constitution was reprinted in *Inprecor*.[27] An endless series of contrasts were drawn in Comintern materials between "Soviet democracy" and "fascism" in the capitalist countries.

3. The impact of the USSR upon the non-Communist states. During the period from 1935 to 1939, the chief current impact of the USSR on the outside world, according to the Comintern, lay in its great influence on the side of peace and in the restraint it imposed upon the aggressive states. This restraint, the Comintern believed, derived from two sources—the capacity of the USSR to wage war and the fear of the aggressors that an anti-Soviet war would mean revolution in their own countries.

The great capacity of the Soviet Union to wage war was boastfully stated time and again. The Manifesto of the ECCI on the twenty-first anniversary of the Bolshevik Revolution referred to the Red Army as "the strongest army in the world," and reminded its audience of the victories won by that army over the Japanese near Lake Hasan in 1938.[28]

The argument that the aggressors refrained from attacking the USSR through fear of internal revolution was not new, but it was given added force during the late 1930s through the Comintern's presentation of the USSR as the protector not only of the world revolution but also of all "peace-loving," "anti-fascist," or "democratic" peoples of the world. It was argued that great masses of people, extending beyond the category of workers and "toilers" to broad strata of the bourgeoisie, were now looking to the USSR for leadership in an anti-fascist crusade. An attack upon the USSR would evoke hostility toward the aggressor not only from those who desired socialism but also from those who were devoted to democracy (under capitalism).[29]

The great importance of the role of the USSR in maintaining peace and postponing the outbreak of war, according to the Comintern, was the gaining of time during which the revolutionary forces in the world could be strengthened. In this sense, any restraint imposed by the USSR upon the capitalist states served the interests of world revolution.

The use of the Soviet armed forces on behalf of the world revolution was not envisaged by the Comintern except in the case of an attack upon the USSR in time of peace; the soldier in the Red Army understood that by guarding the USSR he was fighting for the cause of the workers of all lands.[30] Thus the Red Army was portrayed as a force dedicated to the defense of the Soviet Union and only indirectly to the defense of the world revolution. It may be noted that during this period the Comintern gave wide circulation to the Stalin–Howard interview of March, 1936, during which Stalin had said: "The export of revolution is nonsense."[31] One member of the ECCI made the point even more explicit. "The assertion that the Soviet Union with its Red Army is setting itself the task of carrying the revolution into Europe belongs to the foulest propagandistic inventions of German fascism."[32]

Only in the case of an attack upon the USSR were the Soviet armed forces to assume a clearly revolutionary role outside the USSR. Once attacked, the Red Army would not only crush the invaders "on their own territory," but would demonstrate the meaning of its "international tasks" by helping to liberate those under the "fascist slavery" of the aggressor.[33]

The above statements appear to restrict seriously the possibilities of using the Soviet armed forces on behalf of world revolution, for such activity by military units must await an attack upon the USSR. This conservatism must, however, be considered in the light of the foreign policy of the USSR during this period. It would have been embarrassing, to say the least, for the Comintern especially at that time to have publicized a more positive, offensive role for the armed forces of the Soviet Union. Certainly such a more positive role is clearly stated in materials that were given the highest endorsement by the Comintern, i.e., the writings and speeches of Lenin and Stalin. For instance, Stalin's "The October Revolution and the Tactics of the Russian Communists," written in 1924, unequivocally endorses and repeats Lenin's position that a "victorious proletariat" in one country might in the event of necessity come out with armed force against other (capitalist) states.[34] No purely defensive role is indicated here.

THE PATTERN OF STRATEGY AND TACTICS

In the capitalist societies. At the Seventh Comintern Congress, which convened in the summer of 1935, the major ideas of the period extending roughly from mid-1934 to the autumn of 1939 were crystallized. In his report to the Congress on behalf of the ECCI, Wilhelm Pieck, the German Communist leader, raised the basic question: "What are the prospects of world development, what are the prospects of the world revolution?"[35] In answering this question, he in effect laid down much of the Comintern's line for the next four years. He made the following points: 1) The capitalist system had been "shaken to its foundations" by the Great Depression; 2) the growth of fascism in the capitalist system had brought the world closer to war; 3) the USSR had "become the most powerful and important factor in the world struggle for socialism"; 4) the relation of forces on a world scale had changed to the advantage of socialism and to the disadvantage of capitalism; 5) the revolutionary crisis had not yet fully matured, but was maturing all over the world.[36] In the light of this favorable perspective Pieck and other Comintern leaders emphasized time and again at the Congress, not an early Communist seizure of power, but the necessity of *preparation* for a later seizure of power. In Pieck's words, "No social system falls of itself, however rotten it may be. It must be overthrown. No revolutionary crisis can bring victory to the proletariat if the proletariat cannot organize and win victory."[37] To drive home the need for preparation, the speakers at the Seventh Congress repeatedly read a passage from Stalin's speech at the Seventeenth Congress of the CPSU in 1934, in which the need for preparation for the seizure of power had been stressed by the Soviet dictator. This passage, already cited elsewhere (pp. 87–88), was the selection from Stalin most frequently quoted at the Seventh Congress. During the next four years it remained a favorite of Comintern spokesmen in their efforts to focus the attention of Communists upon thorough *preparation*. Thus, the act of seizing power was pushed further into the future, to be undertaken only after careful and adequate preparatory work.

Certain assumptions underlying the current strategy and tactics of the new period were contradictory to assumptions held during the preceding period. First, the continuing and increasing unrest among the workers and the "toiling masses" did not place on the Communist agenda an early attempt to seize power; rather, as indicated above, preparation for that attempt was emphasized. Second, a qualitative difference existed between democracy and fascism, as two forms of bourgeois rule; democratic rights and institutions under capitalism, however imperfect in the eyes of Communists, were considered beneficial to the working classes and to all "toilers," and were to be defended by Communists and their followers against the onslaught of fascism. Third, the defeat of fascism no longer required the complete destruction of capitalism, but only a purging of that system, as the result of which a "new democracy" was to be created. As will be indicated, none of this meant that capitalism was not to be replaced by socialism ultimately; the immediate aim, however, was not the destruction but the purging of capitalism.

What followed, then, was roughly a four-year period of Comintern history during which the Communist party in each capitalist country was directed to create a broad, anti-fascist, popular movement. This movement had the twin aims of defense of existing democratic liberties against any attack by a fascist movement within the country, and defense of national independence against aggressive fascist states. A more flexible pattern of strategy and tactics replaced the rather rigid and unimaginative pattern of the years 1928–1934. Many interesting ideas and institutions appear during this anti-fascist period in Comintern history, as will be shown below.

Lest the innovations of the new period be overemphasized, it is well to keep always in mind that the new pattern of Communist strategy and tactics was understood by the Comintern as preparation for the ultimate Communist seizure of power. That seizure of power was not abandoned, but only postponed. As stated by Dimitrov, the chief spokesman for the new line in 1935, "We Communists have other ultimate aims than the defense of democracy . . .

but in struggling for our aims we are ready to fight jointly for any immediate tasks which, when realized, will weaken the position of fascism and strengthen the position of the proletariat."[38] The overthrow of world capitalism remained the task of the future. Commenting upon the efforts to create a broad anti-fascist people's movement, an editorial in the Comintern's theoretical journal in 1938 affirmed that this struggle "in its *further development* will inevitably lead to the overthrow of rotting capitalism" (italics mine).[39]

The strategy and tactics of the new period retained the basic aims of Communist activity before the seizure of power: the winning of support from the proletariat and from certain non-proletarian strata, and the defense of the Soviet Union. But new forms were developed to achieve these constant aims as well as the new temporary goal of protecting democracy and national independence from fascism. These new forms were the "popular" or "people's front," the "popular front government," and the "democracy of a new type." In addition to these forms, the new strategy involved also a united front "from above."

The united front "from above," it will be recalled, was an old concept and meant the effort to achieve united working-class action for limited goals through the conclusion of temporary agreements with the Social-Democratic and "reformist" leaders in the proletarian movement. The revival of this type of united front meant a rejection of the tactics employed—so disastrously for the Communists—against the socialists in the years from 1928 to 1934.

The justification for the new approach to the leadership of social democracy was the supposed leftward, pro-Communist tendency in the ranks of the Social Democrats, which was to be exploited to the fullest by the Communists. There still remained, however, in the opinion of the Comintern, a right wing of social democracy that was reluctant to abandon its collaboration with the bourgeoisie.[40] The Comintern's requirement for a united front with the Social-Democratic leadership was an active struggle "*against fascism, against the offensive of capital, against the threat of war, against the class enemy.*"[41] It was not, however, required that the Social Democrats accept the Communist concepts of "proletarian revolution" and "dictatorship of the proletariat." The united front, it may be noted, did not mean that Communists were to forsake public criticism of the "reactionary" sections of social democracy,[42] nor did it mean that Communists were to give up "their independent work in the sphere of Communist education, organization and mobilization of the masses."[43]

The popular or people's front was a still broader movement, centering in the proletarian united front but including peasants, petty bourgeoisie, intellectuals—all in fact who accepted the program of anti-fascism. During the period from 1935 to 1939 the popular front was a front *from above,* i.e., resting upon agreements between Communist, socialist, and bourgeois party leaders.[44]

The popular front government[45] was a most daring and novel concept. It was described as a government resting upon a broad anti-fascist popular movement; in this government Communist parties might participate along with other parties included in the popular front. It was not synonymous with a "dictatorship of the proletariat" and was to appear, to use Dimitrov's phrase, "on the eve" of a Communist seizure of power. It was to be primarily a "government of struggle against fascism and reaction."[46]

Under what conditions was it conceived that such a government could arise? Dimitrov believed that there might develop a political crisis sufficient for limited exploitation by the Communists, but not to the point of a direct Communist seizure of power. Three major conditions for a popular front government were cited by Dimitrov: the bourgeois state apparatus was already to have been "sufficiently *disorganized* and *paralyzed*" to such an extent that the bourgeoisie could not prevent the formation of such a government; "the wide masses of working people" were to be in a state of "vehement revolt *against fascism and reaction, though not ready* to rise in insurrection so as to *fight under Communist Party leadership for the achievement of Soviet power*"; and "a considerable proportion" of the rank-and-file of those parties in the popular front was to have reached the point of demanding "*ruthless measures against the fascists and other reactionaries,*" while working with the Communists and against the anti-Communist section of their own parties.[47]

The remarkable thing about the concept of a popular front government is that it abandoned Communist exclusiveness in relation to other parties and to prerevolutionary governments. The concept permitted the entry of Communists into governments, under certain conditions, *before* the Communist seizure of power. Dimitrov's postulation of an intermediate situation of crisis, occurring prior to a true revolutionary situation (discussed in Chapter IV as a prerequisite of the Communist seizure of power), permitted Communist activity *through* a prerevolutionary governmental structure and not *outside* it, before the final move was made toward a Communist seizure of power. The new pattern for Communist political activity allowed the tapping of hitherto untouched mass support and opened new roads to Communist power.[48]

The function of the popular front government was not to be the destruction of capitalism, but the purging from capitalism of "fascism" and the "economic basis of fascism." The result was to be a "democracy of a new type,"[49] occupying a middle ground between bourgeois democracy and soviet democracy. The economic reforms which were later outlined in various programs in different countries suggest that the "democracy of a new type" was to be a kind of welfare state, involving such reforms as limited nationalization of the economy, tax reforms at the expense of the wealthy, the eight-hour day, minimum-wage and social-insurance laws, and the distribution of land to poor and landless peasantry.[50]

These new concepts and institutions did not emerge overnight. The period from early 1934 to the Seventh Comintern Congress in mid-1935 may be taken as the transitional phase between the sectarianism of the earlier period, 1928–1934, and the anti-fascism of 1935–1939.[51] This sequence of stages in the transitional phase may be identified: 1) a switch from the united front from below to the united front from above, while overthrow of capitalism remains the aim; 2) the development of the idea of a popular front; 3) the change of the immediate aim from the overthrow of capitalism to its purging; and 4) the development of the concept of a people's front government in which Communists might participate. With Dimitrov's speech at the Seventh Congress in 1935 the transition was largely complete.[52]

Coupled with the Comintern's newly assumed, but conditional and temporary, defense of "bourgeois democracy" was its new interest in certain national traditions and its justification of wars of national defense by a nonaggressive capitalist state against the attack of an aggressive capitalist state. The discovery of worthwhile elements in the "bourgeois" tradition of a country led to some interesting examples of Communist patriotism. The French Communists exploited the "principles of 1789"; the American Communists appropriated the heritage of Washington, Jefferson, and Lincoln. Gottwald, the future Communist president of Czechoslovakia, combined class struggle with the Czech national heritage in the following fashion: "When did the Czech nation reach the height of its glory? *In the days of the Hussites when it carried out the revolution, when in plebeian fashion it settled accounts with the Czech lords!*"[53] Had the Communists become nationalistic? To an extent, yes. As Dimitrov declared in 1935, the Communists were "*irreconcilable opponents, on principle*, of bourgeois nationalism in all its forms. But we *are not supporters of national nihilism.*"[54]

Wars among capitalist states were formerly regarded as "unjust" wars, in which the proletariat and "toilers" in general had no reason to fight for national defense. Their activity in such cases was to be directed toward civil war, i.e., toward the overthrow of the bourgeoisie in each country. The new line, developed at the Seventh Comintern Congress and maintained until shortly after the outbreak of World War II, stated that wars of national defense were possible among capitalist states and that the proletarian was to defend his country (although governed by the bourgeoisie) against attack by an aggressive state. According to the resolution of the Seventh Congress on Ercoli's report on war, "the Communist must show that the working class carries on a consistent struggle in defense of the national freedom and independence of the whole people." The resolution further stated:

If any weak state is attacked by one or more big imperialist powers which want to destroy its national independence . . . a war conducted by the national bourgeoisie of such a country to repel this attack may assume the character of a war of liberation, in which the working class and the Communists of that country must intervene. It is the task of the Communists of such a country, while carrying on an irreconcilable struggle to safeguard the economic and political positions of the workers, labouring peasants and national minorities, to be, at the same time, in the front ranks of the fighters for national independence and to fight the war of liberation to a finish.[55]

A Leninist foundation for this line was discovered. It was pointed out that Lenin had affirmed not only the possibility of national wars against imperialism even in Europe, but also the revolutionary character of such wars and the duty of the working classes to support national freedom in such wars.[56] Thus the Comintern urged more than lip service to the cause of national independence. Resistance to the aggressor became the most important political question of the moment.[57]

Obviously there was to be expected a considerably different vocabulary in Comintern literature from that of the preceding period. The words "proletarian" revolution, "dictatorship of the proletariat," "social-fascist," and other basic terms tended in the late 1930s to be crowded out by the increasing use of a less specifically Communist vocabulary, in which figured prominently such terms as "anti-fascism," "democracy," "independence," "peace," and "justice." This is not to suggest that the Comintern's vocabulary changed completely—the old terms were still used—but the vocabulary was "watered down," made less militant, and therefore became more palatable to greater numbers of people.

As was pointed out above, the novel features of the new patterns of strategy and tactics could well create erroneous impressions. Some observers of the world Communist movement made a mistake respecting *means*—and believed that the Comintern now was adopting a program of peaceful, democratic evolution toward Communism. Other observers made a mistake respecting *ends*—and believed that the Comintern had abandoned the idea of struggle for world Communism. A careful reading of the report of the Seventh Congress, as well as of Comintern literature of the next four years, reveals that the Comintern still insisted upon the necessity of a violent overthrow of capitalism by means of a Communist-led revolution and the erection of a Communist dictatorship, and still retained as its fundamental and ultimate goal the establishment of world Communism.[58]

At the Seventh Congress Dimitrov specifically denied that the people's front was a transitional form to socialism and Communism that would make unnecessary a "proletarian" revolution.[59] The "proletarian" revolution remained on the agenda. "We want," he declared, "to draw increasingly wide masses into the revolutionary class struggle and lead them to the proletarian revolution, *proceeding from their vital interests and needs as the starting point.*"[60] The Czech Communist Slansky agreed that the final hopes of the Communists could be realized only "through the revolutionary overthrow of the bourgeoisie."[61] The May Day Manifesto of the ECCI in 1937 announced: "*The knell of capitalism has been sounded. It is an obstacle to human progress, and must be overthrown. Only the revolutionary overthrow of capitalism and its replacement by Socialism will put an end to the exploitation of man by man and to war.*"[62] An editorial in the Comintern journal in 1938 enjoined the Communists to follow Lenin in not losing sight of the "ultimate goals of the proletarian movement," whatever the immediate tasks might be.[63] These examples may suffice to demonstrate that neither world revolution and Communism nor the necessity of a violent overthrow of capitalism were abandoned by the Comintern as basic articles of faith during this period.

One final question may be raised. Since the popular front and the popular front government were to be only temporary arrangements prior to the Communist seizure of power, how were the Communists to break away from their alliances with non-Communists in the front and in the coalition government and proceed to the seizure of all power by way of the "proletarian" revolution? This question is difficult to answer. Certainly it is clear that the Communists were expected to exploit to the utmost the political crisis that had given rise to the popular front and the popular front government. Dimitrov referred to the popular front government as a government "on the eve of and before the victory of the proletariat" and insisted that such a government was "in no way" to restrict the activity of the Communist party.[64] In the opinion of the French Communist leader, Thorez, it was to be a government for the purpose of "leading the masses to the dictatorship of the proletariat, to the soviet republic."[65] Wilhelm Pieck suggested that in the course of the fight against fascism the nature of the mass forces that would participate would be of the greatest importance in solving the question of the form of state power after the overthrow of Hitler.[66] In other words, the possibility might develop that the German Communist Party, in its fight against Hitler, might gain the support it felt necessary for a Communist seizure of power. Unfortunately, Comintern materials do not contain specific statements about the technique of a Communist seizure of power *following* the construction of a popular front or of a popular front government.

In summary, it may be said that the Comintern outlined for the Communist parties in the capitalist countries during 1935–1939 an imaginative, flexible program of strategy and tactics, in which Communists were permitted to exploit the symbols of patriotism, to assume the role of defenders of national independence, to attack fascism without demanding an end to capitalism as the only remedy, and, most important, to enter upon alliances with other parties, on the basis of fronts or on the basis of a government in which Communists might participate. In all of this the fundamental aim of world Communism through violent revolution was retained, and the new pattern of strategy and tactics was pictured as excellent preparation toward that end.[67]

In the colonial, semi-colonial, and dependent societies. The discussion of the new pattern of Communist strategy and tactics in the colonial world can be rather briefly described, as the new Comintern attitudes, described at length above, applied also to the colonies.

Wang Ming, a member of the Presidium of the ECCI, gave the main speech at the Seventh Comintern Congress on the situation in the colonial world. He set as the major task of the Communists in the colonies the creation of an "anti-imperialist united people's front." Such a front would be designed to meet the "savage offensive of imperialism" against the colonies and to coordinate the social unrest and "national-liberation" movements in these areas.[68]

The similarities between the new Communist strategy in the capitalist countries and that in the colonial world may be noted. First, the anti-imperialist united people's front, like the popular front in the capitalist countries, was to be a broad association including several political groups and parties. The front was to rest upon a common struggle by all parties against imperialism and for national independence. Second, the plan for the anti-imperialist people's front assumed that parts of the bourgeoisie could become temporary allies of the Communists, just as the plan for a popular front in the capitalist countries assumed that some socialists and some of the bourgeoisie could become temporary Communist allies. Third, fronts of both types pointed to the creation of people's front governments. Fourth, a temporary period of "new democracy" was foreseen in the colonies, as in the capitalist countries, following the creation of a people's front government. Fifth, direct attempts to attain the ultimate aims of the Communist parties were to be postponed, but not abandoned, in the capitalist countries as well as in the colonial world.

The new pattern of strategy and tactics in the colonies can be better understood by an examination of specific cases. India, China, and Brazil might be selected as typical and important examples, respectively, of colonial, semi-colonial, and dependent societies.

In India, the newly founded Communist Party had already attempted, before the Seventh Comintern Congress, to develop an anti-imperialist front, but those efforts, according to Wang Ming, were at first marred by serious errors. For example, the Indian Communist Party had sought in December, 1934, to establish a front with the Indian National Congress on the basis of a program calling for an Indian Soviet Republic, confiscation of large estates without compensation, and the general strike. These demands went far beyond the proper limits of an anti-imperialist front, Wang

Ming objected. "Such demands on the part of our Indian comrades can serve as an example of how not to carry on the tactics of the anti-imperialist united front." [69] The correct program for India, according to Wang Ming, should involve struggle against the Government of India Act of 1935, as well as struggle against reduction of wages and lengthening of the work day, heavy taxes, and high land rents; in addition, there was to be a constant struggle for democratic liberties and the liberation of all political prisoners. [70]

The rather restrained character of the new program for India probably reflects the Comintern's distinction at this time between aggressive Japanese imperialism and the relatively milder forms of imperialist rule exercised by other capitalist states. England, the imperialist ruler of India, was, of course, catalogued among the "nonaggressive" capitalist states temporarily belonging to the camp of peace.

For China a more militant anti-imperialist front was demanded. Wang Ming proposed that the Central Committee of the Communist Party of China should issue a joint appeal with the Chinese Soviet government *"to all the people, to all parties, groups, troops, mass organizations, and to all prominent political and social leaders to organize together with us an All-China People's Government of National Defence."* [71] This proposal meant a new effort to reach agreement with the Kuomintang, led by Chiang Kai-shek. The new approach in 1935 differed markedly from the extremely bitter attacks upon the Kuomintang during the preceding period. However, even during the Seventh Congress, and after Wang Ming's speech, a Chinese delegate still appealed for a *"broad anti-imperialist and anti-Kuomintang united front"* to fight for a government of national defense. [72] A kind of truce between the Chinese Communists and the Kuomintang was finally achieved in 1937, which was also the year of the Soviet-Chinese Treaty of Nonaggression. Relations between the two parties deteriorated after the spring of 1939, and intermittent fighting between Communist and Kuomintang forces followed. [73]

The implications of the Comintern's new policy for China were developed in subsequent materials published by the Comintern, especially the speeches and writings of Wang Ming and Mao

Tse-tung. Basically, the following picture emerges from this material. China was still in the "bourgeois-democratic" stage of the revolution, and the fundamental goal of this stage was the realization of Sun Yat-sen's famous Three Principles—People's Rights or Democracy, People's Livelihood, and Nationalism. At this stage of the revolution, collaboration with the Kuomintang was temporarily possible and advisable in the struggle to achieve these ends. People's Rights, according to Mao, meant the creation of a democratic state, in which all citizens would have equal rights, including the vote, regardless of their class origins. People's Livelihood, in his opinion, meant not the abolition of private property but full employment; improvement of labor conditions; land for the peasants; low rents, low interest, and low taxes; the opportunity for each citizen to receive education and to develop his own capabilities. Nationalism meant simply resistance to imperialism.[74]

To make collaboration possible, certain concessions were offered by the Chinese Communist Party. Chief among these were the cessation of armed struggle against the Kuomintang, the renaming and broadening of the Communist Soviet government, the re-naming and subordination of the Communist Red Army to the Nanking government, and the end of forcible confiscation of large estates.[75]

It must be noted here that Mao did not regard this second period of Communist-Kuomintang collaboration as permanent nor did he accept Sun Yat-sen's Three Principles as the ultimate goals of Chinese Communism. The bloc of three classes (proletariat, peasantry, and the "democratic strata" of the bourgeoisie) was thought to be correct during the period of the anti-imperialist front. But the Communists were "supporters of the revolution developing to a higher stage," and the temporary alliance with the "revolutionary section of the bourgeoisie" was presented only as a necessary bridge to the future transition to socialism.[76] In that future transition to socialism only the Communist Party could exercise hegemony.

In Brazil, a typical "dependent" country according to the

Comintern's viewpoint, Wang Ming praised the newly formed National Liberation Alliance as a good example of a revolutionary anti-imperialist bloc of classes in Latin America. He pointed to the obligations of the Brazilian Communist Party to consolidate further the united front, to overcome misgivings about the front among "sectarian" members of the Party, and to develop a mass movement in support of the Alliance and to raise this movement *"to the highest forms of struggle for power"* (my italics).[77] This last phrase of course emphasizes once again the dynamic character of the united and popular fronts, in the colonial world as well as in the capitalist world.

At the Seventh Congress, Lacerda, a delegate from Brazil, compared the National Liberation Alliance with the Kuomintang in 1925; each was a bloc of several classes united in a common front against imperialism, "latifundism," and fascism. He pointed out that the Alliance was struggling for a democratic government, which would not be a soviet government.[78]

The imperialist activity of Germany, Italy, and Japan in Brazil was regarded as the only dangerous kind of imperialism at that time. In fact, Lacerda stated that the "slogan of struggle against any and all imperialisms at the present time is in Brazil a Trotskyite slogan, for it divides the anti-fascist ranks and weakens the struggle" against the real enemy—the agents of Germany, Japan, and Italy.[79]

The program of the proposed Brazilian people's government of national liberation involved social reform with limited nationalization. The program called for the repudiation of foreign debts, and the nationalization of enterprises under foreign control that did not "submit to the laws of the People's Government." Social reforms for the proletariat included the eight-hour day, higher wages, a minimum wage, social insurance, nationalization of important public utilities, and the "fulfillment of the other demands of the proletariat." Land reform was to be carried out by the expropriation without compensation of land held by the "reactionary" large landowners and the "reactionary" elements of the church; this land was to be allocated for use by poor workers and peasants. Land that had been taken from the Indians by force was to be returned.

Basic civil liberties, equality of races and nationalities, and separation of church and state were also promised in the program.[80]

The programs for the "dependent" countries of Latin America often exhibited a serious lack of precision. Depending upon the content that might be given certain phrases or words, a more or less far-reaching social transformation might be expected, going far beyond those specific measures actually listed. For instance, the phrase "fulfillment of the other demands of the proletariat," used in the Brazilian program, opens the door to a much more comprehensive social revolution than the fairly modest list of specific labor measures would indicate. Similarly, the word "reactionary"— defined as "those who oppose the emancipation of Brazil and of the people"—permits the most arbitrary and subjective kind of interpretation. These ambiguities reinforce the general impression that the so-called people's fronts, joined and supported by Communists, contained the seeds of development into Communist activity that would have less modest aims.

During this period flexible patterns of strategy and tactics were outlined by the Comintern for its followers in all types of societies. Less exclusively preoccupied for the moment with purely Communist aims and ideals, and more openly associated with the broader symbols of democracy, national defense, independence, and anti-fascism, the Communist parties everywhere blurred their true role in society but created possibilities for greater popular support. As we have seen, the united fronts and people's fronts in the capitalist and colonial countries were clearly and frankly designed by the Comintern as temporary responses to an emergency situation. Looking beyond the period of emergency, the Comintern saw the fronts as valuable and useful arrangements facilitating the extension of Communist influence and thereby aiding the Communists in their struggle for hegemony in the world revolutionary movement.

One final point may shed light on the Comintern's commitment to the popular-front line during these years. In February, 1939, the Comintern leaders considered it advisable to publish—in separate English, German, and French editions—an abridged stenographic report of the proceedings of the Seventh Congress, in order to reindorse the pattern of strategy and tactics proclaimed by Dimitrov in 1935. Whatever shifts might have occurred between 1935 and 1939, either in Soviet foreign policy or in Stalin's interpretation of world problems, it was clear that the ideas of the antifascist popular front had been impressively reaffirmed as basic policy for the international Communist movement.

VII. PREPARATION: STRATEGY

AND TACTICS, 1939-1941

From the time of the Nazi attack on Poland in September, 1939, to the Nazi invasion of the USSR in June, 1941, the cardinal fact was, of course, the outbreak and spreading of World War II, which in a sense had already begun in China in 1937, and which was to embroil the major capitalist countries (with the exception, for the moment, of the United States). The "second round" of wars and revolutions, predicted by the Sixth Comintern Congress in 1928 as an inevitable aspect of the coming end of partial capitalist stabilization, seemed to be at hand.

OVERVIEW OF THE PERIOD

The situation in the non-Communist world. The general course of events in the non-Communist world from the autumn of 1939 to the middle of 1941 needs only the briefest summary here as a background for the discussion of the pattern of Communist strategy and tactics.

The Nazi invasion of Poland on September 1, 1939, provoked British and French declarations of war against Germany two days later, thereby carrying into effect their guarantees made to Poland in the previous spring. Hitler's armies, safeguarded by the Nazi-Soviet Pact of August 23, 1939, moved swiftly to destroy the Polish state and its fighting forces. Soviet troops moved into eastern Poland on September 17, ten days before Warsaw fell to the *Wehrmacht*.

In the west, following a prolonged *Sitzkrieg*, Germany activated the war in April, May, and June of 1940, with complete success on the Continent. She triumphantly brought Denmark, Norway, Belgium, Holland, Luxemburg, and France under her control. The signing of the armistice with France at Compiègne on June 22, 1940, terminated this phase of the war in the west. France, now partitioned and in part occupied, was for the time being eliminated as a belligerent, although a French resistance movement under General Charles de Gaulle developed in certain of France's colonies. There remained the continued refusal of Britain to abandon the struggle. Hitler's subsequent failure to win the Battle of Britain in the fall of 1940 was in part responsible for his decision in December to strike in the east against the Soviet Union.

In September, 1940, the three major aggressor states, Germany, Italy, and Japan, concluded the ten-year Tripartite Pact, illustrating the common agreement of these powers. Following this event, the European signatories of the pact sought to bring southeastern Europe firmly under their control. Land war, renewed by the Italian action against Greece in October, 1940, was further extended by the German invasion of Yugoslavia in April, 1941, following the Yugoslav refusal to accept membership in the Tripartite Pact. Successes in Yugoslavia and Greece rounded out the Axis conquest of southeastern Europe. Japan meanwhile was consolidating her control over French Indo-China.

The isolated position of Britain, subjected to intense air bombardment and submarine warfare, was somewhat mitigated by the growth of interventionist sentiment and action on the part of the United States. The "cash-and-carry" amendment of November, 1939, revised the Neutrality Act to permit sale of arms to belligerents. Less than a year later, in September, 1940, the United States showed its increasing awareness of the dangers confronting world democracy by taking two more steps: the exchange of American destroyers for long-term leases from Britain of naval and air bases and the passage of the Selective Service Act. One half-year later, in March, 1941, the remarkable Lend-Lease Act was signed by President Roosevelt.

The growing involvement of the United States in the war on the side of Great Britain has a kind of parallel in this period in the considerable diplomatic, economic, and propaganda support of the USSR to the Axis camp.

The situation in the Soviet Union. When World War II broke out in September, 1939, the Soviet Union was in the second year of its Third Five-Year Plan. Every effort was made to increase production and to improve the defense of the country. The eight-hour day and the seven-day week were restored in June, 1940. The right to change one's job was at the same time severely curtailed. A system of State Labor Reserves was introduced, providing for the drafting of young persons for vocational training and obligatory work for four years thereafter at the government's discretion. At the same time, the Red Army was enlarged and the authority of the regular army officers was increased.

The signing of the Nazi-Soviet Pact of August 23, 1939, constituted a dramatic reversal of the preceding "anti-fascist" policy identified with Maxim Litvinov. The Pact, superficially a ten-year nonaggression treaty, contained a secret protocol providing in effect for a partitioning of eastern Europe between the USSR and Germany. For the next twenty-two months the Soviet Union associated itself with the fascist camp, and assisted it in a variety of ways. Whatever might have been the diplomatic subtleties of the period, it can be said that the new Soviet Foreign Minister, Viacheslav Molotov, pursued a foreign policy more favorable to Hitler than to the democracies.[1] The period from August, 1939, to June, 1941, was a period of important, although not frictionless, diplomatic and economic collaboration of the USSR with Nazi Germany.

Benefits first accrued to the USSR with the military occupation and annexation of eastern Poland in late 1939. Given a free hand by the Pact in Finland, Estonia, Latvia, Bessarabia, and, by a later amendment, in Lithuania as well, the Soviet rulers exploited the situation to the full. The Winter War of 1939–1940 with Finland resulted in new Soviet territorial gains; in 1940 Estonia, Latvia, and Lithuania were compelled to become Soviet Socialist Republics; and during that same year northern Bukovina and Bessarabia were annexed at the expense of Rumania. These territorial gains were made possible by the "diplomatic revolution" of August, 1939. In the Far East, the long-sought neutrality pact with Japan was realized in April, 1941, lessening Moscow's fears of a possible two-front war.

Although the USSR fulfilled its economic arrangements with Nazi Germany during these years and offered no real resistance to the expansion of the Axis in southeastern Europe, it declined to enter into an agreement to abandon its interests in eastern Europe, particularly in Finland, Bulgaria, and the Turkish Straits. This refusal in November, 1940, deepened the existing mistrust that Hitler felt toward the Soviet Union. The German decision to invade the USSR followed shortly thereafter, but was of course based on larger considerations.

On May 6, not long before the Nazi invasion of the Soviet Union, Stalin became the Chairman of the Council of People's Commissars. Perhaps this move, establishing Stalin more emphatically as the head of the Soviet government as well as of the Communist Party, was an effort to emphasize the unity of Soviet leadership in troubled times.

VIEWS OF THE COMINTERN

The Comintern evaluation of "world capitalism": "the second imperialist war." It was not the German invasion of Poland on September 1, 1939, that inaugurated a new period for the Comintern but rather the signing of the Nazi-Soviet Pact a week before on August 23. The Pact made the war virtually inevitable; both the Pact and the war jarred the Communist parties with surprises. To most Communists, it appeared that the long-expected aggressive war of the fascist states had at last been unleashed upon the nonaggressive capitalist states. The "justness" of an anti-fascist, national war having been repeatedly affirmed by the Comintern, a patriotic stand was at first taken by unsuspecting rank-and-file Communists. "Hitler has unloosed war," wrote a British Communist, "and the people of France and Britain are determined that the war can have only one end—the destruction of fascism."[2] On September 16,

World News and Views carried statements by the Scandinavian Communist parties in support of the war effort in Britain and France. In the latter country the Communists continued with the line of anti-fascist national defense up to September 19.[3]

Four weeks after the signing of the Nazi-Soviet Pact the Comintern disclosed to its followers a surprising new interpretation of the war. The authoritative statement of the new line was given in Dimitrov's article "The War and the Working Class of the Capitalist Countries."[4] Labeling the conflict the "second imperialist war," which he said had actually begun with the attacks on Ethiopia, Spain, and China, Dimitrov proceeded to define the war as follows: "In its character and essence the present war is, on the part of both warring sides, an *imperialist, unjust* war, despite the fraudulent slogans being employed by the ruling classes of the warring capitalist states." The bourgeois class had started the war with the aim of a new repartition of the world. The seemingly nonaggressive states—Britain, France, and the United States—had conducted their policy of retreat and appeasement during the late 1930s to avoid a decisive clash with their rivals and to turn the latter against the USSR. After the fall of Poland, Dimitrov declared, it was precisely the British and French imperialists who were the most eager for the continuation of the war.[5] The Dimitrov analysis was henceforth, until the Nazi invasion of Russia in June, 1941, the basic Comintern line. The war was an imperialist war in which the proletariat could have no interest.

The effect of the Nazi-Soviet Pact is, of course, to be seen in the Comintern's soft-pedaling of German aggression and its severe castigation of the Western democracies. The Comintern illustrated its unmistakable domination from Moscow by the pro-German line it took from September, 1939 to June, 1941.[6] If one were to confine one's reading about this period of World War II to the editorials in *Kommunisticheskii Internatsional*, one would hardly know that such a state as Germany existed and that it was by far the strongest member of one of the two belligerent coalitions.[7] Everywhere, with the announcement of the new Comintern line, the Communist parties abandoned the anti-fascist national defense movement.

Thorez, who deserted the French army after the new line was proclaimed, as late as January, 1941, was still heaping guilt exclusively upon the French bourgeoisie: "In September, 1939, the French bourgeoisie, having earlier given Spain to Franco, having repeatedly betrayed its allies, declared war on Germany under pretext of rendering help to the reactionary lords of Poland, that 'prison of peoples.'"[8]

The extent to which the Comintern accommodated itself to the Nazi-Soviet Pact is illustrated in an editorial that appeared in the Comintern journal only two months before the German invasion of Soviet Russia. No mention whatsoever was made of the word "fascism" and no derogatory remarks were directed toward Hitler. While stating that Yugoslavia was the "object of military attack," the editorial did not identify the aggressor. German interests in the Balkans were described, but without condemnation.[9]

Comintern evaluation of the CPSU and the USSR in the world revolution. As mentioned above, during this phase of World War II the Soviet Union was able to expand it frontiers westward at the expense of its immediate neighbors. The Comintern viewed this expansion favorably as an extension of the revolution to a new part of the world. In his crucial article defining the nature of the war, Dimitrov justified the entry of Soviet armed forces into eastern Poland in terms of the class struggle. Savagely attacking the Polish government as a regime of reaction and terror, oppressing and robbing millions of Ukrainians, Belorussians, and Poles alike, he asserted that the action of the USSR in invading Poland had been dictated by the interests of socialism and of "toilers" all over the world.[10] The titular head of the Comintern praised the first use since 1921 of the Red Army in the cause of expanding the area of socialism.

Another instance of the use of Soviet armed forces was the Winter War with Finland in 1939. This is an especially interesting case, since a puppet "Provisional People's Government" was set up by the Communist Party of the Soviet Union on December 1 at Terijoki, on Finnish soil near the Russian frontier but behind the Soviet military front. This is as good a case as can be found of the use of Soviet military force to export revolution. The high-ranking

Comintern figure, Kuusinen, a member of the ECCI, was placed at the head of this provisional Communist government designed for installation in Finland.[11] In its program, the puppet government promised that it would get help from the Soviet Red Army to overthrow the present Finnish government of "hangmen" and to liberate the Finnish people.[12] The Kuusinen government must have been composed overwhelmingly or totally of Communists. An indirect admission of this was given in the government's program, which contained the promise that, once it got to Helsinki, the government would be reorganized to include representatives of all parties and groups participating in the people's front.[13] Since the Kuusinen government could not get to Helsinki save on the bayonets of the Red Army, it is doubtful that much toleration of non-Communist parties would have been allowed, given a Soviet army of occupation. The Terijoki government was an artificial creation, reflecting only the will of the CPSU and not of the Finnish people, and was abandoned without explanation upon the end of the war. The Communist Party of the Soviet Union, seeking public justification for its aggression against Finland, perhaps hoped that the puppet government would attract real mass support in Finland. It was wrong in this, and correspondingly wrong in its estimation of the Finnish capacity for resistance.

These two cases are good examples of the willingness of the USSR to use even military force to expand the frontiers of socialism (as practiced in the USSR) if the risks did not appear serious. Poland involved almost no risk, for the Germans were anxious to maintain the newly concluded rapprochement. The war against Finland was apparently expected to lead to an easy victory and a satellite Finland; once it was clear that serious embarrassment would develop if the USSR attempted to crush Finnish independence completely, the Kuusinen regime was simply dropped. Of course, the westward expansion of the Soviet Union in 1939–1940 did not have as its *sole* purpose the extension of the frontiers of "socialism." The factor of security was obviously of major importance.

Some contradiction may appear to exist between the Comintern's steadily repeated characterization of the USSR as a bulwark of peace and the military activity of Soviet armed forces in Poland and Finland. In each case, however, the Comintern portrayed the USSR as essentially a *restorer* of order and peace. In Poland the entry of Soviet troops terminated "anarchy" and provided law and order for the population. In Finland Soviet military action was, according to the Comintern, the result of intolerable provocation by Finnish forces.

It may be noted finally regarding the Comintern's attitude toward the CPSU and the USSR that the Comintern continued to assert the inspirational and didactic value of the experience of the CPSU and of the Soviet Union. Stalin's position as supreme theoretician in the Communist world movement was, as usual, consistently proclaimed.

PATTERN OF STRATEGY AND TACTICS

In Comintern materials of the war years a kind of veil was drawn over the more militant and "revolutionary" expressions in Communist vocabulary, with the result that one gets the impression of a certain indirectness or lack of force. The Comintern's repeated use of aggressive words and slogans in earlier periods had given a relative sharpness and clarity to its ideas, in contrast with the muffled tone of its pronouncements during the "second imperialist war." Not only were the tone and language of the Comintern materials more blurred, and consequently more difficult to fathom, but their content was virtually restricted in focus to the war. It seems inappropriate to dignify this content with the word "theory." And it becomes exceedingly arduous to attempt to extract from this material any coherent set of doctrines respecting world revolution.

To explain this change, we must refer once more to Soviet foreign policy and its most important problem of the moment— relations with Germany. The rapprochement of the two countries, considered temporarily advantageous to the USSR, required not only a muting of the extreme anti-fascism of the preceding period but also a toning down of the radical themes of class struggle and world revolution. Typical of the new spirit of Comintern pronouncements was the oft-repeated and rather moderate slogan, "Peace, Freedom, Bread!"

The problem is whether the Comintern's lack of aggressive frankness about its hitherto avowed ultimate aims now meant that it had abandoned those aims. We can reduce the ultimate aims to the preservation and territorial expansion of the Communist system. Do the Comintern materials of the period suggest a withdrawal of these aims, or not?

In attempting to answer this question, we must first sketch the chief elements of Communist strategy during this period. Justifying that strategy was the Comintern's claim that the Communists had been betrayed by their allies in the united and popular fronts. This "betrayal," i.e., the support accorded by the Social Democrats and others to the war effort in individual capitalist countries, made impossible the continuance of the popular front "from above." The new line of 1939–1941 called for the creation of united and popular fronts "from below." "In the present situation," Dimitrov advised, "working-class unity can and must be achieved *from below*, on the basis of the development of the movement of the working masses themselves and in a resolute struggle against the treacherous principal leaders of the Social Democratic parties."[14] Violent attacks upon social democracy and virtual silence about fascism—these are pronounced characteristics of this period.

What was to be the immediate purpose of the people's front from below? Primarily, the struggle against imperialist war. How was the struggle against war to become victorious? Dimitrov answered as follows: "The working class is called upon to put an end to the war after its own fashion, in its own interests, in the interest of the whole of labouring mankind, and thereby to destroy once and for all the fundamental causes giving rise to imperialist wars."[15]

The vague language in which this mission was assigned to the proletariat could only have meant the destruction of the capitalist system, root and branch. The phrase "after its own fashion" could have meant to a Communist only the fashion of "proletarian revolution." By destroying the "fundamental causes" of war there could have been understood only the overthrow of capitalism by a Communist-led revolution.

These are long-range goals of the Communist movement, and their reaffirmation at this time by Dimitrov, albeit in veiled manner, is extremely important. Other evidence supports this reaffirmation. Early in the war, the British Communist Party spoke out with unusual bluntness in calling upon the working class to end the war, destroy the class rule of the bourgeoisie, and establish a socialist society.[16]

The current pattern of strategy for the next few years envisaged the creation of people's fronts against war, people's front governments, and "democracies of a new type" involving limited social reform. How are these goals related to the aim of world revolution?

A program adopted in England by a "People's Congress" which met in January, 1941, supplies one outline of the "new democracy." This was an eight-point program including such modest goals as the increasing of wages and social security, the improvement of air-raid defense, and the "restoration" of trade-union rights, but also such fairly drastic aims as the nationalization of the banks, land, transport, and big industries, the offer of freedom to India and the other colonies, the establishment of friendly relations with the USSR, and the creation of a national government truly representing the interests of the "toiling" population.[17] The last point suggests a question: Could any government other than one controlled by the Communist party truly represent the "toilers," according to Comintern doctrines?

Another typical program was that of the so-called Provisional People's Government of Finland. The points of this program are similar to those listed above, except that a mutual aid pact with the USSR and a people's army are also specified. Did the people's government and program constitute the limits of Comintern intentions in Finland? Or would the Finnish Communists eventually transcend the people's program and move toward socialism and Communism? A Manifesto of the Finnish Communist Party, issued in December, 1939, after the formation of the Kuusinen government, gives us the answer: The new government was to be only the "first step in the advance towards its basic aims of a complete social transformation, which will finally eliminate capitalism and class divisions."[18]

If the reader is still not fully convinced that the Comintern retained its basic revolutionary objectives during this period, let him consult the two exceedingly valuable studies by A. Rossi of the French Communist Party in the early years of World War II.[19] Let him read the chapter on "Social Revolution and National Liberation" in the second of these two works, where Rossi, who has examined thoroughly the French Communist literature of the period, shows how the Party linked the immediate struggle for national liberation with the permanent and unchanging goals of social revolution. And note:

> Until June, 1941, the French Communists are intending to take power (in Vichy France), then wait until the USSR, having achieved in peacetime its aim of military preparedness, can lay down its law to the war-weary belligerents and thus "expand the frontiers of socialism" until one day they will include France. Hitler's sudden attack on the USSR upsets this plan, but without changing the basic character of the Party's long-run intentions.[20]

A few words may suggest Comintern strategy in the colonies, although here the Comintern sources are quite skimpy. In his basic article defining the character of the new period, "The War and the Working Class of the Capitalist Countries," Dimitrov authorized the continuation of the people's front "from above" in the "colonial and dependent countries."[21] However, the front "from above" depended on the attitude of the colonial bourgeoisie toward the imperialist mother country. In India, for example, the Communist Party moved quickly to a front "from below," claiming that the All-Indian National Congress, the leaders of which were Gandhi and Nehru, did not sufficiently fight against Indian involvement in the war.[22] Later, however, the Indian Communists softened their attitude toward the National Congress. According to a report in the Comintern journal, the National Congress was compelled by the "pressure of the masses" to refrain from supporting the British war effort.[23] An anti-British speech by Nehru was quoted with approval in *Kommunisticheskii Internatsional*.[24] The demand for a popular front continued, but no concrete proposal was made directly to the All-Indian National Congress in the form of a program of joint action.

In China during this period the Comintern made efforts to continue the anti-Japanese people's front with the Kuomintang. Basically the same pattern of Communist strategy was pursued as in 1935–1939. The government of the anti-Japanese front was not to be a Communist dictatorship but a coalition government with the Kuomintang and other Chinese political forces, resting on a domestic platform of democracy and social welfare.[25] The maintenance of the anti-Japanese front was by no means easy. In 1940, Chou En-lai felt it necessary to identify and chastise elements in China, chiefly in the ranks of the Kuomintang, who favored capitulation of China to Japan. The "capitulators" were opposed, he said, to the "democratic" regime in the Border Region of Shensi-Kansu-Ninghsia (Communist controlled), and to the Eighth and Fourth Armies (also Communist controlled), but the people of China were inspired by both. The war against Japan, which the "capitulators" were thwarting, was a just war of national liberation and a part of the colonial revolt against imperialism.[26]

It seems clear that, despite the masked character of Comintern literature during this period, the Comintern did not view its pattern of strategy and tactics solely in terms of immediate goals but also in terms of the long-range aspirations of Communism. However frequently was used the relatively colorless slogan "Peace, Freedom, Bread!" the Comintern usually added a footnote to the effect that the genuine and final realization of such aims could occur only under Communist auspices with Communists in power.

VIII. PREPARATION: STRATEGY

AND TACTICS, 1941-1943

From the Nazi invasion of the Soviet Union on June 22, 1941, to the official dissolution of the Comintern in May, 1943, the primary development in the contemporary world was the continuation and the territorial expansion of World War II. The greatest capitalist country, the United States, joined the ranks of the belligerents. The economy of virtually every significant nation in the world became increasingly subordinated to the requirements of warfare. Politics—the winning of victory over the opponent—profoundly altered the normal pattern of peacetime economic activity.

OVERVIEW OF THE PERIOD

The situation in the non-Communist world. After the USSR was forced by the Nazi invasion to join the struggle against Hitler, promises of aid and cooperation were almost immediately forthcoming from the Western democracies. The leading capitalist countries—Great Britain and America—early made arrangements to bolster the Soviet war effort. Britain became an actual ally of the Soviet Union, bound by a military pact. The United States extended Lend-Lease aid to the USSR in September, 1941, three months before Pearl Harbor. As the "arsenal of democracy" and, after December 7, 1941, as a full-fledged belligerent, the United States furnished vast quantities of war matériel and food to the Soviet Union. Ideological differences momentarily paled before the common threat from Nazi Germany.

The great desire of the Western powers to identify themselves with a democratic solution of the war found expression in the

Atlantic Charter of August, 1941. This document, the result of a mid-ocean conference between Churchill and Roosevelt, contained an eight-point program affirming their support of self-determination for all peoples, accessibility to raw materials for all states, improvement of labor standards and social security, disarmament, and the "establishment of a wider and permanent system of general security." Originally a bilateral agreement, the Charter was given the broadest possible support by the Declaration of the United Nations, which was signed by all the major and minor allies on New Year's Day, 1942. Promising not to make a separate peace with Hitler, the signatory powers, Soviet Russia included, committed themselves to the principles of the Atlantic Charter.

During the two years following the German invasion of the Soviet Union, the war against Hitler was carried on in three major contests: the massive struggle on the Russian front, the air bombardment of the heart of "Festung Europa," and the desert war in North Africa. In the Far Eastern conflict, where Russia was not yet a belligerent, the Japanese were able to expand rapidly over Southeast Asia, including Burma, and to conquer most of the Netherlands East Indies.

By the spring of 1943 the unfolding strength of the anti-Axis coalition had made itself felt strongly. The Anglo-American successes in North Africa, the devastating Soviet victory at Stalingrad, and the American conquest of the Solomon Islands in the Pacific—these events taken together foretold ultimate victory for the United Nations. Yet these positive gains did not prevent persistent friction and suspicion among the Big Three. The major issue during these years was that of an Anglo-American cross-Channel invasion of the European continent, continuously demanded by the Soviet leadership. Other thorny problems involved Poland, e.g., the relations between Moscow and the Polish government in exile in London, the Katyn Forest Massacre, and the postwar Polish-Soviet frontier.

To bridge the ideological gulf between the Western democracies and the USSR, much more was required than the vaguely worded Declaration of the United Nations. Much more was required than a common enemy, even of the fearful strength of Nazi Germany. Fundamentally, what was needed was the abandonment of basic philosophical views and of corresponding courses of action. Neither side was interested in, or capable of, such self-abnegation.

The situation in the Soviet Union. We have already spoken briefly of the USSR's participation in the anti-Hitler struggle after June, 1941. We may now mention some of the salient developments within the Soviet Union during this period.

The beginning of hostilities with Germany naturally led to the rapid expansion of the Red Army, already numbering in June, 1941, about six million. Those who were not put into uniform were to work, harder than ever before, at war-connected industries. All male and female citizens of working age were subject to a labor draft, according to a decree of February, 1942. Great care was shown for the preservation and strengthening of the operation of industries vital to the war effort. This concern led to wholesale transfers of factories and machinery to areas remote from the war zone. Military needs took priority over all other considerations.

Supreme direction of the Soviet war effort was placed in the hands of a small State Defense Committee. Stalin was chairman of this body throughout the war.

Spiritual mobilization accompanied military and industrial mobilization. Remarkable efforts were made to evoke the greatest loyalty to the Communist state. Such efforts transcended purely Communist considerations. An intense campaign was directed toward the stimulation of national sentiment and patriotism. Many pre-Revolutionary Russian heroes now were rehabilitated as worthy heroes for the new Communist man. Famous defenders of Russian soil against foreign invaders found fresh recognition. Perhaps chief among these was Alexander Nevsky, who in the thirteenth century had defeated the German Livonian Order in the famous battle on the ice at Lake Chudskoe. New medals and orders were created for military bravery, such as the Order of Kutuzov, who had been the opponent of Napoleon in 1812.

Religion was also employed in the service of the war effort. Anti-religious periodicals were suspended, and the Church answered loyally to the appeal to support the existing regime and help encourage cooperation among the people.

The intensified "nationalism" of the Soviet Union reflected the desperate attempts of the Soviet leaders to mobilize activity on as wide a scale as possible for the war effort. As postwar developments have demonstrated, the wartime revival of traditional patriotism and the relaxation of pressures against the Church did not undermine the Communist philosophical viewpoint. Nor was there created a state in the normal pattern, having only limited external objectives.

VIEWS OF THE COMINTERN

Comintern evaluation of "world capitalism": fascism rediscovered. With the Nazi invasion of the "workers' homeland," the "imperialist war" assumed for Communists an entirely different character. It at once became a just war not only for the USSR and the Comintern but for all "progressive" humanity everywhere. Fascism regained in Comintern materials its former position as the chief object of abuse. Justification of the war effort was very often couched in the broadest, most unrevolutionary terms. The goals of the war, as an editorial in the journal of the ECCI spelled them out, were the defense of human values, civilization, and culture. "Without the rooting out of Hitlerism, there is not, and cannot be, any social, any political, any cultural progress.... Therefore the rooting out of Hitlerism is an *ineluctable, decisive* task of all peoples, and to the solution of this task all else is subordinate."[1] A world front of peace-loving states and peoples in combat with the fascist aggressors was the Comintern's picture of the "new" war.

For the Comintern the war against Hitler thus became a just war. Communists now joined wholeheartedly in the cause of fighting against Nazi Germany. In the pages of the Comintern journals right and wrong were easily judged; states, classes, political parties, and individuals were condemned or praised in the light of their stand on the war. Neutrality was generally condemned, as in the case of the Latin American states,[2] though Sweden was simply urged to pursue a truly neutral policy and to cease making concessions to Germany.[3]

Revolution was pushed out of sight to the point where it could not offend the sensibilities of non-Communist allies in the struggle against fascism and Hitler. The long-range revolutionary goals were less publicized than they had ever been in Comintern history. The basic question for the present study is whether these long-range revolutionary goals were subordinated only for the time being (but preserved for the future) or were abandoned permanently. Many observers in the Western democracies thought these ultimate goals had in fact been discarded and the Soviet Union had at last become a "normal" state, pursuing limited aims only.

In fact, difficulties already noted in the study of Comintern ideas for 1939–1941 are even greater for 1941–1943. To say the least, after the outbreak of World War II the level of Comintern thought—in so far as that thought was expressed in print—sank pathetically low. Granted that the requirements of Soviet foreign policy and war effort made it advisable to mute the revolutionary drums, the virtually complete subordination of the journal *Kommunisticheskii Internatsional* to these requirements is very striking to one who has read through this periodical beginning with the issues of 1928. This journal, between mid-1941 and mid-1943, when it went out of existence, was almost barren of material, for example, on colonial revolution. Not a single article was devoted to China in this period. The other Comintern periodical, *World News and Views*, is equally unsatisfactory in these years. For instance, during the entire year 1942, this weekly did not discuss the subject of world revolution, barely mentioned the existence of the Comintern, and failed to print its customary anniversary message from the ECCI in honor of the Bolshevik Revolution. The unsuspecting reader who compared *World News and Views* of 1942 with *Inprecor* of 1929 would find it hard to believe that both periodicals were press organs of one and the same revolutionary International. Despite these serious difficulties, one can still obtain some worthwhile information and insights into Comintern thinking by a careful reading of the printed materials.

Comintern evaluation of the CPSU and the USSR in the world revolution. To an overwhelming degree, in this period the Comintern presented the CPSU and the USSR simply as the chief forces in the struggle against fascism, while maintaining virtual silence concerning any contributions of the CPSU and the USSR to the cause of world revolution. To be sure, the Soviet Union was consistently and frequently described as a particular kind of state—a socialist state—and, therefore, as the state possessing the most advanced economic and social institutions in the world. The Soviet Union was not, after all, only another anti-fascist state; it was the *best* anti-fascist state and it was the highest product of "universal historical progress."[4]

Even the most explicit statements during this period concerning the relationship between the USSR and world revolution are quite vague and fuzzy pronouncements. For instance, the Soviet Union was credited with the leadership of humanity toward a better future. This kind of restrained statement, devoid of explicitly revolutionary content, was characteristic for the period 1941–1943. It was left for the perceptive reader of the Comintern press to appreciate that the Soviet Union was governed by men who conceived of the "good society" of the future exclusively in terms of Communist doctrine. Though it is impossible to find any precise statement detailing a concrete contribution of the CPSU and the USSR to the cause of Communist-led revolution, it cannot be overlooked that Communist readers were accustomed to interpret such undefined expressions as "leadership of humanity" in a very special way, i.e., in accordance with Marxist-Leninist theory.

Much attention, however, was given to the contribution of the Soviet armed forces to the struggle against Hitler. The Red Army, hitherto rather neglected in Comintern materials, was accorded the most detailed attention after June, 1941. Its military fortunes were fully described in the pages of *Kommunisticheskii Internatsional* and *Inprecor*. The Red Army was not narrowly depicted as a class force, but rather as an army defending the interests of all anti-fascist humanity. A leading editorial in the theoretical journal of the Comintern stated early in 1943 that the aim of the Red Army was the liberation of peoples to enable them to choose their own way of life. There would be, it was promised, no interference by the Red Army in the internal affairs of other peoples.[5] The contribution of the Soviet armed forces was always depicted in such terms—liberation from fascism—and never in terms of the establishment of Communist control and the building of socialism in the liberated country.

Much, of course, was said about the encouragement given by Soviet military victories to the national resistance movements in other countries. "Only after the Red Army had destroyed the legend of the invincibility of the Hitlerite horde," said one writer in the spring of 1943, "did active forms of struggle begin to develop more widely in Austria."[6] Thorez wrote in the same vein: "The victorious offensive of the Red Army has created a situation which puts on the order of the day a national uprising for the liberation of France."[7]

It must not be concluded that the Comintern failed either to present the CPSU as the most dedicated and sincere leaders of humanity or to present the USSR as the most advanced type of society. Quite the contrary. In this sense, while largely abstaining from the specific vocabulary of revolution and socialism and while concentrating upon the immediate problem of the struggle against fascism, the Comintern still propagated the image of Soviet leadership and Soviet society as the best guide and pattern for the future.

THE PATTERN OF STRATEGY AND TACTICS

Underlying the Comintern's new strategy after June, 1941, was the belief that an energetic and unrelenting struggle for victory over Hitler took precedence over all other Communist activity. The popular front "from above" was restored immediately upon the Nazi invasion of Russia in June, 1941. As a broad anti-fascist grouping of any and all opponents of Hitlerite Germany and the other Axis powers, such a popular front had as its most important and immediate objective the winning of victory over fascism. Collaboration within the popular front by Communist parties with other political forces—socialist, bourgeois, Protestant, or Catholic —was fully endorsed by the Comintern. The sole criterion for such collaboration was a common struggle against fascism.

In countries not under Axis domination, Communists were instructed to support the anti-Axis military and political activity of the existing governments, or, where a country still maintained a policy of neutrality, to encourage the development of anti-Axis policies. In those countries that were under Axis domination, Communists were to struggle for the creation of governments resting upon a broad anti-fascist front of national resistance.

The programs of the popular fronts, as well as of governments to be based upon popular fronts, emphasized the tasks of overthrowing fascism, ending the war victoriously, and constructing a society in which "democracy" and an improvement in living conditions would be possible. In these programs, as will be shown, there was no explicit demand for Communists to seize power. Only the vaguest suggestions can be found in the Comintern literature of the period that the Communist party represented something other than a normal political party with objectives that were democratic and limited, rather than undemocratic and unlimited. Obviously, the mobilization of the widest possible anti-fascist coalition of forces demanded the muting of the more radical long-range aims of world Communism. Whether silence in official Comintern publications about these aims meant that they were only temporarily postponed, or that they had been once and for all abandoned by the Comintern, remains, of course, the crucial question.

A look at the salient features of the popular front programs will serve to demonstrate that they were by no means exclusively or specifically Communist in content. In Italy the program of a broad national front of struggle against fascism demanded an end of the war, "economic measures" to prevent future war and poverty, and the right of citizens to participate in the government. The restoration of constitutional guarantees, such as freedom of speech, press, assembly, and religious beliefs, and the abolition of racial legislation were also listed as immediate demands of the popular front.[8]

In Norway, it was proposed that the people's front conduct a struggle for free trade unions, social rights, more food, higher wages, and self-determination and sovereignty.[9] In Yugoslavia, the Titoist forces promised that "the most important questions of public life and state organization will be solved by the freely elected representatives of all the people."[10] The German anti-fascist movement was enjoined to fight for democratic liberties, people's rights, and a "national democratic rejuvenation."[11]

These were typical statements of the period, published in the Comintern press and therefore approved by the Comintern. What did they mean? Did they mean the willingness and intent of the Comintern to forego permanently its earlier ultimate aims and to transform the Communist parties into normal political organizations, aiming at something much more moderate than one-party power and total social transformation?

Apart from the actual evidence of the postwar Yugoslav experience, which has at least given the lie to the Yugoslav promises, the problem of the meaning of the people's front policy of the years 1941–1943 can be examined from two other angles. First, it must be remembered that before the war the Comintern and the Communist parties had always given a very special content to such words as "democracy," "justice," and "people's rights." Throughout the history of the Comintern the Communist definition had differed markedly from the usual meanings attributed by non-Communists to these words. Second, it should be kept in mind that the Comintern, however often during this period it advocated the eradication of fascism and the restoration of democracy, never spelled out the *means* by which such aims were to be realized. To what extent did society have to be reorganized and reconstructed in order to satisfy the Comintern's definition of "democracy"?

One must, then, judge the Comintern's advocacy of "democracy" and "people's rights" in terms of the content previously attributed to these words by the Comintern leadership—a content that was never repudiated by the Comintern. What had the average rank-and-file Communist been led to believe was the true meaning of such a word as "democracy"? What had the rank-and-file Communist been led to understand was the necessary reorganization of society to ensure the the achievement of democracy? In the "genuine" type of democracy, as advocated by the Comintern for years before the war, who should rule? Looking at the programs of the people's fronts from this viewpoint, we inevitably arrive at the conclusion that the Comintern understood in its own special way what genuine democracy meant and how it was to be achieved.

It is worth noting that on several occasions during the period from 1941 to 1943 the proletariat and the Communist party were singled out by the Comintern as the core of the people's front and as the most consistent· elements in the anti-fascist struggle. Ercoli (Togliatti), the leading Italian Communist, reaffirmed the traditional Communist endorsement of the proletariat as the most progressive class, in his discussion of the Italian anti-fascist movement. The chief condition for the success of the anti-fascist struggle, he declared, was the entry into this struggle "of the working masses, of the industrial proletariat of the town and the agricultural proletariat of the village, as the formidable deciding force."[12] Similarly, the English Communist Party was described as the party of the working class and therefore the "only really and effectively independent organization."[13]

With respect to the special case of the anti-fascist resistance movements and the goals of such movements in the Nazi-occupied parts of Europe, there exists one unique bit of evidence—the testimony of a former member of the Presidium of the ECCI, Arvo Tuominen.[14] This former Finnish Communist is the only top-ranking Comintern leader of the period 1928–1943 who has made public any personal recollections. Tuominen, who broke finally with the Comintern in 1940, has asserted that the resistance movements against Hitler constituted in the eyes of the Comintern leadership nothing less than a struggle for world revolution. Referring to the Danish Communists, he has asserted the following:

These leaders had been given Moscow's solemn assurance that the Second World War would bring about the final victory of the Soviet

Union and Communism throughout the world. Thus the resistance movement, as far as Danish Communists were concerned, was nothing but a struggle for world revolution. I myself can confirm that such an assurance was indeed given by Moscow because, at the outbreak of the war, I was the General Secretary of the Finnish Communist Party, an executive of the Comintern and a member of its Presidium; in other words I was one of the relayers and receivers of the assurance.[15]

This unique testimony is the most forthright assertion available of a close link between the resistance movements and the struggle for Communist world revolution. It is, of course, isolated testimony. Yet it is more than probable that Communists were privately encouraged to look upon the fight against Hitler as a stage in the larger struggle for world Communism. Certainly it would seem safe to conclude that for the rank-and-file Communist this presentation of the anti-fascist campaign would have immense appeal.

The Comintern instructed the Communist parties in the colonial countries also to create broad anti-fascist fronts, with programs similar to those of the Communist parties in the capitalist countries except for the additional goal of national independence. The development of an anti-Japanese front naturally occupied the center of the stage.

For the most part, the same problems of interpretation exist for the colonial anti-fascist fronts as for those in the advanced countries. What were the implications of the people's fronts in the colonial sphere? Were these to be permanent arrangements, or merely temporary vehicles designed to facilitate the ultimate acquisition of power by the Communist party? Again the same method of analysis seems justified: What had such terms as "national independence" and "democracy" meant to the Comintern in the past? In the absence of new definitions presented by the Comintern, did not the Communist in the colonial world continue to understand that "genuine" independence and "genuine" democracy depended upon the establishment of Communist power?

Yet the case of China might raise some doubt, for the Chinese Communist Party explicitly denied that it intended to introduce Communism, and insisted that the front with the Kuomintang was to endure even after victory over Japan. Consider Mao's speech of

November, 1941, in which he declared, "We are not out to intro-duce Communism. What is being introduced . . . is the Three People's Principles [of Sun Yat-sen]." He further asserted that the Chinese Communist Party did not pursue a "one-party policy" but stood for "democratic collaboration" with anti-Japanese ele-ments.[16] Such collaboration, it was often affirmed, was to continue after the war of resistance had been won, when the several groups in the front were to undertake the "national reconstruction" of China.[17] The best indication of how permanent such postwar collaboration was to be lies, of course, in the history of postwar China. Yet the use of the phrase "national reconstruction" perhaps also indicates the temporary nature of such collaboration; once the "reconstruction" of China had been completed, a new phase of development would unfold, in which it could be expected that the Communists would move forward toward their own ultimate goals.

The Comintern material on India for this period is even less satisfactory.[18] The removal in 1942 of the ban on the Communist Party of India, illegal since 1934, was greeted with approval by the British Communist Ben Bradley. He stated that the "supreme issue before mankind" was the defeat of Hitler and his allies; victory in the war was the "precondition for the achievement of independence and full democracy" in India.[19] As "independence" and "full democracy" can be realized, for the Communist, only under the essential conditions of Communist leadership and Communist power, the Communist reader of *World News and Views* must have continued to interpret these words according to the special defi-nitions given them for years by the Comintern.

To summarize, it may be said that the Comintern in this period did not look upon efforts toward an early Communist seizure of power as either practicable or helpful to the cause of world revo-lution. However, it did see the energetic and wholehearted par-ticipation of Communists in the struggle for victory over Hitler and fascism as an eminently correct move in the direction of the ultimate aims of the Communist world movement. The struggle against Hitler, it was believed, would preserve and strengthen the Soviet Union as the leader of all "progressive humanity" and promote the reputation of the Communist party as the most ardent opponent of fascism and the most dedicated defender of the people's interests.

The above evidence is sufficient to indicate the degree of subordination of the Comintern and of its press to the requirements of Soviet foreign policy during the war years. The Comintern itself was in the process of being dissolved during this period. In the autumn of 1941 the headquarters of the Comintern had been moved from Moscow to Ufa, the capital of the Bashkir Autonomous Soviet Socialist Republic, about seven hundred and fifty miles to the east of Moscow.[20] In this remote, backward minor capital the "general staff" of the world revolutionary organization lived out its last days. In May, 1943, the Comintern was officially dissolved, thus ending almost a quarter-century of history.

What was the Comintern's explanation of this drastic step? The decision of the Presidium of the ECCI—actually stated in the form of a *proposal* to the several Communist parties—is to be found in the very last issue of *Kommunisticheskii Internatsional*.[21] The document states that the Comintern had ceased to be useful and had even become "a hindrance to the further strengthening of the national workers' parties." The reasons were: 1) "the growth and maturity of the Communist parties and their leading cadres"; 2) the contradiction between an overall international "directing center" and the "fundamental differences of the historical paths of development of the separate countries of the world," which had become apparent even before the war; 3) the struggle against Hitler, which could better be conducted by each Communist party "within the framework of its own country."

The Presidium approved the decision taken in November, 1940, by the American Communist Party to leave the Comintern, and noted that "a number of sections" of the Comintern had raised the question of the dissolution of the Comintern as the "directing center of the international workers' movement." As the Presidium put it, Communists "never were advocates of the preservation of outmoded organizational forms." It then called upon the sections of the Comintern to confirm its proposal that the Comintern be dissolved.

The document dissolving the Comintern bore the names of the following twelve members of the Presidium of the ECCI: Gottwald, Dimitrov, Zhdanov, Kolarov, Koplenig, Kuusinen, Manuilsky, Marty, Pieck, Thorez, Florin, and Ercoli (Togliatti). There followed a statement that "to the present decision are added the following representatives of the Communist Parties: Bianco (Italy), Dolores Ibarruri (Spain), Lehtinen (Finland), Pauker (Rumania), and Rakosi (Hungary)."[22] The document was dated Moscow, May 15, 1943.

Our discussion of the successive broad patterns of the Comintern strategy and tactics is thus brought to an end. The general conclusions on this subject are reserved for the final chapter. We may turn next to the problem of the Communist seizure of power.

PART THREE

The Communist Seizure
of Power

IX. NATURE AND MEANS

In the following discussion it is assumed that all the prerequisite required by Comintern doctrine for the seizure of power have matured. A revolutionary situation exists; and the Communist party, ideologically correct and organizationally sound, has won the support of "decisive strata" among the proletariat, as well as some support among certain nonproletarian groups. The problem is now the carrying out of the Communist seizure of power. The uses and goals of this power are discussed in Part Four.

CHARACTERISTICS

One of the most striking lacunae in Comintern literature is the absence of any comprehensive treatment of the problems involved in the actual seizure of power. Little evidence is to be found on the strategy and tactics of that vital period extending from the first gunfire of the rebels to the final capitulation of the counterrevolutionary forces. But the material that does exist on this question can serve to clarify, at least in part, a number of important questions.

The primary and elementary aspect of the Communist conquest of power was its necessarily violent character. All Comintern materials are in agreement on this point. The restraints imposed by an existing regime through its constitutional and legal systems were to be openly rejected and defied by the revolutionists. The conduct of the revolutionary forces was to shatter all bonds and manifest itself in armed rebellion. "*The conquest of power by the proletariat,*" stated the Comintern Program, "is not a peaceful 'conquest' . . . by means of achieving a parliamentary majority."[1] The refusal of the ruling classes to surrender their position would inevitably compel the recourse to revolutionary violence. The conquest of power required, therefore, "the violent overthrow of the bourgeois power" and the destruction of the entire structure of the bourgeois state.[2]

This position was never questioned or abandoned. The impossibility of a peaceful assumption of power on the part of any Communist-led revolutionary movement was consistently reaffirmed throughout Comintern history. Even upon the inauguration of the popular front period in 1935 at the Seventh Congress, Dimitrov emphatically denied that the new, less aggressive tactics of the Comintern implied the possibility of a peaceful transition from proletarian powerlessness to proletarian power under Communist control.[3]

If violence was an inevitable accompaniment of the Communist seizure of power, unprecedented confusion and disorder were likewise prophesied. In the camp of the revolutionaries, the wide range of special and particular resentments held by different social groups would make impossible a "monolithic" rebellion, despite the leadership of the Communist party and the proletariat. Similarly, the pro-governmental forces would be divided by competing programs aiming at the solution of the crisis. The conquest of power was therefore not thought of as a simple, neat, orderly affair. At the Seventh Comintern Congress, Manuilsky offered extensive comments on the complexity of the revolutionary process and ridiculed those who oversimplified the act of seizing power. He cited Engel's rejection of the idea that the seizure of power would involve a single great and decisive battle between "all official parties united in one lump *here* [and] all the Socialists in one column *there*."[4] Such a scheme, envisaging two clear-cut antagonistic forces, naively and erroneously eliminated all intermediary, vacillating social groups and wrongly assumed a singleness of aim both on the part of the various anti-revolutionary forces and on the part of the revolutionary forces.[5] Manuilsky quoted from Lenin to the same effect:

These are those who imagine that in one place an army will line up and say, "We are for socialism," and in another place another army will say, "We are for imperialism," and that this will be the social revolution. . . .

Whoever expects a "pure" social revolution will *never* live to see it. Such a person pays lip service to revolution without understanding what revolution is.[6]

How lengthy a process was the seizure of power expected to be? No answer is given in available Comintern materials. Even an attempt to suggest an approximate answer to this question requires the making of an almost impossible distinction between the seizure of power and the civil war that was expected to follow it in most cases. Of course, the attempt to seize power is in itself an act of civil warfare. At what point can the seizure of power, as a specific act, be considered to have been accomplished? After the rebels have held power for twenty-four hours, a week, a month, or even years? It is perhaps reasonable to suggest that the seizure of power may be deemed complete when control over the entire country and its people is in the hands of the Communist-led revolutionists and is not effectively contested by either internal or external enemies. From this standpoint the Bolshevik seizure of power in Russia was not the brief activity of November 7 and 8, 1917, but a process lasting from November, 1917, to early 1921, at which time the counterrevolutionary forces abandoned significant efforts at further armed struggle. A prolonged civil war would mean, of course, that the Communists would conduct two simultaneous operations: the carrying through of the seizure of power to completion, and the beginning of the Communist-oriented economic and social transformation in those areas under Communist control.

If the so-called "proletarian" revolution in Russia in November, 1917, required more than three years of civil strife to confirm the Communists' holding of power, then it might reasonably be conjectured that in a smaller but more advanced country, possessing a modern system of communications and transportation, the Communist attempt to seize power would probably meet with either success or failure in less time. It is difficult to imagine that a decision, either favorable or unfavorable, would not come to the

the Communists fairly quickly in those countries where advanced communications systems and modern technology existed. Of course, the above remarks on the duration and outcome of the struggle abstract from the scene the intervention of forces from outside the country.

In colonial countries, where poor communications exist, a more prolonged contest for power might reasonably be expected, especially in the larger colonies. For example, in China the first soviets were established in 1927, but Communist control of the entire mainland was not achieved until 1949. The armed struggle for power lasted more than two decades. An article in *Kommunisticheskii Internatsional* pointed out that by 1935 there had been an effective seizure of power in one sixth of China, while the remainder of the country, including the most important areas, had yet to be won.[7]

ATTENDANT CIRCUMSTANCES: FAVORABLE AND
UNFAVORABLE

We have seen how the Comintern singled out certain phenomena as prerequisites to the seizure of power. Now we turn to a consideration of other, less decisive factors accompanying a seizure of power, the presence of which in themselves would mean neither victory nor defeat, but simply a strengthening or weakening of the chances for success. On this score there exist a number of scattered judgments and implications, which, taken together, help to draw a better picture of the Comintern's understanding of the armed struggle for power.

The spatial factor. On several occasions the spokesmen of the Comintern offered comments on the importance of the factor of space in facilitating or hampering the armed uprising. Very frequent reference was made to the vast areas at the disposal of the Russian Bolsheviks during the years 1917–1921. Repeating both Lenin's and Stalin's appraisals of the factor of space in the Russian Revolution, everyone agreed that the enormous stretches of Russian territory had bestowed important advantages upon the revolutionists, such as maneuverability and the great improbability of an easy knock-out blow from the counterrevolutionists. Commentators who analyzed the defeat of the Hungarian Soviet Republic of 1919 explained that failure partly in terms of the comparatively small size of the country. Bela Kun, who had been the Hungarian Communist leader in 1919, cited not only Lenin's appreciation of the spatial factor in revolutions but also Engels' comments on the difficulties facing the Hungarian revolutionists of 1848–1849 in consequence of the small size of Hungarian territory.[8] This factor, Kun pointed out, returned to plague the Hungarian Communists in 1919.

Apparently many Communists entertained a healthy fear of being isolated in a sea of capitalist countries at the moment of the conquest of power. This feeling was shared not only by the Communist parties of the small states of continental Europe but also by the British Communist Party. Manuilsky dealt with the British case in a speech before the English Commission of the ECCI in 1932. Apparently seeking to reassure representatives of the British Party, he claimed that a proletarian revolution in England would be accompanied by revolution throughout the British Commonwealth, if not also among the other European capitalist states. More specifically, he pointed out that the degree of isolation befalling an English Communist-led rebellion would depend upon the role of the British fleet and the success of Communist work there.[9]

In the colonial and semi-colonial countries, with their relatively underdeveloped systems of communications, the spatial factor would not appear to be so important. But a large colonial country did offer some advantages. The Chinese revolution illustrated the feasibility of a seizure of power in only a part of a large country, in areas remote from the major urban centers and poorly interlaced with roads, rivers, and railroads. The lengthy article by Miro, cited above, was devoted to the problem of establishing such remote soviet regimes in the interior regions of the colony prior to the conquest of power on an all-national scale.[10] The author suggested that the Chinese revolution, which by 1931 had set up a Communist-run soviet-type government in a remote, interior region of China, might serve as a pattern for future colonial revolutions. He pointed out, interestingly enough, that in several past revolutions, the armed uprising had begun in outlying regions while the chief political and economic centers had remained for some time in the hands of the "counterrevolutionists."[11] Miro, of course, overlooks the very basic point that the proletariat will be weakest in outlying rural regions! In his article, Miro recommended that such regions should possess the following characteristics: a terrain hindering swift concentration of enemy forces, a population exploited and resentful, an existing peasant insurgent movement, an adequate, locally produced food supply, and some "primitive" industry to ensure arms repair.[12]

It is certainly worth noting that the Comintern, despite its frequent depiction of the Chinese Communist Party as a model party, refrained from making any clear and unequivocal endorsement of Miro's suggestion, i.e., that the creation of peasant soviets in remote regions, defended by a Red Army, be followed generally in the colonial and semi-colonial countries. The experience of the Chinese Party from 1931 on was never endorsed as the only pattern of development for such countries. There is, in fact, surprisingly little discussion on this theme in Comintern materials.

Although there was universal agreement within the Comintern on the possibility of a seizure of power in any single country, however small, there is some evidence that the Comintern thought in terms of a regional seizure of power embracing several small contiguous states. The Balkan countries were a case in point. At the Sixth Congress, Dimitrov declared that these states were so closely connected that success in any one of them depended directly on the revolutionary situation in the adjacent states.[13] On another occasion a Rumanian Communist spoke of the probability of a "general Balkan-Danubian revolution."[14] A Russian delegate at the Sixth Congress was accused of asserting that a revolution in a single Latin American country was impossible in view of the great subjection of these countries to control by the United States. While rejecting this view, the Colombian Communist Cardenas admitted that the chances of victory would be greater if several countries were simultaneously affected by a revolutionary upsurge.[15]

Revolutionary experience of the proletariat. The Comintern did not believe that there was any substitute for the practical experience gained by the Communist party and the proletariat in daily struggle with the class enemies. The accumulation of such experience was expected to promote feelings of confidence and class solidarity that would stand the revolutionaries in good stead at the time of the attempted seizure of power. The greater the revolutionary experience of the proletariat, the more certain was the Comintern's belief that the decisive struggle for power would be successful. The great value of the Revolution of 1905 for the Russian proletariat and "toiling masses" in 1917 was mentioned time and again. Bela Kun, for example, rationalized the failure of the Hungarian Revolution of 1919 partly in terms of the absence of a "1905" in Hungary.[16] Of course, to some extent the absence of a great revolutionary tradition in a particular Communist party might be balanced by a careful study of the experiences of other parties. As we have seen, the Comintern repeatedly enjoined the parties to master and teach the lessons of Bolshevik experience in Russia.

Military training. In its theses entitled "Measures of Struggle with the Danger of Imperialist Wars," the Sixth Comintern Congress in 1928 strongly insisted on the value of military training for the future revolutionaries. The Congress criticized pacifist campaigns in which refusal of military service was advocated. According to the theses, the Communists were to advise the workers and poor peasants to accept military service as a means of learning the use of arms.[17] "By militarizing the workers and training them in the use of weapons, imperialism itself creates a precondition for the victory of the proletariat in the civil war."[18] The resolution on the question of war at the Seventh Congress in 1935 reaffirmed the incorrectness of refusal to appear for military service.[19] As the French Communist André Marty declared, the Communists will "enter the army in order to acquire a thorough knowledge of how to handle weapons."[20] The lack of such knowledge would be a

serious defect during a Communist uprising. In the case of the
Finnish revolution of 1918, insufficient military training was cited
as one of the reasons for the defeat of the Finnish Communists.[21]

War or peace. As has been noted in Chapter V, the Comintern
considered that the revolutionary situation would develop more
readily in time of war than in time of peace. In making its decision
whether or not to attempt to seize power, the Communist party
would certainly be strongly influenced by the presence or absence
of war. Throughout Comintern literature of 1928–1943, any prediction of war always carried with it the expressed anticipation of
revolution. In the light of this attitude, it seems reasonable to
conclude that the Comintern believed war to be a more favorable
background than peace for the carrying out of a Communist
seizure of power. If a revolutionary situation arose during the
course of a war, it would mean, among other things, that the
existing government could no longer count upon the support of its
armed forces, that it would be faced with masses already trained to
use arms, and that it would have an external danger to cope with
at the same time. Furthermore, if war existed among the capitalist
countries, the "international bourgeoisie" would be unable to
cooperate against the class enemy, the proletariat led by the Communist parties. Here the schism in the bourgeois camp could well
be exploited by the revolutionaries.

If war existed between the USSR and one or more capitalist
countries, an even more favorable factor would be introduced on
the side of the revolutionaries—the armed forces of the Soviet
Union. But this case is treated in the immediately following section,
devoted to the question of the intervention of the CPSU and the
USSR in a Communist attempt to seize power abroad.

At the Seventh Congress in 1935, the Italian Communist Ercoli
(Togliatti), expressed the Comintern view of the relationship
between future war and revolution:

The World War had lasted for two or three years before there were cases
of mass revolts of soldiers at the front and of the population in the rear.
The bourgeoisie must not blame us if this time the interval is much
shorter.... The most objective examination of the international situation

and the mass movement, and of their perspectives, inevitably brings us
to the conclusion that for all capitalist countries the beginning of the war
will mean the beginning of a revolutionary crisis; and during the crisis
we shall fight strenuously at the head of the masses to transform the
imperialist war into a civil war, we shall fight for revolution and for the
conquest of power.[22]

Aid from the CPSU and USSR. The Comintern Program of 1928,
in the section entitled "The Significance of the USSR and its
International-Revolutionary Obligations," states in one short, ambiguous paragraph the obligation of the Communist Party of the
Soviet Union to "render support to all the exploited, to the labor
movement in the capitalist countries, to the movement of the
colonial peoples against imperialism, and to the struggle against
national oppression in whatever form."[23] Unfortunately, a more
detailed statement, spelling out the practical aid of the CPSU in
facilitating the Communist seizure of power in other countries, is
not given in the Program. Nor are other Comintern materials much
more helpful. In such situations, the slight evidence that does exist
must be combined with reasonable speculation and inference in
order to reach an interpretation of the role of the CPSU in Communist seizures of power in other lands. We have, of course, already
discussed the Comintern's view of the role of the Soviet Union and
its Communist Party in helping the world revolutionary movement
prior to the seizure of power.

First of all, it may be recalled that the CPSU possessed a variety
of channels through which to give aid, i.e., through direct contact
with a foreign Communist party, or through the Comintern which
the CPSU controlled, or through the Soviet government. Such aid,
besides ideological guidance and propagandistic support, might
include funds, advisers and leaders, military matériel, and armed
forces. Given these possible channels and these possible types of aid,
what did the Comintern explicitly or implicitly regard as the
proper and possible contribution of the CPSU to the victory of an
attempted Communist seizure of power in another country?

The matter of aid in the form of ideological guidance and
propagandistic support would appear to raise no questions. It

seems virtually incontestable that the CPSU would, immediately upon the beginning of a Communist attempt to seize power in another country, offer every kind of verbal encouragement, including propaganda through its press organs and diplomatic support through its control of the Soviet state. This kind of moral support, as distinguished from tangible aid, would obviously be both cheap and easy to supply. Comintern materials fully support the deduction that such aid would be forthcoming. There would seem to be no problem here.

But when aid means the possible supplying by the CPSU of personnel, military equipment, or even armed forces, there are simply no clear-cut commitments in Comintern literature that the CPSU must or will furnish such aid, either against counterrevolutionary forces within the foreign country in question or against any capitalist states intervening in that country. The lack in Comintern materials of any frequent and explicit assurances of practical aid from the USSR can theoretically be explained in three ways: 1) the relations of the USSR with other sovereign states would have been seriously imperiled by explicit assurances of practical aid to foreign Communist parties, mere verbal support by the CPSU to foreign Communists having caused sufficient trouble; 2) explicit assurances were unnecessary, as all Communists understood that the CPSU would try in any case to give all possible aid; and 3) no blanket decision was ever made by the CPSU.

The problem of support by the CPSU for foreign Communist attempts to seize power may be approached in another way. What limitations, it may be asked, stood in the way of the willingness of the CPSU to use the armed forces of the USSR to aid Communist uprisings in other countries? The only serious limitation would seem to be that imposed by the risk to the CPSU and its control over the Soviet Union. If the supposed "homeland" of the world proletariat were to be seriously endangered by such action, then the CPSU might well refrain from rendering any except moral support. If the consequences of sending some part of the Soviet military machine to aid in a Communist seizure of power elsewhere promised to be war between the USSR and one or more major capitalist states, obviously the risks would have to be calculated carefully. Apart from the matter of possible military destruction and defeat, even the risk of losing sympathy and support from certain countries might deter the CPSU from direct practical intervention in a revolution in another country.

History has shown cases of Soviet willingness to use its armed forces to establish sympathetic regimes. In 1918–1921, there were efforts, some successful, others unsuccessful, to create Communist regimes on the periphery of Soviet Russia. In 1921 units of the Red Army invaded the remote areas of Tuva and Outer Mongolia, establishing Communist control which remains to this day. Again, during the first Russo-Finnish War of 1939–1940, a short-lived puppet Finnish Communist state was constructed at Terijoki, near the Soviet frontier and behind the military front. And, in 1939 and 1940, protected by the Nazi-Soviet Pact, the USSR forcibly occupied extensive areas on its periphery in Eastern Europe (parts of Poland, the Baltic states, Bessarabia, and part of Bukovina).

Comintern endorsement of these uses of Soviet power was consistently expressed. For example, an article in the Comintern journal on the tenth anniversary of the "national-revolutionary movement" in Tuva referred with approval to the support given by the Soviet Red Army in 1921 in the overthrow of the feudal order.[24] Another article mentioned the "last-minute" military training given the Finnish revolutionaries in 1918 by "volunteer Russian instructors."[25] The various explanations given in Comintern materials for the Soviet invasion of Poland in September, 1939, included, as we have seen, the argument that the action of the Soviet armed forces had been dictated by the interests of socialism, since the "reactionary" Polish government had been exploiting millions of "toiling" people. This argument was clearly in terms of the Communist world revolution. To be sure, other explanations were advanced. A report in *World News and Views* emphasized the desire of the USSR to protect the Belorussian and Ukrainian minorities "from the terrors of Nazi invasion."[26] Molotov's official explanation in the same issue of *World News and Views* was somewhat different, and referred to the collapse of

Polish authority and the need to protect the minorities from the consequences of public disorder. In December, 1939, the Finnish puppet Communist government at Terijoki, in its announced program, called upon Finns, with the help of the Red Army of the USSR as "liberator," to overthrow the Finnish government at Helsinki.[27]

Soviet aid to the Loyalist cause during the Spanish Civil War should also be mentioned here. Despite the avowed immediate goals for which such aid was to be used—the defeat of fascism and the creation of a "new type" of democracy—the desired outcome would have greatly improved the position of the Spanish Communist Party and would have increased its ability to push the Spanish revolution to a "higher" stage. Soviet aid did in fact immeasurably increase the influence of the Spanish Communists during the Civil War.[28]

In the light of the historical record of the use of Soviet armed forces to extend the sphere of Communist control, and in the light of the favorable attitude expressed in Comintern literature to these events, it would appear safe to conclude that the lack of frequent and explicit assurances of practical aid by the CPSU did not mean lack of intention and/or willingness to give such aid if the risks were not considered too great.

In case of an attack by one or more capitalist countries upon the USSR, the evidence in Comintern materials is more than convincing that the USSR did not intend to stop at a mere defeat of the attacking power but would also seek to overthrow capitalism in the enemy country. The Comintern time and again informed its member parties that one of their highest obligations was the defense of the USSR. Such defense meant that the Communist party of a country attacking the USSR had the duty of conducting civil war against its bourgeoisie in an effort to overthrow the capitalist rulers.[29] In such a case, the armed forces of the USSR would become allies in the Communist effort to seize power. In 1935, the German Communist Wilhelm Pieck, while stating that the Soviet Red Army in peacetime served "exclusively the cause of defense of the Soviet frontier," added that, if attacked, the Red Army would conduct an offensive war into the enemy's country.

Its victory would mean the liberation of "toilers from fascism, capitalist exploitation, and wars; it would also mean the establishment of Soviet power."[30]

A similar statement is to be found in an unsigned article, "The Army of Peace, Culture, and Victorious Socialism," published in the Comintern information sheet in February, 1939.[31] In case of aggression against the USSR, the article asserted, the Soviet Union would wage an offensive war, in which the "Soviet people will employ armed force to help the workers and the common people of the aggressor countries to overthrow the fascist slavery they hate so much." Another example is the statement of the German Communist leader, Ernst Thälmann, who in 1931 declared that "an anti-Soviet war can lead and will lead only to the overthrow of Hindenburg Germany, to the creation of a socialist soviet Germany."[32]

It may be noted that during the period after June, 1941, when the USSR was at war, the role of the Soviet Red Army as "liberator" was constantly expounded, but the Comintern was always careful to assure that "liberation" meant the destruction of fascism (as distinguished from capitalism) and that the liberated peoples would be free to choose their own way of life. However, such assurances, of course, cannot be understood apart from the events in Soviet-occupied Eastern Europe from 1944 to the present.

In conclusion, two points seem clear and reasonably well established: First, if the USSR were not at war when Communist revolution broke out in another country, it would make the use of its armed forces on behalf of that revolution conditional upon a careful calculation of the risk involved. Second, if the USSR were attacked by a non-Communist country, a combined operation was to develop, in which the Soviet armed forces and a Communist-controlled revolutionary movement in the attacking country were to aim at the defeat of the attacker and the overthrow of its political, social, and economic system.

TECHNIQUES

Useful but brief material on the actual steps in the seizure of power is given in two documents adopted by the Sixth Congress in 1928—the Comintern Program and the theses on "Measures of Struggle with the Danger of Imperialist War."

Confronted with a rising revolutionary tide, the Communist party had the following major tasks: 1) the maintenance and swift increase of its contacts with the discontented classes and strata in society; 2) the development and utilization of more and more radical methods of struggle in order to push the revolution ever to the left; and 3) the preparation of a detailed plan for the seizure of power. Contacts with the masses required the intensification of work amongst all the social categories within the developing revolutionary coalition. Increasingly radical slogans and forms of mass activity were to be employed. The slogans to be used called for workers' control over industry, the formation of peasant committees, the seizure of big landed property, the creation of soviets, the disarming of the bourgeoisie, and the arming of the proletariat.[33]

Soviets, directly elected by the workers, soldiers, and peasants, were always regarded in Comintern literature as the indispensable form of revolutionary government, combining executive and legislative powers in one body. Apparently a demand for the immediate creation of soviets was justified only during the existence of a revolutionary situation.[34] Soviets were considered fully suitable for all types of societies, including backward and colonial countries. As the Communist party was to be a distinct minority in the part of the population that was eligible to vote for the soviets, it may be asked how the party in such a situation was to direct and dominate the seizure of power. If we assume, as we do, that all the prerequisites for a seizure of power existed, then we must also assume that the Communist party had mass support among the proletariat and also among nonproletarian "toilers." Such support would be reflected in the acceptance of Communist leadership and in the election of Communist deputies to the soviets. Assuming also that the ideological and organizational condition of the Communist party was adequate for a seizure of power, the discipline and determination of such a party would be counted on to outweigh numerical shortcomings.

Methods of struggle included the creation of the revolutionary organizational forms mentioned above and their utilization in mass activity beginning with strikes and unarmed demonstrations, and leading to a combination of strikes and armed demonstrations, followed by the ultimate employment of a general strike conjointly with armed insurrection against the ruling classes and their state institutions.[35]

During the transition to increasingly violent forms of struggle, the Communist party was to demand and create a workers' and peasants' militia, organized in a "Red Guard" and in "Red" partisan detachments. "The Red Guard is an organ of rebellion. The duty of Communists in the presence of a directly revolutionary situation is to agitate for and to create such an organ."[36] This militia was to possess a distinct class character and was not to include persons belonging to the "exploiting" classes. Energetic efforts were to be made to disintegrate the "bourgeois" armed forces and thereby to weaken the "counterrevolutionary" camp as much as possible.[37]

The armed uprising was to begin at the most propitious moment, presumably when anarchy within the country had reached a very high point. The precise time of the uprising, according to the Comintern, "can be correctly established only if the closest contact exists between the party and the masses of the revolutionary proletariat."[38]

The armed uprising presupposed a military plan and the decisive execution of that plan by the units of the workers' and peasants' militia. Once begun, the uprising was to be carried through ruthlessly. The rule was to be "no playing with rebellion." Having set the uprising in motion, it was then necessary to prosecute the attack with all vigor until the enemy was crushed. The main revolutionary forces were to be thrown against the main forces of the enemy. Wavering and hesitation would be ruinous. The superiority of the proletarian forces had to be secured at all the vital centers of power and extended rapidly over as large a territory as possible.[39] In this crucial hour the energy and decisiveness of the Communist leadership were to attain maximum importance.

X. THE FORMS OF
COMMUNIST POWER

Like the anarchists, the Comintern leaders believed in the need to destroy the government of the old regime, but, unlike the anarchists, who foresaw a stateless society immediately after the seizure of power, the Comintern insisted upon the need to create at once a new revolutionary government. To be sure, according to Comintern theory, the state was ultimately to "wither away," and the future world society of Communism was not to possess a government. But before the coming of the future world society of Communism, a national government was deemed absolutely necessary for the execution of the many great tasks confronting the Communist-led revolutionaries in each country.

Two types of revolutionary government are identified in Comintern literature: the "dictatorship of the proletariat" and the "democratic dictatorship of the proletariat and peasantry." As employed by Communists, these words have meanings quite different from those which are normally attached to them by non-Communists; both terms as used by Communists mask the actual power position of the Communist party, as will be shown below. The "dictatorship of the proletariat" was considered by the Comintern to be the suitable type of government following the Communist seizure of power in those societies undergoing a "proletarian-socialist" revolution—the advanced capitalist societies and certain societies of medium capitalist development. The "democratic dictatorship of the proletariat and peasantry" was to be the type of government in those societies undergoing a "bourgeois-democratic" revolution—certain societies of medium capitalist development and the colonial, semi-colonial, dependent, and backward societies.

DICTATORSHIP OF THE PROLETARIAT

To understand the term "dictatorship of the proletariat," certain fundamentals in the Comintern's view of the state must be grasped.[1] Political power and the state are for Marxists and Communists not natural but historical phenomena.[2] Historically, the state appears with the division of society into classes, and the ruling class wielding state power has always been, in Marxist and Communist analyses, that class possessing and utilizing the significant means of economic production. Economic power is always the source and basis for political power, which is always exercised for the benefit of the ruling class or classes. Such a concept as democracy was, for the Comintern, without meaning if used abstractly; one must inquire, which class is actually in power? The Comintern claimed that government in the capitalist countries, however disguised by the verbiage and institutional forms of democratic liberalism, was actually in the hands of the capitalists and therefore was not responsive to the will of the people in general. Any and all "capitalist" governments were, in effect, class dictatorships. "Bourgeois democracy," stated the Comintern Program, "with its formal equality of citizens before the law, rests upon a glaring inequality among the classes in the material-economic realm."[3] Liberties and civil rights in the capitalist-controlled state were, therefore, fictions except for the members of the ruling class. In contrast, "proletarian democracy," fostered by the "dictatorship of the proletariat," for the first time in history was to provide the necessary economic and social basis for genuine democracy by abolishing the classes who owned the means of production and by making such means of production the property of all "toilers" in general.

With these considerations in mind, the "dictatorship of the proletariat" may be examined in terms of the following points: 1) the place of the Communist party in the "dictatorship of the proletariat"; and 2) the institutional forms of the dictatorship.

What place was assigned to the Communist party after the successful seizure of power? In the Program of the Comintern, the party, although mentioned only a few times, was assigned an overwhelmingly dominant role and apparently was to be the only political party allowed to exist. There is no mention of any other. The Communist party was to play the "leading role" in the "proletarian dictatorship"; the proletariat was impotent without it. The party was to guide the various mass organizations in the new society—soviets, trade unions, cooperatives, and the Young Communist League.[4]

The role of the Communist party in the "dictatorship of the proletariat" was emphasized even more forcibly in other Comintern literature. In 1933 Kuusinen, citing Stalin as his authority, asserted the importance of the Communist party in the strongest possible terms. The party, he affirmed, was the highest form of proletarian class organization, and absolutely indispensable to the existence and effective work of the "proletarian dictatorship." Its powers were all-embracing; it was not to share leadership with any other parties. It was false and erroneous to differentiate between the "dictatorship of the proletariat" and the leading role of the party.[5] In 1935 another Comintern writer referred to the "maximum strengthening of the Communist party" after the seizure of power. Not a diminishing of the role of the party, but rather an extraordinary growth of its activity would follow the successful armed uprising; the complex tasks inherent in the building of socialism made this growth absolutely necessary.[6]

In the light of this evidence, which is multiplied a hundred- and a thousandfold in Comintern literature, we can only conclude that the "dictatorship of the proletariat" meant in actuality the dictatorship of the Communist party. This dictatorship was to be in fact a minority dictatorship over the non-Communist majority of the population, a dictatorship over proletarians as well as over nonproletarians. Even within the party, the ruling group at the apex exercised an undemocratic control over the lower echelons. What we have, then, with the victorious "proletarian" revolution and the establishment of a "dictatorship of the proletariat," is a dictatorship exercised by a single political party within which the real locus of power is at the top rather than among the rank-and file.

The dictatorship of the Communist party was to be exercised through a new and appropriate governmental structure. The Comintern Program rejected the parliamentary system as an outmoded relic of the capitalist era. As a suitable governmental form for the new era, the Program advocated the soviet system, which existed, of course, in the Soviet Union. Soviets, which simply mean councils, had appeared in the Russian Revolutions of 1905 and 1917, and were regarded as descendants of the revolutionary Paris Commune of 1871. As we know, soviets were to be set up as revolutionary organs on the eve of the Communist seizure of power. Elected by the proletariat and other "toilers," they were to possess, *pro forma*, sole constitutional authority in the new proletarian state. Combining and exercising legislative, executive, and judicial powers, the soviets eliminated the separation of powers found in "bourgeois" governments. The electoral system was to be built on a production basis, rather than a residential basis. Voters were to have the right of recall as well as of electing deputies. The soviet system was to draw the broad masses of the proletariat and other "toilers" into the building of socialism and into the administration of the state. It was announced as the most democratic system of government yet developed by man.[7] The soviet structure alone was advocated, without any exception whatsoever, as the proper constitutional form of the "proletarian dictatorship."[8]

In committing itself to this structure, the Comintern, aware of possible charges of undue "Russification," sought to advertise the soviets as "natural" institutions of universal applicability, despite their Russian origins.[9] The soviet system was "an international world-wide form of the dictatorship of the proletariat."[10] In this, as in other instances, the Comintern labored to achieve two aims—to render full credit to the contributions of the Russian Revolution and to present its achievements as of universal value and applicability.

To summarize: in a newly established "proletarian dictatorship" the Communist party was to wield all effective political power— theoretically in the name of the proletariat and as the embodiment of the proletariat's will, but, in reality, as the sole independent political force, dominating the proletariat as well as other classes.

The use of the term "dictatorship of the proletariat" reflected the Comintern's desire to maintain the fiction of the proletariat as the real driving force of the revolution and as the real ruler over other classes in the new society. Upon examination, the term is exposed as a mask for the dictatorship of the Communist party.

DEMOCRATIC DICTATORSHIP OF THE PROLETARIAT AND PEASANTRY

For those societies which were, in Comintern theory, confronted first of all with a "bourgeois-democratic" revolution, the Comintern employed the formula "democratic dictatorship of the proletariat and peasantry" to designate the appropriate type of government immediately following the Communist seizure of power.

The term "democratic dictatorship of the proletariat and peasantry" was created by Lenin in 1905.[11] It was used in the Comintern Program of 1928 totally without any effort at definition. What precisely did this term mean? Logically, one might infer at least the following: 1) that it meant something other than the "dictatorship of the proletariat," for there would be no need for two labels for the same system of rule; and 2) that the peasantry, explicitly mentioned in the formula, had a significantly greater share in political power than it was permitted to have in the "dictatorship of the proletariat." If, as shown above, the "dictatorship of the proletariat" meant a monopoly of power in the hands of the Communist party, did not the "democratic dictatorship of the proletariat and peasantry" mean that one or more parties representing the peasantry were to share power with the Communist party?[12] If control was to be assigned to the proletariat, i.e., the Communist party, the situation would not be essentially different from that resulting from the "dictatorship of the proletariat." If the two classes were to share power equally, then the peasantry as the numerically larger class would still suffer discrimination. Finally, if power were shared on a truly democratic basis, with every adult in both classes having an equal vote, the peasantry would, of course, be in a position to dominate the new regime.

This latter interpretation appears to be the decisive one; was this, then, what was meant by the "democratic dictatorship of the proletariat and peasantry?"

Three methods may be employed to answer this question. First, we may examine Comintern efforts at a definition. Second, we may resort to inferential analysis, based upon an appreciation of the whole nature of the Communist-led "bourgeois-democratic" revolution. Third, we may consider the Chinese Soviet regime, established in 1931 and proclaimed as a "democratic dictatorship of the proletariat and peasantry."

Unfortunately, Comintern writers and speakers used the term "democratic dictatorship of the proletariat and peasantry" *ad infinitum* without ever bothering with even a simple brief explanation of its content. The conclusion can be either that these individuals did not know themselves what the term meant, or that they did not wish to be frank and thereby risk alienating the peasantry. If an authoritative definition were to be found anywhere, the Program of 1928 would have been the logical place for such a definition, yet none was given. The only really helpful statements are in Manuilsky's speech at the Sixth Congress, entitled "The Situation and Problems of the Communist Party of the Soviet Union." Here Manuilsky clearly indicated that important differences existed between the "dictatorship of the proletariat" and the "democratic dictatorship of the proletariat and peasantry:"

The proletarian dictatorship is a form of government which is based on cooperation with the peasantry but not on the basis of a "democratic" sharing of power. The proletarian dictatorship is not a democratic dictatorship of the proletariat and peasantry. The former stands . . . on the basis of the dictatorship of one class. The latter remains . . . on the basis of sharing power between the proletariat and the peasantry.[13]

Further on in the same speech Manuilsky remarked that, without the leading role of the proletariat, a "proletarian dictatorship" could no longer exist and would become instead "workers' and peasants' democracy." He insisted upon a distinction between these two forms of rule: "All the features which distinguish the proletarian dictatorship from the democratic dictatorship of the proletariat and peasantry remain in force in regard to these two forms of democracy."[14]

It seems possible to deduce from Manuilsky's remarks a system in which the proletariat did not possess the leading role and in which there was a truly democratic sharing of power between the revolutionary proletariat and the revolutionary peasantry. Such a situation would clearly imply the existence of distinct peasant parties—in effect, a multiparty system.

The weakness of the above conclusion, apart from the poverty of evidence supporting it, lies in its obvious contradiction of the leading role, repeatedly emphasized, of the Communist party in the revolutionary process. As we have seen, the hegemony of the Communist party over the revolutionary movement was declared over and over again to be an indispensable prerequisite for the successful seizure of power. That this party (which was declared to be the party of the proletariat) should forgo its leading role and submit to a condition of equality or inferiority with respect to another party or parties representing the revolutionary peasantry —all this is quite unthinkable, notwithstanding Manuilsky's interpretation.

Also, we have to consider the meaning of the "democratic dictatorship of the proletariat and peasantry" in the specific case of the Chinese Soviet regime established in 1931. There is indication here that the Comintern believed the "democratic dictatorship" in China to be unusual and exceptional. An editorial in the Comintern journal in 1931 stated that the "democratic dictatorship of the proletariat and peasantry" in China would be "essentially different from the democratic dictatorship planned by the Bolsheviks in the conditions of the 1905 Revolution." One major difference was that the Communists would constitute a majority in the government.[15] If a Communist majority in such a government was regarded as unusual, the deduction must be that a Communist minority was regarded as normal, and as consistent with Lenin's formula of 1905. Another Comintern editorial in 1931 stated that the "*specific* peculiarity" of the Chinese Soviet system was the monopoly of revolutionary leadership held by the Communist Party, which was "the only ruling party in the Soviet territories of China." The Chinese peasantry, the editorial pointed out, did not create their own party and simply followed the leadership of the proletariat and the Communist Party.[16] The attitude of these Comintern writers—that a Communist majority in the Soviet government and the total absence of other parties constituted exceptional features of the Chinese "democratic dictatorship"— would appear to support the interpretation that the Comintern understood this formula to mean a system in which Communists might well be in a minority. It may be noted, moreover, that the Comintern never publicly generalized from the Chinese experience any conclusion that future "democratic dictatorships" had to follow undeviatingly the Chinese variant. Yet the Chinese experience in establishing and maintaining a Soviet regime was characterized by Pieck, in his major address at the Seventh Comintern Congress in 1935, as "the outstanding event" in the colonial areas since the Sixth Congress in 1928, as "a shining example for the toilers of the whole colonial world," and as "the first model of a colonial revolution in which the ideological, and also, in its initial form, the state hegemony of the proletariat is realized."[17]

All of the above may seem to be nothing but hairsplitting. It seems, however, useful to emphasize the ambiguity of public Comintern statements on this crucial question. This ambiguity suggests embarrassment within the Comintern leadership about the implications of the "democratic dictatorship of the proletariat and peasantry." The Comintern probably did not care to define in clear and unmistakable fashion this particular formula for one or all of the following reasons: 1) it never intended to create a truly democratic system; 2) it offered the formula as a sop in the hope of winning the support or at least the toleration of the middle and poor peasants in those countries where a peasant uprising was indispensable for the Communist seizure of power; 3) it sought to maintain some show of resemblance between the initial period of Communist dictatorship and the bourgeois-democratic stage of Marx by allowing during the initial stage of Communist power a limited representation to "bourgeois" social elements.

Soviets were to constitute the structural form of the "democratic dictatorship of the proletariat and peasantry," and, indeed, were to be the universally applicable form of Communist rule. The existence of soviets in China (especially of the short-lived Canton Soviet of December, 1927), and the later establishment of the Chinese Soviet Republic in 1931, gave practical endorsement to the Comintern's advocacy of soviets, even in the colonial world. It may be pointed out that the Comintern insisted upon the designation of the Chinese soviets as "workers' and peasants' soviets," despite the fact that the Chinese Soviet Republic was created on the basis of rural soviets and in the absence of any Communist control over urban centers. According to an editorial in the Comintern journal, the Chinese rural soviets should "in no case be viewed simply as peasant soviets," for the peasants had accepted Communist (and therefore "proletarian") leadership and principles and were protected by the Communist-led Chinese Red Army.[18] Thus, the rural Chinese soviets were considered genuine workers' and peasants' soviets and the fiction of proletarian hegemony was maintained.

In conclusion, it may be said that the Comintern's insistent demand for the hegemony of the Communist party in preparing and carrying out the seizure of power in the "bourgeois-democratic" revolution is perhaps the most convincing support for the belief that the Communist party would not abdicate that hegemony once power had been seized. In the only practical test between 1928 and 1943 of the real meaning of the "democratic dictatorship of the proletariat and peasantry"—the case of the Chinese Soviet Republic—the Comintern frankly admitted the concentration of power in the hands of the Chinese Communist Party.

We have, then, following the Communist seizure of power in any type of society, a Communist dictatorship exercised through a system of soviets. Now we shall undertake to describe the uses and ultimate goals of Communist power.

PART FOUR

The Uses and Goals of Communist Power

XI. THE TRANSFORMATION OF SOCIETY

With the conquest of power successfully carried out, the Communist dictatorship was to undertake a number of far-reaching measures with the aim of establishing, sooner or later, the final, socialist stage in Marx's scheme of socio-economic development. This period, for Marx, Lenin, and the Comintern alike, was to witness the implementation and flowering of the fondest ideals of the Communist movement—the ennoblement of mankind in a world compounded of material plenty, peace, and equal rights for all. Manifesting a continuous rise to ever higher standards of human welfare and contentment, this period was to be the final stage in man's long journey from primitive communism. It was to possess an unlimited capacity for the satisfaction of the wants and desires of the future Communist man. It was, according to Communist theory, to be the best of all possible worlds.

SOCIAL CHANGE IN THE ADVANCED CAPITALIST SOCIETY

The stages of socialism and communism distinguished. Comintern materials distinguished between two phases within this final stage: a first, socialist phase and a higher, communist phase (the ultimate utopia). In making this distinction, Comintern writers were faithful to Lenin and Marx. It was Lenin who applied the terms "socialism" and "communism," respectively, to the "lower phase" and the "higher phase" of communism, as these latter terms were used by Marx in his *Critique of the Gotha Programme*.[1]

The outlines of the socialist phase are given succinctly in the Comintern Program of 1928.[2] At the beginning of this lower phase, human society, having only recently passed from the capitalist stage, still bears the economic, moral, and intellectual birthmarks of the former society, "from the womb of which it is emerging." A program of wholesale social reconstruction must be undertaken. Even after the creation of a socialist society replacing the former capitalist society, the productive capacity of the new society is not yet mature; distribution must continue to be on the basis of work, rather than on the basis of need, as it is to be later in the communist utopia. Although classes have been abolished, traces of former class divisions will exist for some time. Division of labor persists, as does the distinction between physical and mental labor. During the socialist phase, the antagonism between town and country will persist also, although progressively diminishing. Thus, imperfections and inequalities mar the socialist phase, and only with the removal of these flaws through the further building of socialism will the higher, communist phase be attained.

Government and class rule. It has been shown that the "dictatorship of the proletariat," supposedly established by the Communist seizure of power, was actually a one-party dictatorship exercised by the Communist party independently of the will of the proletariat, and that the soviets, created on the eve of the seizure of power as revolutionary organs of the civil war, were to become the constitutional organs in the new era. We may now examine more closely the nature of politics after the seizure of power.

It may be said at once that the business of administering a modern complex state, to the normal functions of which were now to be added enormously difficult tasks such as centralized economic planning and direction, was not given serious attention in Comintern materials. Yet any "dictatorship of the proletariat" was faced with the acute problem of obtaining sufficient skilled personnel from the ranks of precisely those classes whose intellectual growth, according to Communist claims, had been stunted during the capitalist epoch. Any serious Communist, reflecting upon this problem, must indeed have envied the debonair faith of the anarchists, who, by dispensing with the state, also dispensed with all questions of bureaucracy.

To meet the shortage of qualified "proletarian" personnel, the Program indicated that the new state was to combine a stopgap policy of enlisting the aid of former bourgeois civil servants with a long-range policy of developing socialist administrators through the Communists' own educational system. The Program advocated the utilization of the "organizing skills" of a certain part of the bourgeoisie, the former military officer corps, and the governmental bureaucracy, but only after all resistance from these classes had been quelled. Reference was made to the "technical intelligentsia," which, although brought up in bourgeois traditions, might be won in part and utilized in the work of socialist construction. Encouragement was to be given to any sympathetic or neutral elements among the intelligentsia, while subjecting these elements to the ideological influence of the proletariat, i.e., of the Communist party.[3]

Through a long-range training program, based upon its monopoly of education, the Communist state was able to look forward to a time when its personnel needs could be satisfied from the ranks of workers and "toilers." "Only to the extent that the proletariat [the Communist party] selects its own vanguard elements, for all these 'command posts' of socialist construction . . . will there be realized both the guarantee of victorious socialist construction and the guarantee against bureaucratic decay and class degeneracy."[4]

Comintern materials offer almost nothing on the system of justice and law that was to be inaugurated. It can safely be surmised that the tenets of Marxism-Leninism were to lie at the base of the new system. To safeguard the state and maintain internal order, all arms were to be concentrated in the hands of the proletariat.[5] The Red Guard, originating in the days of the armed uprising, was later to become transformed into a Red Army, which was to be a regular army and no longer an informal popular militia.[6] Only when the Communists had seized power in a number of big capitalist states would the danger of capitalist intervention become sufficiently reduced to permit the substitution of the regular army by a "people's" militia. But whatever the nature of the armed forces, these forces were to bear a class character and were to exclude from their ranks any members of the former exploiting classes.[7]

The temporary persistence of classes after the seizure of power was, as we know, expected to be one of the characteristics of the socialist stage. As long as classes existed, a class struggle would also exist, even in the period of the "proletarian dictatorship." The "exploiters" and other "enemies of the people" were to be immediately deprived of political rights.[8] Ruthless war was to be waged by the dictatorship against the "consistent enemies of the working class," among whom were identified the big bourgeoisie, the landowners, and those parts of the officer corps and the governmental bureaucracy remaining loyal to the former ruling classes.[9] Presumably, either extermination or at least a passive acceptance of the new order were the choices confronting those classified as "enemies of the people."

In relation to the question of the political privileges to be received by the various classes, the following seems clear: political authority and leadership concentrated in the vanguard of the proletariat, the Communist party (the *wielder* of the "proletarian dictatorship"); political privileges bestowed upon the proletariat, as well as its allies and the "neutralized" groups in the seizure of power (the *recipients* of "proletarian democracy"); and denial of political rights to class enemies (the *victims* of "proletarian dictatorship" and *nonrecipients* of "proletarian democracy").

According to the Comintern Program, the superior position which theory accorded the proletariat in the new era was to be bolstered, if necessary, by granting the proletariat a number of "temporary advantages."[10] Presumably, disproportionate representation for the proletariat in the soviets might be one of the advantages.[11] But, the Program continued, the proletariat was to utilize its special position not to maintain and foster narrow class interests but to unite with itself the other categories of "toilers" in the common aim of obliterating all class distinctions.[12]

A clearer picture of the political relationship between the proletariat and other social groups, following the establishment of the "dictatorship of the proletariat," was drawn by Manuilsky in two speeches, one delivered at the Sixth Comintern Congress and the other at the Seventh. In both instances Manuilsky occupied the responsible post of reporter on the situation in the USSR.[13]

His report at the Sixth Congress is much the more candid, and therefore the more valuable.[14] Although directing his attention to the USSR, he clearly implied the applicability of his remarks to all future "proletarian dictatorships." His speech was in the nature of a high-level critique and rebuttal of "Trotskyist" errors. A fairly clear picture of the distribution of privileges among the social groups under the Communist dictatorships emerges. For Manuilsky, "proletarian democracy" was above all else class democracy and meant, certainly in the initial period following the seizure of power, the jealous retention of power in the hands of the proletariat. Whether or not this also meant minority rule was, for him, an irrelevant issue. In Russia, Manuilsky admitted, the "proletarian dictatorship" was the dictatorship of a minority acting in the interests of the majority of "toilers." If the ruling minority had not acted in the interests of the "toilers," Manuilsky claimed, the resulting dictatorship would have been unpopular and unsteady and could not have lasted long.

Manuilsky further clarified the hegemony attributed to the proletariat by pointing out that the alliance with part of the peasantry in the revolution did not necessitate the sharing of power with that class. He denied that the "proletarian dictatorship" was a bloc between two classes on the basis of complete political equality, and defined it rather as a form of government based on cooperation with and judicious concessions to the peasantry, especially in the economic sphere.

The question arises, at what point, if ever, were political privileges to be extended to other classes? Manuilsky at the Sixth Congress stated that the privileges of "proletarian democracy" could and would be extended to additional social groups, given the following conditions: absence of pressure from the outside capitalist world against the socialist state; the willingness of other classes unreservedly to accept proletarian leadership and socialist ideals; and the ability of the Communist party to train the "toiling masses"

politically and to raise them closer to its own level. Given these
conditions, Manuilsky said, the stage of the disappearance of
classes would be reached and, accordingly, "proletarian dictatorship" could be transformed into the most widespread form of labor
democracy.

At the Seventh Comintern Congress, Manuilsky clarified the
meaning of an extension of "proletarian democracy" to other social
groups. In his view, a great expansion of "proletarian democracy"
had occurred in the USSR with the "historical decision of the
Seventh Congress of Soviets—adopted on Comrade Stalin's
initiative—to introduce in our country equal suffrage and direct
and secret ballot."[15] If the introduction of universal, equal, direct,
and secret suffrage in the USSR with the Constitution of 1936 is
a case of the extension of "proletarian democracy," then it is clear
that any such extensions would have no effect upon the position of
the Communist party as the real ruler. If, as Manuilsky declared,
the "Soviet democracy" of the USSR was a higher form of democracy, superior to "bourgeois democracy," then it is again obvious
how undemocratic "proletarian democracy" in practice was. The
endorsement given to the USSR as "a state of fully developed
democracy"[16] should clarify once and for all the profoundly misleading nature of the Comintern's use of the phrases "proletarian dictatorship" and "proletarian democracy."

As will be indicated below, the Comintern expected the role of
the Communist party to increase enormously after the seizure of
power and the assumption of the duties of a ruling political party.
These duties were extraordinarily comprehensive, and it may well
be that the Communist party set for itself a more far-reaching
alteration of society than any other party has ever done. The tasks
and functions of every dictatorship of the Communist party may be
broadly identified as follows:

1. Political: destruction of the sources and instruments of power
enjoyed by the bourgeois class, as well as by the clergy and the
aristocracy; strengthening of the power of the Communist party
and its support among the population.

2. Economic: constriction and eventual abolition of the capitalist system (private ownership of the means of production and the free play of market forces); building of a socialist economy with central planning.

3. Social: construction of a nonclass society of toilers on the basis of the socialization of the means of production.

4. Cultural: entrenchment of Marxism-Leninism as the only truth; displacement of bourgeois codes of morality and religious systems by a code of Communist ethics; achievement of basic changes in human outlook and behavior.

5. International: defense of the Communist state against capitalist aggression; close alliance and cooperation with the Soviet Union and the world revolutionary movement; championship of the cause of the toiling and exploited masses everywhere.

For the Comintern these tasks justified the existence of the "dictatorship of the proletariat" and the expanding role of the Communist party.[17] As Manuilsky indicated at the Sixth Comintern Congress, the tasks of the party after the seizure of power were to become considerably more varied and extensive than in the period before the seizure of power.[18] At the Sixteenth Congress of the CPSU in 1930, Stalin had stressed the need for a steady growth in the power of the Communist state, and this point was taken up subsequently by Comintern writers.[19]

Stalin's remarks on the state are especially interesting because he addressed himself to the specific question of the ultimate disappearance of the state. Friedrich Engels, the collaborator of Marx, had stated in a famous passage that the state would "wither away" during the completion of its task of reconstructing society. The Comintern Program endorsed Engels and asserted that the state, "being the embodiment of class domination, dies out as classes die out."[20] Up until 1930 the process of "dying out" was probably interpreted by most Communists as a gradual dimunition of the state's power as the socialist reconstruction of society progressed. The primarily coercive institutions of the state were to "wither away"—the military forces, police, penal institutions, and the like. Stalin, however, in 1930 declared that the Communist state was to grow and reach the greatest strength ever obtained by any state in history, and only then would it begin to "wither away."[21] But precisely how such an all-powerful state would suffer an ultimate eclipse was never explained.

Economic and social measures. The broad policies underlying the economic and social activity of the "proletarian dictatorship" are easily identified and appear consistent with the spirit of Marxism. Private ownership of the means of production of economic goods, considered as harmful to continued social betterment, was to be curtailed and finally eliminated altogether. The business of substituting public ownership for private ownership was not to be a single abrupt and complete act, but rather a process of some duration. The administration of nationalized property was to be centralized, and overall planned coordination of the various economic units was to replace the anarchy of capitalistic competition. These policies are more or less clearly expressed in Part Four of the Comintern Program, which is entitled "The Period of Transition from Capitalism to Socialism, and the Dictatorship of the Proletariat."[22]

In industry, the Program demanded the confiscation and "proletarian nationalization" of all large industrial enterprises (factories, plants, mines, and electric power stations) belonging to the capitalists. All state and municipal land and enterprises were also to be handed over to the soviets. In one short passage the Program clearly and simply called for the organization of workers' management in industry. But in the sentence immediately following, it complicated matters by referring not only to the establishment of state organs for such management but also to the "closest participation" of the trade unions in management and to an "appropriate role" to be assigned to factory councils. The thorny problem of delimiting spheres of competence for the state organs, trade unions, and factory councils was not fully clarified, either in the Program or in other Comintern materials.[23]

Only the specific functions of the trade unions receive some degree of clarification. The trade unions were described as the "main lever" of the state and a "school of Communism," drawing masses of workers into practical experience in managing industry.

Linked with the state apparatus and influencing its work, the trade unions were to safeguard the everyday interests of the proletariat, to combat bureaucratic abuses in the state apparatus, and to produce, from their ranks, leaders in the work of building socialism.[24]

The outlines of labor legislation are sketched in the Program: a working day of seven hours, and, in certain industries harmful to the health of the worker, of six hours; a five-day work-week in countries with "developed productive forces"; in the future, shorter working days as labor productivity increased; as a rule, no night work or work in harmful trades for women; prohibition of child labor; a maximum day of six hours for young employees up to eighteen years of age, with opportunities for combining employment with schooling. A broad program of social insurance, including insurance for sickness, old age, accident, and unemployment, was to be provided at state expense and administered by the insured. In nonnationalized industry, the private owners would be responsible for this insurance.[25]

In agriculture, immediate confiscation and "proletarian nationalization" was to be applied to all large property in land. Nationalization of all remaining land was to occur subsequently and gradually. Nationalization was to apply not only to the soil but also to any buildings, machinery, livestock, mills, and other inventory on the land. The buying and selling of land even before nationalization was to be forbidden, with the purpose of keeping the land in the hands of the peasants and of preventing speculators from acquiring it.[26]

Mention may be made here of criticisms of the policy of a gradual, rather than an immediate, nationalization of all land.[27] Commenting on the Draft Program of 1928, V. Karpinskii criticized the policy of gradualism and failed to see a reasonable distinction between the condition resulting from the prohibition of trade in land and that resulting from an immediate and complete nationalization of all land.[28] The policy of gradualism was promoted chiefly by the fear of antagonizing the peasantry and transforming it into an active enemy of the new order.[29] Bukharin cynically acknowledged that the prohibition of the sale and purchase of land was "equal to 90–95 percent of nationalization of the land."[30] Denying that Communists were afraid of the peasants, he insisted that, immediately upon the seizure of power in the "proletarian" revolution, the peasants must receive assurance of ownership of their land. Bukharin quoted Marx in support of this point of view. The prohibition of trade in land, according to Bukharin, simply reinforced the guarantee of ownership.

Plans for the disposal of the confiscated land reflected conflicting desires, on the one hand, to preserve large farms intact for collectivized farming and, on the other hand, to win support from the poorer peasants for the new regime by dividing amongst them some of the nationalized land. Estates of special economic importance were to remain undivided and become state, or soviet, farms. Other land of the landlords, especially that formerly tilled by peasants on a tenant basis, was to be parceled out for use, but not ownership, to the poor peasants and to some of the so-called middle peasants. Economic expediency and the need to "neutralize" the peasantry and to win it over to the proletarian regime were to determine the quantity of land that was so distributed.

One category of measures was aimed at improving the lot of those poorest peasants who were regarded as the natural allies of the proletariat. These measures included the annulment of the debts of the "exploited strata" of the peasantry, the combating of usury, the abolition of all agreements resulting in any form of human bondage, and exemption from taxation.

Another category of measures aimed at the improvement of agricultural production: rural electrification, manufacture of tractors, development of improved seed and livestock, extensive credits, and, above all, propaganda on behalf of the advantages of large-scale farming.

Peasant cooperatives of all types (sales, purchasing, credit, and producers') were pictured as the best means of carrying the peasantry over into socialism.[31] Agricultural cooperatives were, therefore, to expand, although "capitalistic" elements in them were to be eradicated.[32] Guided by the state, the agricultural cooperatives would become "one of the principal levers" for the collectivization of the countryside.[33]

Measures in other spheres of the economy may be briefly listed. Under the new regime transportation and communications systems were to fall entirely into the hands of the state. In the financial sphere, the theme of centralization was made quite explicit. There was to be one central state bank, subordinating to itself all the nationalized private, state, and municipal banks of the old regime. Debts owed by the preceding government to capitalists at home and abroad were to be repudiated. Foreign trade was also to become a state monopoly. Domestic trade was to be largely nationalized; the Program stated that wholesale trade enterprises and large retail trade enterprises were to be taken over by the soviets. Among proposed housing reforms were the confiscation of large dwelling units, presumably including apartment houses, hotels, etc., the administration of the confiscated units by the local soviets,[34] the elimination of class residential districts by the settlement of workers in "bourgeois" areas, and the extensive development of public housing construction.[35]

The above economic policies were reflected in the several national programs drawn up by the various Communist parties. In these matters, party programs did not differ essentially from the Comintern Program of 1928.[36]

Having considered the policies and practices of the dictatorship in the socio-economic field, we may now pursue a second line of inquiry. Would the pattern of economic development in the future Communist dictatorships follow that sequence of stages which, historically, Soviet Russia had experienced since 1917? As is well known, Soviet Russia had passed through the following economic phases before World War II: an initial period from November, 1917, to roughly the middle of 1918, during which efforts were made to secure state control over only the "commanding heights" of the economy, while the nonnationalized sector of the economy was relatively extensive; the phase of so-called War Communism, from mid-1918 to March, 1921, characterized by emergency economic measures designed to meet serious military threats; the phase of the New Economic Policy, or NEP, from 1921 to 1928, in effect a partial restoration of private enterprise in production and especially in trade, but with the "commanding heights" of the economy remaining in the hands of the state; and, finally, the Five-Year-Plan period, which witnessed the elimination of almost all private enterprise and the establishment of a highly centralized system of direction and control over the entire economy. The interesting question of the universal applicability of these stages to other countries after the seizure of power was discussed in the Comintern in conjunction with the debate on the Draft Program in 1928.

Respecting the inevitability of a phase similar to that of War Communism in Soviet Russia, there was sharp discussion and disagreement before and during the Sixth Congress. The dominant position, which ultimately found reflection in the Program, was that War Communism, while not inevitable, would be a probable stage in the economic development of the new dictatorships under certain circumstances. These circumstances included such developments as prolonged civil war or military intervention by capitalist states against the new dictatorships. According to Bukharin, a period of War Communism was not to be considered as possible only during the early period of the "proletarian dictatorship"; the necessity might arise at any time.[37] According to Manuilsky, at the same Congress, there even existed the possibility of a return in the Soviet Union to the methods of War Communism, given a sufficiently serious external or internal threat.[38] War Communism was defined in the Program as "the organization of rational consumption for the goal of military defense," in which there would be "intensified pressure" upon the capitalist class and a "more or less complete liquidation of free trade and of market relations." The Program affirmed that War Communism, the purpose of which was the facilitating of a military effort, could not be viewed as a "normal" economic policy.[39]

This view of War Communism as a temporary response to a serious political threat was upheld by both Bukharin and Stalin. Stalin had dealt with the question in his speech of July 5, 1928, to a plenum of the Central Committee of the CPSU. At that time, while rejecting the view that War Communism would inevitably follow the seizure of power, he agreed that the wording of the Draft Program should be changed from an affirmation of the "possibility" of capitalist military intervention and War Communism to the statement of the "probability" of these develop-ments.[40] Bukharin upheld this same line at the Sixth Comintern Congress.[41]

On the other hand, Eugene Varga, a commissar in the Hungarian Soviet Republic of 1919 and subsequently a leading Soviet economist, maintained both before and during the Sixth Congress that War Communism was a much more probable development in the future Communist dictatorships than the Program would indicate. In the case of future Communist states geographically isolated from the Soviet Union, he believed that the phase of War Communism would be necessary for political reasons and also for economic reasons, i.e., the disintegration of the economy before and during the seizure of power.[42] The only way to maintain any kind of production during the initial period following the seizure of power, he affirmed, would be to place all of the economy in the hands of the state by eliminating all private enterprise. Varga's position, for which he was chided by Bukharin, was derived from a very realistic expectation of great political and economic weak-nesses in a new Communist state. Power, he warned, although once gained could still be lost, as in the case of the Finnish, Hungarian, and Bavarian Communist regimes in 1918 and 1919. To introduce the New Economic Policy before the internal enemy had been fully defeated would be equal to support of counterrevolution.[43]

It is important to note that Varga expressly directed his remarks to those future Communist states that would be geographically isolated from the USSR.[44] In a footnote to an article, Varga suggested a different path of economic development for a prole-tarian state bordering on the USSR. Such a state, he wrote, would be able "immediately after the establishment of the dictatorship to join its economy with that of the USSR."[45] This intriguing statement, modestly buried in a footnote, may possibly have re-

flected a general understanding in the Comintern about the fate of
the economies of Polish, Finnish, Chinese, and other future contiguous (to the Soviet Union)"dictatorships of the proletariat."

Unlike War Communism, the New Economic Policy received
endorsement as an inevitable and universal phase in the economic
development of future Communist states. The essence of NEP was
often described as the partial persistence of "market relations,"
a term used by the Comintern to denote economic activity largely
built upon the existence, albeit within certain limits, of private
property, free enterprise, free trade, and the use of money in
buying and selling and in the payment of labor.[46] Market relations
constituted a partial antithesis of a system of economic activity
based on a fully nationalized and fully planned economy. The
Program stated that some market relations would be temporarily
preserved, following the Communist seizure of power, even in the
most advanced capitalist countries, but apparently to the smallest
degree in England. Some delegates to the Sixth Congress revived
a statement by Lenin to the effect that in England it might be
possible to proceed directly to the "socialistic exchange of products," without preserving, even temporarily, capitalist market
relations, but Bukharin considered this view of Lenin to be no
longer tenable.[47] It should be noted that Stalin, already in July,
1928, had endorsed NEP as "an inevitable phase of the socialist
revolution in all countries."[48]

All Comintern materials agreed that NEP would ultimately be
abandoned for a planned economy based upon the complete
nationalization of all means of production. The Program of 1928,
written as it was on the eve of the Russian First Five-Year Plan, did
not describe fully the nature and details of the planning mechanism.
But there is no doubt, in the light of the Comintern's subsequent
multitudinous endorsements of the achievements of the Five-Year
Plans in the Soviet Union, that this path was accepted as the
correct one. Moreover, Comintern materials indicate clearly that
the Soviet Union would not only be the economic model for future
Communist dictatorships but would actively help their development toward a socialist society. Manuilsky, for example, promised

the English Communists that the USSR would help in the building of socialism in England.[49]

One final line of inquiry remains. How dominant and comprehensive was the leadership of the Soviet Union to be in the field of economic development? Did the Comintern, in endorsing the Russian path of development, make allowances for reasonable national variations in the phases of War Communism and NEP and afterward? And was it generally assumed that the Soviet Union would always remain the "most progressive" state, in the sense of being the most advanced along the path of socialist achievement? The direct evidence·is skimpy, but what little exists, when taken together with much indirect evidence, suggests that by 1934, the year of the so-called victory of socialism in the Soviet Union, a turn had been made in Comintern views on these questions. First consider, for example, Bukharin's statement at the Sixth Congress in 1928 that War Communism and NEP under future "proletarian dictatorships" would not be "simple reproductions" of these phases as they had appeared in Soviet Russia. Rather, he said, there would be "numerous variations" of these economic stages. Bukharin went even further at the Sixth Congress to assert that, just as there were varieties of capitalism, there would be different national types of socialism, which would persist for a considerable period of time. However, he cautioned, the methods of building socialism would not differ "completely" from those developed in the USSR.[50] Quite significantly, in 1928 Bukharin foresaw the future displacement of the USSR from its position as the most progressive country, as a result of "proletarian" revolutions in advanced capitalist countries such as Germany. Despite the fact that Communist power had developed first in Soviet Russia, the more advanced starting point provided by German capitalism would permit a Communist-controlled Germany to take the leadership in economic matters. Lenin, Bukharin stated, "had spoken and written many times that after the 'proletarian' revolution in Western Europe, we *again* will be transformed into a backward country, despite the fact that we are now the most advanced country."[51] This remarkable reminder by Bukharin, which would probably have been regarded as treasonable in 1935, is almost unique in Comintern materials from 1928 on. Manuilsky expressed himself in somewhat similar fashion at the Sixth Congress (see p. 272), as did no less a Stalinist than Molotov in a speech printed in *Inprecor* in 1929. Molotov, having referred to the value of the Soviet Russian experience for future "proletarian dictatorships," spoke as follows:

It must not be forgotten, however, that in the case of a victory of the proletariat in one or more advanced capitalist countries, the Soviet Union would come to figure as a backward country which could undoubtedly learn much in regard to the socialist construction of the proletarians of the countries in question.[52]

These remarks of Bukharin, Manuilsky, and Molotov, three of the most important leaders of the Comintern in 1928 and 1929, emphasize that the spokesmen of the Comintern at that time seriously entertained the idea of a future displacement of the USSR as the most progressive country in the world. It is evident that they still appreciated profoundly the fact that Russia had not been an advanced capitalist country in 1917, but rather had been, as the Draft Program of the Comintern indicated, a country of medium or modest capitalist development.

The political implications of these remarks for the continuance of the hegemony of the CPSU in the international revolutionary movement were not even suggested by the two Comintern dignitaries. One can only recognize that by 1928 it would have been exceedingly difficult to displace the CPSU as the leader of the Comintern. And a voluntary abdication of ideological and political leadership on the part of the CPSU seems almost unthinkable.

Certainly by 1935 the Comintern's approach to Soviet Russia had altered. It is extremely doubtful that the earlier views of Bukharin and Molotov could have been expressed at that time. The limitless adoration and adulation heaped by the Seventh Congress upon the Soviet Union and its Communist Party and upon Stalin could have meant only that such views would have been at the very least incongruous, not to say politically dangerous. To be sure, the Soviet Union had been praised in 1928, but such praise had been far short of reflecting a cult of worship. The spirit of the Seventh Congress of 1935 could tolerate only the view that the Soviet Union would always be the pathfinder in the march toward ultimate Communism. Although no one explicitly said as much, the so-called victory of socialism in the USSR, claimed in 1934 by the Seventeenth Congress of the CPSU, did of course elevate the Soviet Union a qualitative notch above any other state in which the seizure of power would occur and in which a NEP period would begin. Considering the much greater degree of ideological conformity and subservience to Soviet Russia within the Comintern in 1935 as contrasted with 1928, one can only conclude that a similar degree of practical conformity to the Soviet Russian model would have followed any Communist seizure of power, even in an advanced capitalist country.

Society and culture. Relatively little information can be found in Comintern materials about such matters as the family, education, religion, or culture in the broad sense. The Comintern's preoccupation with economics and politics crowded out any thoroughgoing discussion of these matters. But the Program of 1928 does give the barest outlines of the policies and reforms that the Communists expected to pursue in these fields. No subsequently published material contradicted the salient features of the social and cultural revolution described in the Program for the phase of socialism.

Respecting family relationships, the Program outlined the following principles and policies: complete equality between men and women before the law and in social life, a fundamental reworking of the law of marriage and of the family, the "recognition of maternity as a social function," the protection of motherhood and infants, the initiation of the social care and upbringing of children in state-operated crèches, kindergartens, and children's homes, and the creation of institutions such as public kitchens and laundries for the gradual relief of women from burdensome domestic work. A planned educational drive was to be undertaken against the ideology and traditions of "female bondage."[53] These brief statements do not in themselves signify either the approval or the disapproval by the Comintern of the family as a permanent social institution. Such radical proposals as the social care and raising of children would certainly reduce greatly the significance of the family. These proposals do indicate also that the Comintern sought to end the dependency of the mother upon the father and to create the basis for self-sufficiency of women. The designation of maternity as a "social function" probably meant, not the disintegration of marriage, but a recognition of the responsibility of the state to share in some measure the expenses of motherhood and child care. It should be noted here that Comintern speakers enthusiastically endorsed Soviet family and marriage arrangements.[54]

In the field of education, the Program demanded an end to the "capitalist monopoly" and instructed the working class to seize all schools, from the elementary through the university level. The Program contrasted the position of the bourgeoisie, which on the eve of its revolution against feudalism had stood culturally at a higher level than the feudal ruling classes, with that of the proletariat, which had been culturally stunted under capitalism. The intellectual development of the proletariat had therefore to follow, rather than precede, the taking of power into its hands.[55] The new proletarian, i.e., Communist, monopoly in education was to be made more effective by such additional measures as the nationalization of the printing industry, the creation of a state monopoly over the publication of newspapers, books, and periodicals, and the nationalization of motion picture houses, theaters, and similar public buildings. With these nationalized means of "intellectual production" there would be created a "new socialist culture on a proletarian class base."[56]

The goals of education during the socialist phase, ranging from the more immediate to the broader, long-term aims, may be summarized as follows: the creation, largely from the ranks of the proletariat, of that body of skilled specialists deemed necessary to the proper functioning of a complex socialist society; the elevation of the general cultural level of the proletarian class; the reeducation of the remaining classes, with the goal of a complete obliteration of all class distinctions; and, in the language of the Program, a "mass change of people."[57]

The Program, specifically mentioning the need for engineers, technicians, and "organizers," as well as specialists in military affairs, science, and art, revealed a strong interest in the development of a technical-scientific intelligentsia. But the broader concern was, of course, with the establishment of Marxism-Leninism as the sole legitimate philosophy and with the engineering of a cultural revolution based upon this philosophy. The engineers of this revolution were repeatedly defined as the proletariat led by its Communist party. The proletariat, or, more realistically, the Communist party, was to utilize the teachings of Marx, Engels, Lenin, and Stalin to eradicate the traditional division of the working class into "advanced" and "backward" sections, to emancipate the peasantry from the backwardness of the countryside, and to re-educate the petty bourgeoisie away from the prejudices of capitalist ownership. The responsibilities of the Communist party and the proletariat extended beyond the proletarian class; other classes were to be transformed into socialist-minded "toilers."[58]

The Program assigned a special place in the cultural revolution to a systematic and undeviating struggle against religion, which was once more dubbed in unoriginal fashion the "opium of the people." No policy of outright suppression of churches and religious bodies was demanded, but religion was to be deprived of state support and denied any participation in the state-operated educational institutions. It is not clear whether religious bodies might conduct their own schools. More ominously, the Program called for the suppression of all counterrevolutionary activity of the churches. Any church or religion that formerly had enjoyed a privileged position was to be reduced to equality with other churches or religions. While granting liberty of worship, the "dictatorship of the proletariat" was to conduct anti-religious propaganda with all available means. No specific mention was made of a balancing right of religious propaganda. Religion, as a system of ideas seeking to explain the universe and man's destiny, was to be replaced by "scientific materialism" as the new and correct world view.[59]

The end result of the educative process undertaken by the Communist dictatorship was to be what the Program termed "a mass change of people." This rather awkward expression, a literal translation of the Russian phrase, *massovoe izmenenie liudei*, was given in the English text of the Program published in *Inprecor* as "a mass change of human nature."[60] Whether this is an accurate translation is doubtful, for Marxist-Leninists have never recognized the validity of the concept of human nature apart from classes, and the term "human nature" is not to be found in the Program. Instead, the Program referred to the "nature" of this or that *class*. In other words, the so-called human nature of an individual depended upon the class to which he belonged. Let us look at the authoritative statement in the Program:

Being in capitalist society a class economically exploited, politically oppressed, and *culturally choked*, the working class only in the transition period, only *after its conquest of state power*, only by destroying the bourgeois monopoly of education and by mastering all science, only in the experience of the greatest constructive work transforms its own nature *[priroda]*. For the mass awakening of Communist consciousness and for the very cause of socialism, there is necessary a *mass change in people*, which is possible only in the practical movement, in the revolution.[61]

Changes in class nature, accomplished during the construction of a socialist society, were not to be confined to the working class. "The proletariat, however, transforms in the process of the revolution not its own nature, but also the nature of *other classes*, first of all the numerous petty-bourgeois strata of town and village, especially the toiling strata of the peasantry."[62] The transforming of people through Communist education and struggle against "antiproletarian" ideologies, was, according to the Program, one of the aspects of the struggle to remove forever the class divisions of society. Purposive and comprehensive, to say the least, was to be the educational program of the Communist dictatorship.

National minorities and colonies. To the Comintern it was patently inconceivable that a satisfactory solution of the national and colonial question could be realized within the framework of the capitalist system.[63] It is in this light that the Comintern's position on minorities and subjugated peoples must be examined.

Once more it is in the Program that the fundamental principles were set forth. This document recognized the right of each nation (*natsiia*), irrespective of race, to full self-determination, including independent statehood. It condemned any kind of discrimination against any nationality, nation, or race, all of whom were to enjoy complete equality with one another. Apart from these broad statements, in which the precise distinction, if any, between "nationality" and "nation," was not clarified, the Program spelled out more fully the measures to be implemented following the Communist seizure of power. The free development of the cultures of those national minorities liberated from capitalism was to be supported by the new proletarian state. Each new dictatorship was to carry out a "consistent proletarian line in the matter of the development of the content of these cultures."[64] That this content was to become "socialist" was reaffirmed in the statement which called for the "socialist transformation" of all formerly oppressed territories, regions, and colonies, "with the goal of creating a lasting basis for genuine and complete national equality."[65]

Was it expected that a young "proletarian dictatorship" would grant full independence, including separation from itself, to a national minority or colony if that minority or colony rejected socialism? On this interesting question, Otto Kuusinen shed some light in his speech before the Presidium of the ECCI in June, 1931. It was not true, he said, that Communists recognized the right of self-determination of peoples only on condition that they agree to "sovietization"; on the contrary, Communists supported this right unqualifiedly. But, he added, "we are convinced that the free right of peoples to self-determination is impossible to achieve and to secure otherwise than on a Soviet basis."[66] Thus genuine self-determination requires a special prerequisite, which can only mean a Communist dictatorship. Obviously the question is not faced fairly, and it seems more than probable that a victorious Communist government would thwart any aspirations for independence by a nationality or colony under non-Communist leadership. The British Communist leader, Harry Pollitt, promised in 1933 that a proletarian dictatorship in his country would remove British troops from Britain's colonies and offer full independence to them. In the next breath he stated that the British revolutionary government would help India, China, Africa, and Ireland to organize and develop a socialist industrial system and to reorganize agriculture on socialist principles.[67] Apparently Pollitt never seriously entertained the notion of any alternative development, i.e., outside of the Communist camp, for the liberated colonies.

In a discussion of the fate of colonies and national minorities "liberated" by a Communist seizure of power in the imperialist country, it must be remembered, of course, that normally the Communist party of the colony or national minority would have been accustomed, before the "liberation," to enjoy close collaboration with and guidance from the Communist party in the mother country. Would not such supervision continue and probably strengthen after the seizure of power in the mother country? Certainly the Communist party in the imperialist country would be inclined to persist in such guidance, justifying its continued tutelage by pointing to the economic inferiority of the colony.

National unity for a people previously divided by the political frontiers of capitalist states would also be made possible as a result of victorious "proletarian" revolutions in those states, according to the Comintern. For example, a German Communist program of 1930 asserted that a victorious Communist revolution in Western Europe would satisfy the desires of those German minorities, presumably in neighboring France, Poland, and Czechoslovakia, which would "express the wish" for union with a Soviet Germany.[68] The same promise was made in a German Communist program of 1934,[69] in an attempt to compete with the nationalist appeals of the political right.

In summary, we may say that, while the Comintern proclaimed the unconditional right of oppressed nationalities to satisfy their national aspirations for liberation, separation, or unification, it pointed to the Communist path of development as the only road to the complete and final solution of the nationality problem. The incompatibility between the assertion of an unconditional right to choose and the assertion of the existence of one single correct choice is obvious. One feels here that the Communists tacitly held to the conviction that it would be quite justifiable to compel nationalities and colonies to limit their political aspirations and to accept only such arrangements as those that recognized the existence of Communist dictatorship.

Relations with the USSR and other Communist states. There is unmistakable evidence, both in the Program and in other Comintern literature, that future Communist dictatorships were not to remain politically or economically isolated but were to constitute a more or less closely knit "Communist bloc." Entry into this community of Communist-ruled states was apparently to occur immediately or soon after the seizure of power. In fact, the Communist parties, prior to becoming ruling parties, would have already become accustomed to participation in an international bloc of Communist parties, i.e., the Comintern. The future bloc of Communist states would be held together in part by this common past experience, but also by common ideals, institutions, and aspirations and, furthermore, by the hostility and menace presented by the capitalist world. This future bloc of states was to be, as the Program stated in one place, an "ever-growing federation of Soviet republics."[70]

Eventually, a "dictatorship of the world proletariat" was to be achieved. The Program pictured the process as follows:

This world-wide dictatorship can be realized only as the result of the victory of socialism in separate countries or groups of countries, when the newly created proletarian republics enter into a federated relationship *[sviaz']* with those already existing, when the network *[set']* of these federated unions *[ob"edineniia]* grows and embraces also the colonies freeing themselves from the yoke of imperialism; when the federation of such republics has finally become the *union [soiuz] of soviet socialist republics of the world*, which will realize the unification *[ob"edinenie]* of humanity under the hegemony of the international proletariat organized as a state [literally: state-organized proletariat].[71]

The phrase "network of these federated unions" seems to suggest the existence, for a time at least, of several different groupings or unions of soviet republics. This implies also that the USSR would exist as merely one of these unions. Yet the programs of the various

Communist parties consistently spoke of the establishment of direct ties between a new Communist dictatorship and the Soviet Union immediately upon a victorious seizure of power. Presumably, the existence of regional federations would not rule out direct ties between individual members of a federation and the USSR. It seems logical to believe that, for convenience's sake, regional multistate federations were expected to appear, following simultaneous Communist seizures of power over a broad geographical area embracing several countries. For example, there might be a federation for Scandinavia and another for the Balkans.[72]

Various party programs published in Western European countries made a special point of promising these close contacts. An election manifesto issued in 1929 by the Communist Party of Great Britain included federation with the USSR as one of its campaign planks.[73] The German Party program of 1934, outlining the Communist solution to Nazi oppression, called for a "fraternal union" with the USSR.[74] The exact nature of such a union with the USSR was, unfortunately, never explained. Would a Soviet Republic of Germany join the USSR on the same basis as the existing constituent republics of the USSR and recognize, among other things, Moscow as the capital of the union? Or would a certain definite measure of autonomy be enjoyed by Germany? Or would a Soviet Germany simply enter into an economic, political, and military alliance with the USSR?[75] Questions of this type were simply never raised or answered in public Comintern materials.

Whatever obscurities becloud the picture of the constitutional relationships between the USSR and future soviet republics, and the relationships of those republics with one another, there is clarity on other points. First, the traditions of Comintern relationships would undoubtedly weigh heavily upon new Communist states and would tend to support continued hegemony by the CPSU. Second, all soviet republics, taken together, would constitute a fraternal Communist bloc and any possible differences within this bloc were clearly expected to be overshadowed by the differences between the Communist bloc as a whole and the capitalist bloc, so long as capitalist states existed. Third, important

political and economic ties would be created amongst the new
soviet republics and with the USSR. A British Communist Party
program of 1935 stated that future economic exchange between
Soviet Britain and other soviet republics, including the USSR,
would involve British exports of coal and machinery and British
imports of food and raw materials.[76] In 1930 a German Party
program promised political and economic ties between a Soviet
Germany and the USSR, "on the basis of which the factories of
Soviet Germany will deliver industrial products to the Soviet Union
and receive food and raw materials from the Soviet Union in
return."[77] Fourth, it is clear that, whatever the precise nature of
the relationship between future soviet republics and the USSR
immediately following the seizure of power, eventually there was
expected to be a merger of all soviet republics into a world federation. Although Comintern materials did not explain the meaning
of "federation," it can be inferred, from the description of the
USSR as a federated state, that a federation for Communists
means much more centralization of power than exists in such a
federal republic as the United States. The continued ascendancy
of the Soviet Union in this world federation, while never explicitly
stated, for obvious reasons, in Comintern materials, was certainly
more to be expected than not, especially in the light of the increasing adulation accorded the USSR in the last fifteen years of
Comintern history.

SOCIAL CHANGE IN THE SOCIETIES OF MEDIUM CAPITALIST DEVELOPMENT

The higher type of societies of medium capitalist development. The reader
will recall that within the category of societies exhibiting a medium
level of capitalist development, there was in Comintern usage a
further subdivision. One group, more advanced politically and
economically in the judgment of the Comintern, was thought to
be confronted with a "proletarian" revolution, albeit one during
which a significant number of so-called "bourgeois-democratic"
tasks were to be solved. The other was considered less advanced

and was assigned a "bourgeois-democratic" revolution, which would, however, develop later into a "proletarian" revolution.

Poland and Hungary may be used as major examples of the first group, since the most detailed evidence exists concerning them. On the important subject of social change after the Communist seizure of power, however, Comintern materials offer less information for these countries than for the advanced capitalist countries. The Comintern, which always placed its major emphasis upon the latter type of countries, quite naturally outlined in some detail, as we have seen, the activities of future Communist dictatorships in these countries. It apparently regarded as unnecessary a largely similar exposition in the case of countries of medium capitalist development that were also confronted with a "proletarian" revolution.

In what respects was the transformation in these societies to resemble the transformation in the advanced capitalist countries following the Communist seizure of power? Communist dictatorships, as we have seen, were to be set up in both types of country.[78] In the economic sphere, the same broad sequence of stages—NEP, socialism, and Communism—were to be followed. War Communism would be a probable phase, as in the case of the advanced capitalist society. The cultural revolution was, of course, to be based upon the same materialist philosophy and was to pursue the same ends. In its foreign policy the Communist dictatorship in the country of medium capitalist development was expected to align itself with the Communist bloc.[79]

What seem to be the major features of the socialist transformation in the countries of medium capitalist development that distinguish this transformation from that of the more advanced capitalist countries? These distinguishing features appear to be twofold in nature: the relatively slower tempo of development toward socialism and Communism, and the relatively greater magnitude of certain problems. The difference in tempo is readily understandable. Progress toward a socialist economy would naturally be slower than in the advanced capitalist countries, for the economic point of departure in the countries of medium capitalist development would be at a lower level. Less large-scale industry, a greater proportion of small enterprises, less capacity to produce capital goods, less centralization—all these would be characteristic initially of the industrial sector of the economy. Similarly in agriculture, the presence here of "semi-feudal remnants" was often discussed in Comintern materials. On the basis of this relative economic backwardness, it seems valid to conclude that the essentially transitional stage of the New Economic Policy would be of greater duration for this type of society. The tempo of socialist construction would be, in the judgment of the Comintern Program, "relatively slow."[80]

One point deserves special attention here. Could the inferior economic development of these countries not be offset to some degree by the helpful intervention of a "proletarian dictatorship" in one or more advanced countries? The close relations with the Communist bloc, involving among other things coordination of the economies of the various units, certainly implies such a possibility. A general principle underlying international Communist relations was that the strong should help the weak. Unfortunately, a detailed treatment of the implications of such aid to a country of medium capitalist development, especially in the acceleration of its economic evolution toward socialism, does not seem to exist in Comintern materials.

There remains the question of the relatively greater magnitude of certain problems—in effect, the unfinished tasks of a "bourgeois-democratic" nature. Three problems appear to be the most important ones here—the agrarian problem, the nationalities question, and the question of the church.

The agrarian policies of the transformation in the higher type of countries of medium capitalist development differed from those appropriate for the advanced capitalist countries in two major respects: 1) the distribution, for use but not ownership, of a greater proportion of the confiscated land to the small, poor, or landless peasantry and, correspondingly, the preservation of a smaller proportion of the confiscated land intact as state farms; 2) the slower rate of the nationalization of peasant land, and of the collectivization of peasant farming, which is a particular instance of the slower tempo of development toward socialism discussed above. In all other respects the agrarian policies were to be almost identical with those to be pursued in the advanced capitalist countries. In fact, the agricultural section of the Polish draft program of 1932 is almost a verbatim copy of the similar passage in the Comintern Program. Although small peasant farming was regarded by Communists as economically inferior to large-scale agriculture, the temporary maintenance and even extension of such peasant farming was deemed politically expedient. The hostility of the Hungarian peasants to the Communist regime of 1919 was more than once called to mind. This hostility, based in great part upon failure to divide and distribute the confiscated estates, had proven to be a mighty counterrevolutionary force.[81]

The nationality question, which loomed large for many of the countries of medium capitalist development, was apparently not to be solved on principles other than those stated above with respect to advanced capitalist countries. The difference seems to have been largely one of the relatively greater seriousness of the question.

Respecting the third "bourgeois-democratic" problem—the liberation of society from dominance by the church—the basic Communist views on religion held true and need not be reexamined here. In countries of medium capitalist development organized religion was generally more strongly entrenched than in the advanced capitalist countries; the task of destroying its political, economic, and cultural position would be, of course, much more difficult, but the aims and means remained the same.

The presence of considerable "unfinished business" of a "bourgeois-democratic" character in these higher countries of medium capitalist development thus set for the future Communist dictatorships greater difficulties than for the Communist dictatorships in the advanced capitalist countries. Those tasks that impersonal historical development had not yet accomplished in full, prior to the seizure of power by the Communist-led revolutionists, were to be worked out purposefully after that seizure by the new rulers. Of course, the accomplishment of these tasks and the further recon-

struction of society along socialist lines was to be facilitated by the
help that the USSR and other Communist dictatorships would
render. However, Comintern evidence on the economic future of
the higher countries of medium capitalist development does not
give the reader that sense of urgency and sacrifice that was associated with the process of industrialization in Russia, a country in
this category in 1917, under the Five-Year Plans. The obvious
explanation for this inattention to matters of pace and tempo must
be given in terms of the changed international situation: in the
future such relatively backward Communist states would not be
dangerously isolated, as the Soviet Union had been, but would
enjoy the fraternal aid and encouragement of more advanced
"socialist" countries.

The lower type of societies of medium capitalist development. We may
now turn our attention to those societies, within the second category,
that were faced with a "bourgeois-democratic" revolution capable
of relatively rapid development by the Communist party into a
"proletarian-socialist" revolution. These countries stood at a lower
economic and political level than those countries discussed immediately above. The agricultural sector of the economy was more
backward and "semi-feudal"; the level of industrial development
was lower; the bourgeoisie had to a lesser extent satisfied its own
political and social aspirations; and the proletariat was inferior in
numbers and political experience. These characteristics, as we have
noted, were not entirely applicable to Japan, where the powerful
role of the monarchy, in the opinion of the Comintern, in effect
negated the relatively large industrial growth of this country.

As we know, the Comintern planned for the Communist party to
seize power in each of these countries long before capitalism had
developed fully, and long before the proletariat had reached the
percentage in the population that a fully developed capitalism
would have required.

Two aspects of the development of these societies following the
establishment of the Communist dictatorship may be discussed: 1)
the nature of the institutions and policies inaugurated with the
seizure of power; and 2) the problem of the subsequent transition

from the "bourgeois-democratic" phase into the "proletarian-socialist" phase.

Marx's "bourgeois-democratic" stage of historical development was, of course, characterized by the full flowering of a capitalist system dominated by the bourgeoisie and resting upon the pillars of private property and freedom of enterprise, contract, and exchange. In contrast, the Comintern's "bourgeois-democratic" stage was not, as we have seen, to be dominated by the bourgeoisie and capitalism, but was to be ruled by a "democratic dictatorship of the proletariat and peasantry," i.e., by the Communist party, whose aims were very different from those held by Marx's bourgeoisie. What then, was to be the program of the "democratic dictatorship"?

Spain, as will be recalled, was classified by the Comintern as a lower type of society of medium capitalist development, i.e., a society undergoing a "bourgeois-democratic" revolution. The "bourgeois-democratic character of the present stage of the Spanish revolution" was especially emphasized during the period of popular fronts,[82] thus reaffirming a characterization given earlier by the Comintern.[83] If the Communists were able to seize power in Spain, what would they do immediately to alter the direction of Spanish life, and, first of all, the direction of Spanish economic development?

We may find in the 1934 Program of the Spanish Communist Party a detailed picture of the anticipated economic system.[84] Among the thirteen points of this program there are several dealing with economic matters. In agriculture, the program called for the confiscation without redemption of all lands owned by the big landlords, the church, the monasteries, the municipalities, and the state; these lands were to be distributed among the "agricultural workers and toiling peasants" for individual or collective use according to their own decision. All debts of peasants to "usurers" and banks were to be annulled, and all "feudal and semi-feudal" obligations were to be abolished. In industry it was stipulated that "big, trustified" industry was to be nationalized, as were to be banks, as well as railroads and other means of transportation and communication owned by "big capital." Other economic measures included governmental action to regulate wages, hours, and social insurance, the latter to be financed by the state or by the "unexpropriated" capitalists.

Communist control was to make possible a number of features that were certainly not characteristic of Marx's bourgeois-dominated "bourgeois" revolution. For one, the wholesale confiscation of large estates constitutes a big difference. The encouragement of collective forms of agricultural production is another. According to the Comintern Program of 1928, however, the tempo of collectivization in this type of country would be comparatively slow.[85] In the industrial and financial sector, there was to be a considerable degree of nationalization, going far beyond the very limited public sector typical of a capitalist economic system.

It may be noted that the Comintern advocated much the same economic policies and measures for the future victorious "democratic dictatorship of the proletariat and peasantry" in the Japanese "bourgeois-democratic" revolution.[86] But some important differences existed. The economic program for Japan did not explicitly call for the nationalization of any industrial enterprises or financial institutions. Instead, it confined itself to ambiguous statements about the introduction of control by Japanese soviets over the banks and over production in the great capitalist enterprises.[87] The unexplainable irony is that in Japan, where the Comintern frequently adjudged the proletariat to represent 50 percent of the population, less radical measures were advocated for industry than in Spain, where one Comintern writer found the proletariat to represent only 5.5 percent.[88] The less industrialized economy of Spain was to be subjected, at least initially, to more far-reaching and radical measures by the "democratic dictatorship" than was Japan's. And in the field of agriculture no statement was made about an immediate collectivization of land in Japan, whereas in the case of Spain the voluntary formation of collectives was suggested.

In other areas of policy, the Spanish program closely resembled that of a "proletarian dictatorship." The right of self-determination, including the freedom to secede from Spain, was to be granted to Catalonia, Biscay, and Galicia, besides the full liberation of all Spanish colonies. A Red Army was to be created and the armed forces of the former regime were to be disarmed and disbanded. "Proletarian solidarity" with oppressed peoples and a "fraternal alliance" with the USSR were also demanded. On these points there is general unanimity in Comintern materials for all countries in this category.

By way of a summary, certain contrasts between this new, Comintern type of "bourgeois-democratic" revolution and that of Marx's classical scheme may again be emphasized. The ruling class and its governing institutions are different: the "democratic dictatorship of the proletariat and peasantry" is exercised by the Communist party through soviets, instead of Marx's dictatorship of the bourgeoisie exercised through a parliamentary system. The economy is profoundly different: instead of the fullest endorsement and scope for private property and free enterprise, there is to be considerable state interference, ranging from controls to outright nationalization of property. In international relations, an orientation toward, and intimate collaboration with, of all things, a socialist bloc, was envisaged for the Communist government that conducted this new type of "bourgeois-democratic" revolution.

The importance of the Comintern's drastic alteration of Marx's "bourgeois-democratic" stage cannot be denied. In terms of sheer numbers, most of humanity, according to the Comintern, was destined to approach socialism and Communism through this preparatory process—the "bourgeois-democratic" stage under Communist control. The reader will recall that such a stage under Communist control was considered by the Comintern to be on the agenda not only for the type of countries we are concerned with at the moment, but also for the societies of the third category—the colonial, semi-colonial, and dependent countries. For example, the Ninth Plenum of the ECCI in its resolution on the Chinese question referred to the existing "bourgeois-democratic stage of the revolution,"[89] over which, of course, Communists and not "bourgeois democrats" were to dominate. The population embraced by such countries undergoing initially a "bourgeois-democratic" revolution was enormous. In the estimation of one writer in 1928, over three fourths of mankind would "come to the dictatorship of the proletariat only in the process of transition from the democratic dictatorship of the proletariat and peasantry. It is understandable how great a significance in these countries is attached to the question of the stages preceding the proletarian revolution."[90] It is certainly obvious how violent is the contradiction that exists between Marx's "bourgeois-democratic" stage and the Comintern's.

Comintern materials were at every point in agreement on one issue: that the "bourgeois-democratic" revolution in the lower type of society of medium capitalist development constituted not an end in itself but a temporary preparatory phase leading to the final stages of socialism and Communism. How, then, was this transition to be effected?

A word may be said initially about the forms this vastly important transitional period would take. Up to 1928 and the drafting of the Comintern Program, there had been two patterns of transition, based upon Lenin's interpretation of the Russian revolutionary movement in 1905 and again in 1917. Mingulin, the author quoted above, described these patterns in his important article, in which he discussed the whole question of the "growing over" *(pererastanie)* of the "bourgeois-democratic" revolution into the "proletarian" revolution. In 1905, according to Mingulin, Lenin had outlined the "growing over" as follows:

The masses of workers and peasants accomplish a democratic revolution, from which grows the revolutionary-democratic dictatorship of the proletariat and peasantry, and complete the bourgeois-democratic revolution, after which the proletariat, to the extent of its forces, develops the revolution into a socialist revolution.[91]

Again according to Mingulin's interpretation of Lenin, a second pattern had appeared in the course of the Russian revolutions of 1917:

The essence of the second form lay in that the bourgeois revolution, carried out by the masses of workers and peasants, ends its first stage, having given power to the bourgeoisie, and there exists after the uprising, along with this power and in some respects subordinated to it, the revolutionary-democratic dictatorship of the proletariat and peasantry in the form of soviets, within which the revolutionary proletariat leads the struggle . . . for a proletarian revolution.[92]

Mingulin complained that the Draft Program acknowledged only the Lenin plan of 1905, while ignoring the system of "dual power" from March to November, 1917. Moreover, he charged, Lenin had insisted upon the possibility of yet other forms of transition.[93] But the probability of a repetition of the pattern of the Russian revolutionary movement in 1917, with its peculiar attribute of dual power, i.e., the coexistence of the Provisional Government and the soviets, did not receive serious attention within the Comintern. Its leadership seems to have considered it much more probable that a Communist party would: 1) attain hegemony in the "bourgeois-democratic" revolutionary movement against feudalism; 2) seize complete power, without sharing it even temporarily with other, hostile, groups; 3) carry out the "bourgeois-democratic" tasks; and 4) begin, sooner or later, the advance toward the "proletarian-socialist" revolution.[94]

What actually was to occur during the process of transition or "growing over" of the Communist-dominated "bourgeois-democratic" revolution into the "proletarian-socialist" revolution? The nature of the transition is difficult to grasp. At some point following the seizure of power those *unfinished tasks* of a "bourgeois-democratic" nature were to be completed. And, at some point following the seizure of power, *new tasks* of a "proletarian-socialist" nature were to be undertaken. Ambiguities arise from the numerous statements in Comintern materials, on the one hand, that there were two distinct stages, each with its own special set of tasks, and, on the other hand, that these stages and tasks imperceptibly merged with one another from the moment when Communists took power. Thus, at times, the Comintern appeared to argue in favor of *A*: the existence of two distinct, separate, and successive stages of socio-economic development; and a great fuss was made over the danger of confusing them. On other occasions, it seemed to insist that no "Chinese wall" separated the two stages, which were regarded as B: integrated parts of a single process of social change, the content of which was progressively less "bourgeois-democratic" and progressively more "proletarian-socialist." Whatever the tasks, it is Communist power that seeks to achieve these tasks, and Communist power is properly (for Marx) restricted to the "proletarian-socialist" stage.

A expresses the insistence upon a clear distinction between the two phases. Such insistence was partially inspired by the desire to avoid charges of "Trotskyism." This term was used here to condemn efforts to compress, by means of an immediate establishment of a Communist dictatorship and an immediate launching of a full-blown socialist program, the socio-economic development of those countries faced with a "bourgeois-democratic" revolution. But, in B, the equally strong insistence upon the merging of these two stages permitted the Comintern to introduce measures of a socialist nature during a stage Marx had pictured as essentially nonsocialist and definitely not ruled by a Communist party. It also permitted a rapid transition to socialism.

Was there any real difference between A and B in the minds of Comintern leaders? Consider Bukharin's speech at the Sixth Congress in reply to the discussion on the Draft Program; contradictory notions were expressed even in this leading theoretician's words. "To mix these [two stages] into one lump," he warned, "is not at all in the Leninist tradition; it is a Trotskyist interpretation of the purest water."[95] Yet he had already asserted that, from the moment of the establishment of the "democratic dictatorship of the proletariat and peasantry," it begins to merge into the "proletarian dictatorship."[96]

On balance, given the socialistic economic program of the "democratic dictatorship," it would appear that B fitted more closely than A the Comintern's general conception of the pattern of development for the lower type of society of medium capitalist development.[97]

What conditions the tempo of the transition from the "bourgeois-democratic" revolution to the "proletarian-socialist"? The

Program speaks of the possibility of a "more or less swift" period of transition for this category of countries.[98] Certainly it was expected to be speedier than the transitional period necessary in the colonies, which would start from a lower stage of development. Comintern leaders, in attempting to describe the prerequisites of the "growing over" process, refer vaguely to the following factors: 1) the degree to which the Communist party and the proletariat have increased their hegemony over the revolutionary movement; 2) the "maturity" of the movement (which perhaps means the same thing); and 3) the degree to which the economic prerequisites for socialist construction have been achieved. Many writers anticipated a class struggle, during which part of the allies of the proletariat, that is, of the Communist party, would either desert or vacillate.[99] Very probably the decisive factor determining the tempo of the "growing over" process would be the extent of aid from the outside, i.e., from already existing Communist dictatorships. The inevitably close economic contacts with the USSR and any future socialist bloc would surely facilitate the transition process. As was pointed out earlier, all Communist dictatorships were to unite in an intimate political and economic union.

SOCIAL CHANGE IN THE COLONIAL, SEMI-COLONIAL, AND DEPENDENT SOCIETIES

The Comintern Program of 1928, in its treatment of the revolutionary process after the Communist seizure of power in the third category of countries, prescribed the following broad course of development: a fairly prolonged "bourgeois-democratic" stage that would "grow over," as a rule only after a "series of preparatory stages," into the "proletarian-socialist" stage.[100]

The Comintern Program spelled out eight special tasks of the Communist-dominated "bourgeois-democratic" revolution in the colonial, semi-colonial, and dependent countries.[101] The undertaking of these tasks would constitute a "preparatory step toward the general tasks of the [later] proletarian dictatorship."[102]

Of these eight tasks, four were of a political nature: 1) the overthrow of the rule exercised by foreign imperialism, the feudal overlords, and the "landlord bureaucracy"; 2) the establishment of the "democratic dictatorship of the proletariat and peasantry" on the basis of soviets; 3) the achievement of full national independence and state unity; and 4) the organization of a revolutionary workers' and peasants' army.

The remaining four tasks concerned economic policy: 1) the cancellation of state debts; 2) the introduction of the eight-hour day; 3) the nationalization of those large-scale enterprises (industrial, transport, banking, and others) belonging to the imperialists; and 4) the confiscation of large privately owned estates and the lands of the churches and monasteries, and the nationalization of all land. Of these economic measures, only the first and second would seem to be consistent with the spirit of Marx's "bourgeois-democratic" stage. It is clear, however, that this "preparatory step" to the "general tasks" of socialist construction already contains significant elements of socialism.

Some of these measures require additional comment. No immediate and full-scale nationalization of industrial and commercial enterprises owned by the native bourgeoisie was indicated in the Comintern Program. However, other Comintern materials called for the nationalization of enterprises owned by the bourgeoisie who had opposed the Communist seizure of power. Apparently, at first, private enterprise was to be tolerated, and the major concern of the government was to protect the worker by an elaborate system of social insurance and by a careful regulation of working conditions. Specific means by which the exploitative aspects of capitalist enterprise would be curtailed were outlined in the programs of several colonial Communist parties.[103] It was expected, however, that, given a continued struggle between the Communist party and the native bourgeoisie, the latter would resort to acts of resistance, including sabotage, whereupon their property would be confiscated. This process of confiscation would ultimately lead to the nationalization of all large-scale industry.[104] Wang Ming, an outstanding figure in the Asian Communist movement, observed neatly that the immediate policy of the Chinese Soviet Republic in

1933 was not one of destroying capitalism but only of preparing conditions for its future destruction.[105]

In agriculture, the confiscated lands were to be turned over for use to the masses of peasantry, usually defined as "toiling peasantry" to differentiate them from counterrevolutionary peasants or kulaks. Although the Comintern Program, it will be remembered, called for the nationalization of all land, it is not clear whether such nationalization would occur immediately. The Chinese Soviet Republic permitted as late as 1933 the purchase and sale of land, under soviet controls, by the peasants.[106] According to Wang Ming, no efforts were to be made to create collective farms on a large scale at the current, "bourgeois-democratic" stage of the Chinese revolution. This was thought to be a task for the later "proletarian-socialist" stage of the revolutionary process.

The picture emerges, in the initial "bourgeois-democratic" stage, of a severely controlled economy in which the Communist dictatorship was to permit the coexistence of a diminishing state-regulated capitalist sector and small peasant farming alongside a nationalized sector (e.g., the confiscated enterprises of the former imperialists and native bourgeoisie) until such time as conditions were thought ripe for the fuller implementation of socialist policies.

In respect to the outside world, close relations were to be established with other Communist-led countries, and especially with the USSR. Federations of former colonies or dependent lands were envisaged in certain areas, e.g., Latin America. Help from "proletarian dictatorships" was thought to be of decisive significance in accelerating the socio-economic development of a colony in which a "democratic dictatorship of the proletariat and peasantry" had been created. The pace at which the capitalist sector in the economy would be constricted and eliminated, while the socialist sector was being expanded, would depend largely on the degree of help from more advanced Communist-controlled states. Indeed, this was precisely the prospect held out for the countries of the third category in the Comintern Program:

With the existence of centers of socialism in the form of Soviet republics and their growing economic might, those colonies falling away from imperialism move in the economic sense toward and gradually unite with the industrial centers of world socialism. They are drawn onto the rails of socialist construction, by-passing the phase of further development of capitalism as the predominant system, and they obtain the possibility for rapid economic and cultural progress.[107]

The above quotation gives the impression that the efforts of a former colony, by itself, were expected to be insufficient to achieve socialism. Generally speaking, Comintern materials supported this conclusion. The Program acknowledged that the colonial countries possessed some industries, but added that the level of industrial development was insufficient, "in the *majority* of cases, for independent socialist construction."[108] Successful building of socialism was to be possible in most cases "only with direct support by the countries of the proletarian dictatorships."

For the majority of the colonies a self-sufficient progress toward socialism was thus considered impossible. Bukharin commented upon this at the Sixth Congress: "If we had a dispute with Trotskyism about the possiblity of building socialism in one country, then this cannot at all be so simplified as to mean that in every country there is everything necessary for the building of socialism. This would be a clumsy and stupid interpretation of our point of view."[109] Bukharin did not think, for instance, that the Chinese proletariat, unaided, could build up socialism.

Other conditions were also necessary for the transition to socialism: a "certain level" of industrial development, of trade-union organization, and of Communist party strength.[110] Stated more elaborately in Comintern materials, the strength of the party meant its size, its fighting qualities, and the level of its class consciousness. It also meant its authority over the nonparty masses, proletarian and peasant alike, and its capacity to raise the organizational and ideological level of the proletariat as a whole and, to a lesser extent, of the peasantry.[111] None of this explains precisely how much power the Communist party had to have in order to carry out the transition to socialism. Did not the Comintern simply intend that, in each country under Communist control, the Com-

munist party was to move as rapidly toward socialism as its
strength would permit?

It is certainly possible to believe that help from more advanced
countries would enable a former colony to avoid some or many of
the painful experiences of high-tempo industrialization and collectivization. Presumably the amount of sacrifice and the degree of
regimentation might well be less than would be required if no help
were received from abroad. On the other hand, the historical
record shows that the Chinese Communist Party, despite aid from
the USSR, has felt it necessary to advance rapidly toward a heavily
industrialized economy at the cost of great sacrifices by its people.
Comintern leaders did not speculate on such matters. However,
more than once statements were made to the effect that the
pioneering experience of the USSR was to lessen the tribulations of
the movement toward socialism in other countries.

For the Communist believer, at any rate, a close association with
the USSR was to facilitate the realization of his idea of progress.
The Sixth Comintern Congress declared that:

Alliance with the Union of Soviet Socialist Republics and with the revolutionary proletariat of the imperialist countries creates for the laboring
popular masses of China, India, and all backward colonial and semi-
colonial countries the possibility of an independent, free economic and
cultural development, *by-passing the stage of the rule of the capitalist order*
or even the development of capitalist relations in general.[112]

SOCIAL CHANGE IN VERY BACKWARD SOCIETIES

The fourth category of societies—often indiscriminately merged in
Comintern materials with the third—embraced those very backward societies that either entirely lacked a proletariat or had only a
very insignificant number of proletarians. Such areas as Tannu
Tuva, Outer Mongolia, Sinkiang, and parts of Africa appear to
belong to this category. These territories, almost completely unin-
dustrialized, possessed essentially agrarian or nomadic economies.

The revolutionary movements in these areas were difficult for the
Comintern to label. The Comintern did not apply the term

"bourgeois-democratic," which technically required the existence of at least a few bourgeois and proletarians. We may consider the two examples of Tannu Tuva and Mongolia, where in 1921 Russian Red Army units effectively established control.

An article in the Comintern journal in 1931 spoke of the tenth anniversary of the "national-revolutionary movement" in Tuva.[113] Without mentioning the existence of a proletariat, the author saw the movement as the effort of peasants supported by the Red Army to overthrow the "feudal order" and establish "genuine democratic-revolutionary" statehood. After the successful "revolution," the "feudal order" had been "liquidated" and a "people's revolutionary power" had been created. The country was described as a "people's republic." The author of the article felt that, with the support of the USSR, Tuva would undoubtedly be able to skip the capitalist stage, and to pursue a "noncapitalist" path to socialism.[114] Perhaps the Comintern felt that no party designated as "Communist" could properly exist in the absence of any proletariat whatever; at any rate another name—the People's Revolutionary Party—was used to designate the Tuva group having a pro-Communist orientation. In 1935, this group was admitted as a section of the Comintern, but only with the rights of a "sympathizing" party.[115]

The case of Mongolia appears similar, although there existed a small proletariat and a small bourgeoisie.[116] Here there developed, according to the Comintern, a national movement of the "toiling masses," led by a modest proletariat and by the poor peasants, against foreign rule as well as against native landlords and bourgeoisie. In actuality, the movement was led by a People's Revolutionary Party, founded in 1921. The fact that this party did not formally call itself a Communist party did not indicate a non-Communist attitude but simply reflected the backwardness of the country and the very small size of the proletariat. The Party continues even today to call itself the People's Revolutionary Party.

With the help of Soviet Russian Red Army units, a pro-Soviet regime came to power in 1921. Thus a "noncapitalist" path was made possible:

In close alliance with the world proletariat movement the Mongol peasantry has found in itself sufficient revolutionary forces, not only to achieve national liberation, not only to overthrow the power and to undermine the income of the feudal lords, but also to turn decisively toward a noncapitalist (i.e., socialist) path, the path of limiting and squeezing out capitalist elements and successfully establishing a new socialist kolkhoz-cooperative social order.[117]

The Communist-oriented People's Revolutionary Party henceforth directed the political and social evolution of Mongolia. In 1929, in the interests, it was said, of the agricultural proletariat and the poor and middle peasants, the property of the secular feudal lords was confiscated. In 1930, a campaign was begun to confiscate the property of the Buddhist church, the "most powerful branch" of Mongol feudalism.[118] By 1931, it was claimed that one third of all the "toiling" population was organized in peasant cooperatives.[119]

The developments in these two countries illustrate the pattern anticipated by the Comintern: a largely peasant and nationalist movement directed by a local party of Communist character is able, with the help of a Communist dictatorship abroad, completely to bypass the stage of capitalism. In the case of Tuva and Outer Mongolia, decisive aid came from the Russian Communist Party at the very beginning—at the moment of the seizure of power by the local party. It is not clear whether the Comintern believed that outside help was necessary in every case for the act of seizing power. But outside help was considered indispensable for the subsequent advance of the revolutionary movement toward a socialist path of development. As Bukharin explained, in such backward areas there existed no proletariat that could make history turn in this direction.[120] An outside proletariat, in actuality a foreign Communist dictatorship, was to be the catalytic agent. This emphasis upon the unique, almost miracle-performing power of even a foreign proletariat, i.e., a foreign Communist party, once again underscores the Comintern's appreciation of this class in the making of history. Bukharin envisaged such peasant and backward areas as a kind of world village, which would be drawn onto the path of socialist development by close contact with the international Communist-led proletariat, just as the rural areas in the Soviet Union were brought into the work of building socialism through the direction of the Communist Party of the Soviet Union.[121]

To summarize: Comintern materials indicate that even in extremely backward areas, in which bourgeoisie and proletariat did not exist or were very insignificant, a Communist-oriented party could seize power, declare national independence, undertake reforms (especially agrarian), and, with the necessary assistance of a foreign Communist party ruling a more advanced country, step forth upon a "noncapitalist" path of development. The virtue of backwardness permitted these countries to by-pass the "exploitation" and "oppression" of a capitalist stage of development, given the proper kind of outside help. Yet that outside help, from a ruling Communist party, could well mean that the national independence of the backward country existed only in form, and not in reality. Drawn into such a world system as described by Bukharin, the backward areas might find themselves forever denied genuine independence. This was surely the case with Tannu Tuva and Outer Mongolia.

XII. COMMUNISM AS THE

ULTIMATE WORLD SOCIETY

Any inquiry into the nature of Communism as the highest and ultimate form of human society advocated by the Comintern is a frustrating intellectual task. The obscurities and gaps that mar Comintern theory in its entirety are never so apparent as here. Although the Communist utopia was the final justification of all that was urged and undertaken in its name, only a fragmentary description of its broad outlines may be found in Comintern literature. Yet its major importance in Comintern theory obviously cannot be denied. The Communist utopia provided the necessary rationalization for the whole arduous revolutionary process, from the moment of its inception by an embryonic Communist party until the work of the seizure of power and of the transitional period had reached a triumphant end.

Beyond the scanty material offered by the Sixth Congress, which attempted to describe the Communist phase in the Program of 1928, very little relevant evidence exists. Given the paucity of available material, the student must be satisfied with only partial answers, amplified to a reasonable degree, however, by conjecture and inference. It is of no particular comfort to be reminded of the un-Marxist character of any attempt to blueprint in detail the future society. Manuilsky, speaking at the Seventh Congress in commemoration of the fortieth anniversary of the death of Friedrich Engels, was content to revert to this position. "Engels," he declared, ". . . more than once poured ridicule on those who, departing from the soil of science, tried to philosophize on the 'architectonics of future society.' More than once he wrote that he was quite at ease about the 'peoples of future society who at all events will not be more stupid than we are.' "[1] However, without waiting for the people of the future to tell us their situation, we may now attempt to shed some light on the Communist utopia.

POWER AND FREEDOM

The Comintern always agreed that a major distinctive feature of world-wide Communism of the future would be its stateless character. On this issue, it followed, as is well known, the statements of Marx, Engels, and Lenin. The great tasks of the "proletarian dictatorship" having been achieved, the state would "wither away."

The state is, for the Comintern, basically an instrument of class rule; it is always used by one class against other classes, and it exists so long as classes exist. With the disappearance of class divisions in society, there will also disappear "the organs of class rule, and, in the first place, state power. It, being the embodiment of class rule, dies out as classes die out. With it gradually die out all rules of compulsion whatsoever."[2] This is stated in the 1928 Program.

The state is used here to denote the aggregate of the means of class rule and coercion—such as the police, the courts, the penal institutions, and the armed forces. There is yet to remain, after the dying out of the state, an administrative apparatus to run the economy. In Engels' famous phrase, "The government of persons is replaced by the administration of things and the direction of the process of production."[3] Thus, in the ultimate Communist society there are to be no means of force by which members of society are compelled to act or refrain from acting; there is only to be an administrative apparatus to run the economy.

These, then, are the essentials of the Comintern's position concerning the public institution normally designated as the "state" or the "government." Deceptively, they suggest a voluntary society, in which coercion is no longer needed or employed, and in which all members of society are enlightened to the point that they cooperate without disharmony and conflict.

Before examining in detail the position of the Comintern on the question of power and freedom in Communist society, we may point out that the issue of power appears to exist so long as human beings live in organized communities. The very existence of society, especially a highly developed and complex society such as world Communism would be, requires decision-making. There must be some way of arriving at decisions and some way of seeing that these decisions are implemented and obeyed, so that people will act in accordance with these decisions and not in some other fashion. In other words, there must be an institution possessing the authority to exercise power—the power required for the making of decisions and for their enforcement. The only imaginable alternatives would seem to be either pure anarchy—which would be the negation of society—or a society of super-intelligent and super-cooperative human beings who, spontaneously and simultaneously, always are able to perceive the best possible line of policy and activity and to cooperate fully in its implementation. Such alternatives, in the light of the historical record, can only seem fantastic.

The phrase "the administration of things and the direction of the process of production" clearly rejects the idea of a spontaneously and magically functioning economy in which nothing needs to be administered or directed. Right away, there is the problem of decision-making. How should the economy be administered? Along what path should it be directed? Someone or some group must decide. How are the administrators selected? How are differences among the administrators resolved? How are differences between the administrators and the rest of the populace resolved? The problem of power and the coercion of human beings, not "things," remains. Unless, of course, we are to have the super-intelligent, super-cooperative beings noted above.

It is useful to present at this point the Comintern's own understanding of the nature of public administration under Communism. In the socialist phase, one of the functions of the state is the management of a centralized, planned economic system. Communism would inherit this economic system, which would have made Communism possible. In the words of Manuilsky, "the political functions of the state will die out, but the functions of social planning and control will not die out [under Communism]; on the contrary, they will increase in importance."[4] The Program is clear on the point that the economic system under Communism would be "rational" and not chaotic. The world system of Communism would witness "planned utilization of all its material resources and painless economic development on the basis of an unrestricted, planned, and rapid upsurge of productive forces."[5] Moreover, there would be the "application of the most perfect methods of statistical accounting and planned economic regulation."[6]

It seems clear that the problem of how to get people to do some things and not do others is not eliminated by the anticipated reduction of the agencies and function of public authority to mere economic administration.

It may moreover be noted that the noneconomic activities of a society also require decision-making. The present scope of the noneconomic activity of governments, no matter how broadly the sphere of economics is interpreted, is of course quite large. When one looks at the scope of the noneconomic activity of the Soviet Russian government, one sees the most extreme case of the expansion of governmental power. To reduce public administration solely to economic administration, as the Comintern seemed to do, debonairly erases huge problems of administration in many other fields, problems that will in fact persist.

Who then, is to exercise power under Communism? Not the proletariat, because: 1) according to Comintern theory all classes have disappeared; and 2) according to our earlier analysis the Communist party, and not the proletariat, exercises power in the socialist stage.

Would the Communist party continue to exist and wield power?

If we momentarily assume that prior to the establishment of the Communist society the party actually is the vanguard of the proletariat and expresses the proletariat's will, then, logically, we must accept the disappearance of the party in the Communist phase, along with the disappearance of the proletariat as a separate class.

It is interesting that Comintern materials almost never mentioned the ultimate disappearance of the Communist party. The Program did not do so. But one Comintern figure (and only one to my knowledge) did express himself on this important matter—Lozovsky, the leader of the Red International of Trade Unions. In a speech during the debate on the Draft Program at the Sixth Congress, Lozovsky (bravely?) committed himself as follows: "As classes disappear and consequently the state withers away, there will also disappear the political party of the proletariat."[7] Thus Lozovsky postulated the voluntary abdication of absolute power by a political party that has been exercising it in totalitarian fashion to transform everything in society, from the ownership of the means of production to the outlook, desires, and needs of human beings. From Lozovsky's remarks, it would appear that the Communist party will forgo under Communism the special and unique role of hegemony which it enjoys even before the seizure of power, and which it continues to enjoy in the socialist phase. And it would seem that the party was to disappear willingly.

Assuming that the Communist party does disappear, will it be possible for some other public organization to take charge of the administration of the society? Again it is Lozovsky who offered an interesting idea. At the Sixth Comintern Congress he outlined an important role for the trade unions in the future Communist society. During the phase of socialism, he said, the trade unions were to become powerful administrative organs, ultimately concentrating in their hands the entire management of the whole economy. Here Lozovsky based himself upon the Program of the All-Russian Communist Party, adopted in 1919. With the dawn of the Communist phase, the state was indeed to disappear, Lozovsky said, and organs for economic administration would assume the most important place. These organs would already have been amalgamated with the trade unions, which were to exist under Communism in a "new, modified form, as the organs for accounting, production, and distribution."[8] Communist society, Lozovsky insisted, would not be an organization-less society. "The Communist society is the highest form of organization for toiling mankind. A society without power does not mean disorganization."[9]

In the light of events in the USSR after 1928 and the mediocre role assigned there to the trade unions, it is difficult to accept Lozovsky's enthusiastic forecast, especially as it was not explicitly endorsed by the Comintern. In actual fact, the Comintern never addressed itself as a body to the question of the existence of trade unions under Communism. At any rate, it is clear that Lozovsky's scheme does not eliminate the problem of power and decision-making.

Thus far the disappearance of the state has been discussed on the assumption that a world-wide "dictatorship of the proletariat" exists. But Stalin raised the question of Communism in one country and of the existence of the state under such circumstances. In March, 1939, in his report to the Eighteenth Congress of the CPSU, he declared that the Soviet state would exist in the period of Communism if the "capitalist encirclement" of the Communist area were not liquidated.[10] He thus offered a kind of justification for the existence of a state under Communism in an "isolated" USSR. Presumably, until such time as Communist rule had been established at least in all the important capitalist states, Stalin's remarks were to be applicable.[11]

On balance, did the Comintern present a convincing picture of a voluntary abdication of power on the eve of Communism by the Communist party, which had been exercising a monopoly of power during the socialist phase? The answer must be in the negative. Doubtless many, probably most, Communists believed vaguely in a distant future stateless society. But nowhere was there given a reasonable justification for such a belief. From a society ruled in all aspects by a highly centralized and highly disciplined party to a society without government and coercion—such is the evolution which the Comintern Program predicted, but did not explain. The word "state" might disappear from Communist vocabulary, but the problem of power would remain. One almost feels the impulse to search in Comintern materials for yet another revolution—the "missing" revolution, occurring on the threshold of Communism, by which the totalitarian rule of the Communist party would be terminated.

The Program claimed that a new freedom was to be acquired under Communism. This was the freedom of mankind to decide its own fate. "For the first time in history mankind takes its fate in its own hands."[12] Manuilsky spoke in much the same vein at the Seventh Congress:

Man is the creator of socialism, the creator of a new social system. For the first time in history man has been put in his proper place. He is the smith forging his own destiny and his own history, he is the master of the socialist machine. *Socialism exists for him: he himself is the great goal of Socialism.*[13]

This new freedom would mean that mankind, instead of destroying human lives and resources in warfare, "will devote all its energy to the struggle with the forces of nature, to the development and elevation of its own collective might."[14] The use of the word "collective" is worth noting, for it is free man as a cooperating member of society, and *not* free man as an individualist pursuing primarily personal interests, that is to live in the ultimate society of Communism. Other remarks of Manuilsky, in reference to the USSR, developed this theme more explicitly:

In a socialist country the creation of a well-to-do cultured and happy life is not the work of a single person. In our country happiness is not based on the shifting sands of chance or luck; it is not the lot of the most crafty, the most insolent and shameless persons elbowing everyone out of their way. We are solving the problem of the happiness of the socialist man by our collective effort. . . . And only such an enormous collective effort is capable of solving this problem.[15]

Man's problems were to be solved only by the collective action of enlightened and socially conscious men and women, and not by the individual seeking his way alone. The fullest realization of individual talents and happiness, yes, but only by means of the highest degree of collective activity—such was the Comintern formula. (A living contradiction, as Stalin would have said.)

Again the problem of power and freedom presents itself. The great emphasis upon collective action suggests: 1) the need for organization, leaders, and power to mobilize collective action, the action of society, of the masses, of the group, but never of the

individual alone; and 2) the necessary submission of the individual
to the group. Man's freedom is obviously curtailed.

THE ECONOMY

The Comintern envisaged the existence under Communism of a
flourishing economy, scientifically planned and regulated, and
capable of satisfying all the needs of the new Communist man.
Under Communism the following slogan would prevail as a reality,
according to the Comintern: "From each according to his ability,
to each according to his needs!" This, of course, is the formula
used by Marx in his *Critique of the Gotha Programme* as one very basic
characteristic of the ultimate utopian society.

Something of the nature of this economic system has been
indicated already in the discussion of power and freedom. There
was to be, of course, complete socialization of industry and collectivization of agriculture, though the precise form of the rural
collective was never specified. The Program is rhapsodical about
the excellence of the Communist economic system: no private
ownership of the means of production, therefore no exploitation of
man by man, and no want and no poverty. Planning and rational
utilization of resources, close cooperation between science and the
economy, the encouragement of research—"all these will secure
the maximum productivity of social labor and will liberate in turn
the energy of mankind for the powerful growth of science and
art."[16]

Harold Laski has wisely commented that the formula "From
each according to his abilities, to each according to his needs"
defies precise definition.[17] The reason is that abilities cannot be
measured, and needs vary. An objective test of abilities and needs
is required. And, it may be added, if differences in abilities and
needs are to be taken into account, who is to identify and measure
these differences?

In the classless Communist society, according to the Program,
labor "will cease to be only a means for livelihood and will become
the prime vital need."[18] There would disappear "the hierarchy of

people according to the division of labor, and with it also the contradiction between mental and physical labor." Presumably, this requires, among other things, the creation through education of a common, positive attitude toward work. It is not clear whether all persons would be expected to do both physical work and mental labor, although this seems to be implied. It is difficult to see how the division of labor could be eliminated. As R. N. Carew Hunt points out, it is impossible to end the division of labor "as long as the technology is retained, since men will still have to discharge the same functions whether their factory belongs to society or to the capitalist."[19] Moreover, there must be someone who has the power to assign others to the various jobs. The decision-maker appears again.

If we assume the Comintern's prediction of a coming world-wide existence of Communism, it appears that there would be no attempt by individual countries at economic self-sufficiency. We have noted that a successful Communist seizure of power in a given country would mean the establishment of close economic cooperation with other countries that were already socialist. This cooperation would continue under Communism. The Program referred to the "most expedient utilization of the forces of nature and of the natural conditions of production in separate parts of the world."[20] This suggests a kind of international division of labor, determined by a decision-making body which would, of course, take account of the geographical distribution of natural resources. It is interesting to note that Manuilsky at the Sixth Congress rejected autarky as a permanent goal of the USSR when he said:

We are an isolated economic system. We are compelled to rely solely upon our internal division of labor . . . . We know that the victory of the proletariat in other capitalist countries will compel us to reorganize our economy on the basis of an international division of labor. When the international revolution is brought about, it will not be the international duty of our Party and of our working class to establish independent branches of industry, which today make us independent of capitalist markets. It will be the business of the highly industrialized countries to combine their work with that of our more backward country on the basis of a greater increase of productive forces and an international division of labor. All this is indisputable truth, to which no politically mature person can object.[21]

It is clear that Comintern spokesmen were more ready to extol the benefits of the future Communist economy than to explain precisely how that economy was to be administered. The painful silence respecting the practical implementation of their utopia once more reminds us of the Comintern's inability or unwillingness to clarify the thorny problem of authority and power.

SOCIETY, CULTURE, AND THE NATURE OF MAN

The Comintern Program presented Communism as an unending era of social justice, cultural growth, and freedom for all on an equal basis. In such an era, war would be forever eliminated and permanent peace would prevail. The individual and society would enjoy an ever-ascending standard of living. There would be no hindrances that might hamper the continued flowering of the good life for all.

Society, according to the Program, would no longer consist of antagonistic classes but would become instead "a single association of world labor."[22] There would be no class ideologies; one philosophy would be accepted by all—dialectical, scientific materialism. Culture would become the possession of all, and there would be the "harmonious development of all the talents inherent in mankind."[23] Although the Program did not explicitly say so, it implied the disappearance of distinctive national cultures, for it predicted a "new culture of humanity united for the first time" which would destroy all state boundaries and would be based upon "clear and transparent relations among people."[24] An unprecedented cultural growth under Communism, it was promised, would be made possible by the development of new productive forces, which would not only raise the living standards of society but would also reduce to a minimum the time devoted to material production. Mankind, reeducated in the spirit of Communism, would have a whole new outlook upon life, society, and social obligations.[25]

The nonexistence of classes under Communism is one of the

most unrealistic promises of Communist theory. If private *ownership* of the means of production (the Communist explanation for classes) were abolished, there would yet remain a group of leaders, directors, and administrators who effectively control the means of production and use them for purposes that might or might not correspond to the interests of all. The formal abolition of private property need not alter the existence of a basic division of society into two groups, one exercising control over productive forces (and over the rest of society's undertakings as well) and the other deprived of such control. In the absence of genuine democratic mechanism for the selection, appointment, and removal of the administrators of the productive process, the "class" divisions remain.

The Comintern's description of culture in the Communist era was replete with promises of cultural advantages and opportunities. Yet it must be emphasized that there would be only one philosophical basis for the culture of society—the philosophy of "dialectical materialism." The range of intellectual inquiry is thus already severely limited. Truth is ascertainable and its fundamental principles have already been discovered. The subsequent scientific and cultural advance of mankind must proceed within the limits of this philosophy, or, more accurately, within the limits of the official philosophy as defined by the decision-makers of society. The new Communist man would certainly not be free to adopt any other philosophical system. As the Program stated, the new culture would "bury forever every kind of mysticism, religion, prejudices, and superstitions."[26]

We have discussed the task of transforming human nature, which the Comintern Program set for the Communist dictatorship in the period following the seizure of power. On the eve of the Communist phase, the proposed transformation would have been completed, for the absence of the "state" presupposed, on the part of man, a voluntary and spontaneous conduct in accordance with Communist ideals. A new pattern of human wants and needs would have been created in the process of Communist reeducation during the initial socialist phase. Society would have discarded old prejudices and replaced them with new attitudes (prejudices?). Man would have lost selfish instincts and would have become willing to work for the good of all society.

Carew Hunt remarks that "the assertion that human nature will undergo such a transformation is a genuflexion to mythology."[27] Human nature is certainly a difficult and elusive concept. One may identify at least three kinds of theories of human nature: first, the "ethical," which describes the nature of man essentially in terms of the doctrines of a religion or philosophical world-view; second, the "natural," which offers an explanation of human nature purely in terms of psychology and biology, without the inclusion of judgments of value; and third, the "sociological," which sees man as primarily the product of conditioning from his environment. As noted earlier, the Comintern Program avoided the term "human nature" and spoke rather of the "nature of classes." The Program's interpretation of human nature was essentially "sociological"; there existed no constant immutable human nature, based either on an Eden-like "fall from grace" or on a set of instincts and drives inherent in the psychological and biological make-up of all human beings.

If we cannot satisfactorily probe the inner mystery of human nature, we can yet observe the overt conduct of man. Can the the patterns of human behavior be changed through social conditioning, as the Comintern believed? If we adopt a common-sense definition of human nature as a pattern of behavior based on deeply rooted propensities, we can assume the Comintern position was that these propensities and resulting patterns of behavior could be altered, given the proper kind of reeducation. The formerly "incorrect" or "imperfect" (from the Communist point of view) nature of man exhibited such dominant characteristics as egotism, competition, and self-interest. The desired characteristics of the new Communist man would include altruism, cooperation, and community interest.

As H. B. Mayo writes, the Marxist (and Comintern) view of human nature "comes down to very little: that self-interest has dominated human behavior through history, but that once capitalism is abolished, man will transcend self-interest and be 'naturally' good."[28] While no empirical test, of course, can be made of the validity of this faith in "regeneration," the evidence of man's history is a weighty testimony casting serious doubts upon the idea of such a change. But even if history appears to support belief in the essential immutability of man's nature, still no absolutely conclusive proof exists that man's pattern of behavior cannot ever be changed, given suitable meaures of reeducation and reorientation. It may be added that the Communists are not by any means the first or only reformers who have announced the goal of transforming and improving man's nature.

THE FATE OF THE USSR

According to the general outlines of the future Communist utopia as sketched in the Program, it would seem that the USSR, like other proletarian dictatorships, is destined to disappear as a separate political entity. It would become a part of the world-wide Union of Soviet Socialist Republics, which, as a "state," would disappear ultimately. The international division of labor, the universal culture under Communism—these also point to the ultimate extinction of the Soviet Union as such, though no Comintern figure explicitly said so. In a clear sense, however, the USSR would leave a permanent imprint upon the future society. By pathfinding the way toward socialism, "achieved" in 1934 in the USSR, and by moving thereafter in the direction of Communism, it enjoyed throughout the life of the Comintern a monopoly in the practical business of building socialism and Communism. Between 1928 and 1943, the Comintern saw no alternate routes whatsoever. The postwar world, of course, has seen interesting developments in the problem of alternative routes to Communism. But during the history of the Comintern, the Soviet Russian path was declared to be the sole example for the world proletariat and its several Communist parties. If the Soviet Union were ultimately to disappear as a distinct entity, at the very least it would have created a new world in its own image.

PART FIVE

Conclusions

XIII. CONCLUSIONS

One overall conclusion may be stated at the outset. The dominant theme permeating all Comintern doctrines and directives is the theme of *Communist power*—the struggle for Communist power and the uses and goals of Communist power. It seems indisputable that the great preoccupation of individual speakers and writers, of meetings and congresses, and of the official organs of the Comintern is a preoccupation with the problem of Communist power. Politics, not economics, is then the central focus. In Comintern materials economic factors receive only secondary emphasis. These factors hold an inferior place in the speeches and writings of the Comintern theoreticians, and consequently their treatment is often inadequate and blurred. Regardless of the type of society and regardless of the specific kind of revolution that seemed appropriate to the Comintern, in each and every society the basic issue was considered to be the same: how to gain all effective power for the Communist party, which was and is a very special kind of party. As H. H. Fisher has stated it, the Communist revolution is to be engineered through "the accumulation of total power by a small self-perpetuating, carefully recruited, strictly disciplined paramilitary organization."[1]

If Communist power is the great goal, the means of acquiring and retaining power are necessarily of the utmost importance. The exploitation of immediate social unrest and nationalist discontent, the formation of temporary alliances even with elements in the enemy camp, the swift change-over in strategy and tactics to meet new challenges, the injection of a new and undemocratic content into traditionally democratic concepts—these techniques and others are developed and perfected. The atmosphere of the power struggle, even when purely legal means are employed, is for the Communist an atmosphere of perpetual tension, from which no genuine compromise is desired or considered possible. The line between legal and illegal means is for the Communist not the real issue; what matters is that the means bring success, and only in this light are means to be judged.

In Comintern theory, the first stage of the revolutionary process is the stage of preparation for the seizure of power. Basing itself on an acceptance of Marxism-Leninism as the only correct explanation of social change, past, present, and future, the Comintern presented the world as essentially a duality comprising a socialist (i.e., Communist-ruled) sector and a nonsocialist sector. On the one hand, the Soviet Union was pictured as an operating vindication of the claims of Marxism-Leninism—a country moving under Communist leadership in the direction, first, of socialism and, later, after the "victory of socialism" in 1934, in the direction of Communism. On the other hand, the "capitalist-dominated" world was pictured as the battleground for Communist activity on behalf of drastic social change in the direction of socialism and Communism. This nonsocialist sector of the world was complex, embracing a gradation of countries: advanced capitalist societies, societies of medium capitalist development (among which Comintern theory further distinguished two types), colonial, semi-colonial, and dependent societies, and very backward societies. The nonsocialist or "capitalist-dominated" sector was declared to be unproductive, inefficient, and inhumane. It was presented as ruled by a capitalist imperialism that was moribund and decaying, subject to violent crises, and prone to resort to war as a "way out." A fundamental antagonism existed between the socialist and the nonsocialist sector. This antagonism, however, was not to be permanent and would "inevitably" be removed by the victory of the socialist sector.

There is ample evidence for the assertion that this same picture of the world was drawn faithfully and constantly in Comintern literature from 1928 down to 1943. At no time was it suggested that "coexistence" of the two sectors—the socialist and the non-socialist—was possible on a permanent footing. Nor was the essentially critical view of the capitalist system as outmoded and unproductive ever modified. The "necessity" and "inevitability" of the universal replacement of all nonsocialist societies by socialist societies was constantly affirmed. The socialist sector, i.e., the Soviet Union, was never subjected to criticism and its "proletarian" character was never called into doubt.

From the major constants in the Comintern theory of the two worlds, we now pass to the major variables. With respect to the nonsocialist sector, the only important variable concerns the phenomenon of fascism. In the period from 1928 to about 1934, fascism was presented as the final, desperate manifestation of the political rule of the capitalist bourgeoisie; where fascism existed, it was to be followed immediately by the socialist era. In the years after 1934, fascism lost for the Comintern its character as the ultimate stage in the capitalist era; it *might* be replaced by a more democratic stage, falling within the capitalist era and preceding the socialist era. This reinterpretation of fascism held true for the subsequent years down to 1943.

As far as the socialist sector is concerned, two variables may be singled out. For one, it is worth noting that the extremely favorable attitude held by the Comintern in 1928 toward the USSR steadily deepened and broadened, so that the Comintern's recognition of the importance of the USSR in the world movement had, by 1943, vastly expanded even in comparison with the very positive Comintern view of 1928. The other point to note is that after 1934, the presentation of the USSR in neutral or non-Communist terms, i.e., as "democratic" and "peace-loving," received much attention and sometimes even greater attention, than the presentation of the USSR as a socialist society. As has been suggested this presentation did not reflect a change in the basic aims of the Comintern but only in tactics.

The prerequisites of the seizure of power included a situation of severe crisis, permeating the entire society, and the existence of a Communist-led revolutionary movement. The necessity of these prerequisites was consistently proclaimed. There is, however, considerable difficulty in attempting to find out clearly what the Comintern meant by these prerequisites. The revolutionary situation was only briefly defined, always in the familiar Leninist formula, and was devoid of recognizable criteria. The Comintern was content to describe such a situation as one in which a nation-wide crisis prevails, with the result that the "ruling circles" are unable to continue their rule and the masses of the people refuse to accept their condition and are resolved to change it. Admittedly, it would be impossible to judge such a socio-political situation in quantitative terms. But when the Comintern rejects the idea that a revolutionary situation existed in Germany in 1933, for instance, it exposes itself to the charge of extreme arbitrariness in its interpretation of social phenomena. The vagueness of the Leninist formula, copied so faithfully by the Comintern, permits a highly subjective approach to any situation of unrest and instability, and invites abuse of the right of interpretation. It obviously gives the widest possible latitude to the Communist, whose interpretation is not constrained by the existence of specific criteria.

According to the Comintern, the revolutionary situation might arise in a society of weakly developed capitalism as readily as in a highly developed capitalist society. To use the Comintern's words, the revolutionary situation would develop at the "weakest link" in the chain of world capitalism. Viewed by the Comintern as a system that was decadent on a *world* scale, i.e., from the point of view of its overall, world-wide development, the capitalist system was theoretically removable in any single country, if only it could be demonstrated that at a given time the country was the "weakest link" and a "revolutionary situation" existed. Every Communist was educated to live with the idea that the near future might bring a revolutionary situation in his country; the Communist did not then simply await passively the maturing of capitalism in his country.

An additional prerequisite of the seizure of power was the existence of a Communist party possessing certain minimum standards and supported by certain social strata. To say the least, this prerequisite received copious attention in Comintern doctrines and directives.

In Comintern evidence, the Communist party becomes the vanguard of the revolutionary movement all over the world. Without its leadership the revolutionary movement cannot be successful. The party must have certain organizational characteristics, copied from the Communist Party of the Soviet Union. It must attain and demonstrate a mastery of Marxism-Leninism, the official philosophy of the CPSU. And it must have a "correct," i.e., favorable and receptive, attitude toward the Soviet Union—its past experience, its present situation, and its future development. This ruled out the possibility that there could ever exist an orthodox Communist party holding a critical or hostile attitude toward the Soviet Union. Hostility toward the USSR was *ipso facto* clear indication of an incorrect understanding of Marxism-Leninism.

The Communist party was not considered, in Comintern theory, as an effective force in itself. It had to receive broad popular support of some kind, primarily from the proletariat, but also from other groups—the peasantry, the petty bourgeoisie, and the national minorities. But just how much support? Here the evidence is quite vague. Consider the problem of proletarian support. The term "majority of the proletariat" was used to express the necessary degree of support for the Communist party, but this term was expressly defined as signifying not a majority of the class as a whole but only a majority of the "decisive strata." These decisive strata, which were said to be found in important key industries and cities, constituted a very elusive category, defying quantitative measurement.

In addition to its proletarian allies, the party needed support from the peasantry, the petty bourgeoisie, and—where these existed—from national minorities. Support from these groups was considered more important in the more backward societies than in the more advanced societies. Again, just how much support? It seems safe to say, in the case of the peasantry, that the Comintern felt the need of the support of the majority of the poor peasants. But where is the line to be drawn between poor, middle, and well-to-do peasants? The experience of Soviet history shows that the most arbitrary definitions have been applied at various times. The extent of the support needed from the petty bourgeoisie and from the national minorities was even more vaguely expressed.

It should be noted that the Comintern did not mean mass support of the Communist party's *ultimate* program, but support only of the *immediate* program outlined by the party at the time of crisis. Popular support did not necessitate support of fundamental Communist ideals and ultimate aims; of these aims the various social strata might well remain ignorant until after the seizure of power.

Yet one point is clear: the Comintern did not believe in a *putsch* or *coup d'état*. It believed that mass unrest and widespread support for the Communist party were essential prerequisites of the seizure of power. The party's seizure of power was not to be an act of an isolated political élite but rather the act of a party having fairly strong contact with and support drawn first from the workers and second from other "toilers." It is doubtful that the Comintern's concern for considerable mass support in a seizure of power can be written off as hypocritical; the masses were necessary, but in their proper, subordinate place.

Preparation for the fulfillment of these prerequisites (the development of a Communist party and the creation of considerable popular support) was to be undertaken against the background of the changing national and international situation. From 1928 to 1943, considerable alterations, switches, and reversals were made in Comintern strategy and tactics. From 1928 to 1934, the Comintern held to what may be fairly called an inflexible, sectarian line. The strategy and tactics of the united front "from below" segregated Communists from all other political groupings, postulated "social-fascists" (the Social Democrats) as the main enemy, and seriously underestimated the strength of fascism (which was understood simply as a futile and weak last effort by capitalism to avert an immediately threatening revolution). From 1935 to 1939, the popular front "from above" remarkably emancipated Communist activity from the restrictions of the preceding period. Collaboration with other anti-fascist political groupings was encouraged, with the recognition of the possibility that such collaboration might result in the formation, with Communist participation, of popular front governments. Such a government, opening up unprecedented opportunities for Communists to hold ministerial posts *before* the Communist seizure of power, was to direct its main blow against fascists, defined as the worst elements of "finance capital." The Comintern presented such a government, aiming immediately at the creation of a "new democracy," as a dynamic arrangement facilitating the extension of Communist influence and therefore also the achievement of ultimate Comintern aims. From November, 1939, to June, 1941, the popular front was outlined as a popular front "from below," and the war of fascist Germany and Italy with other capitalist states was presented simply as another imperialist war. Communists were directed to create popular fronts, which would oppose, not fascism, but the war as such, and would not aim immediately at socialism but at the "new democracy." From the Nazi invasion of Soviet Russia in 1941 to the dissolution of the Comintern in May, 1943, the pattern of strategy and tactics involved essentially a restoration of the pattern of 1935–1939, the popular front "from above," aiming immediately at the overthrow of the Axis camp. Again, cooperation with other anti-fascist political groupings was demanded and the immediate aim was again that of a new democratic capitalism purged of fascist elements.

Does Comintern theory explain such wide vacillation? From 1928 to 1934, both fascist and Social Democratic forces drew fire, but the heaviest fire was directed against the Social Democrats. The Comintern maintained that a new "third period" in the postwar development of world capitalism had begun and that this period would witness a new round of wars and revolutions. Revolution was "just around the corner." From 1935 to 1939, the Comintern insisted that the same trends were continuing and that the prospects for revolution were getting better and better, but drew the following startling conclusions: 1) fascism was now the main enemy and should get all the practical attention of the Communist parties, 2) Communism and social democracy, as well as bourgeois anti-fascist parties, could profitably ally in a common anti-fascist struggle, and 3) a "new democracy," not a Communist seizure of power, was the immediate goal. The obvious query is: if the prospects for revolution were steadily improving during 1935–1939, why should the Communist parties have accepted less ambitious goals than those of the preceding period? If the working class, as the Comintern asserted, was day by day becoming more revolutionary-minded, why was alliance with social democracy, not to speak of bourgeois parties, so strongly emphasized as an absolutely necessary strategy? If capitalism was becoming more and more hated by the "toiling" masses, why should the Comintern have advocated merely a limited purge and not an outright over-throw of capitalism?

Of course, the international situation in 1935–1939 and Soviet foreign policy make understandable the Comintern strategy and tactics of these years, but the point is that the *Comintern evidence* itself does not adequately explain the switch that took place in 1934–1935. If the basic tendencies in the capitalist world in 1935–1939 were the same as those of 1928–1934, differing only in their greater intensity, then the same pattern of strategy and tactics should have been carried out in 1935–1939 as in 1928–1934. The switch in 1934–1935 in the pattern of strategy and tactics can be rationalized only if new and different fundamental tendencies in world capitalism were discovered by the Comintern, which was not asserted, or if the Comintern condemned completely the basic pattern of strategy and tactics for 1928–1934, which was not done. True, the Comintern did criticize the "sectarianism" of the period 1928–1934 and the underestimation of fascism during those years, but it never asserted that its own broad strategical pattern was basically erroneous and harmful. Of course, to condemn the prescribed pattern of strategy pursued for five or six years is to admit a profoundly serious mistake in the application of the Marxist-Leninist tools of analysis, or even radical defects in the tools themselves. In actual fact, the line followed in the period 1928–1934 was a complete failure.

Another criticism may be stated. The Comintern promised consistently down to the outbreak of war in 1939 that the Communists would struggle to turn imperialist war into a war for the overthrow of capitalism. Yet when the "imperialist" nature of World War II was proclaimed (down to June 22, 1941), the Comintern prescribed a rather tame and lifeless peace movement as the Communist line, and the demand for the overthrow of capitalism as well as fascism is virtually muted.

The insufficiency of Comintern theory with respect to the explanation of sudden changes in the pattern of strategy and tactics is only too obvious in the case of the changing attitude toward fascism. After having seriously underestimated the fascist threat in 1928–1934, the Comintern preached an intensified anti-fascist crusade in 1935–1939, then abruptly abandoned this crusade during the first year and a half of World War II. All in all, Comintern theory is perhaps weakest in its explanation of such shifts in strategy and tactics.

The role that the Comintern evidence assigned to the CPSU and the USSR in the preparation of the prerequisites for a Communist seizure of power in other countries was clearly stated in so far as this role meant ideological guidance, inspiration, and moral support. Certainly study by the various Communist parties of the theory and practice of Soviet Communism was advocated time and again. The influence of the Soviet Union as a "practicing" socialist community was always considered of great weight in attracting support in other countries for the Communist cause. Comintern materials consistently pointed to the restraining pressure exercised by the USSR upon other states to keep them from launching wars. The "peace policy" of the USSR was always interpreted as an important factor in strengthening the world revolutionary movement, for, it was claimed, such a "peace policy" permitted both the USSR—the "bulwark" of world revolution—and the foreign Communist parties to grow stronger and prepare better for the inevitable future conflicts with the class enemy, world capitalism.

Practical aid from the USSR and its Communist Party, such

as funds and equipment, were simply not advertised in Comintern materials.

Now we may turn to the salient features of Comintern evidence on the seizure of power. Change from a nonsocialist society to a socialist society required, according to Comintern materials, a violent wresting of power, by Communists and their supporters, from the hands of the "ruling circles" of the society. Peaceful, evolutionary transitions were considered impossible. For relatively advanced societies, the Comintern prescribed a "proletarian-socialist" revolution; for relatively backward societies, a "bour-geois-democratic" revolution which would eventually "grow over" into a "proletarian-socialist" revolution. In each, violence was to be an inevitable feature.

The Comintern was certainly constant in its view that violence was a necessary and inevitable aspect of this basic social change. The whole weight of the evidence from 1928 to 1943 supports this conclusion. Comintern materials consistently rejected a democratic peaceful transition from one social stage to another. It thus also rejected the relevance and usefulness, for such a transition, of all the democratic techniques developed in the nineteenth and twentieth centuries. Essentially its case rested on the simple-minded and unsatisfactory assertion that the will of the people (who must "inevitably" come to perceive the superiority of a socialist system) cannot be realized by peaceful means in the milieu of a nonsocialist society. There is something old-fashioned and narrow-minded about this very basic and strongly held belief: it denies the genuine democratic gains of the last century and asserts stubbornly that nothing in political techniques has changed since the days of Metternich. The authoritarian nature of the Comintern and the Communist parties was, of course, quite incompatible with demo-cratic processes. Unused to genuine democracy within their ranks, the Communists could hardly be expected to practice democracy outside their party.

Change from a nonsocialist society to a socialist society was always to be under Communist control and direction. This was to be true of every type of society. Even in countries where the development of capitalism was weak and where a "bourgeois-demo-cratic" revolution stood as the first step on the agenda, the revolutionary movement was to be throughout under the control and direction of the Communist party. Thus the Comintern, at least from 1928 on, denied to the bourgeoisie of the world any leading role whatsoever in the change from the feudal stage of development to the capitalist stage. The conclusion reached by Lenin and Trotsky in 1905, that the Russian bourgeoisie could not lead its "own" revolution, was generalized to apply to all countries faced with a "bourgeois-democratic" revolution. The simplification is obvious: only Communists can lead a society to a higher (in Communist eyes) stage of development. Essentially the major "progressive" force in all societies is the same—the Communist party.

Relatively little detailed evidence is to be found on the practical problem of carrying out the Communist seizure of power. Some essential organs of revolt were to be created—the soviets and the Red Guard. In this connection the importance of military training for the proletariat and other "toilers" was strongly emphasized. A background of war, despite the availability of men and weapons to the existing regime that war affords, was always considered to be more favorable than peacetime conditions.

The question of practical aid to be given by the Soviet Union to a Communist-led revolt in another country is certainly one of the most important and intriguing problems in Comintern theory. The absence of explicit assurances in Comintern theory that the Soviet Union would send its armed forces to aid such revolts certainly must not be taken to signify a noninterventionist attitude on the part of the Comintern or the CPSU. Comintern evidence is full of praise for the historical record of the expansion of "socialism" with the help of Soviet arms between 1918 and 1941. The omission in Comintern theory of clear-cut provisions for Soviet military aid has at least two explanations: 1) the public Comintern argument that revolution cannot be artificially "exported" but must be genuinely produced by "objective" and "subjective" factors operating in each country; and 2) the probable undercover argument in the Comintern that theory must necessarily be reticent or silent on certain issues in order to avoid embarrassing the Soviet Union in its conventional international relations. In the case of an attack by an "imperialist" country upon the USSR, however, there was a clear promise by the Comintern that the USSR was not only to defend itself but to seek to overthrow capitalism in the enemy country, with the help of a Communist revolution within that country. Presumably, in such a case the impact of a Soviet offensive against an "imperialist" country was expected to be sufficient to cause a "revolutionary situation" in which the Communist party of that country could act in an armed uprising with Soviet help.

Comintern materials discussed two types of Communist government that may be established by a victorious seizure of power— the "dictatorship of the proletariat" and the "democratic dictatorship of the proletariat and peasantry"—the former being applicable in the "proletarian-socialist" revolution and the latter being applicable in the "bourgeois-democratic" revolution. Yet no real effort was made to provide an adequate statement of any essential difference between these dictatorships, in so far as the actual locus of power is concerned. On the basis of the evidence reviewed in the body of the text, one is led to that conclusion which the Comintern did not state in so many words: Communists were to dominate both types of dictatorships, and the only genuine difference between the types lay in the nature of the immediate tasks to be undertaken by the respective dictatorships. The long-range task— the building of a Communist society—remained, of course, the common ultimate task of all Communist dictatorships. The evidence fails to convince us that either type of dictatorship would be democratic, as this word is understood in normal non-Communist usage.

The uses and goals of Communist power can be divided into two parts: the immediate measures to be undertaken to direct a non-Communist society along the path of socialist development, and the nature of the ultimate Communist society. On the whole, the Comintern materials are more adequate in their treatment of the former question than of the latter. Yet several gaps and obscurities remain.

As to the measures to be undertaken by the Communist dictatorship following the seizure of power in a "proletarian-socialist" revolution, the Comintern presented a fairly comprehensive outline of the most important steps. Some questions were, however, never clarified. A major example is the problem of the "withering away" of the state, a process promised in Comintern theory and one apparently to be completed before the advent of the ultimate Communist utopia. No indications are given as to how this process will manifest itself; we are left simply with the assurances that the most powerful state in the history of the world—a virtually omnipotent and omnipresent state—will voluntarily abdicate.

When Comintern theory deals with the "bourgeois-democratic" revolution the problem of word-meanings becomes almost indescribably difficult. For societies undergoing initially this type of revolution, Comintern theory assigned to the term "bourgeois-democratic" an unexpected and novel content. This kind of "bourgeois-democratic" revolution was admittedly not to be bourgeois in any important sense; nor was it to be democratic, despite Comintern claims to the contrary. The seizure of power was to result in Communist domination over a temporarily mixed economy possessing both a nationalized sector and a capitalist sector. The capitalist sector, controlled by the Communist government, was to be progressively eliminated in measure as socialist construction developed. Perhaps the persistent use by the Comintern of the label "bourgeois-democratic" is the most glaring example of distortion of terms, in which the original meaning is completely displaced by new Communist content.

A serious difficulty lies in the nature of the transition in these societies from a "bourgeois-democratic" revolution to a "proletarian-socialist" revolution. On the one hand, Comintern theory emphasized that these were distinct phases not to be indiscriminately telescoped into one another. On the other hand, Comintern evidence often points out that once power had been seized, the Communist dictatorship had to initiate immediately some tasks of a "proletarian-socialist" nature. No "Chinese wall" separated the two revolutions. A major characteristic of Comintern theory is to be observed here once again: the main issue is Communist power, and theory devoted more attention to placing Communists in power than to clarifying their subsequent exercise of power.

In its very fragmentary discussion of the ultimate Communist utopia, Comintern theory leaves completely unresolved at least three questions of huge importance. One of these questions is the familiar one of power and decision-making. Comintern theory asks us to believe that this problem will be nonexistent simply because the state will have "withered away." Yet administrators will remain: economic experts and planners must be selected in some fashion and must be endowed with authority to make and enforce decisions. Decision-makers will also exist in other, noneconomic fields. Yet any faithful member of the Comintern would object to our criticism on the grounds that a basic transformation of human nature will have been accomplished by the time the state of Communism has begun, and that man's new nature will eliminate the need for coercion or the power to enforce decisions.

This point brings us to the second major inadequacy of theory respecting the ultimate utopia. We are presented with a great promise, as yet unproven and highly optimistic, that man's nature can and will be changed (for the better, of course) during the process of socialist construction. This promise is truly grandiose and inspiring, but must remain an article of faith.

Another major difficulty arises with respect to the problem of any continuing separate identity of the USSR. There is no explicit statement that the USSR as such will disappear, although we are promised that ultimately one world-wide "dictatorship of the proletariat" will emerge. But, in the light of the emphasis in Comintern materials upon the need to study Soviet experience with care and to imitate the NEP and the Five-Year Plans, and probably also War Communism, is it not reasonable to conclude that what the Comintern expected was an expansion of the Soviet Union to include all new "proletarian dictatorships"?

So far we have recapitulated some of the major elements of Comintern evidence on the problem of world revolution. Now we may offer some overall conclusions respecting Comintern evidence as a whole.

It is clear that the Comintern evidence embraced several levels of thought, ranging from what may legitimately be called "theory" to purely propagandistic and sloganized statements. Its uneven quality presents a serious problem in judgment to the student. Obviously greater weight had to be given to the more lofty pronouncements of the Comintern, such as the Program of 1928, than to the relatively primitive clichés of sheer propaganda. Yet even the slogans were revealing, and careful examination of them permits some exposure of underlying beliefs and assumptions. On the whole, the level of Comintern theory deteriorated during the period under study, and especially during 1939–1943. Yet even then Communists the world over continued to read the same "classics" as before.

In addition to its uneven character, there is an obviously "scholastic" quality running through Comintern evidence. By "scholastic" we mean the negative connotation of that term: the recourse to authoritative writings, to "scripture," as the method of proof. Again and again the great "teachers"—Marx, Engels, Lenin, and Stalin—are cited *pro* or *con* a particular point. Their writings and speeches are apparently considered more convincing than logical argumentation based on free and objective inquiry. One fact must not be overlooked: the leaders of the Comintern did not present Comintern theory as a set of doctrines originating in 1919 with the founding of the Comintern. The fundamentals of Comintern theory were regarded as having been worked out earlier, first by Marx and Engels, and later by Lenin. Comintern theory was a development, under changed conditions, of an already well-defined theory with a history dating back to the 1840s. Thus for many important problems Comintern theory simply incorporated certain formulations arrived at by the early "teachers." These formulations were not debated or examined critically; they were adopted wholesale and repeatedly reindorsed. The "tyranny of scripture" continued under the new "teacher," Stalin. The Comintern Congress of 1935 was perhaps the most convincing display of the sacrifice of objective inquiry; Stalin's writings and speeches alone constituted the requisite proof of the correctness of certain formulations.

Another serious cause of weaknesses, especially sins of omission, lies in the domination exercised by the Soviet Union during the whole history of the Communist International. That the control exercised by the USSR had a negative impact on the level of Comintern thought, in so far as this thought was made public, is demonstrable in several ways. In the first place, the actuality of the USSR as a sovereign state necessarily imposed certain restraints upon the development of Comintern doctrines and directives into a complete, consistent, and frankly stated body of theory. Any public pronouncements had to be circumspect in particular areas where the national interests of the USSR were concerned. In such areas, theory often degenerated into vague propagandistic slogans. Obscurities, even gaps in the doctrine of revolution were the result. If the USSR had not existed, if there had been no *state* under Communist rule, then Comintern evidence would most certainly have constituted a "purer" body of theory, untrammeled by considerations of Soviet national interest.

Second, the actuality of the USSR had a deleterious effect upon the development of Comintern theory due to the overwhelming power possessed by the USSR in the Communist world movement. As the only Communist party that ruled a state, the CPSU had immense resources unavailable to any other Communist party. It is not surprising, therefore, that the CPSU enjoyed hegemony in doctrinal matters and that opposition to this hegemony was weak and easily erased. The CPSU was not simply *primus inter pares*; its predominance was uncontested, and all other Communist parties were equally impotent. Thus Comintern theory became quite largely the product of the Stalinist CPSU rather than the joint achievement of theoreticians from several parties.

Third, the existence of the USSR adversely affected the development of Comintern thought by substituting Soviet experience for critical inquiry. Great segments of the Comintern evidence, especially those dealing with the seizure of power and the subsequent uses of power, had only the experience of the USSR and the CPSU to provide practical guidance. All too often, instead of undertaking an independent examination of a problem, a Comintern spokesman would advocate careful study of the experience of the USSR. The serious matter of differences in the social, economic, and political development of various "capitalist" countries simply was not given due examination. The generalization of Soviet Russian experience became a common practice. To be sure, there occurred frequent warnings in Comintern materials respecting the dangers involved in ignoring national differences and in applying Soviet Russian practice to foreign areas too mechanically and indiscriminately. But the failure to develop a body of detailed literature showing theoretical alternatives to the Soviet Russian experience reveals an abject capitulation before the authority of the practical experience of the USSR.

It is obvious that a special and continuing problem facing Comintern spokesmen was the problem of the relationship between Comintern strategy and the strategy of the Soviet foreign office. During the period from 1928 to 1934, the two strategies diverged markedly: the "harder" strategy of the Comintern was extremist, militant, and uncompromising, whereas the "softer" strategy of the Soviet foreign policy sought reduction of international tension as a factor favoring foreign trade as well as "socialist reconstruction" at home. The "harder" line of the Comintern certainly intensified the old fears and suspicions of foreign governments and must have hampered to some degree the effectiveness of the "softer" line then pursued by the Soviet government. After 1934 the two strategies show a close similarity, and the Comintern fully supported the changing foreign policies of the USSR.

What explains the divergence in strategies in 1928–1934? One explanation often given is that the "left" turn taken within the Soviet Union in 1927–1928 was simply reflected in the Comintern, since the CPSU controlled both entities. Just as the Soviet leaders combated the "moderates" in the CPSU and launched a strenuous program of industrialization and collectivization within the USSR, so they proceeded to combat "moderates" in the Comintern and to enforce the most militant, sectarian strategy possible for the Communist parties. The fact that Comintern intransigence and militancy hurt the reputation of the USSR and weakened confidence in it either was not fully understood by the CPSU or was regarded as simply inevitable and unavoidable. Very probably the Soviet leaders had not yet come to realize how useful the Comintern might be as an auxiliary of the Soviet foreign office.

Another kind of explanation may be offered. The Comintern leadership, i.e., essentially the leadership of the CPSU, was accustomed, by the very nature of its basic philosophy, to thinking in stages. The Soviet Union was thought to be in the socialist stage; for the most part, other countries were thought to be in the capitalist or feudal stages, with a few areas in a pre-feudal stage. The immediate goals of the CPSU no longer included the seizure of power, but this aim was the indispensable goal of all other Communist parties. As long as the existence of the USSR, the "proletarian homeland," was not threatened seriously, the Communist parties in other countries were to work actively toward accelerating the creation of conditions for a seizure of power. But when the USSR was thought to be in serious danger, as in the period from 1935 to the end of the Comintern in 1943, the primary activity of the Comintern was to be in the direction of insuring the continued existence of this "proletarian base," so important to the movement as a whole. The requirements of Soviet strategy might even lead to such a situation where the strong possibility of a successful Communist seizure of power would not be tested, as in Spain during the Civil War, and a more limited goal would temporarily be imposed on the Communist party. Facing this problem of the interrelation of the world revolution and the Soviet Union, the disciplined Communist, accustomed to accept the theory of an identity of interests and the obligation to put the safety of the "proletarian base" first above all else, probably did not see a serious conflict of interests. But the problem remains. M. N. Roy has stated it in this fashion: "The contradiction was between the post-revolutionary tasks of the Communist Party of the Soviet Union and the pre-revolutionary problems which confronted the rest of the International."[2]

Another broad characteristic of the content of Comintern thought between 1928 and 1943 is the tendency to reduce the restrictions imposed by "objective laws" upon Communist activity. As is well known, Lenin's modification of Marxism had been in the direction of emancipating the activity of the Communist party from certain restrictive preconditions defined by Marx. The Bolshevik seizure of power in November, 1917, is a case in point, for as a "proletarian" revolution this political event was quite premature in a society with an underdeveloped capitalism and a relatively insignificant proletariat. Comintern evidence continued and strengthened this Leninist trend. This is to be observed, for instance, in the question of prerequisites of the Communist seizure of power. The formula "majority of the proletariat" came to mean not a numerical majority but a majority of the "decisive strata" of the proletariat. A majority of the "decisive strata" could, of course, be considerably smaller than a majority of the proletarian class as a whole. The "decisive strata" are difficult to define, and a "majority" of the "decisive strata" defies any useful explanation.

But it was in the great strategical and tactical switch of 1934–1935 that the emancipation of the Communist party was achieved. It was then that Communists received permission, under suitable circumstances, to join "bourgeois" governments, during the capitalist era and before the Communist seizure of power. The prohibition against this important kind of political activity was withdrawn. The popular-front strategy instructed Communists to join in coalition governments of an "anti-fascist" character in time of national crisis. This new line also instructed the Communists to exploit national traditions and patriotic sentiments. A new and lasting flexibility characterized Communist activity.

From 1935 to 1939 and again from 1941 to 1943, the activity and influence of Communists was further enhanced by the relative blurring in Comintern public statements of the fundamental aims of world revolution and world Communism and the greatly increased emphasis upon the portrayal of Communists as anti-fascists and as defenders of peace and democracy, even under capitalism. This façade made cooperation with Communists appear more acceptable to non-Communists, and suggested, albeit wrongly, to many that Communists were abandoning their more far-reaching and drastic aims.

This misinterpretation of Communist aims raises the final and all-important question in our judgment of the Comintern evidence. Should the materials examined in this study lead to the conclusion that the Comintern ever abandoned, as its fundamental goal, a world revolution under Communist direction and control? In so far as the printed materials of the Comintern are available, and in so far as the answer is based upon their content alone, this answer must be in the negative. The Comintern never gave up the struggle for the great transformation of the world that it had begun in 1919. The evidence for this is quite adequate for the years down to the outbreak of World War II. During the war years, first out of consideration for the Nazi-Soviet Pact and then out of consideration for the anti-Nazi war effort, the aim of world revolution was only indirectly expressed. But expressed it was, for the Comintern was never silent on the subject of the superiority of socialism, the superiority of the USSR, and the superiority of the leadership offered by the Communist parties. All other systems, societies, and political forces were presented as being to a greater or lesser extent inadequate and inferior. The slogans of "Peace," "Victory," and "Democracy" were always linked with the slogan of "Socialism." The prospect of developing a purged and democratic capitalism, free of fascism, was indeed held out, but a careful reading of the evidence will support the conclusion that such a regime, in the Comintern's view, was to be only temporary. Ultimately socialism, and later Communism, would come, and, of course, according to Comintern theory, only under the control and guidance of Communist parties.

For roughly fifteen years the shaping of Communist doctrine for millions the world over was performed through the agency of a Communist International dominated by Stalin. This monolithic era may well turn out to be the period of greatest unity ever enjoyed by world Communism. Indeed, it may be regarded as the second chapter in the history of the international movement. The years from 1917 to the late 1920s constitute the first chapter, during

which Soviet Russian absolutism was achieved by the eradication
of all independent-minded Communists; the years following World
War II, during which the disintegration of Soviet Russian hegemony began, are the third chapter. In brief, the stages are consolidation, monolithism, and polycentrism. Yet, whatever the phase of
historical development of Communism, its leaders have always
emphatically concurred on one point—the overweening importance of a correct world view, sharply differentiating mankind into
two irreconcilable camps of believers and nonbelievers. To ignore
the actuality and content of this world view is to fail in an understanding of Communism.

Notes and
Bibliography

ABBREVIATIONS

Inprecor	International Press Correspondence
KI	Kommunisticheskii Internatsional
Kun, KIVD	Kun, Bela, ed., Kommunisticheskii Internatsional v dokumentakh
VI kongress	VI kongress Kominterna
VII Congress	VII Congress of the Communist International
X plenum	X plenum ispolkom Kominterna
XI plenum	XI plenum IKKI
XII plenum	XII plenum IKKI
XIII plenum	XIII plenum IKKI

NOTES

I. The Problem: Pages 3-15

1. Technically, during the period under study the correct title was All-Union Communist Party (Bolsheviks). I prefer the use of the clearer title given in the text (official since 1952) and its abbreviation, CPSU.

2. If one excludes the insignificant Asian puppet states created under Russian Communist auspices in 1921 and 1922, the Mongolian People's Republic and the Tuvinian People's Republic, both of which were quite isolated from the outside world.

3. Russell, "The End of the Idea of Progress," *The Manchester Guardian Weekly* (March 19, 1953), p. 11.

4. Stalin, *Sochineniia*, I, xiv–xv.

II. Foundations of the Comintern: Pages 16-43

1. On the founding of the International, see the documentary study, *Founding of the First International*, originally published in 1934 by the Marx-Engels-Lenin Institute. There is no satisfactory history of the International, but from the Marxist-Communist viewpoint there are Stekloff, *History of the First International*, and material in Foster, *History of the Three Internationals*. See also Postgate, *The Workers' International*, pp. 11–83, and Valiani, *Storia del Movimento Socialista*. Vol. I: *L'Epoca della Internationale*.

2. From the Provisional Rules of the Association, as given in *Founding of the First International*, p. 40.

3. Balabanoff, *My Life as a Rebel*, p. 113.

4. The best studies of the Second International are by Joll, *The Second International*, and Cole, *A History of Socialist Thought*. Vol. III (in two parts): *The Second International 1889–1914*. See also Lenz, *The Rise and Fall of the Second International*. Earlier editions of this work by a German Communist appeared in German and Russian. Zaidel', *Ocherki po istorii vtorogo internatsionala (1889–1914 gg.)*, is very useful for the

Communist appreciation of the various currents in Marxist thought during this period. For the Second International during World War I, see Fainsod, *International Socialism*.

5. See the excellent study of Bernstein's life and thought by Gay, *The Dilemma of Democratic Socialism*.

6. For a self-portrait, see *Die Volkswirtsschaftslehre der Gegenwart in Selbstdarstellungen*, pp. 117–50.

7. Fainsod, *International Socialism*, pp. 14–15.

8. Meyer, *Marxism: The Unity of Theory and Practice*, p. 135.

9. *Ibid.*, p. 136.

10. In brief, Lenin insisted upon the need for a highly organized and disciplined leadership; Luxemburg relied upon the "spontaneous" activity of the working classes.

11. See Carr, *The Bolshevik Revolution 1917–1923*, III, 567.

12. Besides Fainsod's indispensable study, already cited, see also the valuable documentary volume by Gankin and Fisher, *The Bolsheviks and the World War*.

13. For Lenin's comments, see his report, "Mezhdunarodnyi sotsialisticheskii kongress v Shtutgarte," *Sochineniia*, XII, 78–83. All references in this study to Lenin's works are to the third edition. The Russian text of the Bebel resolution as amended is on pp. 444–46. For the English text, see Joll, *The Second International*, pp. 196–98.

14. Gankin and Fisher, *The Bolsheviks and the World War*, p. 140.

15. *Ibid.*, p. 141.

16. *Ibid.*

17. Lenin's thinking on the subject of a new International during the first year of the war, up to and including the first Zimmerwald Conference of September, 1915, has been recently examined in detailed fashion by Phillips, "Lenin and the Origin of the Third International: July 28, 1914, to September 8, 1915."

18. Lenin, *Sochineniia*, XX, 130.

19. Deutscher, *The Prophet Armed*, p. 217.

20. Gorter, *Der Imperialismus, der Weltkrieg und die Sozialdemokratie*, pp. 146–47 and Chapter XI. The first edition (Dutch) contained an author's note, dated October, 1914.

21. Zaidel', *Ocherki po istorii vtorogo internatsionala*, p. 209.

22. For the Left radicals in Germany, see Frölich, *Rosa Luxemburg: Her Life and Work*, pp. 197–205.

23. See van Ravesteyn, *De Wording van het Communisme in Nederland, 1907–1925*. Among the Tribunists were the poet Herman Gorter, the astronomer Anton Pannekoek, and David Wijnkoop, all future founders of the Dutch Communist Party.

24. Lazitch, *Lénine et la IIIe Internationale*, p. 48. This work was first

published in Geneva in 1950, with the author's name given as Branislav Stranjakovitch.

25. Besides Lenin, there were Zinoviev, Berzin, Radek, Höglund, Nerman, Platten, and Borchardt. Gankin and Fisher, *The Bolsheviks and the World War*, p. 348; Fainsod, *International Socialism*, p. 68.

26. Gankin and Fisher, p. 349.

27. See the autobiography of the secretary of the Zimmerwald movement, Balabanoff, *My Life as a Rebel*, p. 137.

28. Two periodicals were subsequently issued by the International Socialist Committee: a *Bulletin* (Berne), 1915–1917, and the *Nachrichtendienst* (Stockholm), 1917–1918. Gankin and Fisher, *The Bolsheviks and the World War*, p. 756.

29. Lazitch, *Lénine et la IIIe Internationale*, pp. 60–63. It is impossible, for this reason, to accept Isaac Deutscher's view that Lenin "carried with him the second conference of the Zimmerwald movement." Deutscher, *The Prophet Armed*, p. 235.

30. Fainsod, *International Socialism*, p. 212.

31. Lenin, *Sochineniia*, XXIV, 723. Stalin was present for the Russians.

32. *Ibid.*, p. 724.

33. *Ibid.*, p. 753.

34. The eight parties included the Russian, Hungarian, German-Austrian, Lettish, and Finnish Communist parties, and the Polish Communist Labor Party, the Revolutionary Social-Democratic Federation of the Balkans, and the Socialist Labor Party of America. Fainsod, *International Socialism*, p. 202. As Fainsod points out, the real drive for a conference came from the Bolsheviks, regardless of the apparent effort to give the invitation a broad sponsorship.

35. *Ibid.*, pp. 201–3.

36. Lenin, *Sochineniia*, XXIV, 725.

37. Carr, *The Bolshevik Revolution, 1917–1923*, III, 121.

38. Kun is evidently in error when he writes that the Statutes were adopted at the First Congress; there is no indication of this in the official record of the Congress. Kun, *KIVD*, p. 1. At the fifth session of the First Congress a proposal establishing certain governing organs of the Comintern was adopted; this proposal called for a definitive constitution to be presented at the next congress. See *Der I. Kongress der Kommunistischen Internationale*, pp. 220–21.

39. For the text, see *Blueprint*, pp. 33–40.

40. *Inprecor* (June 5, 1928), p. 321. The text of the 1924 Statutes is in Kun, *Komintern v rezoliutsiiakh*, pp. 11–19.

41. For the text, see Kun, *KIVD*, pp. 46–51; *Blueprint*, pp. 249–58; *Inprecor* (November 28, 1928), pp. 1600–1.

42. Although a decision was taken at the Seventh Congress in 1935 to

revise the Statutes in time for the next World Congress, in fact no more congresses were held and no evidence has been found of a fourth set of Statutes. See *VII Congress*, p. 604.

43. In 1919, 1920, 1921, 1922, 1924, 1928, and 1935.

44. Article 4 of the Statutes of 1920.

45. Article 7 of the Statutes of 1924 and Article 8 of the Statutes of 1928.

46. Articles 8 through 11 of the Statutes of 1928.

47. At the Third Congress, for instance, those having a decisive vote were actually in a minority. Kun, *KIVD*, p. 163.

48. Article 8 of the Statutes. Kun, *KIVD*, p. 48; *Blueprint*, p. 252. For the impending Sixth Congress, the Ninth Plenum in February, 1928, arranged the following distribution of votes: RSFSR—50 votes; Young Communist International—30 votes; France, Germany, Czechoslovakia, Italy—25 votes each; Great Britain, China, United States—20 votes each; Poland—15 votes; India, Sweden, Ukrainian SSR—10 votes each; Bulgaria, Yugoslavia, Finland, Norway, Argentina—7 votes each; Japan, Indonesia, Mexico, Belorussian SSR—5 votes each; Hungary, Belgium, Austria, Canada, Rumania—4 votes each; Holland, Australia, South Africa, Switzerland, Georgian SSR, Azerbaijan SSR—3 votes each; Chile, Denmark, Spain, Estonia, Latvia, Lithuania, Greece, Portugal, Turkey, Palestine, Persia, Egypt, Brazil, Columbia, Ireland, Korea, Uruguay, Cuba, Ecuador, Armenian SSR—2 votes each; Syria—one vote. The actual representation at the Sixth Congress deviated slightly from these figures. For details, as given by Piatnitsky, see *Inprecor* (November 21, 1928), p. 1532.

49. *Der I. Kongress der Kommunistischen Internationale*, p. 201.

50. *Blueprint*, p. 37.

51. Carr, *The Bolshevik Revolution, 1917–1923*, III, 393.

52. At the final Seventh Congress in 1935 an ECCI of forty-seven full members and thirty-three candidates was elected. For the list, see *Kommunisticheskii Internatsional: Organ ispolnitel'nogo Komiteta Kommunisticheskogo Internatsionala*, no. 23–24 (1935), p. 159.

53. Tivel', *Chetvertyi kongress Kominterna*, p. 65. Trotsky had already enunciated this conception of the International when he wrote on the eve of the Second Congress that the Comintern "is not an arithmetical sum of national workers' parties. It is the Communist Party of the international proletariat." Trotsky, *The First Five Years of the Communist International*, I, 85.

54. Kun, *KIVD*, p. 48.

55. *Ibid.* There was right of appeal by a section to the next congress, but in the meantime the section was required to carry out the decision.

56. Apparently, only a World Congress could admit *full* members.

57. Tivel' and Kheimo, *10 let Kominterna*, p. 366.

58. Stalin, "O pravoi opasnosti v germanskoi kompartii," *Sochineniia*, XI, 309.

59. There are no published records of ECCI plenums after 1933.

60. *Inprecor* (November 21, 1928), p. 1533.

61. The Fifth Enlarged Plenum in 1925 was attended by 281 delegates, of whom 136 had a decisive vote; in 1924 an ECCI of only 35 members had been elected. At the Ninth Plenum of 1928, which was regular, the decisive vote was limited to the members of the ECCI.

62. *Inprecor* (November 21, 1928), pp. 1533–34.

63. Kun, *KIVD*, p. 50.

64. *KI*, no. 23–24 (1935), p. 160. Many well-known political figures were in the Presidium in 1935, e.g., Stalin, Gottwald, Dimitrov, Cachin, Kolarov, Koplenig, Kuusinen, Manuilsky, Marty, Wang Ming, Okano, Pieck, Pollitt, Thorez, Foster, and Ercoli (Togliatti).

65. Carr, *The Bolshevik Revolution, 1917–1923*, III, 132.

66. *Inprecor* (April 15, 1926), p. 446.

67. The Statutes are quite silent about the powers of the Political Secretariat as a "deciding organ." See Kun, *KIVD*, p. 50.

68. Tivel' and Kheimo, *10 let Kominterna*, p. 365. The following Länder-secretariats existed immediately after the Sixth Congress:

1. Central European (Germany, Czechoslovakia, Austria, Hungary, Switzerland, Holland).
2. Balkan (Bulgaria, Yugoslavia, Rumania, Greece).
3. Anglo-American (England, South Africa, Australia, New Zealand, United States, Canada, Ireland, Philippines).
4. Scandinavian (Sweden, Norway, Denmark, Iceland).
5. Polish-Baltic (Poland, Latvia, Lithuania, Estonia, Finland).
6. Romance (France, Italy, Belgium, Spain, Portugal, Luxemburg).
7. Latin-American (Mexico, etc.).
8. Eastern (China, Japan, Korea, India, Indonesia, Turkey, Palestine, Egypt, Persia, Indochina).

69. *KI*, no. 23–24 (1935), p. 160.

70. Nollau, *Die Internationale*, p. 109. Nollau gives a rather full treatment of the Comintern organization, pp. 104–50.

71. Lenin, it may be noted, was elected Honorary Chairman of the Comintern in 1923. *Rasshirennyi plenum ispolnitel'nogo Komiteta Kommunisticheskogo Internatsionala (12–23 iiunia 1923 goda): Otchet*, p. 4.

72. *Puti mirovoi revoliutsii: Sed'moi rasshirennyi plenum ispolnitel'nogo komiteta Kommunisticheskogo Internatsionala (22 noiabria–16 dekabria 1926)*, I, 14.

73. *Ibid.*, II, 468. The Plenum's decision acknowledged the necessary constitutional formality of seeking subsequent confirmation for this action at the coming Sixth Congress.

74. The title of president (chairman) is ascribed to Bukharin by Foster, *History of the Three Internationals*, p. 361, and by Gitlow, *I Confess*, p. 549.

75. Gitlow refers to Molotov as Bukharin's successor in the chairmanship of the Comintern, *I Confess*, p. 549.

76. Technically speaking, this office was not new for the Bulgarian Kolarov was General Secretary in 1922–1923. *Bol'shaia Sovetskaia Entsiklopediia* (2d ed., 1953), XXI, 580. The office apparently lapsed thereafter.

77. The Russian text is in Kun, *KIVD*, pp. 100–4, and in Lenin, *Sochineniia*, XXV, 575–79.

78. Kun, *KIVD*, pp. 201–25.

79. *Ibid.*, p. 220. Italics in the original.

80. *Ibid.*, p. 221. My italics. It is clear that the system of dual responsibility of executive organs, so characteristic of the Soviet Party and governmental structures, was carried over into the Comintern.

81. The Russian is "obmen . . . rukovodiashchimi silami," which apparently refers to the (temporary?) exchange of personnel at the top level to facilitate multiparty cooperation.

82. For the text of this part of the Statutes, see Kun, *KIVD*, pp. 50–51, and *Blueprint*, pp. 257–58.

83. *VII Congress*, pp. 566 and 604.

84. The two volumes by Borkenau are indispensable: *World Communism* and *European Communism*. In addition, see among others: Ypsilon, *Pattern for World Revolution*; Ruth Fischer, *Stalin and German Communism*; and Gitlow, *I Confess*.

85. *Inprecor* (April 26, 1929), p. 435.

86. *Inprecor* (February 18, 1929), p. 327.

87. Gitlow, *I Confess*, p. 516. Gitlow remarks: "Under the statutes of the Communist International, its representatives had the power to make any ruling they desired and it was our duty as members of the Communist International to accept them as binding upon us."

88. *Kommunisticheskii Internatsional pered VII vsemirnym kongressom: Materialy*, p. 593. It should be pointed out that the ICC also ruled informally on an undeclared number of cases through the medium of "oral decisions." The British Communist McCarthy, reporting one example of prolonged chastisement, writes: "In 1931 practically the entire Central Committee of the Greek Party was in Moscow for over a year, to my certain knowledge, while the Comintern painfully and slothfully went over their mistakes and resolved on disciplinary action." *Generation in Revolt*, p. 200.

89. Kun, *KIVD*, p. 48.

90. *Inprecor* (September 14, 1934), p. 1266.

91. Borkenau, *European Communism*, p. 227. Borkenau is, however, in error when he says that the same fate befell the Yugoslav Party. A

serious purge, but not dissolution, did begin in 1937. See the political report by Tito in *V kongress Komunisticke Partije Yugoslavije: Izvestaji i referatii*, pp. 47–48, and Dedijer, *Tito*, p. 115.

92. Much interesting material on the Lenin School is given in the memoirs of the Finnish ex-Communist Tuominen, *Kremls Klockor*, pp. 21–43. Some description of the courses in 1931 is in McCarthy, *Generation in Revolt*, pp. 117–18. See also Burmeister, *Dissolution and Aftermath of the Comintern: Experiences and Observations, 1937–1947*, pp. 4–10.

93. Kardelj, later to become Tito's foreign minister, gave lectures at the KUNMZ on Comintern history. Dedijer, *Tito*, p. 104.

94. *Ibid.*, p. 103.

95. *Ibid.*, p. 116. The acceptance of these subsidies was, it is claimed, discontinued by Tito after his accession to party leadership in 1937.

96. For example, Tito ascribes to Manuilsky alone the decision that no Yugoslav should be elected to full membership in the ECCI at the Seventh World Congress. Dedijer, *Tito*, p. 105. Manuilsky's powerful influence is described at length in Ravines, *The Yenan Way*.

97. Borkenau, *European Communism*, pp. 226–29.

98. Such was the decision of Ignazio Silone. See his account of high-handed procedure at the Eighth Plenum in May, 1927, in Crossman, *The God That Failed*, pp. 107–13.

99. Kun, *KIVD*, pp. 61–65.

100. Mingulin, *Pervyi kongress Kominterna*, pp. 51–52.

101. Kun, *KIVD*, p. 1.

102. Trotsky, *The Third International After Lenin*, p. 311.

103. Tivel' and Kheimo, *10 let Kominterna*, p. 48.

104. Kun, *KIVD*, p. 1.

105. *Inprecor* (April 17, 1924), p. 229.

106. The draft can be found in *Le Programme de l'internationale communiste*, pp. 33–55.

107. *Inprecor* (August 12, 1924), p. 609.

108. *Inprecor* (June 6, 1928), p. 549.

109. Stalin, *Sochineniia*, XI, 362.

110. For the text, see *KI* (June, 1928), pp. 49–79, and *Inprecor* (June 6, 1928), pp. 549–64. The text is also given in the official report of the Sixth Congress. See also *VI kongress*, III, 156–92.

111. Stalin, *Sochineniia*, XI, 141–56. The resolution of the July Plenum called upon members of the CPSU to submit their emendations directly to the Program Commission, thus indicating that discussion was not terminated by the Plenum's approval of the Draft. *Ibid.*, p. 204.

112. Stalin charged that "certain circles around the Comintern" had labeled the Draft Program as "too Russian," but he absolved the July Plenum of any such sin. *Ibid.*, p. 150.

113. Ypsilon, *Pattern for World Revolution*, pp. 118–19.

114. One faction of the badly split American Communist Party was accused by the other faction of drawing arguments from a hundred-page criticism of the Draft Program "belonging to the pen of former comrade Trotsky." *VI kongress*, I, 282.

115. Trotsky, *The Third International After Lenin*, p. 346. This volume includes both the criticism of the Draft Program and the letter.

116. *VI kongress*, I, 99.

117. *Ibid.*, p. 100.

118. Günther, *Shestoi kongress Kominterna*, p. 26. The commission subdivided into a "broad" commission, where issues were initially debated, and a "narrow" commission, which apparently decided upon the precise wording. See Bukharin's remarks, *VI kongress*, V, 132.

119. *Ibid.*, p. 132.

120. As discussed in Chapter V, a major "sin" of Bukharin was his alleged belief that capitalists could so organize national economies that internal conflict would disappear.

121. See, for example: Ypsilon, *Pattern for World Revolution*, p. 117; Trotsky, *The Third International After Lenin*, p. 311; and Souvarine, *Stalin*, p. 484.

122. Schifrin, "Die Bekenntnisse der Komintern," *Die Gesellschaft* (January, 1929), pp. 44–46.

123. Lazitch, *Lénine et la IIIe Internationale*, p. 212.

124. *Inprecor* (December 11, 1930), p. 1200.

125. Florinsky, *World Revolution and the USSR*, p. 178.

126. Ebon, *World Communism Today*, p. 21.

127. Souvarine, *Stalin*, p. 484. Bukharin's stress on the "collective" nature of the work of the Sixth Congress in revising the Draft Program may have been an ironical recognition of Stalin's interference. *VI kongress*, V, 132.

128. Stalin, *Sochineniia*, XI, 202–4.

129. "15 let Kommunisticheskogo Internatsionala (tezisy dlia dokladchikov)," *KI* (March 10, 1934), p. 139.

130. Stalin, *Sochineniia*, XI, 362.

131. Kabakchiev, *Kak voznik*, p. 235.

132. *XVI s"ezd vsesoiuznoi kommunisticheskoi partii (b): Stenograficheskii otchet*, p. 427. Molotov noted that the Program had been translated into thirty-three languages.

133. "Rech' t. Dimitrova pered fashistskim sudilishchem," *KI* (April 1, 1934), p. 15.

134. *Inprecor* (May 11, 1934), p. 779.

135. *Inprecor* (June 22, 1934), p. 948.

III. REVOLUTIONARY PROSPECTS AND STRATEGY, 1919–1928:
PAGES 44–57

1. This paragraph and the next three are based on these documents,
See Kun, *KIVD*, pp. 53–66.

2. Lenin made this identification in his well-known brochure of 1916.
Imperialism, the Highest Stage of Capitalism, wherein he equated the term
"imperialism," as used by the Englishman J. A. Hobson, with the term
"finance capital," as used by the Austrian Rudolf Hilferding. Stalin
employed the same identification in his speech at the Seventh Enlarged
Plenum of the ECCI in 1926. *Sochineniia*, IX, 101–2 and elsewhere.

3. Kun, *KIVD*, p. 61.

4. *Ibid.*, pp. 66–73.

5. Lazitch, *Lénine et la IIIe Internationale*, p. 118. The same view is
expressed in the explanatory note on the First Congress in Stalin,
Sochineniia, I, 429. See also Komor, *Ten Years of the Communist International*, p. 14.

6. Borkenau, *World Communism*, p. 191. For the text, see Lenin,
Sochineniia, XXV, 171–249.

7. Kun, *KIVD*, pp. 113–19 and 120–26.

8. *Ibid.*, pp. 104–11.

9. *Ibid.*, pp. 100–4.

10. For the theses of the Second Congress on the national and
colonial questions, based on Lenin's views, see Kun, *KIVD*, pp. 126–30.
The "Supplementary Theses" on pp. 130–32 were based on the views
of M. N. Roy, the Indian delegate.

11. *Ibid.*, p. 129.

12. *Ibid.*, pp. 132–39.

13. *Ibid.*, p. 166.

14. *Ibid.*, p. 181.

15. *Ibid.*, p. 183.

16. See the discussion of the mood of the Congress in Carr, *The
Bolshevik Revolution, 1917–1923*, III, 441–46.

17. Kun, *KIVD*, p. 415.

18. *Ibid.*, p. 529.

19. *Ibid.*, p. 530.

20. *Ibid.*

21. *Ibid.*, pp. 303–10.

22. For good brief accounts of this collaboration, see especially Louis
Fischer, *The Soviets in World Affairs*, II, 632–79, and North, *Moscow and
Chinese Communists*, pp. 66–97.

23. Kun, *KIVD*, p. 701.

24. Carr, *The Bolshevik Revolution, 1917–1923*, III, 448.

25. *Ibid.*
26. Kun, *KIVD*, p. 198.
27. Trotsky, *The First Five Years of the Communist International*, I, 267–68.
28. Kun, *KIVD*, p. 327.
29. *Ibid.*, pp. 699–717. On the "war scare" of 1927, see Louis Fischer, *Soviets in World Affairs*, II, 739–42.
30. Kun, *KIVD*, p. 411.
31. *Ibid.*, p. 412.
32. *Ibid.*, p. 411.
33. Kabakchiev, *Kak voznik*, p. 159.
34. *Ibid.*, p. 161.
35. Kun, *KIVD*, p. 479. Italics in the original.
36. *Ibid.*, pp. 478–79.
37. *Ibid.*, pp. 472–95. The document lays heavy stress upon the Leninist-Bolshevik tradition throughout, but a small concession is made to the merits of a few outside this tradition: Paul Lafargue, a son-in-law of Karl Marx; Jules Guesde, "when Guesde was still a Marxist"; the Chartists; Wilhelm Liebknecht and August Bebel; and Plekhanov, "when he was still a Marxist." *Ibid.*, p. 480.
38. The story of the diminishing faith of the Comintern in the immediacy of world revolution is traced in an article by Florinsky, "World Revolution and Soviet Foreign Policy," *Political Science Quarterly*, XLVII (June, 1932), 204–33.

IV. Prerequisites: Pages 61–112

1. See the interesting debate on the peculiarities of revolution in dependent areas presented in *Kommunisticheskii Internatsional* in 1935: V. Miro, "Bor'ba za sozdanie vnutrennikh sovetskikh raionov v polukolonial'nykh stranakh," *KI* (January 1, 1935), pp. 38–45; and Li, "K voprosu ob usloviiakh sozdaniia vnutrennikh sovetskikh raionov v polukolonial'nykh stranakh (otvet t. V. Miro)," *KI* (January 10, 1935), pp. 40–51.
2. Federn, *The Materialist Conception of History*, pp. 1–3.
3. *Ibid.*, p. 2 (Federn's eleventh proposition).
4. Stalin, *Problems of Leninism*, p. 21. The eleventh edition is used in this study.
5. Kun, *KIVD*, p. 9.
6. Stalin, *Problems of Leninism*, p. 21.
7. "Tailism" *(khvostizm)* means, for Communists, a passive waiting upon or lagging behind events, rather than a conscious effort to lead, control, and even accelerate the revolutionary process.

8. A. Martynov, "Lenin, Liuksemburg, Libknekht," *KI* (January 10, 1933), p. 14.

9. Deutscher, *The Prophet Armed*, p. 156.

10. Used, for example, in the title to Chapter I of the Comintern Program, in which the concept is discussed. See Kun, *KIVD*, pp. 4–9.

11. "Kak ispol'zovat' chrezvychaino blagopriiatnuiu situatsiiu, kak preodolet' otstavanie," *KI* (April 20, 1931), p. 10.

12. *X plenum*, I, 118.

13. "Put' Kominterna," *KI* (1929), no. 9–10, p. 12.

14. Kun, *KIVD*, pp. 29–30.

15. *Ibid.*, p. 29.

16. In the sense employed, for example, by Clarke in his well-known volume, *The Conditions of Economic Progress*.

17. Kun, *KIVD*, p. 29.

18. The Draft Program of 1928 had singled out only Russia (before 1917) and Poland. *Inprecor* (June 6, 1928), p. 559.

19. *Inprecor* (June 6, 1928), p. 559.

20. *VI kongress*, III, 150.

21. Kun, *KIVD*, p. 29.

22. *VI kongress*, III, 35.

23. *Ibid.*, p. 47.

24. "Proekt programmy kompartii Pol'ski (sektsii Kommunisticheskogo Internatsionala)," *KI* (August 30, 1932), p. 71.

25. Kun, *KIVD*, p. 9.

26. On this dictatorship, see Borkenau, *World Communism*, pp. 108–33.

27. *Kommunisticheskii Internatsional pered VII vsemirnym kongressom: Materialy*, pp. 149–50.

28. This and the remaining quotations in the paragraph are from the "Otkrytoe pis'mo k chlenam kommunisticheskoi partii Vengrii," printed in *KI* (November 22, 1929), pp. 67–69.

29. *VI kongress*, III, 107.

30. *XII plenum*, II, 83.

31. *Ibid.* In Pieck's report to the Seventh Congress in 1935, he pinpointed the beginning of the Spanish "bourgeois-democratic" revolution to the year 1931, when the monarchy was overthrown. *VII Congress*, p. 42.

32. Ercoli, "Ob osobennostiakh Ispanskoi revoliutsii," *KI* (October, 1936), pp. 14–16.

33. See the analysis in the Comintern editorial, "Polozhenie v Iaponii i zadachi KPIa," *KI* (March 30, 1932), pp. 3–12.

34. See Kuusinen's report, *XII plenum*, I, 23.

35. Swearingen and Langer, *Red Flag in Japan*, p. 26.

36. *Ibid.*, pp. 43–44. The reasons for this change are unclear. It is doubtful that the change was based solely on a desire of the Comintern to purge the Japanese theses of "Bukharinist" elements, as the authors suggest. With Bukharin's participation, a number of countries had been assigned a particular type of revolution, which continued to be held applicable by the Comintern even after Bukharin's downfall. Bukharin's supposed sins lay in other fields.

37. Magyar *et al.*, *Programmnye dokumenty kommunisticheskikh partii vostoka*, p. 241.

38. *Ibid.*

39. *Ibid.*, p. 241.

40. The report, apparently not published in the Comintern periodicals, is given in Mif and Voitinskii, *Sovremennaia Iaponiia*, pp. 26–38.

41. *Ibid.*, p. 32.

42. *Ibid.*, p. 33.

43. *Ibid.*, p. 34.

44. *Ibid.*

45. *Inprecor* (June 6, 1928), p. 559.

46. Kun, *KIVD*, p. 30.

47. *VI kongress*, IV, 220.

48. Kun, *KIVD*, p. 30.

49. For a critical analysis of Marx's five stages, see Federn, *The Materialist Conception of History*, Chapter V. For a full-scale discussion of the "Asiatic mode of production," see Wittfogel, *Oriental Despotism: A Comparative Study of Total Power*, especially Chapter IX.

50. Kun, *KIVD*, p. 30.

51. *Ibid.*

52. *Ibid.*

53. *Ibid.*, p. 763.

54. *Ibid.*

55. Perhaps Abyssinia fell in this category. See the description given by Ercoli (Togliatti) at the Seventh Comintern Congress: "Abyssinia is an economically and politically backward country. No trace of a national-revolutionary movement or even of a democratic movement has yet been in evidence there. It is a country, moreover, in which the transition from a feudal regime, the substructure of which is semi-independent tribes, to a centralized monarchy is taking place rather slowly." *VII Congress*, p. 413.

56. In Comintern usage, the "national bourgeoisie" is the native-born bourgeoisie of a colony or any other backward society under the control of imperialist countries; a foreign-born bourgeoisie, representing the imperialist countries, is also present in the colony. The "national bourgeoisie" vacillates between two loyalties: to the patriotic anti-

imperialist struggle and to the bourgeois class of which the "national bourgeoisie," like the foreign-born bourgeoisie, is a part.

57. Kun, *KIVD*, p. 30.

58. Lenin, *Sochineniia*, XXV, 165–250.

59. A. Martynov, "Problema pererastaniia mirovogo ekonomicheskogo krizisa v politicheskii," *KI* (December 20, 1930), p. 8.

60. See, for example, the theses entitled "Measures of Struggle with the Danger of Imperialist Wars," adopted at the Sixth Comintern Congress, which stated in part: "A revolutionary situation must exist, i.e., a crisis among the ruling classes, provoked, for example, by military defeats. There must be an *extraordinary* worsening in the situation of the masses and in their oppression, and an increase in the activity of the masses and in their readiness to fight for the overthrow of the government by way of revolutionary action." Kun, *KIVD*, p. 808.

61. Schlesinger, *Marx: His Time and Ours*, p. 256.

62. Kun, *KIVD*, p. 43.

63. *Ibid.*, p. 41.

64. *Ibid.*

65. Lenin, "Chto delat'?" *Sochineniia*, IV, 359–509. Lenin, utilizing certain writings of Karl Kautsky, said the proletariat by itself could attain only a "trade-union consciousness," which would lead the proletariat to struggle for higher wages and better working conditions but not for the overthrow of capitalism.

66. See, for example, the article by V. Knorin, a member of the ECCI, entitled "II s"ezd RSDRP i mezhdunarodnaia sotsialdemokratiia," *KI* (August 10, 1933), pp. 3–11; and Manuilsky's remarks at the Seventh Comintern Congress, *VII Congress*, pp. 262–63.

67. *Ibid.*, pp. 51–52. See also Stalin, *Problems of Leninism*, p. 481.

68. Kun, *KIVD*, p. 3.

69. *XIII plenum*, p. 583.

70. *VII Congress*, p. 277.

71. *Ibid.*, p. 273.

72. In Communist thinking, there are two basic categories of heresy involving deviation from or opposition to the orthodox line of the party. These categories are labeled "left" and "right." While the difference between the two is not always clear, generally speaking a "left" deviation or opposition is seen as an excessively sectarian, and therefore detrimental, concern for doctrinal purity regardless of the demands of real-life situations. Correspondingly, a "right" deviation or opposition is seen as a willingness to sacrifice doctrinal purity and to compromise opportunistically with real-life situations. Thus the "left" sins in the direction of unrealistic revolutionary zeal and is often overly optimistic, while the "right" is excessively cautious and prone to view

pessimistically the possibilities for revolutionary changes. Both "left" and "right" are, of course, deviations from the party line, which is always "correct," however fickle it may appear to the bewildered non-Communist.

73. See also, on the "right" deviation in this period, Lentsner, *O pravoi opasnosti v Kominterne*, and Nordman and Lenskii, *Pravyi uklon v Kominterne*.

74. One Communist who reportedly opposed this Pact was the Hungarian Laszlo Rajk, who was consequently expelled from the Communist Party. Later, he reentered the party during the resistance movement against Hitler, and became one of the foremost leaders in the "Hungarian People's Democracy"; he was executed as a traitor in 1951, but was given a "posthumous rehabilitation" in 1956. "Rajk rehabilité," *Est et Ouest* (May 1–15, 1956), p. 7.

75. *XI plenum*, I, 41.

76. *VII Congress*, p. 355.

77. Kun, *KIVD*, pp. 38–40.

78. Revolutionary syndicalism has much in common with anarchism but departs from strict anarchism in its concession that the trade union is a beneficial and necessary organizational form, both prior to and during the future workers' utopia.

79. On Garveyism, see Edmund David Cronon, *Black Moses: The Story of Marcus Garvey and the Universal Negro Improvement Association* (Madison, University of Wisconsin Press, 1955).

80. Kun, *KIVD*, pp. 40–41.

81. Communists were not immune to the influence of fascism, as is perhaps best shown by the case of Doriot, the French Communist. Ypsilon, *Pattern for World Revolution*, pp. 211–18.

82. At the Seventh Congress in 1935 Dimitrov observed that "the most reactionary variety of fascism is the *German type* of fascism." *VII Congress*, p. 126.

83. "Mirovaia partiia proletariata novogo tipa," *KI* (March 10, 1934), pp. 3–7.

84. *Ibid.*, p. 3.

85. *Ibid.*, p. 7.

86. *Inprecor* (March 8, 1929), p. 224.

87. Kun, *KIVD*, p. 35.

88. *VII Congress*, pp. 602–3.

89. *Ibid.*, p. 427.

90. *Ibid.*, p. 56.

91. The most important documents include: "The Conditions of Entry into the Communist International (the 21 conditions)," adopted at the Second Congress in 1920; "The Organizational Structure of the Communist Parties, the Methods and Content of Their Work," adopted

at the Third Congress in 1921; and "The Reconstruction of the Parties on the Basis of Production Cells," adopted at the Fifth Congress in 1924. These documents are in the collection edited by Kun.

92. Kun, *KIVD*, p. 202.

93. *Ibid*. Historically, this term had currency in Bolshevik circles at least as far back as 1905. In 1919 it was given a final definition and incorporated into the Rules of the Russian Communist Party. See Moore, *Soviet Politics—the Dilemma of Power*, pp. 64–70.

94. Kun, *KIVD*, p. 204. The party member was also expected to pay membership dues and subscribe to the party newspaper.

95. *Ibid.*, p. 219.

96. The Fourth Congress declared that "not one Communist party can be regarded as a serious and solidly organized mass Communist party unless it has stable Communist cells in the factories, plants, mines, railroads, etc." *Ibid.*, p. 302.

97. See the very interesting discussion of the problem of the "proletarian base" in the Chinese Communist Party in Schwartz, *Chinese Communism and the Rise of Mao*, pp. 191–99.

98. For example, the People's Revolutionary Party of the very backward and remote country of Tuva, lying to the northeast of Mongolia, was in 1935 admitted as a section of the Comintern "with the rights of a sympathizing party." *VII Congress*, p. 604. Tuva was annexed by the USSR during World War II.

99. A noted political scientist, Raymond Aron, has recently discussed the distinction between the term "proletariat" as used to denote industrial workers and Toynbee's use of the term to denote a state of mind characterized by feelings of dehumanization, disinheritance, and exclusion from society; with Marx, he points out, these two definitions coincided. See Aron, "Workers, Proletariats, and Intellectuals," *Diogenes*, no. 10 (1955), pp. 31–46. It is obvious that the Comintern, despite the great improvement in the lot of the industrial workers since the mid-nineteenth century, faithfully continued to follow Marx in its understanding of the term "proletariat."

100. Kun, *KIVD*, p. 41.

101. *VII Congress*, p. 264.

102. *Inprecor* (June 28, 1928), p. 664.

103. "I maia–I avgusta," *KI* (June 20, 1929), p. 4.

104. "Bol'shevistskii ogon' po opportunizmu," *KI* (August 30, 1932), p. 6. See also in the same issue the article by Al Griunberg and Vl. Kuchumov, "Teoriia i taktika t. Iablonskogo."

105. A. Martynov, "Perekliuchenie na boevuiu takticheskuiu ustanovku—perekhod na 'russkii put'," *KI* (October 30, 1932), p. 29.

106. *X plenum*, I, 43–49.

107. The important resolution of the Second Comintern Congress, "Role of the Communist Party in the Proletarian Revolution," stated that prior to the seizure of power "the Communist party as a rule will have in its organized ranks only a minority of the workers." Kun, *KIVD*, p. 105.

108. *XI plenum*, I, 398–99.

109. O. Piatnitsky, "O sovremennom polozhenii v Germanii," *KI* (July 10, 1933), p. 51.

110. *X plenum*, I, 47.

111. *Ibid.*, p. 48.

112. Mingulin, "Ocherednye voprosy KP SASSh," *KI* (October 20, 1933), p. 92.

113. Kun, *KIVD*, p. 42.

114. *X plenum*, I, 46.

115. For a typical statement, see T. Neibauer, "Nasha rabota sredi melkoburzhuaznykh srednikh sloev," *KI* (March 20, 1931), p. 32.

116. For example, Thorez, at the VII Congress in 1935, stated: "It is undeniable that the masses of the people in town and country, the middle classes and the peasants in particular, play a very important historic role. But this role is never an independent one, however; they either fall under the influence of the big bourgeoisie, of capital, and become the tool of its policy, or they ally themselves with the working class." *VII Congress*, p. 214.

117. Kun, *KIVD*, pp. 132–33.

118. *XI plenum*, I, 347.

119. *Ibid.*, p. 408.

120. Kun, *KIVD*, p. 42.

121. "Ideologicheskie oshibki i probely pri provedenii reshenii XI plenum IKKI," *KI* (February 20, 1932), p. 13.

122. L. Magyar, "Agrarnaia politika diktatury v Vengrii," *KI* (March 22, 1929), pp. 21–22.

123. P. Iskrov, "Kompartiia Bolgarii pered reshaiushchimi boiami," *KI* (November 20, 1932), p. 37.

124. "Nereshennye zadachi ispanskoi revolutsii (k IV s"ezdu KP Ispanii)," *KI* (January 30, 1932), p. 30.

125. B. Boshkovich, "IV s"ezd KPIu," *KI* (January 25, 1929), p. 43.

126. It is well known that Lenin and Trotsky, in their appraisals of the 1905 Revolution in Russia, concluded that the bourgeoisie was unable to carry through successfully the "bourgeois-democratic" revolution in Russia and that this job must be done by other, more revolutionary classes. See Carr, *The Bolshevik Revolution*, 1917–1923, I, 53–60.

127. P. Iskrov, "KP Bolgarii zavoevala bol'shinstvo proletariata," *KI* (August 10, 1933), p. 28. At this time (1933), the Party had only

3,832 members. See G. Alikhanov, "Ob organizatsionnom sostoianii kompartii na Balkanakh," *KI* (April 20, 1934), p. 66.

128. Kun, *KIVD*, p. 29. Other possible allies are not mentioned in the Program.

129. A. Martynov, "Strategiia i taktika v bor'be s kulachestvom," *KI* (September 20, 1932), p. 21.

130. B. Boshkovich, "Kompartiia Iugoslaviia v usloviiakh voennofashistskoi diktatury," *KI* (July 31, 1930), p. 55.

131. *Inprecor* (May 10, 1929), p. 493.

132. *XI plenum*, I, 209.

133. O. Kuusinen, "O natsional'nom voprose v kapitalisticheskoi Evrope," *KI* (August 20, 1931), pp. 13–16.

134. Seton-Watson, *From Lenin to Malenkov*, pp. 123–26.

135. Kun, *KIVD*, p. 849.

136. See especially the speeches of Kuusinen, the main reporter on the colonial question at the Sixth Congress, in *VI kongress*, IV, 6–30 and 505–29. He referred to the hegemony of the proletariat in the colonial revolutionary movement as the "leading idea" of the theses on this question. *Ibid.*, pp. 505–6.

137. Kun, *KIVD*, p. 853.

138. *Ibid.*

139. *VI kongress*, IV, 525–26.

140. V. Vasil'eva, "V preddverii indokitaiskoi revoliutsii," *KI* (February 20, 1931), p. 60.

141. Based largely upon the theses on the revolutionary movement in the colonial and semi-colonial countries adopted by the Sixth Congress in 1928. See Kun, *KIVD*, pp. 832–70 and especially pp. 846–50.

142. *Ibid.*, p. 346.

143. According to the Program of 1928, temporary agreements might be made with the bourgeoisie, but "only in so far as it does not hamper the revolutionary organization of the workers and peasants, and [in so far as the bourgeoisie] carries on a genuine struggle against imperialism." Kun, *KIVD*, p. 43.

144. "The *peasantry* along with the proletariat, and as its ally, is the driving force of the revolution." *Ibid.*

145. *Ibid.*, p. 347.

V. STRATEGY AND TACTICS, 1928–1934: PAGES 113–139

1. For an expert analysis of 1929, see Galbraith, *The Great Crash*.

2. Quoted by Galbraith, *The Great Crash*, p. 6.

3. Sharp and Kirk, *Contemporary International Politics*, p. 368. "This act forced other nations to adopt a variety of short-term expedients, the

cumulative effect of which was to destroy most of the domestic protective value of each, thereby leaving all the countries in a worse condition than before. More than this . . . the Smoot-Hawley tariff was instrumental in placing the world in the worst possible condition, psychologically, for any serious consideration of the cooperative, long-term measures which alone might have sufficed to save the day."

4. *Year Book of Labour Statistics, 1943–44*, p. 250.

5. Galbraith, *The Great Crash*, p. 172.

6. See the Stalinist account, *History of the Communist Party of the Soviet Union: Short Course*, pp. 320–21.

7. Often termed in Communist literature the "anti-party bloc of Trotskyites and Zinovievites." *Ibid.*, pp. 280–85.

8. Often termed the "Bukharin-Rykov anti-party group." *Ibid.*, pp. 291–95. Rykov was then Chairman of the Council of People's Commissars, i.e., he held Lenin's former post in the Soviet government.

9. The ablest, and mutually antithetical, biographies of Stalin are Deutscher's *Stalin: A Political Biography* and Souvarine's *Stalin: A Critical Study of Bolshevism*.

10. Kun, *KIVD*, p. 769.

11. *Ibid.*, pp. 769–93.

12. *Ibid.*, p. 769.

13. *Ibid.*, p. 770.

14. *Srashchivanie:* growing together, merging.

15. Kun, *KIVD*, p. 770.

16. Perhaps a good example in the Comintern's view of the "growing together" of economics and politics would be the political organization of German business during the Nazi era into a hierarchical structure operating "in a twofold capacity: as a self-governing body and as an organ of the state." Neumann, *Behemoth*, p. 201. "From a juristic point of view, the organizations have a twofold task, as does every self-governing body in German law. They carry out genuine functions of self-government and they also carry out state functions that are delegated to them by the public authorities."

17. *Inprecor* (February 25, 1928), p. 214.

18. See Neumann, *Behemoth*, pp. 181–86. For a clearer analysis of state capitalism, see also the conclusions of an American political scientist: Pollock, "State Capitalism: Its Possibilities and Limitations," *Studies in Philosophy and Social Science*, IX, 200–25. State capitalism, he believes, is a more accurate term than "managerial society," "administrative capitalism," "neo-mercantilism," "state socialism," etc., for designating that form of capitalism in which "the state assumes important functions of the private capitalist" and in which "profit interests still play a significant role." *Ibid.*, p. 201. State capitalism, which

may be either totalitarian or democratic, is not socialism. It differs, however, from capitalism in at least two crucial aspects: 1) the autonomous market is deposed from its controlling function, which is taken over by a system of direct controls; 2) these controls are vested in the state, which uses old and new devices, including a "pseudomarket" for regulating production and consumption.

19. Kun, *KIVD*, p. 12.

20. *Ibid*.

21. *Ibid*.

22. Borkenau states that the Comintern's swing to the left in 1928 "was carried through in the context of the intra-party factional struggle in Russia, and in no other context whatsoever." *European Communism*, p. 72.

23. Stalin's report is in Volume X of his *Sochineniia*; his remarks on the third period are found on pp. 271–91. Bukharin's speech can be found in *Inprecor* (December 29, 1927, and January 5, 1928).

24. See, for example, O. V. Kuusinen, "Novyi period i povorot v politike Kominterna (pod rukovodstvom tov. Stalina)," *KI* (January 24, 1930), pp. 3–19; and the remarks of Wilhelm Pieck at the Seventh Comintern Congress, *VII Congress*, p. 17.

25. Stalin, *Sochineniia*, XII, 19–26.

26. At the Tenth Plenum the chief speakers were Manuilsky, Molotov, Kuusinen, and Thälmann. These four may have temporarily constituted a kind of quadrumvirate at the apex of the Comintern; the collective character of their work was given recognition. See "Na pod"eme (Itogi X plenuma IKKI)," *KI* (July 31, 1929), p. 3. Manuilsky led the onslaught against Bukharin.

27. Among the chief Comintern personalities condemned as "right" deviationists, there were, besides Bukharin, Serra (Italy), Humbert-Droz (Switzerland), and Gitlow (U.S.A.). All four were removed in July, 1929, from the Presidium of the ECCI. In the opinion of the Comintern's Stalinist majority, the common sins of all of these leaders of the "right" deviation were an overestimation of the strength of capitalism in the third period and an underestimation of the possibilities for Communist revolution.

28. This charge is quite incorrect. Bukharin explicitly predicted wars and catastrophe for the capitalist countries in his speech at the Fifteenth Congress of the CPSU. See *XV s"ezd vsesoiuznoi kommunisticheskoi partii (b): Stenograficheskii otchet*, p. 57. Borkenau errs in stating that, to Bukharin, "the third period meant that capitalism was in a process of enormous expansion, which was a clear advance on the prewar standard." *World Communism*, p. 336. He further states that "to facilitate the final destruction of Bukharin and his followers a war atmosphere was

created." *Ibid.*, p. 337. But a "war atmosphere" had already been created in 1927, and Bukharin himself repeatedly and strongly emphasized the danger of war at the Sixth Congress.

29. The "errors" of Bukharin, both in the USSR and in the Comintern, were described in the Plenum's resolution removing him from work in the Comintern. See Kun, *KIVD*, pp. 911–12.

30. An adequate judgment of Bukharin's actual position on these matters must await an extensive analysis of several of his writings, beginning at least with his book *Economics of the Transitional Period*, published in 1920. Such an analysis falls outside the scope of this study. A judgment based solely on Bukharin's writings and speeches as a Comintern dignitary would be partial and risky. Bukharin was not a free agent at the Sixth Comintern Congress, and his draft of the theses on the international situation (not available to the author) was corrected in about twenty places by the Russian delegation at the Congress. See Stalin, *Sochineniia*, XII, 20. For a comprehensive list of Bukharin's works, see Sidney Heitman, compiler, *An Annotated Bibliography of Nikolai I. Bukharin's Published Works* (Fort Collins, Colorado, 1958).

31. Kun, *KIVD*, pp. 876–81.

32. *Inprecor* (May 28, 1929), p. 544.

33. *Inprecor* (May 28, 1929), p. 556.

34. *Inprecor* (August 28, 1929), p. 917.

35. *Inprecor* (August 28, 1929), p. 930. Interestingly, Varga praised in this quarterly report the "great work on business cycles" of W. C. Mitchell of Columbia University.

36. Kun, *KIVD*, p. 915.

37. *Inprecor* (February 20, 1930), pp. 125–26.

38. *XI plenum*, I, 5.

39. *XII plenum*, III, 163.

40. *XIII plenum*, p. 589.

41. *Ibid.*, p. 4.

42. *Socialism Victorious*, p. 299.

43. For a recent summary of the evidence on such practical aid, see Nollau, *Die Internationale*, pp. 133–50.

44. "Stalin (k piatidesiatiletiiu so dnia ego rozhdeniia)," *KI* (December 31, 1929), pp. 7–12. For the first time it was claimed that Stalin had played the biggest role in formulating the Program: "The theoretical exactitude with which Stalin edited the Program . . . has led to this, that hardly anyone who has fallen from the Marxist-Leninist position has succeeded in seizing upon this or that 'unclear' formulation in the Program." *Ibid.*, p. 12.

45. "Ideologicheskie oshibki i probely pri provedenii reshenii XI plenuma IKKI," *KI* (February 20, 1932), p. 23.

46. A. Martynov, "Kak Lenin v epokhu pervoi revoliutsii borolsia za ee 'pererastanie' i protiv tsentrizma," *KI* (December 30, 1931), p. 21.

47. The only "enlarged" meeting of the Presidium for which a record exists.

48. Kun, *KIVD*, pp. 947–51.

49. *Ibid.*, p. 995.

50. "Novaia pobeda mirnoi politiki SSSR—Novyi uspekh mirovogo proletariata," *KI* (December 10, 1932), pp. 3–11.

51. Kun, *KIVD*, pp. 990–91.

52. Reinberg, "Nekotorye uroki vooruzhennykh vosstanii no Vostoke," *KI* (June 29, 1928), p. 75. My italics.

53. Kun, *KIVD*, p. 799.

54. *XIII plenum*, p. 594.

55. See Kun, *KIVD*, pp. 755–63.

56. *Ibid.*, p. 782.

57. *XII plenum*, III, 165.

58. *XIII plenum*, p. 21.

59. *XII plenum*, III, 165.

60. For the pertinent theses and parts of these dealing with the trade-union question during this period, see Kun, *KIVD*, pp. 782–83, 888–908, 921–25, 982–90.

61. *XIII plenum*, p. 312.

62. Kun, *KIVD*, pp. 884–88, 921–23.

63. *Ibid.*, pp. 963–64, 976–79.

64. *Ibid.*, p. 959.

65. *Inprecor* (March 9, 1933), pp. 261–62.

66. See *Inprecor* (March 31, 1933).

67. *Inprecor* (April 28, 1933), pp. 427–28.

68. *Inprecor* (January 5, 1934), p. 15.

69. For the most recent and the most thorough treatment of this collaboration and its failure, see Brandt, *Stalin's Failure in China, 1924–1927*.

70. See the interesting discussion of "proletarian hegemony" in the excellent work by Schwartz, *Chinese Communism and the Rise of Mao*, pp. 113–15. This phrase, Schwartz affirms, "means that only the proletariat is to be allowed a separate political voice . . . that is, that the Communist Party alone is to monopolize the heights of political power." *Ibid.*, pp. 113–14. This statement equates hegemony with dictatorship, and is certainly applicable to the situation *following* the seizure of power. *Prior* to the seizure of power, such a definition of hegemony seems to be too strong.

71. Kun, *KIVD*, p. 43.

72. See, for example, the Resolution on the Chinese question, adopted

by the Sixth Plenum of the ECCI in 1926. Kun, *KIVD*, pp. 619–23.

73. "The Kuomintang is in China precisely that specific Chinese organizational form in which the proletariat collaborates directly with the petty bourgeoisie and the peasantry." From "Questions of the Chinese Revolution," adopted by the Eighth Plenum of the ECCI in May, 1927. See Kun, *KIVD*, p. 723.

74. *Ibid.*

75. The first soviets in China were created in 1927.

76. The above paragraphs are based on the theses. See Kun, *KIVD*, pp. 456–60.

77. On the history of the Chinese Soviet Republic from its founding to its formal dissolution in 1937, see North, *Moscow and Chinese Communists*, pp. 147–80, and McLane, *Soviet Policy*, pp. 5–100.

78. Kun, *KIVD*, p. 905.

79. *Ibid.*, pp. 959–60.

80. *Ibid.*, pp. 981, 992.

81. Borkenau, *World Communism*, p. 374. See this basic and invaluable work, *passim*, for the history of the Comintern during these years.

82. For the story of German Communism from 1929 to 1933, see the detailed study of Flechtheim, *Die Kommunistische Partei Deutschlands in der Weimarer Republik*, pp. 150–84. Flechtheim points out that the German Communist Party in 1932 and 1933 did propose to other parties and organizations joint action (the united front "from above") against the Nazis; such proposals came too late, inspired no confidence, and resulted in nothing. *Ibid.*, p. 178. See also Anderson, *Hammer or Anvil*, pp. 127–59.

VI. STRATEGY AND TACTICS, 1935- 1939: PAGES 140–165

1. For data, see Seton-Watson, *From Lenin to Malenkov*, p. 170, note 1. See also Khrushchev's "secret" speech at the Twentieth Congress of the CPSU in February, 1956, in Gruliow, *Current Soviet Policies II*, pp. 172–88.

2. "Germaniia—glavnyi podzhigatel' voiny," *KI* (March 10, 1935), p. 5.

3. *Inprecor* (March 10, 1937), p. 283.

4. *Inprecor* (April 17, 1937), p. 411.

5. *VII Congress*, p. 126.

6. *Inprecor* (January 5, 1934), p. 20.

7. L. Magyar, "Fashizm, voina i mirnaia politika Sovetskogo Soiuza," *KI* (February 10, 1934), p. 25.

8. A typical grouping of the anti-fascist forces for peace in 1936 included the USSR, the proletariat of the capitalist countries, the "working masses," the colonial and semi-colonial peoples, and, signifi-

cantly listed last, the governments of those capitalist countries momentarily opposed to war. "Front mira dolzhen pobedit'!" *KI* (July, 1936),
pp. 5–6.

9. "Stalin: 'We do not always and in all conditions take a negative
attitude towards the League. . . . Despite the withdrawal of Germany
and Japan from the League—or perhaps because of it—the League may
well become to a certain extent a brake to retard or prevent military
actions.'" *Inprecor* (January 12, 1934), p. 43.

10. R. Magnus, "Protiv lzheneitraliteta v skandinavskikh stranakh,"
KI (September, 1938), p. 64.

11. *World News and Views* (January 28, 1939), p. 68.

12. See, for example, *VII Congress*, p. 18.

13. An amusing point may be noted. The abridged stenographic
report of the Seventh Comintern Congress, in recording the names of
those delegates elected to the Presidium of the Congress, carefully noted
the applause evoked by the calling out of each name. The sensitive
nature of this business is indicated by the use of a refined scale of grada-
tions. For instance, Foster (U.S.A.) received only "applause"; Marty
(France) "loud applause"; Dimitrov (the General Secretary) "stormy
applause, ovation, shouts of 'Hurrah!'" while Stalin received "stormy,
prolonged applause, ovation, shouts of 'Hurrah!'" *Ibid.*, p. 6.

14. See D. Manuilsky, "Stalin i mirovoe kommunisticheskoe dvizhe-
nie," *KI* (April, 1937), p. 64; and O. Kuusinen, "Twenty Years of the
Communist International," *World News and Views* (March 18, 1939),
p. 242.

15. This history of the CPSU, according to Mikoyan's speech at the
Eighteenth Congress of the CPSU, came "almost entirely from Stalin's
pen." *World News and Views* (March 23, 1939), pp. 286–87. See also
D. Manuilsky, "Kratkii kurs istorii VKP(b) za rubezhom," *KI*
(August–September, 1939), pp. 132–37.

16. Gruliow, *Current Soviet Politics II*, p. 185.

17. *Inprecor* (June 29, 1934), p. 960.

18. *VII Congress*, p. 278.

19. "Istoricheskii Plenum Ts. K. Vsesoiuznoi Kommunisticheskoi
Partii (bolshevikov)," *KI* (March 3, 1937), p. 34.

20. *VII Congress*, p. 276.

21. *Ibid.*, p. 279.

22. *Ibid.*

23. "O lozunge ovladeniia bol'shevizmom i ob izuchenii istorii
russkoi sektsii Kominterna," *KI* (May, 1937), p. 8.

24. *VII Congress*, p. 525.

25. "Vozzvanie Ispolnitel'nogo Komiteta Kommunisticheskogo Internatsionala," *KI* (October–November, 1937), pp. 11–12.

26. *VII Congress*, p. 537.

27. *Inprecor* (December 12, 1936), p. 1483.

28. *World News and Views* (November 5, 1938), p. 1204.

29. See McKenzie, "The Messianic Concept in the Third International, 1935–1939," in Simmons, *Russian and Soviet Thought*, pp. 516–30.

30. G. Ernst, "Maslo i pushki," *KI* (February 10, 1936), p. 70.

31. The interview was reprinted in *KI* (March 25, 1936), pp. 7–11.

32. V. Florin, "Bor'ba protiv fashizma—eto bor'ba za mir," *KI* (July, 1936), p. 17.

33. *World News and Views* (February 25, 1939), p. 166.

34. Stalin, *Problems of Leninism*, pp. 115–17.

35. *VII Congress*, p. 64.

36. *Ibid.*, pp. 64–71.

37. *Ibid.*, p. 71.

38. *Ibid.*, p. 553.

39. "K tret'ei godovshchine VII kongressa Kommunisticheskogo Internatsionala," *KI* (August, 1938), p. 22.

40. *VII Congress*, pp. 176–77.

41. *Ibid.*, p. 143.

42. *Ibid.*, p. 577.

43. *Ibid.*, p. 575.

44. *Ibid.*, pp. 149–50.

45. Dimitrov at the Seventh Congress used both the term "united front government" and the term "people's front government" without making any distinction. Presumably, the latter would include all antifascist parties, not simply the Communist and Social-Democratic. In terms of functions, Comintern literature reveals no distinctions between these two governments. As the term "popular front government" was by far the more frequently used in Comintern literature of the period, this term is employed in the present study.

46. *VII Congress*, p. 174.

47. *Ibid.*, pp. 174–75. Italics in the original.

48. For further discussion, see McKenzie, "The Messianic Concept in the Third International, 1935–1939," in Simmons, *Russian and Soviet Thought*, pp. 523–25.

49. The phrase "democracy of a new type" was frequently used in Comintern materials of the period. It is employed here as a convenient term denoting the reforms of a popular front government.

50. For examples of such programs, see James Campbell, "Bor'ba za narodnyi front v Velikobritanii," *KI* (June 6, 1938), pp. 48–55; N. Zakhariadis and G. Nikis, "Bor'ba i uspekhi narodnogo fronta v Gretsii," *KI* (March 25, 1936), pp. 68–82; and M. Thorez, "Narodnyi

front vo Frantsii i zadachi KPF," *KI* (September, 1936), pp. 46–56.

51. On the beginnings of the new pattern of strategy in France, see Borkenau, *European Communism*, pp. 115–62.

52. There is some (contradictory) evidence of a serious struggle within the Comintern leadership before the new pattern of strategy and tactics was adopted. Borkenau presents Manuilsky as the leading exponent of the new "line," and states that Manuilsky "stood quite alone," opposed by Piatnitsky and Bela Kun. See *European Communism*, p. 123. On the other hand, Eudocio Ravines, a former Peruvian Communist, states that Manuilsky was very unenthusiastic about the new "line" when it was being discussed in 1934; in his opposition he was supported by Kuusinen, Pieck, and Gottwald. Ravines reports that Dimitrov was wholly in favor of the idea of a popular front, and was supported by the French and Chinese Communists and by Earl Browder. See Ravines, *The Yenan Way*, especially pp. 113–16 and 145–46.

53. *VII Congress*, p. 322.

54. *Ibid.*, p. 181.

55. *Ibid.*, p. 593.

56. "Delo Lenina bessmertno," *KI* (January, 1939), p. 11. Lenin's position was given in his critique of Rosa Luxemburg's "Junius pamphlet," written in 1916. See Lenin, *Sochineniia*, XIX, 178–90.

57. See, for example, I. Ercoli, "Soprotivlenie agressoru—osnovnoi vopros v politicheskoi zhizni Frantsii," *KI* (July, 1939), p. 16.

58. See also my discussion of this issue, "The Soviet Union, the Comintern and World Revolution: 1935," *Political Science Quarterly*, LXV (June, 1950), 214–37.

59. *VII Congress*, p. 178.

60. *Ibid.*, p. 192.

61. *Inprecor* (August 28, 1935), p. 1071.

62. *Inprecor* (May 1, 1937), p. 446.

63. "Vernost' leninizmu—zalog dal'neishikh pobed," *KI* (February, 1938), pp. 10–11.

64. *VII Congress*, p. 174.

65. M. Thorez, "K s"ezdu kompartii Frantsii," *KI* (January 10, 1936), p. 34.

66. Wilhelm Pieck, "O narodnom fronte v Germanii," *KI* (August, 1937), p. 33.

67. On the history of the popular front in Spain and France, where it received its greatest development, see Borkenau, *European Communism*, pp. 163–220; for Spain the fullest account is Cattell, *Communism and the Spanish Civil War*.

68. *VII Congress*, pp. 280–85.

69. *Ibid.*, p. 299.

70. *Ibid.*, pp. 299–300.

71. *Ibid.*, p. 288. Mao Tse-tung at this time was chairman both of the Chinese Soviet Republic, since its inception in November, 1931, and of the Central Committee of the Chinese Communist Party, since January, 1935. See Brandt *et al.*, *Chinese Communism*, pp. 37–38.

72. *Inprecor* (December 12, 1935), p. 1666. The Chinese Communists slowly and reluctantly moved toward the united front with Chiang Kai-shek. For this story, see McLane, *Soviet Policy'* pp. 61–100.

73. Brandt *et al.*, *Chinese Communism*, pp. 239–40.

74. Mao Tse-tung, "Novyi etap razvitiia antiiaponskoi natsional'noi voiny i zadachi kompartii Kitaia," *KI* (April, 1939), pp. 107–8. This was Mao's speech at the Sixth Enlarged Plenum of the Central Committee of the Chinese Communist Party in November, 1938.

75. Mao Tse-tung, "Zadachi obshchenatsional'nogo antiiaponskogo edinogo fronta v Kitae na dannom etape," *KI* (September, 1937), p. 69. See also Wang Ming, "Kliuch k spaseniiu kitaiskogo naroda," *KI* (March, 1937), pp. 49–56.

76. See Mao's article, cited *ibid.*, pp. 70–73.

77. *VII Congress*, p. 296.

78. *Inprecor* (December 2, 1935), pp. 1601–2.

79. F. Lacerda, "Fashistskii perevorot v Brazilii," *KI* (December, 1937), p. 52.

80. "The Programme of the Brazilian People's Government of National Liberation," *Inprecor* (April 18, 1936), p. 504.

VII. STRATEGY AND TACTICS, 1939–1941: PAGES 166–177

1. See Rossi, *The Russo-German Alliance, August 1939–June 1941*. He cites, as partial evidence, Soviet support of the German peace campaign of late 1939, Soviet protests against the British blockade, Soviet pressure on Turkey not to conclude a mutual assistance pact with Britain and France, and Soviet opposition to Roosevelt's Lend-Lease bill (p. 210).

2. *World News and Views* (September 9, 1939), p. 960. In the same issue, R. Bishop called for a new government, since a "people's war" needed a "people's leadership." *Ibid.*, p. 963.

3. Rossi, *Les communistes français pendant la drôle de guerre*, p. 46.

4. G. Dimitrov, "Voina i rabochii klass kapitalisticheskikh stran," *KI*, no. 8–9 (1939), pp. 24–34. This issue actually appeared in October, and not in August or September as the number would seem to indicate. See also *World News and Views* (November 11, 1939), pp. 1079–83.

5. *World News and Views* (November 11, 1939), pp. 1079–80.

6. See Borkenau, *European Communism*, pp. 233–64, for Communist activity in this period.

7. See, for example, "Novaia faza imperialisticheskoi voiny." *KI*, no. 5 (1940), pp. 3–9. In the American edition, however, there appeared an article by F. Florin, in which Germany, along with England and France, was condemned for its war guilt. See D. IJ. Dallin, "Komintern v voine," *Novyi Zhurnal*, no. 1 (1942), pp. 254–55.

8. M. Thorez, "20 let kompartii Frantsii," *KI*, no. 1 (1941), p. 35.

9. "Ko dniu mezhdunarodnoi proletarskoi solidarnosti," *KI*, no. 4 (1941), pp. 11–12.

10. G. Dimitrov, "Voina i rabochii klass kapitalisticheskikh stran," *KI*, no. 8–9 (1939).

11. Another high-ranking Finnish Communist, Arvo Tuominen, who was a candidate-member of the Presidium of the ECCI, at this time refused to leave Stockholm and go to Moscow to become a minister in the Terijoki government. See his memoirs, *Kremls Klockor*, pp. 338–41.

12. "Programme of People's Government of Finland," *World News and Views* (December 9, 1939), p. 1130.

13. *Ibid.*

14. *World News and Views* (November 11, 1939), p. 1082.

15. *World News and Views* (November 11, 1939), p. 1083. The harsh slogan, "Turn imperialist war into civil war," while not used in the Comintern's public propaganda during this period, was freely used within the ranks of the Communist parties, according to Douglas Hyde, a former high-ranking British Communist. Letter to author, June 14, 1955.

16. "Zadachi kompartii v novoi politicheskoi obstanovke (deklaratsiia TsK kompartii Anglii)," *KI*, no. 1 (1940), p. 124.

17. L. Little, "Narodnyi kongress v Anglii," *KI*, no. 1 (1941), p. 87.

18. "Manifesto of the Communist Party of Finland," *World News and Views* (December 9, 1939), p. 1133.

19. Rossi, *Les communistes français pendant la drôle de guerre* and *A Communist Party in Action*.

20. Rossi, *A Communist Party in Action*, p. 53.

21. *World News and Views* (November 11, 1939), p. 1081.

22. Masani, *The Communist Party of India*, p. 78.

23. K. Kattel', "Indiia v usloviiakh voiny," *KI*, no. 1 (1941), p. 64.

24. *Ibid.*, pp. 67–68.

25. The difficulties in maintaining the anti-Japanese front during this period are described in McLane, *Soviet Policy*, pp. 137–55.

26. Chou En-lai, "Protiv opasnosti raskola i kapituliatsii v Kitae," *KI*, no. 3–4 (1940), pp. 101–5.

VIII. STRATEGY AND TACTICS, 1941–1943: PAGES 178–191

1. "Edinyi front narodov gitlerovskogo fashizma," *KI*, no. 6–7 (1941), p. 16.

2. *World News and Views* (January 17, 1942), p. 47.

3. *World News and Views* (October 31, 1942), p. 431.

4. *World News and Views* (November 7, 1942), p. 435.

5. "Velikaia armiia velikogo naroda," *KI*, no. 2–3 (1943), p. 10.

6. F. Shilling, "Avstriia v gitlerovskoi voine," *KI*, no. 2–3 (1943), p. 38.

7. M. Thorez, "Nastuplenie Krasnoi Armii i osvoboditel'naia bor'ba frantsuzskogo naroda," *KI*, no. 2–3 (1943), p. 17.

8. *World News and Views* (December 19, 1942), p. 482.

9. *World News and Views* (February 28, 1942), p. 136.

10. "Edinyi antigitlerovskii front narodov," *KI*, no. 2–3 (1943), p. 61.

11. *World News and Views* (December 12, 1942), p. 475.

12. M. Ercoli, "Fashistskaia Italiia nakanune bankrotstva," *KI*, no. 1–2 (1942), p. 36.

13. *World News and Views* (May 23, 1942), p. 243.

14. Actually a candidate-member of the Presidium, elected shortly after the Seventh Comintern Congress of 1935. See Lazitch, *Les Partis communistes d'Europe, 1919–1955*, p. 42.

15. Tuominen, "The North European Communist Parties," *Occidente*, XI (May-June, 1955), 204.

16. *World News and Views* (January 3, 1942), p. 13.

17. *World News and Views* (December 19, 1942), p. 486.

18. For the history of Indian Communism in this period, see Masani, *The Communist Party of India*, pp. 80–86, and Overstreet and Windmiller, *Communism in India*, pp. 191–222.

19. *World News and Views* (August 1, 1942), p. 326.

20. Leonhard, *Child of the Revolution*, p. 163. The author describes his stay at the Comintern school in Ufa on pp. 163–239.

21. The last issue of the *Kommunisticheskii Internatsional* was no. 5–6 in 1943. For the document dissolving the Comintern, see pp. 8–10.

22. Leonhard is thus inaccurate when he states that the foreign Communist leaders in Ufa in 1943 "were not brought in to sign the documents." *Child of the Revolution*, p. 219. He mentions Dolores Ibarruri, Ana Pauker, and Rakosi as being at Comintern headquarters at that time.

IX. NATURE AND MEANS: PAGES 195–209

1. Kun, *KIVD*, p. 18.

2. *Ibid.*

3. *VII Congress, p.* 178.

4. *Ibid.*, p. 263.

5. *Ibid.*, p. 262.

6. *Ibid.*, p. 263.

7. V. Miro, "Bor'ba za sozdanie vnutrennikh sovetskikh raionov v

polukolonial'nykh stranakh," *KI* (January 1, 1935), p. 39. "The revolution has been victorious on different parts of the periphery, before the forces of the counterrevolution have been smashed in the main centers."

8. B. Kun, "K godovshchine proletarskoi revoliutsii v Vengrii," *KI* (March 22, 1929), p. 9.

9. "K voprosu o revoliutsionnom vykhode iz krizisa v Anglii (Rech' tov. Manuil'skogo na diskussii po angliiskomu voprosu)," *KI* (February 29, 1932), pp. 16–17.

10. V. Miro, *KI* (January 1, 1935), pp. 38–45.

11. *Ibid.*, pp. 39–40. The American Revolution, he asserted, had begun with its base in Virginia, while the chief centers, New York and Boston, were in the hands of the British. Similarly, the nationalist movement in Turkey under Kemal Atatürk had begun in 1919 in eastern Anatolia and only in 1923 succeeded in gaining Istanbul.

12. *Ibid.*, p. 44.

13. *VI kongress*, I, 270.

14. S. Titov, "O pravoi opasnosti i primirenchestve v rumynskoi kompartii," *KI* (June 28, 1929), p. 45.

15. *VI kongress*, IV, 437–38.

16. B. Kun, "K godovshchine proletarskoi revoliutsii v Vengrii," *KI* (March 22, 1929), p. 4.

17. Kun, *KIVD*, p. 806.

18. *Ibid.*, p. 817.

19. *VII Congress*, p. 594.

20. *Ibid.*, p. 468.

21. "Grazhdanskaia voina v Finliandii," *KI* (February 3, 1928), p. 3.

22. *VII Congress*, p. 446.

23. Kun, *KIVD*, p. 35.

24. A——n, "K desiatiletiiu natsional'no-revoliutsionnogo dvizheniia Tuvy," *KI* (August 31, 1931), p. 35.

25. "Grazhdanskaia voina v Finliandii," *KI* (February 3, 1928), p. 3.

26. *World News and Views* (September 23, 1939), p. 986. The author obviously had not yet received word to abandon the "antifascist" line.

27. *Inprecor* (December 9, 1939), p. 1130.

28. The story of Soviet aid to Loyalist Spain is detailed in Cattell, *Communism and the Spanish Civil War*.

29. See, for example, the theses on "Measures of Struggle with the Danger of Imperialist Wars," adopted at the Sixth Comintern Congress, in Kun, *KIVD*, especially pp. 808–11; the resolution on "The Tasks of the Communist International in Connection with the Preparations of the Imperialists for a New World War," adopted at the Seventh Congress, in *VII Congress*, especially p. 595; and Togliatti's remarks, *ibid.*, p. 448.

30. Wilhelm Pieck, "Nasha bor'ba protiv shovinizma i imperialisticheskoi voiny," *KI* (July 1, 1935), pp. 35–36.

31. *World News and Views* (February 29, 1939), p. 166.

32. *XI plenum*, II, 203.

33. Kun, *KIVD*, p. 43.

34. At the Second Comintern Congress in 1920, it was decided that
soviets could be created only under the following conditions: a mass
revolutionary upsurge, an intensified economic and political crisis with
power slipping from the rulers' hands, and the "serious resolve" of the
Communist party and "significant strata" of the proletariat to begin a
systematic planned struggle for power. *Ibid.*, p. 112.

35. *Ibid.*, p. 43.

36. *Ibid.*, p. 820.

37. *Ibid.*, p. 808.

38. *Ibid.*

39. *Ibid.*

X. The Forms of Communist Power: Pages 210–218

1. See also the discussion in Carew Hunt, *Marxism*, pp. 104–19 and
138–64.

2. *Ibid.*, p. 106; F. L. Neumann, "Approaches to the Study of Political
Power," *Political Science Quarterly*, LXV (June, 1950), 166.

3. Kun, *KIVD*, p. 19.

4. *Ibid.*, p. 27. In one instance, the possibility of multiparty rule
following the seizure of power was mentioned by a high-ranking Comintern official. Dimitrov, at the Seventh Congress in 1935, spoke as follows:
"It is not impossible, of course, that in some country, immediately after
the revolutionary overthrow of the bourgeoisie, there may be formed a
Soviet government on the basis of a government bloc of the Communist
party with a definite party (or its left wing) participating in the revolution. After the October Revolution the victorious Party of the Russian
Bolsheviks, as we know, included representatives of the Left Socialist-
Revolutionaries in the Soviet government." *VII Congress*, p. 174. As we
well know, also, the short-lived coalition government of 1917–1918 did
not involve any significant sharing of power with the Left Socialist-
Revolutionaries.

5. O. Kuusinen, "Kommunisticheskii Manifest," *KI* (October 20,
1933), pp. 39–40.

6. Ia. Tsitovich, "II kongress Kommunisticheskogo Internatsionala,"
KI (July 20, 1935), p. 168.

7. Kun, *KIVD*, pp. 18–19.

8. See, for example, "Programma sovetskoi vlasti kompartii Anglii,"

KI (April 10, 1935), pp. 43–45, and "Programma osvobozhdeniia germanskogo rabochevo klassa i germanskogo trudovogo naroda," *KI* (June 1, 1934), pp. 60–63. Actually, the Draft Program of 1928 termed the soviet structure the "most suitable" form, as a rule, of proletarian state power. This seemed to suggest the possibility of alternative forms, and Dengel at the Sixth Congress asked for a clarification. *VI kongress*, III, 47. But no clarification was ever given, and the final version of the Program again used the phrase "most suitable." See Kun, *KIVD*, p. 18. However, no alternative forms were ever mentioned in Comintern materials. Again Soviet Russian experience won a victory.

9. O. Kuusinen, "Kommunisticheskii Manifest," *KI* (October 20, 1933), p. 36.

10. *Ibid.*, p. 37.

11. For Lenin's first elaboration of this term, see his *Sochineniia*, VII, 183–95. See also the discussion in Wolfe, *Three Who Made a Revolution*, pp. 291–98.

12. This is what Lenin meant, in the opinion of Wolfe, *Three Who Made a Revolution*, p. 292, and of Schwartz, *Chinese Communism and the Rise of Mao*, p. 89.

13. *VI kongress*, V, 72. It may be remembered that the word "democracy," placed in Comintern materials within quotes, means either that such democracy is false or, as in the above quotation, that the term is used in a formal, constitutional sense, e.g., to indicate the existence of universal suffrage.

14. *Ibid.*, p. 79. Cf. Bukharin's remark at the same congress: "At the same time the dictatorship of the proletariat and the peasantry is not yet the dictatorship of the proletariat—as the sole vehicle of power." *Ibid.*, III, 149.

15. "U preddveriia novoi revoliutsii v Kitae," *KI* (August 10, 1930), p. 15. See also *Kommunisticheskii Internatsional pered VII vsemirnym kongressom*, pp. 79–80.

16. "Revoliutsionnyi krizis v Kitae i zadachi kitaiskikh Kommunistov," *KI* (November 10, 1931), p. 10. See also Wang Ming, "Sovety v Kitae kak osobaia forma demokraticheskoi diktatury proletariata i krest'ianstva," *KI* (November 1, 1934), p. 26.

17. *VII Congress*, pp. 50–51.

18. "Revoliutsionnyi krizis v Kitae i zadachi kitaiskikh kommunistov," *KI* (November 10, 1931), p. 11.

XI. The Transformation of Society: Pages 221–263

1. Marx, *Critique of the Gotha Programme*, pp. 10, 80–83.
2. Kun, *KIVD*, p. 16.

3. *Ibid.*, pp. 25–26.

4. *Ibid.*, p. 28.

5. *Ibid.*, p. 19. Apparently, the poor peasants also were entitled to bear arms, since the Red Guard was made up of workers and the lower strata among the peasants.

6. *Ibid.*, p. 820.

7. *Ibid.*

8. *Ibid.*, p. 19.

9. *Ibid.*, p. 25.

10. *Ibid.*, p. 18.

11. Such was, of course, the case in Soviet Russia before the 1936 Constitution.

12. Kun, *KIVD*, p. 19.

13. He shared this charge with Varga at the Sixth Congress, but was the sole reporter on the Soviet Union at the Seventh.

14. This and the following two paragraphs are based on Manuilsky's report on "The Situation in the Communist Party of the Soviet Union," in *VI kongress*, V, 55–85.

15. *VII Congress*, p. 515. This decision of course was incorporated in the Soviet Constitution of 1936.

16. *Ibid.*, p. 598.

17. There is no evidence to the effect that the Communist party was to increase its membership rapidly following the seizure of power. Manuilsky pointed out to the Sixth Comintern Congress that the CPSU had enlarged its membership "with the greatest caution" and had rejected "fantastic" proposals that the Party absorb the whole of the proletariat in two or three years. See *VI kongress*, V, 83.

18. *Ibid.*, V, 81–83.

19. See, for example, V. Knorin, "K itogam XVII konferentsii VKP (b)," *KI* (February 10, 1932), p. 18.

20. Kun, *KIVD*, p. 15.

21. Carew Hunt, *Marxism*, p. 117. Stalin: "The highest development of state power with the object of preparing the conditions for the dying out of state power—this is the Marxist formula." *Sochineniia*, XII, 369–70.

22. Kun, *KIVD*, pp. 16–31.

23. *Ibid.*, p. 20. The obscurity here can of course be removed by accepting state organs, trade unions, and factory councils as different forms of one and the same sovereign "proletarian" power, possessing a single "general will." But that conflicts do arise among these forms, Soviet history amply demonstrates.

24. *Ibid.*, p. 26.

25. *Ibid.*, p. 22.

26. *Ibid.*, pp. 20–21.

27. See, for example, V. Karpinskii, "Ob agrarnoi chasti proekta," *KI* (June 29, 1928), pp. 52–57.

28. *Ibid.*, p. 54.

29. See A. Martynov, "Vopros k natsionalizatsii zemli v proekte programmy Kominterna," *KI* (July 13, 1928), pp. 33–34, and Bukharin's remarks, *VI kongress*, III, 146–49.

30. *Ibid.*, p. 146.

31. Kun, *KIVD*, pp. 20–21.

32. The Program openly expressed the fear that cooperatives might become the "bulwark of counterrevolutionary activity and sabotage." *Ibid.*, p. 27.

33. *Ibid.*

34. This is the only instance where the *local* soviets are expressly indicated as the administrators of confiscated property; in all other cases the reference is simply to "soviets."

35. Kun, *KIVD*, pp. 20–22.

36. See, for example, the British program of 1935, "Programma sovetskoi vlasti kompartii Anglii," *KI* (April 10, 1935), pp. 43–58, and the German program of 1930, "Programmatic Declaration of the C.P. of Germany on the National and Social Emancipation of the German People," *Inprecor* (August 28, 1930), pp. 825–27.

37. *VI kongress*, III, 152.

38. *Ibid.*, V, 77.

39. Kun, *KIVD*, p. 25.

40. Stalin, *Sochineniia*, XI, 146–49.

41. *VI kongress*, III, 152.

42. E. Varga, "Perekhodnyi period ot kapitalizma k sotsializmu," *KI* (June 13, 1928), p. 97.

43. *Ibid.*, p. 102.

44. See also his remarks at the Congress, *VI kongress*, III, 62–68.

45. E. Varga, "Perekhodnyi period ot kapitalizma k sotsializmu," *KI* (June 13, 1928), p. 98.

46. Kun, *KIVD*, p. 25.

47. *VI kongress*, III, 153.

48. *Sochineniia*, XI, 146. Stalin asserted also in this speech that Lenin had actually launched the NEP period early in 1918, before the outbreak of widespread civil war compelled its temporary abandonment in favor of War Communism. *Ibid.*, pp. 146–47.

49. "K voprosu o revoliutsionnom vykhode iz krizisa v Anglii (Rech' tov. Manuil'skogo na diskussii po angliiskomu voprosu)," *KI* (February 29, 1932), p. 19.

50. *VI kongress*, III, 154.

51. *Ibid.*, p. 153.
52. *Inprecor* (April 19, 1929), p. 409.
53. Kun, *KIVD*, p. 22.
54. See Manuilsky's remarks, *VII Congress*, p. 514.
55. *Ibid.*, p. 28.
56. *Ibid.*, p. 23.
57. *Ibid.*, p. 28.
58. *Ibid.*
59. *Ibid.*, pp. 28–29.
60. *Inprecor* (December 31, 1928), p. 1760.
61. Kun, *KIVD*, p. 28.
62. *Ibid.*
63. See, for example, the remarks of Manuilsky at the Seventh Comintern Congress in 1935, *VII Congress*, pp. 512–13.
64. *Ibid* ., p. 22.
65. *Ibid.*, p. 23.
66. O. Kuusinen, "O natsional'nom voprose v kapitalisticheskoi Evrope," *KI* (August 20, 1931), p. 16.
67. H. Pollitt, "God posle XII plenuma IKKI i bor'ba kompartii Anglii," *KI* (October 20, 1933), p. 51.
68. *Inprecor* (August 28, 1930), p. 826.
69. "Programma osvobozhdeniia germanskogo rabochego klassa i germanskogo trudovogo naroda," *KI* (June 1, 1934), p. 63.
70. Kun, *KIVD*, p. 31.
71. *Ibid.*, p. 18.
72. Hansen of the Norwegian Communist Party discussed the possibility of a "Soviet Scandinavia" at the Thirteenth Plenum of the ECCI. See *XIII plenum*, p. 258.
73. *Inprecor* (May 10, 1929), p. 475.
74. "Programma osvobozhdeniia germanskogo rabochego klassa i germanskogo trudovogo naroda," *KI* (June 1, 1934), p. 63.
75. The word *soiuz* may be translated as "union," as in Soviet Union, or as "alliance," as in treaty of alliance.
76. "Programma sovetskoi vlasti kompartii Anglii," *KI* (April 10, 1935), p. 58.
77. *Inprecor* (August 28, 1930), p. 826. It is noteworthy that both the German program of 1930 and the British program of 1935 conceived of the USSR as a weakly industrialized country, exporting agricultural products in exchange for industrial goods.
78. One of the most serious mistakes of the Hungarian Communist regime in 1919 was considered to be its failure to oust the Social Democrats completely from any share in power. See B. Kun, "K godovshchine proletarskoi revoliutsii v Vengrii," and L. Magyar,

"Agrarnaia politika diktatura v Vengrii," in *KI* (March 22, 1929), p. 5 and p. 12. A Polish delegate at the Sixth Congress did suggest the possibility of a temporary coalition with revolutionary peasant parties after the Communist seizure of power, but no other evidence exists in Comintern sources to support his idea. See *VI kongress*, III, 35.

79. The 1932 draft program of the Polish Communist Party states that the future Polish Soviet Republic would "conclude a union *[soiuz]* with the USSR and with every nation liberated from capitalism, on the basis of a revolutionary unification *[ob"edineniia]* and centralization of military and economic forces for the struggle against imperialism and for the building of a socialist economy." See "Proekt programmy kompartii Pol'shi," *KI* (August 30, 1932), p. 76. This useful document is closely patterned after the Comintern Program of 1928.

80. Kun, *KIVD*, p. 30.

81. L. Magyar, "Agrarnaia politika diktatury v Vengrii," *KI* (March 22, 1929), p. 25. For a detailed treatment of the Communist agrarian policy in Hungary in 1919, see Borton, "The Hungarian Revolutions of 1918–1919 in Relation to the Agrarian Problem," especially pp. 110–52.

82. "Otkrytoe pis'mo tsentral'nykh komitetov kompartii Ispanii, Frantsii i Italii," *KI* (May 10, 1935), p. 11.

83. See, for example, the editorial appearing shortly after Alphonso XIII's withdrawal from Spain in April, 1931: "Ispanskaia kompartiia v revoliutsionnoi obstanovke," *KI* (May 20, 1931), pp. 4–12.

84. "Platforma sovetskoi vlasti kompartii Ispanii," *KI* (November 1, 1934), pp. 40–41.

85. Kun, *KIVD*, p. 31.

86. See the important theses of the West European Bureau of the Comintern on the Japanese Party in *Programmnye dokumenty kommunisticheskikh partii vostoka*, pp. 237–55.

87. *Ibid.*, p. 244.

88. N. Majorsky, "The Spanish Revolution," *Inprecor* (May 21, 1931), p. 482.

89. Kun, *KIVD*, p. 763.

90. I. Mingulin, "O pererastanii burzhuazno-demokraticheskoi revoliutsii v proletarskuiu v proekte programmy," *KI* (August 13, 1928), p. 42.

91. *Ibid.*, p. 41.

92. *Ibid.*

93. It may be noted that Dimitrov in 1935 suggested in one brief remark that a people's front government might become the government of the "democratic dictatorship of the working class and the peasantry." *VII Congress*, p. 368.

94. It is true, however, that one writer expressed regret that the Spanish revolution of 1931, which set up a republic, did not witness the

creation of workers' and peasants' soviets in addition to the bourgeois government. *Inprecor* (May 21, 1931), p. 481. This would have meant a situation very similar to the "dual power" of 1917 in Russia.

95. *VI kongress*, III, 150.

96. *Ibid.*, p. 149.

97. See N. Majorsky's appraisal: "*Lenin said that the bourgeois-democratic and the socialist revolutions are not separated from one another by a Chinese wall. The first develops into the second. The second consolidates the work of the first. The fight and only the fight decides how far the first succeeds in developing into the second.*" *Inprecor* (May 21, 1931), p. 482.

98. Kun, *KIVD*, p. 29.

99. See, for example, I. Mingulin, *KI* (August 13, 1928), p. 41. He cited in particular the wealthy and the middle peasants.

100. Kun, *KIVD*, p. 30.

101. *Ibid.*, p. 31.

102. *Ibid.*

103. See, for example, the following: "Proekt platformy deistviia kompartii Indii," *KI* (January 20, 1931), pp. 74–81; "Platforma deistviia kompartii Korei," *KI* (June 10, 1934), pp. 18–26; "Programma deistviia indokitaiskoi kompartii," *KI* (December 10, 1932), pp. 52–60.

104. Kun, *KIVD*, p. 31.

105. Wang Ming, "Ekonomicheskaia politika sovetskoi vlasti v Kitae," *KI* (August 20, 1933), p. 22.

106. *Ibid.*

107. Kun, *KIVD*, p. 31.

108. *Ibid.*, p. 30. My italics.

109. *VI kongress*, III, 20.

110. Kun, *KIVD*, p. 845.

111. *Ibid.*, p. 853.

112. *Ibid.*, p. 836.

113. A——n, "K desiateletiiu natsional'no-revoliutsionnogo dvizheniia Tuvy," *KI* (August 31, 1931), pp. 35–38.

114. *Ibid.*, pp. 36–38. Tuva was incorporated into the USSR during World War II.

115. *VII Congress*, p. 604.

116. See V. Kuchumov, "K desiatiletiiu mongol'skoi revoliutsii," *KI* (June 30, 1931), pp. 14–18.

117. *Ibid.*, p. 15.

118. *Ibid.*, p. 16.

119. *Ibid.*, p. 15. A Five-Year Plan was actually begun in 1931, but abandoned the next year. Only in 1948 was long-term overall planning resumed. See R. Rupen, "Notes on Outer Mongolia Since 1945," *Pacific Affairs*, XXVIII (March, 1955), 71–79.

120. *VI kongress*, III, 21.
121. *Ibid.*, p. 22.

XII. COMMUNISM AS THE ULTIMATE WORLD SOCIETY: PAGES 264–276

1. *VII Congress*, p. 274.
2. See Kun, *KIVD*, p. 15.
3. Quoted in Carew Hunt, *Marxism*, p. 108.
4. *VI kongress*, V, 75.
5. Kun, *KIVD*, p. 15.
6. *Ibid.*, pp. 15–16.
7. *VI kongress*, III, 89.
8. *Ibid.*
9. *Ibid.*
10. This speech was published in *KI* (March, 1939), pp. 5–37. See also Stalin, *Problems of Leninism*, especially pp. 656–63.
11. An interesting reference to an earlier Stalinist position on the military defense of an isolated Communist society was made by V. Knorin, "K itogam XVII konferentsii VKP(b)," *KI* (February 10, 1932). He quoted Stalin as affirming in 1925 the theoretical possibility of the existence of a "socialist militia" in a classless, stateless society. *Ibid.*, p. 18.
12. Kun, *KIVD*, p. 15.
13. *VII Congress*, p. 510.
14. Kun, *KIVD*, p. 15.
15. *VII Congress*, p. 510.
16. Kun, *KIVD*, pp. 15–16.
17. Laski, *Communism*, p. 178.
18. Kun, *KIVD*, p. 15.
19. Carew Hunt, *Marxism*, p. 131.
20. Kun, *KIVD*, p. 15.
21. *VI kongress*, V, 63.
22. Kun, *KIVD*, p. 15.
23. *Ibid.*
24. *Ibid.*, p. 16.
25. *Ibid.*
26. *Ibid.*
27. Carew Hunt, *Marxism*, p. 137.
28. Mayo, *Democracy and Marxism*, p. 232.

XIII. CONCLUSIONS: PAGES 279–299

1. Fisher, *The Communist Revolution*, p. 55.
2. Roy, *The Communist International*, p. 73.

NOTE ON SOURCES

The source materials for this study of Comintern theory are quite unevenly distributed within the fifteen-year period from 1928 to 1943. By far the greater amount of the total available material dates from the years before 1934, and relatively little evidence exists for the last decade of the Comintern's doctrinal development. To some extent this unequal distribution is offset by the generally repetitious nature of the materials, so that the greater quantity of evidence for the first five or six years under study does not always mean a proportionately more thorough treatment of a problem in theory. However, on the whole, both the range of topics discussed and the quality of the treatment accorded these topics in Comintern materials are more satisfactory for the period before 1934.

The primary sources may be briefly noted. There are, first, the stenographic reports for the congresses that were held—the Sixth Comintern Congress in 1928 and the Seventh in 1935. The report of the Sixth Congress was issued in six volumes in the Russian language. All these volumes were used except the sixth, which contained the resolutions and theses of the Congress; these documents are readily available in other works. There is also a German-language edition in four volumes.

For the Seventh Congress no complete report was ever published. An abridged report did appear in 1939 in English, French, and German. In the Publishers' Preface to this report no reference is made to an earlier report, and no evidence has been found by the present writer that a stenographic report of the Seventh Congress was ever published prior to 1939. Contemporary reports were, however, published in the issues of *Pravda* and *International Press Correspondence*, and these reports were used to supplement the English stenographic record of 1939. It may be noted here that nothing of serious importance was omitted from the English publication, although some material critical of the Western democracies and of Chiang Kai-shek was left out. In the 1936 report that was published in London, only sixteen speeches are included, but with full text. The reports given in the two periodicals simply bear out the overwhelming unanimity exhibited during the Seventh Congress.

Full use was also made of the stenographic reports of the four plenary meetings of the Executive Committee of the Communist International during this period—the Tenth in 1929, the Eleventh in 1931, the Twelfth in 1932, and the Thirteenth in 1933. There is no published record of any subsequent plenary meetings of this committee.

A useful collection of Comintern documents, covering the period from 1919 through 1932, appeared in 1933 under the editorship of Bela Kun, the Hungarian revolutionary who was executed in the USSR in the late 1930s but recently and posthumously exonerated by the Soviet leaders. This thousand-page volume—an extension of earlier collections of a similar nature—includes many decisions, theses, and manifestoes of the several congresses and of the plenary meetings of the Executive Committee; it contains also a helpful list of omitted documents.

The initial decade of Comintern history is covered in the first two volumes (1956, 1960) of the valuable series now in progress under the editorship of Jane Degras, *The Communist International, 1919–1943: Documents* (New York, Oxford University Press).

The two periodicals of the Comintern should be mentioned. The more important by far was the organ of the Executive Committee of the Comintern, *Kommunisticheskii Internatsional*, which appeared from 1919 to 1943. At various times editions in other languages appeared, which frequently omitted articles appearing in the Russian edition but only rarely contained items not appearing in the Russian edition. The Russian edition is by far the most complete and useful. Unsigned editorials in this journal reflected the views of the Comintern Executive Committee. The other Comintern periodical, *International Press Correspondence* or *Inprecor*, was a weekly news-sheet of about twenty pages, published in several different languages. First appearing on September 24, 1921, it functioned as a service for the press of the Communist parties and contained chiefly news items rather than articles devoted to theory. It is helpful, however, in its extensive reporting of the meetings of Comintern bodies, as well as those of the Communist Party of the Soviet Union. With the issue of July 2, 1938, it assumed a new name, *World News and Views*. *Inprecor* was not without its inaccuracies, as witness the somewhat premature report, in its issue of March 30, 1930, of the death of Mao Tse-tung.

Two other Comintern publications should be noted. Prior to the convening of the World Congresses of 1928 and 1935, the Comintern issued surveys of the developments within the international Communist movement since the preceding congress. These surveys contain useful data on the work of the central Comintern organs and on the activity of most of the Communist parties.

BIBLIOGRAPHY

COMINTERN SOURCE MATERIALS

WORLD CONGRESSES

Der I. Kongress der Kommunistischen Internationale: Protokoll der Verhandlungen in Moskau vom 2. bis 19. März 1919. Hamburg, Verlag der Kommunistischen Internationale, 1921. (The date March 19 is a misprint, as the last session of the Congress was on March 6.)

VI kongress Kominterna: Stenograficheskii otchet (VI Congress of the Comintern: Stenographic report). 6 vols. Moscow, Leningrad, Gosudarstvennoe izdatel'stvo, 1929. German edition: *Protokoll des 6. Weltkongresses der Kommunistischen Internationale, Juli-September 1928.* 4 vols. Hamburg, Carl Hoym Nachfolger, 1929.

VII Congress of the Communist International: Stenographic Report of Proceedings. Moscow, Foreign Languages Publishing House, 1939. French edition: *VIIe Congrès mondial de l'Internationale communiste: Compte rendu abrégé.* Moscow, Editions en langues étrangères, 1939. German edition: *VII Kongres der Kommunistischen Internationale: Gekrüztes stenographisches Protokoll.* Moscow, Verlag für Fremdsprachige Literatur, 1939.

Report of the Seventh World Congress of the Communist International. London, Modern Books, 1936.

PLENUMS OF THE ECCI

Rasshirennyi plenum ispolnitel'nogo Komiteta Kommunisticheskogo Internatsionala (12–23 iiunia 1923 goda): Otchet (Enlarged Plenum of the Executive Committee of the Communist International [June 12–23, 1923]: Report). Moscow, 1923.

Puti mirovoi revoliutsii: Sed'moi rasshirennyi plenum ispolnitel'nogo komiteta Kommunistcheskogo Internatsionala, 22 noiabria–16 dekabria 1926 (The Paths of World Revolution: The Seventh Enlarged Plenum of the Executive Committee of the Communist International, November 22—December 16, 1926). 2 vols. Moscow, 1927.

X plenum ispolkoma Kominterna (X Plenum of the Ispolkom of the Comintern). 4 vols. Moscow, Gosudarstvennoe izdatel'stvo, 1929.

XI plenum IKKI: Stenograficheskii otchet (XI Plenum of the ECCI: Steno-

graphic report). Vol. I, Moscow, Partiinoe izdatel'stvo, 1932. Vol.
II, Moscow and Leningrad, Gosudarstvennoe Sotsial'no-Ekonomiche-
skoe Izdatel'stvo, 1931.
XII plenum IKKI: Stenograficheskii otchet (XII Plenum of the ECCI:
Stenographic report). 3 vols. Moscow, Partizdat, 1933.
XIII plenum IKKI: Stenograficheskii otchet (XIII Plenum of the ECCI:
Stenographic report). Moscow, Partizdat, 1934.

OTHER COMINTERN MATERIALS

Blueprint for World Conquest as Outlined by the Communist International.
Washington and Chicago, Human Events, 1946.
The Communist International Between the Fifth and Sixth World Congresses,
1924–1928. London, Communist Party of Great Britain, July, 1928.
International Press Correspondence. Vols. 8–23 (1928–1943). Changed name
to *World News and Views* with vol. 18, no. 33 (July 2, 1938). Weekly.
Kommunisticheskii Internatsional: Organ ispolnitel'nogo Komiteta Kommunis-
ticheskogo Internatsionala (Communist International: Organ of the Exe-
cutive Committee of the Communist International). Vols. X–XXV.
Moscow, Izdatel'stvo Ts.K. V.K.P.(b) "Pravda," 1928–1943.
Weekly, 1928–1929; thrice monthly, 1930–1935; twice monthly,
January–July, 1936; monthly, July, 1936–May, 1943. From January,
1940, the issues are numbered but not dated.
Kommunisticheskii Internatsional pered VII vsemirnym kongressom: Materialy
(The Communist International before the VII World Congress:
Materials). Moscow, Partizdat Ts.K. V.K.P. (b), 1935.
Kun, Bela, ed. *Komintern v rezoliutsiiakh* (The Comintern in Resolutions).
2d ed Moscow, 1926.
—— *Kommunisticheskii Internatsional v dokumentakh: Resheniia, tezisy i*
vozzvaniia kongressov Kominterna i Plenumov IKKI, 1919–1932 (The
Communist International in Documents: Decisions, Theses, and
Manifestoes of the Congresses of the Comintern and of the Plenums
of the ECCI, 1919–1932). Moscow, Partiinoe izdatel'stvo, 1933.
Magyar, L., P. Mif, M. Orakhelashvili, and G. Safarov, eds. *Programm-*
nye dokumenty kommunisticheskikh partii vostoka (Program Documents of the
Communist Parties of the East). Moscow, Partiinoe izdatel'stvo, 1934.

GENERAL WORKS

Anderson, Evelyn. *Hammer or Anvil: The Story of the German Working-Class*
Movement. London, Victor Gollancz, 1945.
Aron, Raymond. "Workers, Proletariats, and Intellectuals," *Diogenes,*
no. 10 (1955).

Balabanoff, Angelica. *My Life as a Rebel*. New York, Harpers, 1938.
Bol'shaia Sovetskaia Entsiklopediia (The Great Soviet Encyclopedia). 2d ed. Vol. XXI. Moscow, 1953.
Borkenau, Franz. *European Communism*. New York, Harpers, 1953.
—— *World Communism*. New York, Norton, 1939.
Borton, Vivian. "The Hungarian Revolutions of 1918–1919 in Relation to the Agrarian Problem." Unpublished master's essay, Department of History, Columbia University, May, 1950.
Brandt, Conrad. *Stalin's Failure in China, 1924–1927*. Cambridge, Harvard University Press, 1958.
Brandt, Conrad, Benjamin Schwartz, and John K. Fairbank, eds. *A Documentary History of Chinese Communism*. Cambridge, Harvard University Press, 1952.
Burmeister, Alfred. *Dissolution and Aftermath of the Comintern: Experiences and Observations, 1937–1947*. New York, Research Program on the U.S.S.R., 1955. Mimeographed Series No. 77.
Carew Hunt, R. N. *Marxism: Past and Present.* New York, Macmillan, 1954.
Carr, E. H. *The Bolshevik Revolution, 1917–1923*. Vols. I and III. New York, Macmillan, 1951 and 1953.
—— *The Interregnum*. New York, Macmillan, 1954.
Cattell, David T. *Communism and the Spanish Civil War*. Berkeley and Los Angeles, University of California Press, 1956.
Clark, Colin. *The Conditions of Economic Progress*. 2d ed. London, Macmillan, 1951.
Cole, G. D. H. *A History of Socialist Thought*. Vol. III: *The Second International, 1889–1914*. London, Macmillan, 1956.
Crossman, Richard, ed. *The God That Failed*. New York, Bantam Books, 1952.
Dallin, D. J. "Komintern v voine," *Novyi Zhurnal*, no. 1 (1942).
Dedijer, Vladimir. *Tito*. New York, Simon and Schuster, 1953.
Deutscher, Isaac. *The Prophet Armed*. New York, Oxford University Press, 1954.
—— *Stalin: A Political Biography*. New York and London, Oxford University Press, 1949.
Ebon, Martin. *World Communism Today*. New York, McGraw-Hill, 1948.
Fainsod, Merle. *International Socialism and the World War*. Cambridge, Harvard University Press, 1935.
Federn, Karl. *The Materialistic Conception of History*. London, Macmillan, 1939.
Fischer, Louis. *The Soviets in World Affairs*. 2 vols. Princeton, Princeton University Press, 1951.
Fischer, Ruth. *Stalin and German Communism: A Study in the Origins of the State Party*. Cambridge, Harvard University Press, 1948.

Fisher, H. H. *The Communist Revolution: An Outline of Strategy and Tactics.* Stanford, Stanford University Press, 1955.

Flechtheim, Ossip K. *Die Kommunistische Partei Deutschlands in der Weimarer Republik.* Offenbach A. M., 1948.

Florinsky, Michael. *World Revolution and the U.S.S.R.* New York, Macmillan, 1933.

——"World Revolution and Soviet Foreign Policy," *Political Science Quarterly,* vol. XLVII (June, 1932).

Foster, William Z. *History of the Three Internationals.* New York, International Publishers, 1955.

Founding of the First International. New York, International Publishers, 1937.

Frölich, Paul. *Rosa Luxemburg: Her Life and Work.* London, Gollancz, 1940.

Galbraith, John Kenneth. *The Great Crash, 1929.* Boston, Houghton Mifflin, 1954.

Gankin, Olga Hess, and H. H. Fisher. *The Bolsheviks and the World War.* Stanford, Stanford University Press, 1940.

Gay, Peter. *The Dilemma of Democratic Socialism.* New York, Columbia University Press, 1952.

Gitlow, Benjamin. *I Confess.* Cambridge, Harvard University Press, 1948.

Glaubauf, F. *Tretii kongress Kominterna* (The Third Congress of the Comintern). Moscow, Izdatel'stvo "Proletarii," 1929.

Gorter, Hermann. *Der Imperialismus, der Weltkrieg und die Sozialdemokratie.* Munich, 1919.

Gruliow, Leo, ed. *Current Soviet Policies II. The Documentary Record of the 20th Communist Party Congress and Its Aftermath.* New York, Praeger, 1957.

Günther, G. *Shestoi kongress Kominterna* (The Sixth Congress of the Comintern). Moscow, Izdatel'stvo "Proletarii," 1929.

History of the Communist Party of the Soviet Union: Short Course. New York, International Publishers, 1939.

Joll, James. *The Second International, 1889–1914.* London, Weidenfeld and Nicolson, 1955.

Kabakchiev, Kh. *Kak voznik i razvivalsia Kommunisticheskii Internatsional (Kratkii istoricheskii ocherk)* (How the Communist International Arose and Developed [Short Historical Sketch]). Moscow and Leningrad, Gosudarstvennoe izdatel'stvo, 1929.

Komer, I. *Ten Years of the Communist International.* London, Modern Books, 1929.

V kongress Komunisticke Partije Jugoslavije: Izvestaji i referati (V Congress of the Communist Party of Yugoslavia: Statements and Reports). Moscow, Kultura, 1948.

Laski, Harold J. *Communism.* New York, Holt, 1927.
Lazitch, Branko. *Lénine et la IIIe Internationale.* Neuchatel and Paris, Editions de la Baconnière, 1951.
—— *Les Partis communistes d'Europe, 1919–1955.* Paris, Les Iles d'or, 1956.
Lenin, V. I. *Sochineniia* (Works). 3d ed. Moscow, Partizdat Ts.K. V.K.P., 1929–1937.
Lentsner, N. *O pravoi opasnosti v Kominterne* (On the Right Danger in the Comintern). 2d ed. Moscow, Moskovskii rabochii, 1929.
Lenz, Josef. *The Rise and Fall of the Second International.* New York, International Publishers, 1932.
Leonhard, Wolfgang. *Child of the Revolution.* Chicago, Regnery, 1958.
McCarthy, Margaret. *Generation in Revolt.* London, Heinemann, 1953.
McKenzie, Kermit E. "The Messianic Concept in the Third International, 1935–1939," in Ernest J. Simmons, ed., *Continuity and Change in Russian and Soviet Thought.* Cambridge, Harvard University Press, 1955.
—— "The Soviet Union, the Comintern, and World Revolution: 1935," *Political Science Quarterly,* vol. LXV (June, 1950).
McLane, Charles B. *Soviet Policy and the Chinese Communists, 1931–1946.* New York, Columbia University Press, 1958.
Marx, Karl. *Critique of the Gotha Programme.* New York, International Publishers, 1938.
Masani, M. R. *The Communist Party of India.* New York, Macmillan, 1954.
Mayo, H. B. *Democracy and Marxism.* New York, Oxford University Press, 1955.
Meyer, Alfred G. *Marxism: The Unity of Theory and Practice.* Cambridge, Harvard University Press, 1954.
Mif, P., and G. Voitinskii, eds. *Sovremennaia Iaponiia: Sbornik pervyi* (Contemparary Japan: First Miscellany). Moscow, Izdanie Instituta MKh i MP, 1934.
Mingulin, I. *Pervyi kongress Kominterna* (The First Congress of the Comintern). Moscow, Izdatel'stvo "Proletarii," 1929.
Moore, Barrington, Jr. *Soviet Politics—the Dilemma of Power.* Cambridge, Harvard University Press, 1951.
Narvskii, I. *K istorii bor'by bol'shevizma s liuksemburgianstvom* (For a History of the Struggle of Bolshevism with Luxemburgism). Moscow, Partiinoe izdatel'stvo, 1932.
Neumann, Franz. "Approaches to the Study of Political Power," *Political Science Quarterly,* vol. LXV (June, 1950).
—— *Behemoth: The Structure and Practice of National Socialism.* London, Gollancz, 1943.
Nollau, G. *Die Internationale: Würzeln und Erscheinungsformen des proletarischen Internationalismus.* Köln, Verlag für Politik und Wirtschaft, 1959.

Nordman, K., and G. Lenskii. *Pravyi uklon v Kominterne* (The Right Deviation in the Comintern). Leningrad, "Priboi," 1930.

North, Robert C. *Moscow and Chinese Communists.* Stanford, Stanford University Press, 1953.

Overstreet, Gene D., and Marshall Windmiller. *Communism in India.* Berkeley and Los Angeles, University of California Press, 1959.

Phillips, Wayne. "Lenin and the Origin of the Third International: July 28, 1914, to September 8, 1915." Unpublished master's essay, Department of History, Columbia University, 1953.

Piyade, Moshe. *About the Legend That the Yugoslav Uprising Owed Its Existence to Soviet Assistance.* London, 1950.

Pollock, Frederick. "State Capitalism: Its Possibilities and Limitations," *Studies in Philosophy and Social Science,* vol. IX, 1941.

Postgate, R. W. *The Workers' International.* London, Harcourt, Brace and Howe, 1920.

Pravda, 1935.

Le Programme de l'internationale communiste. Paris, Libraire de l'Humanité, 1924.

"Rajk rehabilité," *Est et Ouest* (May 1–15, 1956).

Ravesteyn, D. W. van. *De Wording van het Communisme in Nederland, 1907–1925.* Amsterdam, P. N. van Kampen, 1948.

Ravines, Eudocio. *The Yenan Way.* New York, Scribner's, 1951.

Rossi, A. *A Communist Party in Action: An Account of the Organization and Operations in France.* New Haven, Yale University Press, 1949.

—— *Les communistes français pendant la drôle de guerre.* Paris, Les Iles d'or, 1951.

—— *The Russo-German Alliance, August 1939–June 1941.* Boston, Beacon Press, 1951.

Roy, M. N. *The Communist International.* Bombay, V. B. Karnik, 1943.

Rupen, Robert A. "Notes on Outer Mongolia Since 1945," *Pacific Affairs,* vol. XXVIII (March, 1955).

Russell, Bertrand. "The End of the Idea of Progress," *The Manchester Guardian Weekly* (March 19, 1953).

Schifrin, Alexander. "Die Bekenntnisse der Komintern," *Die Gesellschaft* (January, 1929).

Schlesinger, Rudolf. *Marx: His Time and Ours.* London, Routledge and Kegan Paul, 1950.

Schwartz, Benjamin I. *Chinese Communism and the Rise of Mao.* Cambridge, Harvard University Press, 1952.

Seton-Watson, Hugh. *From Lenin to Malenkov.* New York, Praeger, 1953.

XV s"ezd vsesoiuznoi kommunisticheskoi partii: Stenograficheskii otchet (XV Congress of the All-Union Communist Party: Stenographic report). Moscow, Gosudarstvennoe izdatel'stvo, 1928.

XVI s"ezd vsesoiuznoi kommunisticheskoi partii: Stenograficheskii otchet (XVI Congress of the All-Union Communist Party: Stenographic report). Moscow, Gosudarstvennoe izdatel'stvo, 1930.

Sharp, Walter R., and Grayson Kirk. *Contemporary International Politics.* New York, Rinehart, 1940.

Socialism Victorious. Moscow and Leningrad, Co-operative Publishing Society of Foreign Workers in the USSR, n.d.

Souvarine, Boris. *Stalin: A Critical Study of Bolshevism.* New York, Longmans, Green, 1939.

Stalin, I. V. *Problems of Leninism.* 11th ed. Moscow, Foreign Languages Publishing House, 1940.

—— *Sochineniia* (Works). 13 vols. Moscow, Gosudarstvennoe izdatel'stvo politicheskoi literatury, 1946–1951.

Stekloff, G. N. *History of the First International.* London, Lawrence, 1928.

Swearingen, Roger, and Paul Langer. *Red Flag in Japan: International Communism in Action, 1919–1951.* Cambridge, Harvard University Press, 1952.

Tivel', A. *Chetvertyi kongress Kominterna* (The Fourth Congress of the Comintern). Moscow, Izdatel'stvo "Proletarii," 1929.

Tivel', A., and M. Kheimo. *10 let Kominterna v resheniiakh i tsifrakh* (Ten Years of the Comintern in Decisions and Figures). Moscow and Leningrad, Gosudarstvennoe izdatel'stvo, 1929.

Touminen, Arvo. *Kremls Klockor.* Helsingfors. Söderström, 1958.

—— "The North European Communist Parties," *Occidente*, vol. XI (May–June, 1955).

Trotsky, Leon. *The First Five Years of the Communist International.* 2 vols. New York, Pioneer Publishers, 1945–1953.

—— *The Third International After Lenin.* New York, Pioneer Publishers, 1936.

Valiani, L. *Storia del Movimento Socialiste.* Vol. I: *L'Epoca della Prima Internazionale.* Florence, La Nuova Italia, 1951.

Die Volkswirtsschaftslehre der Gegenwart in Selbstdarstellungen. Leipzig, Verlag von Feliz Meiner, 1924.

Wittfogel, Karl A. *Oriental Despotism: A Comparative Study of Total Power.* New Haven, Yale University Press, 1957.

Wolfe, B. *Three Who Made a Revolution.* New York, Dial Press, 1948.

Year Book of Labour Statistics, 1943–1944. Montreal, International Labour Office, 1945.

Ypsilon. *Pattern for World Revolution.* Chicago and New York, Ziff-Davis, 1947.

Zaidel', G. *Ocherki po istorii vtorogo internatsionala (1889–1919 gg.)* (Essays on the History of the Second International [1889–1919]). Leningrad, 1931.

Index

INDEX